Stained Glass

from

Shrigley & Hunt

of

Lancaster and London

by

William Waters

Centre for North-West Regional Studies
University of Lancaster 2003
Volume Editor: Marion McClintock

This volume is the 50th in a series published by the
Centre for North-West Regional Studies University of Lancaster.
Series Editor: Jean Turnbull

Text copyright © William Waters 2003
Designed, typeset, printed and bound by J W Arrowsmith Ltd, Bristol

British Library Cataloguing in Publication Data.
A CIP catalogue record for this book is available from the British Library

ISBN 1-86220-140-4

Contents

Listing of plates and figures   v

Introduction and copyright   1

Chapter 1   The entrepreneur: Arthur William Hunt   5

Chapter 2   'The model of what stained glass ought to be'   14

Chapter 3   Commissions and clients   29

Chapter 4   The Twentieth Century: a changing order   40

Appendix A Chronology   53

Appendix B Artists and craftsmen associated with Shrigley and Hunt   57

Appendix C Select Bibliography   63

Select Gazetteer   66

Index to people and places   86

DEDICATION

FOR VICKY, SARAH AND ALEX

LISTING OF PLATES AND FIGURES

PLATES   *Gathering*

Christ Church, Latchford, Cheshire (1887)   Front cover
St. Peter and St. Paul, Pickering, Yorkshire, North Riding (1878)   Back cover
1. All Saints, Silkstone, Yorkshire, West Riding (1875–76)   between pages 8 and 9
2   (a) and (b) St. James, Bolton near Bradford, Yorkshire, West Riding (1876)
3   (a) and (b) All Saints, Hindley, Lancashire (1878)
4. St. Luke, Dunham-on-the-Hill, Cheshire (c.1880)
5. St. Catherine and St. Paul, Hoddesdon, Hertfordshire (1880)
6. St. John, North Bovey, Devon (1880)
7. Matlock Town Hall, Derbyshire (1881)
8. St. Peter, Quernmore, Lancashire (1881)
9. St. Nikolai, Orebrö, Sweden (1881)
10 (a) and (b) St. James, West Derby, Lancashire (1883)
11 (a) and (b) St. James, West Derby, Lancashire (1883)   between pages 24 and 25
12. Parish Church, East Hoathly, Sussex (1883)
13. St. John, Walton near Warrington, Lancashire (1883)
14. St. Paul, Oswaldtwistle, Lancashire (1884)
15. St. Paul, Bedford, Bedfordshire (1884–85)
16. Parish Church, Eastwood, Glasgow (1884–85)
17. St. Barnabas, Great Strickland, Cumbria (1885)
18. St. Mary, Ware, Hertfordshire (1885)
19. All Saints, Upper Stondon, Bedfordshire (1885)

20. St. Margaret, Hornby, Lancashire (c.1885)
21. All Saints, Hertford, Hertfordshire (1885)   between pages 40 and 41
22. Pownall Hall, Wilmslow, Cheshire (1886 onwards)
23. All Saints, Harthill, Cheshire (1885–87)
24 (a) and (b) St. Wilfrid, Grappenhall, Cheshire (1887)
25. Bettws, Cardiganshire (1887)
26. Cartmel Priory, Cartmel, Cumbria (1887)
27 (a)and (b) St. Oswald, Winwick, Lancashire (c.1887)
28. Mansfield College, Oxford (1889)
29. Holy Trinity, Bolton-le-Sands, Lancashire (1891)
30. Kilncroft, Hest Bank, Lancashire (1891–93)   between pages 56 and 57
31. Town Hall, Barrow-in-Furness, Cumbria (1893)
32 (a) and (b) St. Catherine, Burbage, Leicestershire (1894)
33 (a) and (b) Christ Church, Lancaster, Lancashire (1895)
34. Christ Church, Lancaster, Lancashire (c.1896)
35. Christ Church, Lancaster, Lancashire (c.1896)
36. St. George, Preston, Lancashire (1897)
37. Christ Church, Over Wyresdale, Lancashire (c.1897)
38. St. Anne, St Annes-on-Sea, Lancashire (c.1899)
39. St. Mary, Higham Ferrers, Northamptonshire (1899)
40. St. Wilfred, Melling, Lancashire (1905)   between pages 72 and 73
41 (a) and (b) St. Mary, Norton-sub-Hamdon, Somerset (1905)
42. St. Cuthbert, Aldingham, Lancashire (c.1905)
43. St. Nicholas, Wallasey, Cheshire (1919)
44. St. John the Baptist, Clayton near Bradford, Yorkshire, West Riding (1918)
45. St. James, Brindle, Lancashire (1950)
46 (a) and (b) Designs for St. Gregory the Great, Ruislip, Middlesex (1967)
47. St. Barnabas, Heapey, Lancashire (1969)
48. St. Oswald, Preesall, Lancashire (c.1972)
49. (a) and (b) St. Oswald, Preesall, Lancashire (c.1972)

FIGURES

pages

1. Studio portrait of Arthur William Hunt   6
2. The early Hoddesdon workshops   7
3. Shrigley and Hunt at Castle Hill, Lancaster   9
4. Longlands, Lancaster   11
5. Hunt family group, 1897   11
6. Longlands drawing room   12

pages

7. Trinity College, Cambridge (H. Holiday, 1870s) — 15

8. St. Mary, Lapworth, Warwickshire, 1872 — 18

9. Dürer's 'The Suffering Christ' — 19

10. St. John, Halifax, Yorkshire, West Riding (wood engraving of 1840) — 20

11. Jesus College, Cambridge (Burne-Jones, 1873) — 22

12. (a) and (b) St. John, Silverdale, Lancashire (1886) — 23

13. Workshop catalogue (1879) — 24

14. St. Michael, Rampside, Lancashire (c.1892) — 25

15. Tiles by John Milner Allen — 26

16. Tile of alternating pattern — 26

17. St. Edmund, Holme Pierrepont, Nottinghamshire: tile pattern — 26

18. St. Peter, Newton-le-Willows, Lancashire (1898–1901) — 30

19. Dumbarton Town Hall (1906) — 33

20. Photograph of model used for mural design — 37

21. All Saints, Thelwall, Cheshire: cartoon — 38

22. All Saints, Margate, Kent (after 1909) — 42

23. All Saints, Burton-in-Lonsdale, Yorkshire, West Riding (1908) — 43

24. Hunt family at Longlands, 1918 — 44

25. St. Bartholomew, Wilmslow, Cheshire (1925) — 45

26. Lancaster Photographic Society, 1892 — 46

27. Harry Harvey in 1998 — 49

28. Jo Fisher c.1978 — 51

29. 'Notes on Stained Glass', 1936 — 56

30. St. John the Baptist, Thaxted, Essex (Gamon and Humphry, c.1915) — 58

31. All Saints, Hollingbourne, Kent (Prest, 1904) — 60

32. Shrigley and Hunt works supper (c.1890) — 62

33. St. Michael, Steeple Claydon, Buckinghamshire — 67

34. (a) and (b) All Saints, Boxley, Kent (1913) — 73

35. Brindle, Lancashire: gouache of design — 74

36. Croft, Warrington, Lancashire: watercolour of St. Cecilia (1952) — 75

37. St. Paul, Warton, Lancashire (1889) — 79

38. St. James, Scarborough, Yorkshire, North Riding (1901) — 83

INTRODUCTION

At the height of its fame in the late Victorian era, the company of Shrigley and Hunt ranked among the leading designers and manufacturers of stained glass in Britain, rivalling the better-known contemporaries such as William Morris and Company, or James Powell of Whitefriars. At the beginning of the twenty-first century, however, the name of Shrigley and Hunt means little to the average person and not much more to the historian of stained glass. The company deserves much more recognition. Its neglect is largely due to the fact that, unlike their better-known competitors, their designers did not double up as fine artists and the firm did not remain nationally active beyond the early twentieth century. Shrigley and Hunt's story is rather one of an emergence from provincial obscurity into a position of national high regard, followed by a period of slow decline and a return to a local level of operation, albeit of some merit.

Its success relied on a marriage between sound business acumen and talented designers. The firm's founder, Arthur William Hunt, who was a builder's son apprenticed to a stained glass business, possessed a shrewd business sense, knowledge of the trade and a good eye for artistic talent. In a clever move he bought an existing decorating business in Lancaster and he was able to tap into a market that could exploit the opportunities opened up by the industrial and commercial expansion in the North West. His foresight proved accurate and he rapidly exploited the domestic and ecclesiastical demands for artistic decoration.

The success of the enterprise owed quite as much to the artists Hunt chose as it did to his own energies. Carl Almquist and Edward Holmes Jewitt in particular had genius as individual designers and were also able to work as part of a team. They rank among the best of late-Victorian stained glass designers, belonging to the group of artists that followed in the wake of the Pre-Raphaelites with Burne-Jones and Henry Holiday at their head. These artists of the second generation explored the decorative qualities of the medium, while also freeing the figure from some of its historicist tendencies. Moving away from the earlier mediaevalism, they pioneered a more realist style loosely inspired by Renaissance or classical precedents. Often drawing from the model they took steps towards raising the status of stained glass to a fine art, thus upgrading the position of the designer within the arts. In doing so they also increased the accessibility of the Biblical narratives, by selecting easily understood allegories or simply presented stories.

Under Hunt, Almquist and Jewitt were encouraged to develop their talents freely and in doing so they attracted the custom of architects and laymen alike, helping the firm to attain a position equal to any of their national compatriots. Almquist had a studio opened in London for him, which led to recognition in the capital and the Home Counties, providing yet another chance to expand the business. At the height of its fame Shrigley and Hunt was patronised by some of the greatest architects of the day. Paley and Austin, the Lancaster-based architectural practice, was their most important client, while G. F. Bodley, Sir Arthur Blomfield, Richard Norman Shaw and Alfred Waterhouse were numbered among the others. Private commissions poured in from the wealthy magnates of the North West, not just the Storeys, Williamsons, Garnetts and Fosters from around Lancaster itself, but business leaders on Merseyside, the Wirral and Manchester, including the Manchester brewers Henry Boddington, and Sir Gilbert Greenall of Warrington.

Shrigley and Hunt's demise in the twentieth century paralleled that of other family businesses in which the original proprietor's incapacity to allow new blood into the directorship, stifled development, while his too-tight control and over-disciplined leadership meant his sons lost their enthusiasm and looked elsewhere for a career. George, a talented artist and the natural successor, left to begin his own firm and the other sons joined the army or went abroad. Unfortunately, in spite of freelance artists being employed, the impetus was lost and the firm turned out mediocre work in the period between the World Wars.

Inevitably, a commercial firm is first and foremost committed to projecting a corporate identity, leading to problems in attributing windows to individual artists. Shrigley and Hunt, like all the other large nineteenth century stained glass houses and in spite of the two special talents the company nurtured, was not keen to promote the artists themselves except in their role as part of a design team. In the interests of commerce the firm wished to present a uniform style, characterising itself rather than any particular individual. In deciphering the *oeuvre* of Shrigley and Hunt, therefore, and sorting the windows into recognisable separate styles, it is necessary to understand the processes by which they were made. The initial sketch was often made as a joint effort of two designers, while the cartoon that followed could be the work of another. Further complications arise when existing cartoons were re-used, sometimes redrawn by apprentices and, of course, styles could be diluted by the transference of a design on to the glass by the glass painters. However there are clues in the firm's records which help in detecting an individual designer's work.

In the early years between 1873–85 Almquist and Jewitt tended to work separately, establishing a body of cartoons. From c.1885–1914, on occasions when money allowed, and a commissioner requested a superior window, then a single artist could be responsible for all stages in production. Composite windows that carry the work of a number of artists but in which the original cartoons are unaltered, allow for a comparison of styles. Windows were designed by freelance artists in two main periods; 1875–80 and 1905 onwards.

However there are many locations where a secure attribution is difficult and, lacking confirmation from archival sources, no absolute decision can be made. The complexities of attribution are exemplified in the case of the window at Finsthwaite, commissioned by Austin and Paley in 1894. Jewitt spent sixteen hours on the watercolour design, Almquist was responsible for the figure cartoons which took him a total of seventy hours' work, but the account books show that Gamon also spent thirty-seven hours and Prest another thirteen-and-a-half hours on the cartoons. As birds feature prominently in the windows Gamon made when he left to start his own firm, one can assume he was responsible for the doves in the Finsthwaite window.

As would be expected there is a concentration of windows by Shrigley and Hunt in the north of England, with the largest number in the northern counties and the North West in particular. Those counties at a great distance from London or Lancaster naturally patronised local firms, or preferred to draw on the larger London glass houses. Shrigley and Hunt's work is rarely found in Cornwall, Devon, Suffolk or Kent, but good examples are to be found in Cheshire, Hertfordshire, Bedfordshire and Yorkshire. For reasons discussed in the text there are some fine examples thinly distributed across Scotland. Wales, too, is fortunate to have a few splendid windows. The metropolitan areas, with their concentration of wealth, were well served but the ravages of war, vandals and recent activities of the demolition men have taken their toll. Many windows have been destroyed in London, Manchester and Glasgow.

The book is arranged to give an account of the development, range and personalities of the business, with particular concentration on the period 1880–1910 in Chapters 1 to 3, while Chapter 4 relates how the company met the challenges and difficulties of the twentieth century beyond World War 1. After a chronology, a listing of artists and a bibliography, comes the Gazetteer, the heart of the book, where critical comment on particular work is given in the context of the selected *oeuvre* of Shrigley and Hunt's work.

It was while researching the influence of Edward Burne-Jones on nineteenth-century stained glass in Britain[1] that I came across the work of Shrigley and Hunt. It was well known that Carl Almquist, who worked for the firm, had been a pupil of Henry Holiday and thus had access to Burne-Jones' working methods, but it rapidly became evident that his work and that of the rest of the firm deserved closer study. In no way was it derivative; the firm had a character all of its own.

At first it had been my intention to concentrate on the two chief designers, Almquist and Jewitt, but the more I studied, the more the whole activity and output of the firm appeared substantial. As I grew to appreciate the energy underlying the production, so Arthur Hunt, the entrepreneur behind the firm, began to take centre stage. This book is, I hope, a tribute to his indefatigable spirit and taste. Through his efforts the firm grew to be amongst the greatest of its age and but for his early death might have continued without the slump between the World Wars. Tribute should also be given to the vision of Joseph Fisher in the final period of the firm, when he took on a failing concern and once again raised the standard.

My gratitude is owed to a great many people who have encouraged me and given the details that helped construct the book. Firstly, to those members of the Hunt family who generously spared their time and tolerated my interrogations. There my special thanks go to Mrs Isobel Hunt, the only living person with a direct experience of the original firm, as well as to Chris Gartside, Peter Hunt, Stephen Hunt, Mrs Denis Hunt, Mr and Mrs Schooling and Fiona Prior. John Hughes and Annie Ellis gave me invaluable information about twentieth century practice; Susan Ashworth of Lancaster City Museums was magnanimous with time and information. For the period when Joseph Fisher ran the firm I am deeply grateful to Mrs Doris Fisher and Mr and Mrs Stuart for their hospitality and allowing me free access to the material in their possession. The staff of Lancashire Record Office, Hertfordshire Record Office, Lancaster Central Library (with particular thanks to Susan Wilson), and Rachel Moss of Moss Galleries, London have been most helpful. My thanks also go to Chris Morley and Brian Cargin for allowing me access to relevant material, to Birgitta Lövgren, Joseph Carr and Martin Harrison for information and to my daughter Sarah for advice and patience in discussion of the text. At the University of Lancaster I am grateful to Jean Turnbull, Michael Winstanley and Stephen Wildman for expert information and advice, and to Marion McClintock for her close understanding of my text and her sustained effort in bringing this volume to fruition. I also thank Kathryn Lambert and Christine Wilkinson for their patience with the many editings of the text and for their care in assembling text and illustrations. Lastly I thank the incumbents and wardens of the churches and houses I have visited for allowing me access to the windows themselves.

All opinions presented in the book are my own, although I am deeply aware that all the forementioned friends contributed ideas and facts that led to their formation.

William Waters
Crosby, Maryport, 2003

Notes

[1] Martin Harrison and Bill Waters, *Burne-Jones* (Barrie & Jenkins, London, 1973, second edition, 1989).

Copyright

CHAPTER 1

THE ENTREPRENEUR: ARTHUR WILLIAM HUNT

THE HUNTS OF HODDESDON

*B*orn into a culture in which the work ethic was esteemed as the route to progress through society, Arthur William Hunt (1849–1917) (Fig. 1), the inspiration behind the firm of Shrigley and Hunt, was destined from infancy to enter the building profession or an allied career. His family had been occupied as builders in the Hoddesdon area of Hertfordshire since 1719. Inevitably, Arthur's future would be bound up with the processes of construction and decoration. Jonathan Dunn had established the building firm but after William Hunt, Arthur's grandfather, had married Dunn's daughter-in-law it passed into the Hunt family's ownership, to remain there until its ultimate closure in the 1920s.

Hoddesdon was a pleasant environment in which to be born. In the mid-nineteenth century the town was still small, stretching along the main road from London to Cambridge. Earlier it had been a convenient stopping place since it offered hospitality by means of numerous coaching inns, some of which survive to this day. Only seventeen miles separated the town from the metropolis, enabling its inhabitants to enjoy the pleasures of both city and country life. 'Beautifully situated on rising ground backed by extensive woods',[2] Hoddesdon lies on the River Lea which is met by the River Stort a mile upstream. Meandering within its broad valley, the river creates numerous backwaters whose fishing was made famous by Isaak Walton's enthusiasm in the seventeenth century.

As the nineteenth century advanced the new wealth generated by industrial and commercial advance opened up great opportunities for creative entrepreneurs. John Hunt, Arthur's father, took advantage of the growing demand and expanded the firm's undertakings from plumbing and painting in the 1830s, to glazing, paperhanging, gas fitting (he was agent for the Hoddesdon Gas Company) and fire insurance as well as the primary function of building. In the mid-nineteenth century the family increased their social status within the local community. The children

Fig. 1   A studio portrait of Arthur William Hunt.

Fig. 2 The early workshops at the rear of Hogges Hall in the High Street, Hoddesdon, after J. A. Hunt had taken over control of the firm in 1869 (reproduced from David Dent, *Hoddesdon's Past in Pictures*) (Ware, Rockingham Press, 1992).

consequently benefited from a happy, god-fearing if disciplined life (their father was a lay reader at Hoddesdon Church), set against a thriving business. Living on site, their home was a large two-storied Georgian house facing Hoddesdon High Street, quaintly named Hogges Hall (Fig. 2). John had his sons sent to board at a school in nearby Bishop's Stortford. At his death in 1869 he left a widow, four sons and four daughters. He died leaving property in Hoddesdon and neighbouring Broxbourne, from which his widow was able to derive a reasonable income.

All four of his sons entered the building trade. John as the eldest inherited the firm, Arthur began his stained glass and decorating business, Thomas practised as a builder and Samuel became a plumber. Each achieved success within their spheres and later were to pass on mutually advantageous contacts and commissions to each other. John developed his father's firm far beyond its original scope and became the head of a building company with a national reputation. During the time the firm was operating many large contracts were successfully carried out including All Saints, Hertford, Tonbridge Chapel and St. John's, Stansted among churches; new buildings for Highgate, Haileybury and Felsted schools; the large Sanatorium at Bures, Suffolk, and also the Hearts Convalescent Home, St. Leonards. They also built or reconstructed many country houses. At one time they had some three hundred men on their books.[3]

John's capacity for hard work, his commercial accomplishments and his keen business sense were shared by his brothers, especially Arthur, who succeeded in creating an equally impressive parallel stained glass manufactory.

EARLY YEARS

What caused Arthur to develop his initial interest in artistic stained glass and tilework is unclear. Approximately six miles south of Hoddesdon, also lying on the River Lea, is the Norman church at Waltham Abbey, a notable landmark within the locality. From 1859 William Burges was involved in redesigning the interior, particularly the east wall, which included a large spectacular stained glass window designed by Burne-Jones and made by Powells of Whitefriars. Arthur's father's attention may have been caught by the addition of such an important work of art to a local edifice. Alternatively William Morris also grew up in nearby Essex and it may have been through this connection that Arthur's interest grew. The Morris family were wealthy and owned various mansions in the area, and as such they would have been known to local builders. It is possible that Arthur, therefore, having a keen interest in the decorative arts, was sent to the Morris firm because of its reputation within the vicinity. Hunt family tradition has it that Arthur first began his training with Burne-Jones, probably at Morris, Marshall, Faulkner and Company.[4]

What is certain, however, is that Arthur was later apprenticed to the firm of Heaton, Butler and Bayne of Cardington Street, Hampstead Road, London.[5] During that time he lodged in Oak Hill Lane, Hampstead, combining his work with periods of study at The National Art Training School under the direction of R. W. Herman (1815–1886) at South Kensington.[6] When Arthur Hunt entered Heaton, Butler and Bayne's workshop, they were undergoing a change in the style of their designing. Henry Holiday (1839–1927), who incidentally had also designed a window for Waltham Abbey in 1867, was supplying cartoons, which were helping to forge a new approach in the presentation of stained glass that was more representative of the age. Formal Gothicism was becoming a thing of the past and, following the example of Morris' company, Holiday's designs developed a looser iconography based upon Renaissance precedents and a closer anatomical study of the figure. Also following Morris' example, young designers of stained glass in the more progressive workshops were as likely to be recruited from the schools of fine art as from the craft-based, works apprentices. In 1871, with these ideas colouring his judgement, Arthur Hunt came to the end of his apprenticeship. He was then courting Jane Marion Caroline Matthews, daughter of the proprietor of the decorators and furnishers E. Matthews and Sons of Oxford Street, London. He was also looking for a business which would support a family and allow him to develop his artistic ambitions.

Northern England in the late 1860s held great promise for an aspiring domestic and church decorator. It was a time of extensive church building and the emergent aesthetic movement led to an increased demand for decorative interiors both secular and ecclesiastical. How Arthur discovered the firm of Joseph Shrigley of Lancaster is not definitely known, although their account books show that they had dealings with a J. Shrigley's of London, possibly a relative who may have been known to the Hunts of Hoddesdon. Shrigley's of Lancaster ran a painting, carving and gilding firm which had its

Plate 1 All Saints, Silkstone, Yorkshire, West Riding
(1875–76)

Plate 2 (a) and (b)   St. James, Bolton near
Bradford, Yorkshire, West Riding (1876)

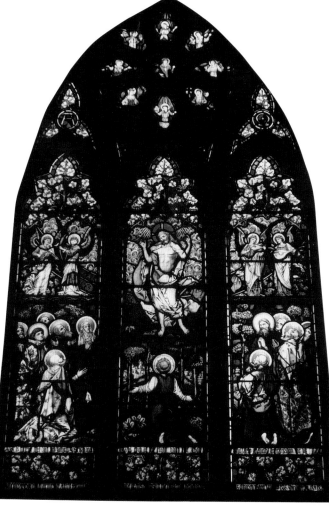

Plate 3 (a) and (b)   All Saints, Hindley, Lancashire
(1878)

Plate 4 St. Luke, Dunham-on-the Hill,
Cheshire (c.1880)

Plate 5 St. Catherine and St. Paul, Hoddesdon,
Hertfordshire (1880)

Plate 6   St. John, North Bovey,
Devon (1880)

Plate 7   Matlock Town Hall, Derbyshire
(1881)

Plate 8   St. Peter, Quernmore, Lancashire
(1881)

Plate 9   St. Nikolai, Orebrö, Sweden (1881)

Plate 10 (a) and (b) St. James, West Derby, Lancashire (1883)

Fig. 3 Shrigley and Hunt's works, Castle Hill, Lancaster. The showrooms with stained glass were on the ground floor, and the studios were on the top floor. In March 2003 the glass furnaces in the basement were rediscovered and are to be put on display.

origins in the mid-eighteenth century. Quite early on they had specialised in church decorating and mural painting. When her husband died in 1836, the widowed Ellen Shrigley had formed a business partnership with James Williamson for some ten years until 1847, when her son Joseph was old enough to assist her.[7] After her death the firm had passed to Joseph. When he died prematurely in 1868, his widow Eliza, with eight young children to rear, was desperate to sell the business. Negotiations with Arthur began around 1872 (he was still living at home in 1871[8]), resulting in Arthur taking over as manager of the newly-named Hudson (Mrs Shrigley's maiden name) and Shrigley the next January. Having secured a working base in Lancaster, Arthur settled there in 1873. He was married on 9 June 1874 at St. George's Church, Kensington and the couple moved into 22 West Road, Lancaster. Jane brought with her a sizeable legacy, giving Arthur much-needed capital. The same year Arthur took sole charge of the business and paid £44 per annum for rent of the firm's premises on Castle Hill, together with a yearly purchase instalment. His final payment of £1,000 in July 1878 bought complete ownership of the firm henceforward called Shrigley and Hunt, and with it the opportunity to pioneer in the North of England those innovations he had recently acquired in the South (Fig. 3).[9]

THE FIRM IN LANCASTER AND LONDON

Arthur possessed a shrewd business sense but also set a hard-working example. He was continually away canvassing, either in London or the provinces searching out wealthy clients. Often away for weeks at a time, he targeted areas by lobbying local solicitors, architects and clergy.

He inherited and successfully retained an important local client base of Shrigley's patrons which included many wealthy families who would prove advantageous to the new firm.[10] On taking over the firm he made no radical policy changes; rather his intention was gradually to increase the range of the services he had to offer, the firm advertising itself in 1875 as 'Church and House Painters and Decorators, Paperhangers, Carvers and Gilders, Stained Glass and Heraldic Painters, Castle Hill, Lancaster'.[11] Initially, Shrigley and Hunt had to subcontract the manufacture to stained glass workshops elsewhere. A London firm, Baillie and Mayer of 18 Wardour Street, who had made up Charles Eamer Kempe's (1837–1907) windows in the late 1860s, was engaged and, although the practice was not uncommon, it had obvious drawbacks largely arising from lack of supervision on the part of the contractor. January 1875, therefore, saw the erection of kilns for firing glass and tiles, the alteration of the building for a glazing shop and the preparation of a glass painting room in Lancaster.[12] Once these were operating, all the stained glass was executed on the premises. William Eaves (1844–1907) who worked for the firm from about 1874 as chief glass painter and manager of some twenty personnel in the workshop, ensured that the team responded by using their skills to develop a whole series of superlative windows in the late 1880s and 1890s, which proved to be the high point in the firm's history.

By the end of the 1870s Hunt had opened a London office at 28 John Street, Bedford Row, partly to retain the services of one of his chief designers, Carl Almquist, but also to interview southern clients. Being on the main line railway, Lancaster was less than a day's journey from London and Arthur came to an arrangement with the railway company by which he was able to board any train he required, even if not scheduled to stop at Lancaster. Any packages sent would be received the following day. All windows were made and assembled at Lancaster but completed panels were exhibited for inspection by clients at both Lancaster and London show rooms.[13]

Arthur Hunt's commercial skills were coupled with a fine artistic intelligence. He had absolute faith in his designers and backed their judgement when clients called them into question. The business prospered. Over the first twenty years the firm recorded a yearly increase in trade, which was reflected in its healthy bank balance. Order books were full, the artists saw a gradual increase in their income and more staff were taken on.

By 1884 Arthur was confident enough to entrust the design of a large new house to the local architects Paley and Austin. 'Longlands' was an impressive redbrick, gabled house with tall chimneys standing within its own landscaped gardens in a salubrious suburb to the west of Lancaster. In fine Victorian style it had a conservatory, croquet lawn and tennis court. Well-proportioned but unostentatious, the house enjoyed a fine view of the city and was to serve Arthur amply with his increasing family and servants, including a nanny and gardener. Life at 'Longlands' was that of an

Fig. 4 Exterior of Longlands, Lancaster, home of Arthur Hunt and his family, built to a design by Paley and Austin in 1884.

Fig. 5 A Hunt family group at Longlands in 1897.

Fig. 6   Interior, drawing room of Longlands. Note the Shrigley and Hunt tiles in the fireplace.

upper middle-class family. A man of culture, Arthur surrounded himself with art and decoration typical of the period. His walls, covered with Morris wallpapers, were tastefully hung with paintings and drawings by local painters and the finest cartoons by his artists. His furniture displayed a collection of De Morgan vases, tiles and dishes and not surprisingly the windows were filled with the best stained glass. The house served as an impressive backdrop for the entertainment of clients (Figs. 4, 5, 6).[14]

Over the years he established himself as a leading public figure in Lancaster's social life. Widely respected, he was a church warden at the Priory Church, a freemason, an active committee member of the Storey Institute and a member of the local hunt. All his children rode and their horses were stabled at Halton Green Farm, an eighty-three acre holding which he had bought and rented out. Arthur Hunt's family grew almost yearly. His wife gave birth to twelve children between 1875 and 1895, although three died before they reached adulthood. Of the remaining nine, two were girls who were taught locally. Arthur, with an eye to the future, had the seven boys well educated. After preparatory school, at Dunchurch in Warwick-shire, they attended Sedbergh School before continuing to Wadham College, Oxford. They were required to spend periods working in the business, presumably with a view to inheriting joint responsibility for it after their father's death.[15]

Unfortunately this was not to be the case as shall be outlined later.

Notes

2   *Kelly's Directory of Hertfordshire* (1890).

3   H. F. Hayllar, *The Chronicles of Hoddesdon: From the Earliest Times to the Present Day* (Hoddesdon, T. Knight & Company, 1948).

[4] At the time AWH is thought to have been with MMF & Co. Daniel Cottier, a young Scottish designer had connections with the firm, the two might well have been known to each other and this may explain the subsequent Scottish activities of Shrigley and Hunt during the 1880s.

[5] Letter Book, Lancashire Record Office (LRO), DDSR 2/7 letter 25 October 1907 AWH to Prof. Church.

[6] Notes made by Aileen, wife of Oliver Hunt, private family collection in Lancashire and *Building News*, 2 December 1887, p.849.

[7] Philip Gooderson, *Lord Linoleum: Lord Ashton, Lancaster and the Rise of the British Oilcloth Industry* (Keele University Press, 1996), pp. 66–7.

[8] Census 1871.

[9] Margaret Edwards, *The Studios of Lancaster Artists in Stained Glass* (Lancaster City Museum Monograph, 1974).

[10] Information about the personalities and entrepreneurs who shaped Lancaster economy in the second half of the nineteenth century is scattered amongst a variety of sources, including the following: W. Farrer and J. Brownhill, *The Victoria County History: Lancaster,* Constable, vols 2 (1908) and 8 (1914); 'Cross Fleury', *Time-Honoured Lancaster: Historic Notes on the Ancient Borough of Lancaster,* Eaton and Bulfield (1891 reprinted with an index, 1974); (ed.) A. White, *A History of Lancaster* (second edition, Edinburgh University Press, 2001); and Bulmer's *History and Directory of Lancaster and District* (undated, but c.1912).

[11] *Kelly's Directory for Lancashire*, 1875.

[12] MS 8030, Lancaster Central Library.

[13] Letters, LRO.

[14] Longlands survives today but sadly has lost much of its original character due to modernisation.

[15] 21 December 1917, Obituary, *Lancaster Guardian*; Sale documents, Halton Green Sale, 12 October 1918.

CHAPTER 2

'The model of what stained glass ought to be'

Artist Designers, Carl Almquist and Edward Holmes Jewitt

PROGRESSIVE STAINED GLASS IN THE LATER NINETEENTH CENTURY

When Hunt first took over the firm, the Queen Anne Movement was at its height. Its aims were to remove the heaviness of the Gothic Revival style and to replace it with light and delicacy in the design of buildings and their interiors. Concurrently the Aesthetic Movement championed art-for-art's-sake, redefining an earlier almost obligatory religious base, and declaring (especially after the impact of Darwin's theories), that art had no need for a moral credo. Radical ideas such as these were to alter profoundly the fine arts and their consequences were greatly to affect the practice of ecclesiastical decoration.

Obviously, serious-minded designers of stained glass responded. Back in 1861, the newly formed Morris, Marshall, Faulkner and Company had begun to introduce these ideas and were derided for doing so by the Gothicists who called the group orientated towards fine art as 'a set of amateurs who are going to teach us our trade'.[16] But they were to eat their words. Burne-Jones, the foremost of the group, influenced all later stained glass production.[17] He reinterpreted mediaeval iconography, drawing upon Renaissance and later images, whilst making the figures more psychologically complex. Henry Holiday, who took over Burne-Jones' position at Powell's of Whitefriars, developed along similar lines. A few quotations from a lecture he gave in 1871 convey Holiday's ideas:

> They [earlier 19th century makers of stained glass] perceived that the drawing in these figures [in mediaeval glass] was that of a vigorous but primitive school … Bad drawing could be obtained without difficulty and as for the colour, they could greatly improve upon that of the old glass, for clearly the brighter the colours were the better must they be. The great advantage of this system was that it was not necessary that an artist should come near

the windows…if anyone wishes to see how noble are these experiments [in modern glass], let him visit Waltham Abbey, the east windows of which were designed by Mr. Jones, and executed by Messrs. Powell of Whitefriars. They are equal to the finest thirteenth century work, but differ from the glass of other modern workmen in this respect, that while the glass of the prevailing style preserved none of the beauty of colour or conception of the old work, and imitated only the archaic drawing which they simply caricatured, Mr Jones affected no archaisms but reproduced marvellously a splendour of colour which is seen only in the greatest early glass. [18]

Holiday's enthusiasm for forging a style to suit the age in which he lived was unbounded (Fig. 7). He gradually developed more realism in his windows, lightened his palette and simplified the lead lines. He was always uncomfortable with the work shop system of leaving his cartoons to be executed by inexperienced or inadequate draughtsmen. As a remedy he and an architect, Thomas Graham Jackson (1835–1934), co-operated to improve the situation:

… in January 1870 we got up a life class…in one of the galleries in Powell's works at Whitefriars… we mustered from fourteen to twenty including Norman Garstin, a painter and some of Powell's own draughtsmen. Maw Egley [a Royal Academy painter] used to coach us and set the model. Reginald Thompson, now a physician at St. George's and the Brompton Hospital, used to give us lectures on artistic anatomy with demonstrations.[19]

Fig. 7   In 1871 Henry Holiday received a commission through Heaton Butler and Bayne to fill the windows of Trinity College Chapel at Cambridge with stained glass. The fifteen windows, all with eight figures, were too much for a single artist to design and execute cartoons, and hence Almquist and Wooldridge were both enlisted on the project.

The same rationalist ideas that were revolutionising the arts had their impact upon religion; practical Evangelism began supplanting the high church Anglo-Catholicism, which in turn demanded new ideas in ecclesiastical decoration. The remote, dark and mysterious images of Gothicist windows were no longer in demand and gave way to light, intelligible figures of Christ and his saints performing charitable acts that were appealing in their accessibility. Static icons looked old fashioned; Christ became portrayed as a credible human being.

At first Shrigley and Hunt were to manifest the modernist ideas by using pastel coloured glass overlain with pale enamels, with Almquist and Jewitt's figures typically embodying the new ideas of figure drawing and design. Later, at the end of the century, when the High Church Movement re-emerged, some churches required a return to darker interiors, and the firm again accommodated to the new requirements. Still adhering to their liberated figure drawing, they altered their pattern surrounds and draperies and used darker, richer colours. Canopies and pedestals, much loved by the Gothic Revivalists of the first half of the century, and still favoured by conservative clients, were banished by progressive designers but then occasionally re-introduced. Paley and Austin often required them, when they worked in their Perpendicular style, to blend in with the architectural details. Like most of the stained glass houses, Shrigley and Hunt's windows varied when they worked closely with a particular architect, some having a greater impact than others, depending upon their ideas of light, colour and style. The interaction could prove dramatic as at Mansfield College Chapel, Oxford (with G. F. Armitage) (Plate 28), or at Stanton church, Gloucestershire (with Blomfield), where the architect required a colourful pair of windows that took into consideration the existing mediaeval east window.

FREELANCE ARTISTS

As far as is known Arthur Hunt did not design for his firm.[20] His success owed much to the quality of the designers he worked with from the 1870s. His policy in the first few years was to employ well-known freelance artists, including John Milner Allen, Henry Holiday, Alex Skirving and H. Bone (possibly the designer of the Royal Windsor tapestry factory).

The best known of these was John Milner Allen. He was an experienced designer who had worked for many stained glass firms, including Heaton, Butler and Bayne, and his work included most notably the series of windows in Plymouth Guildhall – now destroyed. By the time he worked for Shrigley and Hunt between 1874 and 1882, however, he was becoming out-moded. Only one of his windows survives, at St Mary Magdalene's church in Broughton-in-Furness, which consists of three lights portraying symbolic plants, although there are other known but as yet untraced domestic examples. Allen also designed tiles for the firm and, more importantly, in 1878 he produced cartoons for the new Preston County Office murals which were his most important commission to be executed by them.[21]

As mentioned earlier Henry Holiday worked for Heaton, Butler and Bayne, and no doubt became known to Arthur Hunt there. His sole contribution to the new firm's output was a single sketch for a window in 1875 for the east window of St. John's church at Calder Vale, depicting the life of Christ over five lights.[22] Unfortunately this unique window no longer exists; it was removed and replaced with a Last Supper design in 1906, almost certainly because of enamel deterioration.[23]

Two other designers were hired in the 1880s; G. Porter[24] and William J. Tipping. Neither of them achieved the stature of the chief designers. Arthur Hunt was not impressed, especially by the more reactionary work of Tipping who soon left to work in Germany. Porter's main contribution was in copying mediaeval decorative patterns and borders for reference, but his own work too is of a conservative nature. Presumably these artists were hired to develop more variety, thus increasing the firm's appeal to a wider range of clients. By this time, his business had become more established and Arthur's design policy had clarified. Carl Almquist and Edward Holmes Jewitt took over completely, eliminating the need for freelance talent. For the next thirty years Shrigley and Hunt established a distinctive style of glass which was greatly admired and became a very successful business.

CARL ALMQUIST (1848 – 1924)

When Arthur left Heaton, Butler and Bayne, he had become friendly with a young Swedish pupil of Henry Holiday named Carl Almquist, whom he persuaded to submit designs for his new firm. The arrangement was to prove highly significant for them both.

In the summer of 1870 the twenty-two year old Swede had come to England, financed by the Royal Chamber of Commerce, Stockholm, in order to study the production of stained glass, as there was nothing of the kind in Sweden. He carried a letter of introduction to Axel Herman Haig (1835–1922) who worked as a draughtsman in the office of the architect William Burges (1827–81). Burges, a friend of Henry Holiday, recommended the young man and thus Almquist at once found himself a pupil of one of the foremost stained glass artists of his day. Almquist wrote home enthusiastically in December 1871:

> [Mr Holiday] designs the most splendid windows, his colours especially are so beautiful and I think he is certainly one of the best if not the best glasspainter in England and I think it is very fortunate that I came to him and not to one of those large firms where the most wretched things very often are executed. Even Heaton, Butler and Bayne, who generally execute our cartoons, and who are considered as one of the best firms in London, do not do good work when they furnish the design themselves.[25]

In the evenings Almquist worked for Henry Ellis Wooldridge (1845–1917), one of the designers for James Powell of Whitefriars (Figure 8), who had been a pupil of Burne-Jones. Consequently Almquist was fortunate in that he absorbed progressive ideas from the finest contemporary designers of the day at the very start of his formal training. His skills developed dramatically; by December 1870 Holiday wrote of him:

I have much pleasure in testifying to the ability you have shown and the rapid progress you have made during the time you have been working with me. Judging from the improvement in your drawing after so short a period, I think it likely that at the end of the first year I may be able to offer you a small salary for the second.[26]

In December 1873 Almquist was in Lancaster for the first time:

Some time ago I got commission [sic] through a friend here who has a decorating establishment to paint some figures on a couple of doors belonging to a certain Mr Pearson of Storrs Hall. … My friend Mr Hunt here gets a good many windows to dispose of and he says that if I will work for him he will be glad to give them to me to design. I have got one now for a church at Burnley in Yorkshire…he is…thinking of getting up a stained glass manufactory of his own here in which case he would require the services of resident artist, and I might possibly make arrangements to come and stay here in that case.[27]

A number of options were now available to Almquist. He had experience working for some of the best firms of the time including Holiday, Powell and Company (Fig. 8), and Heaton, Butler and Bayne, as well as another less progressive firm, Burlison and Grylls of Langham Place. Holiday tried to persuade him to remain on his staff permanently but Almquist eventually decided to move to Lancaster and become a member of Hunt's new team.

During these early years Arthur Hunt relied heavily upon Almquist. Not only did he design stained glass but he was responsible for tile design, church decoration and patterns of all kinds. He was also required to paint *in situ* and he once travelled with Arthur to Tullamore in central Ireland to discuss the installation of windows. Initially Almquist was paid separately for each piece of work but from 1876 he received a retaining fee in addition.

Fig. 8 St. Mary, Lapworth, Warwickshire, a panel from a three-light east window depicting St. John and the Virgin Mary, designed by H. E. Wooldridge and made by Powell's of Whitefriars in 1872. During that year Almquist spent time in the evenings as a pupil of Wooldridge, and he later used the figure of St. John as a type for the west window of St. John, Silverdale (1886).

Almquist moved up to Lancaster in 1876 and lived there until 1878, but the limitations imposed by a provincial life irked him so much he felt he had to return to London. Arthur Hunt obliged him in this, as Almquist explained in a letter of 1879:

> We have now opened an office in London for the convenience of transacting business in the South of England. After having been about two years in Lancaster I commenced to get extremely tired of the place and determined again to return to London; chiefly for the sake of the opportunities for study that one has here and the entire absence of which makes a country town such as Lancaster anything but a desirable place of residence to anyone like myself who wishes to improve and make progress.[28]

Fig. 9 Dürer's 'The suffering Christ before the people', c.1497–1500 from 'The Great Passion', used by Almquist as a model for All Saints, Harthill (see Plate 23).

That the office was opened in London basically to retain Almquist within the firm is confirmed in a letter from Arthur in 1889 about the London premises:

> I should not feel justified in giving them up so long as the business gradually prospers & while my artist friend for whom they were opened continues to work in them.[29]

Over the years various apprentices spent time at the London office assisting Almquist, including Gilbert Gamon (1871–1941), George Hunt (1878–c.1945), G. S. Payne (active with Shrigley and Hunt 1903–9),[30] and Jewitt's son Austen in the early years of the twentieth century.

Almquist's time in Lancaster, however, was most productive and influential. Arthur had brought with him a group of skilled craftsmen that were able to execute the windows (and tiles) with an accomplishment that matched the best contemporary work. Examples at Silkstone in Yorkshire, Garstang in Lancashire, Menai Bridge in Anglesey, and Bolton near Bradford, show a mastery of figure drawing and effective design in the disposition of the figures together with a thoroughly up-to-date re-interpretation of iconography. They also show a lessening influence of his masters Holiday and Wooldridge although, like his former teachers, one can detect an admiration for Botticelli and Florentine artists of the fifteenth century; elsewhere he demonstrates an alternative preference for the art of Dürer and his followers (Fig. 9). There is a freshness in Almquist's drawing which is reflected in the restrained leading, subtle colours and in the secondary pattern work. Contact with Scottish glass designers in the early 1880s had a profound impact upon his use of colour and strengthened his resolve to further modernise the design. The figures become more powerfully drawn and splendidly rich in colour. His wish to remove the vestiges of Gothicism is given further evidence by his use of the figure to occupy the whole area of the window, leaving no room for anachronistic elements such as canopies and pediments (see Plate 9). (In his later work he left such details, when required, to be added by the Lancaster workshop, his cartoons remaining at the figure stage.) Like his Scottish counterparts he allowed his themes to dominate the eye, making few concessions to the architectural context. Almquist's mature style was to benefit from his ability to absorb and develop a variety of such influences.

EDWARD HOLMES JEWITT, 1849–1929

With the expansion of the business, Arthur Hunt recruited managers for the Lancaster workshops and offices and the London office and studio, and added a second young and versatile artist into his studio in September 1877; Edward Holmes Jewitt. He was to contribute as wide a range of designs as

Fig. 10   Wood engraving by Orlando Jewitt of St. John, Halifax, c.1840. His nephew, E. H. Jewitt, designed an important set of windows there for Shrigley and Hunt in the 1870s.

Almquist and from the time he was first engaged, Edward received equal pay with his colleague, thus having equivalent status as a chief designer (and not the subordinate role to Almquist previously assumed).

Edward was the nephew of the famous early nineteenth-century book engraver Orlando Jewitt (1799–1869) for whom Edward's father Henry worked (Fig. 10). Edward's early childhood was spent in Headington, Oxfordshire where his family worked upon various books on local antiquities for Thomas Combe, a noted patron of the Pre-Raphaelites. He grew up surrounded by engraving tools that were used chiefly to illustrate books on ecclesiology, 'concerned with the architecture of the church buildings, their decoration and internal arrangement'.[31] The Jewitts were later responsible for illustrating architectural volumes by A. W. N. Pugin (1812–52) and G. E. Street (1824–81) among others. Their subject matter required detailed knowledge of antiquarianism and iconography, an expertise which Edward acquired and which he was to employ effectively in the service of Shrigley and Hunt.

It is not known how Jewitt and Arthur Hunt met. In 1856, when Edward was aged eight, Orlando Jewitt took the family to London to join the staff of *The Building News*. At present, there is no indication as to Edward's employment in his early years or how he made the transition from book illustration to stained glass. Possibly he trained as a stained glass artist in the same circles as Arthur and Almquist. When he joined Shrigley and Hunt in 1877, aged twenty-nine, he was a mature practitioner. At first he domiciled in Lancaster, then Morecambe, but later settled in Station Road, Hest Bank, on the coast to the north of Lancaster, and remained there all his life. It was his habit to walk the five miles into work every day, a trait which sometimes annoyed Arthur Hunt who would have preferred him to spend more time during busy periods at the drawing board.

Jewitt's background in engraving is revealed by his drawing technique. The lines he uses in his earlier work are delicate and convoluted, his draperies are fine and fold back on themselves in the manner of Flemish paintings. His use of enamel for shadings and to give volume is also softer and more subtle than his colleague. Unlike the more neo-classical Almquist whose drapery has long tubular folds, Jewitt's are angular and contorted. Later, after years of working together, their cartoon style became much closer, although naturally they still retained individual characteristics.

A WORKING PARTNERSHIP

Over the years Almquist and Jewitt evolved a method of collaborating which overcame the difficult situation of having workshops divided by nearly 300 miles and produced what were in effect joint designs. Jewitt most frequently interviewed clients, discussed the required subject matter, recommended the correct iconography and was chiefly responsible for the choice of coloured glass to be used. Clients could however also be interviewed at the London studio by Almquist:

> Since opening these premises we have found them of great use both as a convenience for
> Mr Hunt, who has often to come up to London on business and for architects and other
> customers in London who also wish to employ us and who before had no means of

communication except through the post whereas now everything can be done through a personal interview, which is always much better.[32]

The system later adopted was for Jewitt either to supervise or himself draw and paint a small watercolour version of the projected window to be submitted to the client; once approved, either he or Almquist would draw a full-sized cartoon. Almquist produced the greater bulk of cartoons from c.1890. Jewitt had greater responsibility not only for the colour of each particular window but also for selecting the raw materials with the makers of the glass. His refined sensitivity to its qualities was an important contributory factor to the consistent excellence of Shrigley and Hunt's windows. This letter is typical of many he exchanged with suppliers, Powell's, Hartley Wood and Chance:

> We have examined your samples of ant[ique] rubies referred to in yr. letter and re[ceive]d by us, and whilst acknowledging that they are fine glasses we do not think they compare with samples sent in 03 of ruby with a fine large streak in the metal which is what we always look for. However what we are wanting is r[uby] on blue of which we do not like yr. sample for it is too sudden in transition in colour turning gradually from pale to dark then stopping at a black ridge and breaking again into pale.
>
> These sudden breaks from pale to light always cause great waste in cutting and are useless to us. Perhaps you have sent us an unfortunate sample.[33]

In overcoming the difficulties inherent in the division of the business between two locations, the two artists gradually developed the style that became characteristic of Shrigley and Hunt. Neverthe-less, there continued inevitable difficulties that occasionally arose from working at such a distance and with shared responsibilities. These are indicated in a letter from Jewitt to Almquist of 6 March 1907:

Fig. 11 Jesus College, Cambridge. South transept, detail of a five-light window designed by Burne-Jones and executed by Morris and Co. (1873). An important benchmark in nineteenth century stained glass, the Burne-Jones designs for this window had a profound effect on subsequent stained glass.

Fig. 12 (a) and (b) St John, Silverdale, Lancashire: west window, Nativity (Almquist, 1886). Almquist's sources range from Della Robbia, as shown by a comparison of the central angel in frieze and window, to Burne-Jones and Dürer (see Fig. 9). The Della Robbia photograph belonged to the workshop.

You must not think because I do not reply at length that I do not appreciate yr[sic] remarks (though there are one or two I do not wholly agree with) it opens up many questions that I frequently want to discuss with you about wh[sic] could be so much better done in an hour's conversation than by correspondence, considering how very much of the success of the work depends on mutual understanding as almost everything goes jointly through our hands we do not meet to air views freely as we shd[sic] do. I do not press you to come north though I shd[sic] welcome you if you cd[sic] be induced to do so but if you cannot I will seek an early opportunity of coming to town to have a talk with you . . . .[34]

'THE MODEL OF
WHAT STAINED GLASS OUGHT TO BE'

Both Almquist and Jewitt were capable of creating superlative works of art on their own. Examples include 'The Life of Hezekiah', a three-light window in the south wall at St. Catherine's Church, Burbage, Leicestershire by Jewitt (Plate 32(a) and (b)), and the east window of four lights at St Mary's Episcopalian Church, Aberfoyle by Almquist, showing the early life of Christ.

Nevertheless, it was the partnership which produced most of the masterpieces, especially during the 1880s. Like their contemporaries, Morris and Co. and Powell's, they were developing a dense, highly colourful style that left the paler colours of the previous decade behind. Situated within walking distance of the two rival companies, the London studio facilitated Almquist's study of the designs emerging from their competitors. The admiration for Burne-Jones by both designers is evident in the character of their work during this period. A comparison of the angels in St James, West Derby, Liverpool (1883) by Jewitt (Plate 10) with Burne-Jones' 'Angels of the Hierarchy' (1873–5) in Jesus College Chapel, Cambridge (Fig. 11) and of Almquist's 'Faith' in St. Paul's Church, Bedford (1884) (Plate 15) with Burne-Jones' 'Faith' in Christ Church, Oxford (1871) bears this out. Burne-Jones' working methods could also be studied at the Grosvenor Gallery in Bond Street where he exhibited cartoons and studies each year in their annual summer and winter exhibitions. In the 1881 winter Grosvenor Gallery show Burne-Jones exhibited his 'Last Judgment' cartoons for Easthampstead church. Almquist, clearly inspired by this example, created two masterworks, one for Latchford, Gloucestershire in 1887 and one for Grappenhall, Cheshire the following year.

It was common amongst the stained glass artists to borrow ideas from Renaissance masters, since the pressure of inventing new designs daily exhausted even the most fertile imaginations. Examples of Almquist's

Fig. 13 An early Shrigley and Hunt catalogue of designs (1879). This involved considerable effort from the design team (including J. M. Allen and A. Skirving), and was well received by the architectural press.

24

Plate 11 (a) and (b)   St. James, West Derby, Lancashire (1883)

Plate 12   Parish Church, East Hoathly, Sussex (1883)

Plate 13 St. John, Walton near Warrington, Lancashire (1883)

Plate 14   St. Paul, Oswaldtwistle, Lancashire (1884)

Plate 15 St. Paul, Bedford, Bedfordshire (1884–85)

Plate 16 Parish Church, Eastwood, Glasgow (1884–85)

Plate 18   St. Mary, Ware, Hertfordshire (1885)

Plate 17   St. Barnabas, Great Strickland, Cumbria (1885)

Plate 19 All Saints, Upper
Stondon, Bedfordshire (1885)

Plate 20 St. Margaret, Hornby, Lancashire (c.1885)

borrowing from Dürer can be seen at Harthill (1885–87) (see Fig. 9, above, and Plate 23) and from Della Robbia at St. John, Silverdale (Fig. 12(a) and (b)). Jewitt, who interviewed clients more often and at this time produced fewer cartoons, appears not to have leaned too heavily on his forbears. His knowledge of iconography gained at an early age from his father and uncle proved a most reliable resource. Although there are passing references to the Burne-Jones type, and to Flemish art, his cartoons are more idiosyncratic, and less Pre-Raphaelite, with an emphasis on more specific character interpretation of the individuals depicted.

ART TILES

From the outset, art tiles – individually designed and painted tiles – were also an important part of Shrigley and Hunt's production, as they had been an important part of Morris and Co.'s output. Those of Shrigley and Hunt, which are very similar to the Morris output, would appear to substantiate the theory that Arthur Hunt had some contact with the firm or even began an apprenticeship with them.

Family tradition also holds that Arthur Hunt was trained as a tile designer at Heaton, Butler and Bayne's studio, from where he had first-hand experience in production methods on a commercial scale. His interest in the Morris tradition is confirmed by his amassing a large collection of William De Morgan tiles for reference. An early catalogue of designs (Fig. 13) included repeating patterns, floral designs, panels (depicting typical Japanoiserie, storks and chrysanthemums, Renaissance putti, classical figures) and sets characteristic of the period such as seasons, country sports, virtues and muses. For many years the firm used imported blanks from Minton's

Fig. 14 St. Michael, Rampside, Lancashire. East window, The Crucifixion, Lambert and Moore (c.1892). William Lambert was one of the original workers for Arthur Hunt in the 1870s. He was responsible for painting and firing tiles. His name continues in the account books until the mid 1880s. Lambert and Moore are reported in 1891 as having recently started as glass and tile painters. Their name appears on the east window of St. Paul, Scotforth, Lancaster in 1893 which, together with the isolated example of the Rampside east window, points to their having been active for a short while only, especially as Lambert occurs in the bankruptcy lists for 1895.

Fig. 15 (*top left*) Page from a workshop catalogue of tiles, from which clients could order by quoting the reference numbers at the top. These tiles were designed by John Milner Allen in 1875 and depict Prometheus and Epimetheus (private collection).

Fig. 16 (*top right*) A typical Shrigley and Hunt six-inch repeating pattern.

Fig. 17 (*left*) Tile panel of 1877 by Shrigley and Hunt for St. Edmund, Holme Pierrepont, Nottinghamshire. It depicts vine leaves and corn-on-the-cob on either side of an inscription, and is still *in situ*.

which were over-painted and fired at the works. They can be recognised by a stencil mark applied to the reverse, which comprises an 'S' superimposed upon an 'H'. Later tiles were however impressed with a device (using the same initials) into the wet clay, indicating that the firm was able to manufacture as well as to decorate their tiles. Arthur Hunt recruited William Lambert[35] (Fig. 14) from the Potteries especially to oversee this department.

The same designers were involved in tile work as those who made stained glass designs, notably J. M. Allen (Fig. 15), Almquist, Jewitt and W. Tipping. Like Morris and Co., Shrigley and Hunt issued pattern and figure tiles. Some of the latter were clearly based upon Burne-Jones' device of spreading the image over two six-inch tiles (Fig. 16). During the 1870s and 1880s Shrigley and Hunt's tiles were extremely popular. They certainly generated a substantial part of the firm's income and helped to support stained glass production during these early stages. At that time the demand for hand-painted tiles to be used in furniture and fire surrounds was at its height. Many of the high-class cabinetmakers had accounts with Shrigley and Hunt as the following list for 1876 shows:[36]

Edwards and Sons	Gt. Marlborough St. London	
W. L. Burton and Sons	London	£27
Longdon & Co.	Sheffield	£7.6.9
Benham & Sons		£74.16.6
Gray & Son	Edinburgh	
W. G. Skelton & Co.		£8.18
Jackson and Graham	London	£19.6.6
Barnard Bishop and Barnard	Norwich	£35.16
Wippell & Sons	Exeter	£11.2.6
Marsh Jones and Cribb	Leeds	
Falkirk Iron Foundry		
Crace and Son	London	

Later, in the 1880s, the firm capitalised on the Scottish market, selling large quantities to architects in Glasgow and Edinburgh for use in their building projects. On rare occasions tiles were used as part of church decoration; like Powell's and Morris and Co., Shrigley and Hunt used them primarily to decorate church sanctuaries. An early hand-painted tiled reredos exists at Holme Pierrepont in Nottinghamshire depicting emblematic botanical subjects (Fig. 17). An unusual combination of a tiled reredos by Heaton, Butler and Bayne, below a window by Shrigley and Hunt, also survives at Bolton-near-Bradford.

When mass production was introduced by the pottery industry, the demand for expensive hand-painted tiles significantly decreased. Around 1900 production was reduced to a trickle, since only very wealthy clients could still afford them, and tiles were no longer manufactured by Shrigley and Hunt after the 1914–18 war.

Notes

[16] L. F. Day (1845–1910), heard during his period at the stained glass workshop Lavers & Barraud, 1866. L. F. Day, 'William Morris and his Art', *Easter Annual of the Art Journal* (1899), p.2.

[17] Harrison and Waters, *Burne-Jones*, op. cit., pp. 48–52.

[18] H. Holiday, 'Stained Glass Aesthetically Considered', *The Architect*, 25 March 1871, pp.159–61. Lecture given at the London Institution.

[19] B. H. Jackson, *Recollections of Thomas Graham Jackson (1835–1934)* (Oxford University Press, 1950), p.116.

[20] It is possible that he designed pattern tiles – his training at Heaton, Butler and Bayne is said (by the family) to have been orientated towards tiles.

[21] Windows by J. M. A. now destroyed: St. Mark's Bradford, St. Peter's Walsden and Didsbury Chapel. Anthony Hewitson, *History of Preston* pub. 'Chronicle Office, Preston' (1883) (the building was known as Preston County Offices).

[22] There is no evidence to support the claim that the Holiday windows in Whittington, Lancashire or Finsthwaite, Cumbria were made by Shrigley and Hunt.

[23] Many of the early windows had to be replaced owing to the use of borax as a flux, which becomes water-soluble. Virtually all of the stained glass firms suffered because of this fault, which was remedied by replacing the borax with iron. Shrigley and Hunt volunteered to replace many of their early windows during the 1890s, which sometimes leads to confusion in dating their style.

[24] Dates unknown; worked for Shrigley and Hunt in the 1880s.

[25] Quoted in C. A. to A. Kjellström, Letter 11 December 1871, Orebrö Local Archive Collection, Sweden.

[26] Orebrö Collection, Letter 15 December 1870.

[27] Ibid.

[28] Ibid, Letter 15 September 1879.

[29] A. W. H. to Mr Burder (?), 4 February 1889, LRO.

[30] G. S. Payne was Almquist's secretary for a short period and acted as the executor of his will, after his death. He came from Heaton, Butler and Bayne to join Shrigley and Hunt.

[31] F. Broomhead, *Orlando Jewitt* (pub. Private Libraries Association, 1995), p.55.

[32] Orebrö Collection, Letter 15 September 1879.

[33] Jewitt to Messrs. Chance, 20 March 1905. LRO, DDSR 2/4.

[34] LRO, Preston, DDSR 2/6.

[35] Dates unknown, worked for Shrigley and Hunt c.1873–late 1880s.

[36] List of tile accounts, No. 25 Shrigley and Hunt Account Book, LRO, DDSR 1/1.

CHAPTER 3

COMMISSIONS AND CLIENTS

W hile Almquist and Jewitt provided the artistic inspiration for the firm, Arthur Hunt adopted a variety of strategies to obtain commissions and deal with clients. His relationships with architects and patrons, and his involvement in exhibitions, contribute to our understanding of the ways in which designs were created and business deals cemented.

ARCHITECTURAL COMMISSIONS

As early as 1858 Joseph Shrigley had had an account with E. P. Paley, the renowned Lancaster architect, so he and his partner Herbert Austin were a natural choice for Arthur Hunt to collaborate with. Beginning in a small way in the late 1870s, the mutually advantageous cooperation developed to become an important factor in the firm's prosperity, especially when collaboration between architect and stained glass firm was at its height from the mid-1890s until World War I. Their involvement, convenient since their offices were only yards apart, resulted in a particular style of window. Obviously the architects were desirous of continuity with their interiors. They demanded a formal two-dimensional presentation, often with canopies and pedestals, a centrally-placed figure surrounded by pale glass to allow light into the building. Frequently the windows give a dark impression that is pierced by a greenish-yellow glow. However Paley and Austin did not work exclusively with Shrigley and Hunt, as is exemplified by the inclusion in their church at Pilling in Lancashire of a large east window by Burlison and Grylls, and a west window by Mayer of Munich (c.1889). Here Shrigley and Hunt's contribution was reduced to a supporting role as they provided works only for the north nave wall.

Over the Pennines, the Yorkshire-based architects Demaine and Brierley paralleled Hunt's relationship with Paley and Austin in Lancashire. They first employed the firm in 1888, commissioning windows for St. Olave's, York (see Gazetteer). A close relationship ensued which lasted into the early years of the new century. More colourful windows than those demanded by Paley and Austin are characteristic of this partnership, the most notable examples being those at Pocklington, Yorkshire, East Riding (see Gazetteer) and St Peter's at Makerfield, Newton-le-Willows, Lancashire, the west window being particularly fine (Fig. 18).

The firm also had dealings with George Faulkner Armitage (1849–1937), more a furniture designer and interior decorator than architect. He is best known for his association with the Century Guild at Pownall Hall, Wilmslow, Cheshire, the home of Henry Boddington, the wealthy brewer. The house was a magnificent palace of art, furnished with the Guild's art furniture, sculptured fireplaces, decorative friezes and painted panels. It was here that Shrigley and Hunt were commissioned, through Armitage, to make virtually all the stained glass that fills almost every room. There were signs of the zodiac in the hall, classical heads in the sitting room, and nursery rhymes and scenes upstairs. On the stairs are the superbly colourful 'Four Winds', one of the finest secular windows produced by the firm using striped ruby glass and expressive leading (Plate 22).[37] Mansfield College Chapel, Oxford was another collaboration with Armitage. Arthur Hunt noted that the four figure subjects here were 'very fine cartoons in the perpendicular style' (Plate 28).[38]

Sir Arthur Blomfield (1829–1899), who was responsible for commissioning glass in Pampisford near Cambridge, Stanton in Gloucestershire, Aldington in Kent and a comprehensive scheme in Trent church, New Barnet, Hertfordshire, was another architect who regularly utilised the firm during the same period.

Fig. 18   St. Peter, Makerfield, Newton-le-Willows, Lancashire, detail of four-light west window showing Asaph and Solomon (Jewitt, 1898–1901): see also Gazetteer.

ADVERTISING, EXHIBITIONS AND COMPETITIONS

Advertising became an important dynamic of nineteenth-century capitalism but only at the outset did Arthur Hunt apparently see the need to engage in self-promotion, by utilising the architectural press to announce his firm's presence. As early as 1875 he was planning an impressive trade catalogue, eventually issued in 1879. Devised on a large scale it involved J. M. Allen and Alexander Skirving in a design that comprised nineteen large line drawings on quarto sheets. The catalogue immediately caught the attention of the architectural press. *The Building News* was enthusiastic:

> …but we miss the artistic feeling [in a catalogue by another stained glass firm – Gibbs and Howard] … which we find in the lithographic drawing of the plates in the … volume published by Shrigley and Hunt … there is a sympathetic touch which is thoroughly in character with the spirit of the work illustrated … Of the designs themselves we may say that they are in nearly every instance both suitable and good combining the quaint effect peculiar to the treatment of old glass with the improved modern drawing of the figure… Such books as these … are worthy of their publishers, and can but add to the credit of their authors.[39]

Having proved so successful at launching his firm on a national level, Arthur's decision not to publish a further catalogue until 1906 comes a surprise, but he later prided himself that his reputation was largely spread by word of mouth. Family and business contacts fulfilled the demand for propagation. As the firm's reputation grew, information about its activities appeared more frequently in the columns of *The Building News*, *The Builder*, *The Architectural Review*, and *The Architect* without the need for blatant self-promotion.

An insight into Arthur Hunt's ambitions for his firm and its artists is given by the fact that between 1882 and 1910 he exhibited thirty-six designs for windows at the Royal Academy in London. Stained glass was beginning to break out of the classification as a lesser art and to be taken more seriously. It became the custom for stained glass designers to rank their work with the fine arts, and naturally the best of them desired their work to hang in the galleries of the Royal Academy. It not only made a statement of their aspirations but opened the possibility for more creative and prestigious commissions.

As early as 1875 Shrigley and Hunt were represented in exhibitions at Alexandra Park, London, and at York and Preston. The following year Arthur's father-in-law's firm, E. Matthews and Sons, had included stained glass and tiles in their display at the Centennial Exhibition in Philadelphia, presumably to encourage and publicise his son-in-law's youthful enterprise. This impressive *tour de force* from Matthews was made solely to display fashionable interior decoration, in one of a series of temporary rooms created specially for the exhibition.

The Dickensian window, which Hunt contributed, had been commissioned for the exhibition and was unlike any further windows he created. Twelve years later, however, his public display was far more complex and sophisticated. Manchester celebrated the Queen's Jubilee in 1887 with:

> exhibition buildings...of brick, iron and glass which Messrs. Maxwell and Tuke, of Manchester, have imparted an architectural significance that would do credit to any capital in Europe.[40]

Shrigley and Hunt was represented by a large number of exhibits, hoping to capitalise on the prestigious location. They executed the glazing for the whole of the Council Chamber at Manchester with heraldic glass. The approaching corridor contained domestic figure glass and two religious subjects in perpendicular style. Exhibited elsewhere were panels of secular and religious figures, flowers, quarries and borders. They also contributed cartoons, drawings and photographs.

The following year (1888) Glasgow hosted the largest exhibition since 1862. Opened by the Prince and Princess of Wales, it spread over sixty acres in Kelvingrove Park and was a brilliant success that was recognised internationally. Arthur Hunt had already established a profitable trade, mostly in tiles, with Scottish architects and wished to develop it further. James Sellars of Campbell Douglas and Sellars had won the contract to design the exhibition. They had had some dealings with the firm in the 1870s and in 1885 had commissioned an important set of windows for the Sick Children's Hospital in Glasgow. Arthur was thus in a strong position to take advantage of his contacts and to present the firm's work to a Scottish audience.

He mounted a striking display. Rising to the occasion he showed eight medallion portraits within wreaths and scrolls of Scottish worthies and their associated coats of arms in the Bishop's Palace, together with a repeat of Almquist's magnificent design of St. Michael which had been made for Bettws Church, Derry Ormond, mid-Wales in the previous year (Plate 25). At the entrance to the ladies' tea room he exhibited a four-light window in the Renaissance style with figures representing 'Welcome the Coming', 'Speed the Parting', 'Friendship', and 'Hospitality'. As at Manchester he also included working drawings and designs.

Despite the firm's best efforts, however, not many contracts were issued from Scotland, the reason being that, although the firm's work equalled the highest standards of the time, the rising native Scottish school of stained glass, well represented at the exhibition, was dominant north of the border. The notable exceptions were Almquist's design for Eastwood parish church, obtained through Campbell Douglas and Sellars (Plate 16); Aberfoyle Parish Church, where his powerful two-light east window had a definite 'Scottish' massiveness to it; and Dumbarton Town Hall, where Robert Anderson's commission resulted in two exceptionally fine windows (Fig. 19), part of a contemplated complete set of windows that fell short owing to lack of funds. Of course, there are other examples in Scotland but many are later and mediocre – the earlier examples in Glasgow are now regrettably lost. Likewise in Edinburgh, after initial success with an agency held by Wm. Scott Morton and Sons, who sold tiles and domestic stained glass, sales declined after the death of Scott Morton. Be that as it may, contact with the Scottish school had a profound impact, especially upon

Almquist, who for a few years in the 1880s evolved a new style clearly influenced by the rich colours and the liberated massive figure drawing of his Scottish contemporaries.

Later, at the turn of the century, Arthur was thwarted when he attempted to secure a place in the competition for the windows in the Anglican Cathedral at Liverpool. He imagined that he had a good chance of landing this substantial contract since G. F. Bodley, who was on the judging committee, had already worked with him and two of Arthur's sons had been articled in Bodley's office. In December 1904 Shrigley and Hunt were making a window for Bodley in St. Matthew's Church, Westminster. A co-adjudicator was Richard Norman Shaw (1831-1912), who was also being subtly lobbied by the firm. By this time, however Arthur began to have grave suspicions that he would not succeed in overcoming the usurping of Burlison and Grylls, who were rivals for Bodley's contracts, noting that:

> at present we are out in the cold for wh. there is no reason whatever except that B[urlison] & G[rylls] are in touch every day with Bodley & we only partially.[41]

Arthur's schemings came to nothing. The firm was not even represented at the competitors' exhibition and the contract was won by Powell's and by Morris and Co., probably due to their existing reputation. The resultant windows were mediocre, enlivened only by Brown's design made by Powell for the east end. The loss of this important contract was a hard blow for Shrigley and Hunt, since orders for stained glass were slowing down at this time.

SECULAR AND DOMESTIC STAINED GLASS

When Morris, Marshall, Faulkner and Co. exhibited at the 1862 and 1864 South Kensington exhibitions in London, a considerable portion of their display had been made up of secular stained glass. In fact Morris had, in initiating the company, built on his experience of decorating his own home, 'Red House' in Bexley Heath, which had been built

Fig. 19   Dumbarton Town Hall, two windows from a set of six (Almquist, 1906): see also Gazetteer.

33

from the designs of his friend Philip Webb. An important part of their prospectus had been given over to secular work:

> Mural decoration, either in pictures or in pattern work, or merely in the arrangement of colours, as applied to dwelling houses, churches or public buildings. Stained glass especially with reference to its harmony with mural decoration.

Their first major commission, the 'Green Dining Room' of 1866 in the South Kensington Museum, had set a precedent which subsequent decorators were unable to ignore. Situated at such a public location, its significance had immediately been recognised. There were no gothic references, no distant moral or religious undercurrents; it was purely decorative. The windows had contained a set of six maidens in classical draperies picking or carrying flowers, designed by Burne-Jones. A panelled dado almost six feet high had encompassed the walls, decorated at intervals with figures also designed by Burne-Jones. Arthur Hunt, when he studied at the Art School situated in the Museum, therefore had plenty of opportunity to study the new scheme, especially if we accept he had spent time working with Morris and Co. before he was apprenticed to Heaton, Butler and Bayne.

When Almquist, a few years later, spent time at the Art School, the dining room had become famous. Through Daniel Cottier, a decorative artist who studied with Morris and Co. in the early 1860s, the style spread to Scotland and created a demand that Shrigley and Hunt were able to some extent to supply. In 1870, when Almquist first became a pupil of Henry Holiday, he had been invited to assist with the murals that Holiday was designing in the Great Hall of Rochdale Town Hall. Both he and Wooldridge, who was also assisting on the murals, had agreed with Holiday in dismissing the reformed gothic figures in the stained glass as passé (designed by R. T. Bayne (1837–1915)). However, in the stained glass on the ground floor of the building there was a set of maidens symbolising the seasons, designed by J. M. Allen (later an employee of Arthur Hunt), which stemmed directly from the windows in the Green Dining Room. In the few years since 1866, the new style had become a fashion and was beginning to reach the north of England.

Soon after its establishment, therefore, Shrigley and Hunt had become known for their interior decoration. Arthur Hunt deliberately built upon the existing firm's reputation as decorators of distinction. At first they had taken mundane but lucrative commissions for painting, varnishing, paperhanging and general work which smaller firms would undertake. In many cases, however, they worked for the very same wealthy middle-class customers that were later to commission secular and ecclesiastical stained glass. Opening the London offices gave them access to a more sophisticated and advanced market, allowing Almquist and later Jewitt to develop their talents as designers in the 'aesthetic' manner.

Gregory and Co., the high class furnishers based in Regent Street, London, not only worked closely with Shrigley and Hunt from c.1877 until the 1890s, but commissioned stained glass for their own showrooms which included a figure of 'Fame' and an Aesop fable 'Fox and Magpie'. Liberty and Co. also employed the firm to supply a leaf design for their shop window, also in Regent Street.

An important commission came from Maurice B. Adams (1849–1933), a luminary in the field of aesthetic architecture, and editor of *The Building News*. He was joint architect of the Bedford Park Estate, a development putting into practice the latest architectural ideas concerning suburban planning which introduced light interiors with emphasis upon tasteful interior decoration. Because Shrigley and Hunt were at the centre of the new movement, they had a reputation as suppliers of domestic stained glass to the more progressive clients of their day. The commission at 1, Marlborough Crescent, Bedford Park, Adams' own house, consisted of stained glass window blinds with a set of heads of maidens representing 'The Seasons', a design that set a precedent for many subsequent profitable contracts.

Throughout the country it became fashionable for some of the larger houses to use stained glass as an important part in their overall decorative schemes. Even the more modest houses generally had an inner door, vestibule screen and side panels, and the upper lights of the windows in drawing room, dining room and study glazed simply in colours. More ambitious patrons had more elaborate arrangements incorporating figure subjects, often in series which were most often found in library, stairs or drawing room. The finest total decoration was supplied to Henry Boddington of Pownall Hall, Wilmslow, Cheshire, from 1886 (see above, p.30). Other fine examples were to be found at 'Oakhurst', Colwyn Bay, at the home of W. Foster, Jnr. in Nottingham (through the architect Albert Bromley), at 'The Oaks', Millom (in Cumbria), and at Smedley's Hydropathic Establishment, Matlock (now the County Offices) (Plate 7).

Also through the Lancaster studio came large amounts of work from Merseyside. The large town houses belonging to the Holts, Frederick Leyland, G. S. Pickard, R. Alexander and H. W. Meade King, all contained extensive figurative windows as part of their interior decoration. Both new and old wealth were frequently responsible for placing heraldic and armorial windows to ornament either library or staircase. There are fine examples in Thurland Castle, near Lancaster, Lorton Hall near Cockermouth, Walton Hall near Warrington, and 'Aultshellach' near Inverness, to name but a few. Many town halls throughout the British Isles boast heraldic windows by the firm.

In Scotland the firm built up an association with the major architect Campbell Douglas. The collaboration had begun earlier in the 1870s with a commission for figures representing 'Painting', 'Architecture', and 'Sculpture' to fill windows in an unspecified Glasgow building. Through him they were responsible for a number of secular commissions, the most notable being an example of 1893 at 4, University Gardens, Glasgow. In Edinburgh, a suite of windows and a tiled fireplace at 3 Rothesay Terrace for the owner of *The Scotsman*, J. R. Finlay, was installed in 1884 and did much to enhance the reputation of the firm in the city.

The highly profitable secular interior decoration business was at its peak between 1879 and 1899 and for those twenty years a substantial income flowed into the firm. However, after 1900 tastes changed and, like the tile business, the demand for domestic stained glass fell rapidly, so that by 1910 it had virtually stopped and the firm became almost wholly ecclesiastical.

THE FIRM AND ITS CLIENTS

Only rarely can the stained glass artist have a completely free hand. He is a craftsman and, unlike the fine artist, he must take the client's wishes as the base upon which to build. Therefore the end product varies according to the level of demands made and is to a greater or lesser extent a compromise. Stained glass artists accept this and absorb it into their *modus operandi*. When Arthur Hunt met the clients, often with one of the artists, he would evolve a subject, its themes and treatment. A small watercolour (most often made by Jewitt) was shown to them, alterations were added where necessary and the design was then passed on to the cartoon studio.

There were varying degrees of quality available to clients depending upon the money they had available. Top of the range, and the most expensive, were the windows involving a specially designed cartoon utilising the best glass. Even then constraints could be placed upon the artist since the architectural space had to be taken into consideration – whether the position was high or low or on a north or south wall – and a style had to be adopted that was sympathetic to the architecture. After some years' existence, the firm had assembled a large number of stock cartoons for less expensive commissions, since re-use of these allowed for cheaper production. Single figures with simple patterned backgrounds cost the least, since apprentices could reduce or adapt them to any window size.

Each commission was different. Unlike William Morris, Arthur Hunt had no scruples about filling windows in ancient churches. Memorial windows in old churches were generally single commissions for a specific occasion by a member of the public and were usually confined to one window. When working with an architect it was a different matter, since there was often ample money and more than one window was frequently required. Working closely together meant that the artist quickly understood the architect's requirements and was then able to allow himself a certain amount of sympathetic artistic freedom. At times the company was commissioned to make a total glazing scheme. Such opportunities were in fact rare, however, since money frequently ran short in the early stages, as at St. Mary's, Leigh, Lancashire and St. James', Scarborough (with Paley and Austin), St. Peter's, Makerfield, Newton-Le-Willows (with Demaine and Brierley), and Dumbarton (with Robert Anderson). A rare total scheme survives at Trent Church, New Barnet (with Sir Arthur Blomfield), although slightly marred by some additional inferior work from the firm, executed in the 1920s.

St. George's, Preston was a major commission and is a unique survival in that all the windows are by Shrigley and Hunt, as well as an entire set of mural decorations executed between 1885 and 1914 (Plate 36). It should be better known because it is a glorious example of late-Victorian church decoration surviving in its entirety. A further reason for its importance was the use of new techniques that were adopted over the twenty-year period. Particularly interesting was the use of photography as a short cut in the process. Models were posed in the studio, photographs then taken and used as cartoons (Fig. 20). An indication of how important the project was at the time is demonstrated by the fact that Almquist travelled up from London to supervise, bringing his artist friend A. C. Weatherstone to assist.

Fig. 20 A surviving photograph used in the production of the mural at St. George the Martyr, Preston (Plate 36). Compare the photograph with the mural figure second from the right.

The firm executed many such decorative projects but the purges of the last 100 years have erased most of them, including those at Crosby Ravensworth, Singleton and Thelwall, Cheshire (Fig. 21). Mural painting was not their strongest point as the artisans who executed them from cartoons were often not sufficiently skilled. But as they were mostly seen from a distance they could be really effective. A contributory factor to their rarity was the firm's habit of painting on linoleum rather than directly on to the walls, leading to the mural painting perishing over time in the damp conditions of most British churches.

Working directly with lay clients, or for that matter the clergy, could prove taxing. Their interference in the process of manufacture could be especially disruptive. During the planning of the preliminary watercolour sketch, comments might be welcomed, as the following discussions about designs at Christ Church, Lancaster, in November 1896 suggest: : 'diaperbook held by S. Peter (too black) St. John Bapt. To be less clothed, & show camel hair, reconsider Noah'.[42] Sometimes, a client's input could be significantly fuller. Notes on the order book for the east window, at Copp, near Eccleston, Lancashire in August 1884 read:

> The wood of the cross to be carried up higher behind the angel's wings, being at present too stunted; the cross beam to be shortened that the extremities appear. The line of the clouds not to be so sharp – the marks of the nails in our Lords hands and feet & of the spear in his left side to appear distinctly. The inscription INRI to be on the scroll on the top of the cross. Scroll too stiff and inartistic – There is a great sameness in the figure of S. Anne and the B.V.M. and their affinities about identical – this difficulty would be omitted by transposing the figures of S. Anne and S. Thomas so as to have a male and a female at each side of the cross instead of 2 males at one side and 2 females at the other – the inscription being below should be S. Anne Daes. The small circular light at the right represent the sun eclipsed in addition to the omega and will the corresponding light at the left contain the moon with alpha (?) S. John's expression to be improved – tree roots defective – bottoms of trees in sidelights not thick enough. S. Thomas' spear too stiff and vertical Crown of thorns more in forehead & traces of blood to be seen.[43]

Fig. 21 Original cartoon for the chancel arch at All Saints, Thelwall, Cheshire (charcoal on paper, 83"× 27", private collection). This depicted Christ in Majesty, surrounded by Angels and Saints, whose iconological source originated from mediaeval chancel arches depicting The Last Judgement.

Later on in the process, clients' intervention must have been extremely annoying, yet Jewitt always dealt with it calmly and tactfully as is evident in his reply to Rev. Davidson in a letter of April 1905 about All Saints, Barnacre, Lancashire:

> The four figures are not intended as portraits, that is to represent the Saints as they appeared on Earth but rather as glorified Saints as they would have been designed by an artist of the 15th century to accord with the architecture of the building.

The extract in reference to St. Kentigern, though it points out that he always wore his [vestments?] over a goatskin dress as he went about his ordinary duties does not, we think mean that he did not vest fully for divine service.

The omission of these vestments wh. give so much life and beauty to the glass of this period would part the window of colour and its character wh. we are still most anxious to retain as being quite that of the church for which it is designed. The same arrangement applies to the mitres without wh. who can know that these Saints are Bishops?[44]

Arthur Hunt's patience was less evident, however, and clearly ran out with a Mr Hibbert who had commissioned a window for Aldenham Church, Hertfordshire, in November 1906:

…he harps upon what he calls the 'pink' flushing of the flesh in certain lights though he admits that the tone of the flesh is right & white when standing opposite to the window. We contend that because the effect is too warm when seen in a side-light from a certain point it is not fair to condemn the window on that a/c and inasmuch as you have been graciously pleased to express your satisfaction with it we venture respectfully to ask your service as to the course we shd. adopt to obtain a settlement desiring to balance our books.[45]

As the letter suggests, however, the clients had the upper hand until they had settled the account. Whoever dealt with them required diplomatic skills.

Notes

[37] Today these are obscured by a fire escape.

[38] Shrigley and Hunt, Inventory of Cartoons, LRO, DDSR 11/2.

[39] Lancaster Central Library Cuttings Box. Jewitt's family connections with the Journal may well have had some involvement in this.

[40] *Magazine of Art* (1887), p.281.

[41] Letter Book, LRO, DDSR 2/3.

[42] Note from the order book on the Baptistry windows in Christ Church, Lancaster, November 1896, LRO, DDSR 5/2.

[43] Note from the order book on the east window, Copp Church, August 1884, LRO.

[44] Letter Book, LRO, DDSR 2/3.

[45] Letter Book, LRO, DDSR 2/5.

CHAPTER 4

THE TWENTIETH CENTURY: A CHANGING ORDER

FINANCIAL, FAMILY AND ARTISTIC CRISES

No business is independent from the general economic climate. Despite its reputation, Shrigley and Hunt like any other became affected by the rise and fall of world trade and by changing tastes. The early years of the twentieth century witnessed a decline in the activities and profitability of the firm. Sensing a potentially serious problem, Arthur responded by looking for a partner to develop the practical side of the business, to create a greater variety and introduce some capital. As early as 1897 he had applied for a £2,000 overdraft. In 1903 the artist Ion Pace, who had considerable experience designing stained glass, was approached but the negotiations fell through. After various attempts, including an appeal to Gilbert Gamon, he finally gave up in 1912.

The reasons for his search were not entirely financial. Almquist had always been reluctant to work solely for Shrigley and Hunt as Arthur had wished: he was ambitious and would have liked to have been more widely known. From Almquist's first employment Arthur had held him on a tight rein, even preventing him from returning to Sweden for a vacation, citing the pressure of work. Later Almquist found difficulty in being confined to the London studio as the following letter from Arthur shows:

Referring to your remarks to me in a hansom cab some weeks ago when you said that if I wd. renew the arrangement existing last year of £100 retaining fee for your exclusive services you would work every day at the studio in John Street instead of working where and when you liked as stipulated in your letter 21 March last with a retaining fee of £50 only.

Plate 21 All Saints, Hertford, Hertfordshire (1885)

Plate 22   Pownall Hall, Wilmslow, Cheshire (1886 onwards)

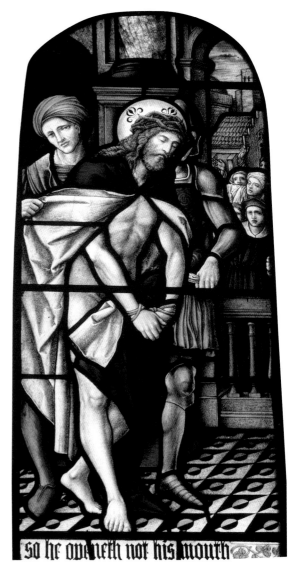

Plate 23   All Saints, Harthill, Cheshire (1885–87)

Plate 24 (a) and (b) St. Wilfrid, Grappenhall, Cheshire (1887)

Plate 25   Bettws, Cardiganshire (1887)

Plate 26   Cartmel Priory, Cartmel, Cumbria (1887)

Plate 27 (a) and (b)   St. Oswald, Winwick, Lancashire
(c.1887)

Plate 28   Mansfield College, Oxford (1889)

Plate 29 Holy Trinity, Bolton-le-Sands, Lancashire (1891)

Now I want to say that I would rather pay the 100 for work at John St. than 50 for working elsewhere for I conceive that the existence of your work in progress on the easel at John St. even during your absence was valuable and your presence when you are able to work at all, this is worth from my point of view fully £50 a year more than equally good work done where you are and easily accessible. I think this is a clear statement of my views upon your suggestion last week that you should work partially at home & I can only say do as you please but I shd. prefer the more expensive way & at your convenience shall be glad to hear your decision.

A more probable reason for this plea was because of Almquist working freelance for other firms – probably Burlison and Grylls – whose windows contain Almquist-like figures at this time.[46]

Arthur's relationships with his family could be fraught. He was a strong disciplinarian and an autocrat and this helps to explain why the plans he had for his sons to succeed him were never carried out. Three of his sons initially worked for the business, but they found his strictures too confining: they were treated much the same as the apprentices and were given very limited payment and little or no freedom in any creative or managerial decisions. Arthur's regime, based on his own training at Heaton, Butler and Bayne, was not as acceptable to his offspring as it had been to him; their public school and Oxford education had led them to expect more preferential treatment. They became alienated from their father and this ultimately caused the decline of the firm. Oliver, who found his father's service oppressive, left for life in Canada to practise as an architect, having spent time articled to George Frederick Bodley (1827–1907), the famous Gothic revival architect. Arthur Edward, who also trained with Bodley, and George, became partners in the firm. It was George who had a natural aptitude for stained glass design and who should have taken over the business after his father's death. He had entered the studio in 1896, and spent time working with Almquist in London and with Jewitt in Lancaster, before he became a junior partner in 1905. He acquired considerable experience and his cartoons show real talent. But he and his father grew estranged, mainly over commitment to the firm and about remuneration. He left in 1909 and never spoke to his parents again. The rest of his life was spent at the head of his own stained glass company in the south of England (Fig. 22).

Arthur faced these dilemmas with equanimity. The years 1906–07 were particularly bad. However his staff were extremely proficient and a number of apprentices were appointed which helped to secure a more settled future. Arthur Edward took an active role in the running of the office in Lancaster and, like his father, spent periods travelling and interviewing prospective clients. By 1914 the firm was beginning to show signs of a recovery from threats, financial or otherwise.

ARTISTS AND DESIGNERS

Despite the difficult times, the firm's designs in the first decade of the century remained of a continuing high standard, unlike many of their chief rivals. Powell's, Burlison and Grylls, and

Morris and Co. were in decline by this time, and their output had become stereotyped. Powell's occasionally produced inspired work under the direction of J. W. Brown (1842–1928); otherwise their work was mediocre until the 1920s modernist revival. Morris and Co. had lost Burne-Jones, who had died in 1898, and with him their creative genius.

Shrigley and Hunt were almost alone, therefore, in continuing to develop a post-Victorian stained glass art form. Their colour during this period was particularly memorable, especially their use of deep gold obtained by skilful manipulation of the kiln when firing back painted silver salts on to the glass. Facilitated by Arthur Hunt's conviction in their talent and masterful craftsmen in the workshops, his designers were encouraged to produce windows that allowed them to develop artistically and, unlike other firms, they continued to experiment and develop original ideas. Like their contemporaries they had to cater for the taste for more narrative windows but they were not inevitably led, as in the majority of other cases, to predictable Biblical illustration. Because of Jewitt's grounding in iconography, Shrigley and Hunt had remained faithful to the tradition of images, but reinterpreted them with great originality. The scheme in 'The Shepherd's Church' at Abbeystead, Wyresdale, by Almquist (Plate 37),

Fig. 22 All Saints, Margate, Kent; detail of worshipping angels in Te Deum window, designed by George J. Hunt and made at his studio in 2 Sydney Grove, Old Hendon, London. At first he showed the benefit of having studied under Almquist and Jewitt, as seen in these windows at Margate, but his later work (e.g. St. Margaret's, Rochester) became weak, probably as a consequence of his isolation.

and the remarkable windows in Christ Church, Lancaster, notably Jewitt's 'Christ at the Door' (Plate 33 (b)), demonstrate that they continued imaginatively to interpret the art of figurative and pictorial stained glass well into the twentieth century, when the great London studios were becoming either sentimental and conservative or even obsolete. As a result of the quality of both its established and new designers, the London studio in John Street retained a considerable reputation in the early years of the twentieth century. In contrast to the artists of the new Arts and Crafts Movement, with which it was now competing, its artists remained only distantly involved in the actual manufacture of the window.

At the turn of the century the younger generation, in a further attempt to raise the craft to the level of a fine art, believed that artist and craftsman should be one and the same.[47] Shrigley and

Hunt, although being an artistic manufactory and not a large industrial glasshouse, had always held that the artists should at least supervise the selection and painting of the glass used, and were thus not entirely opposed to the ideas of the new movement. Yet there were some feelings of antipathy towards it, as indicated in Arthur Edward's report of a church in the Liverpool area in which:

> the East window is by Whall,[48] the colouring being dazzling white, with a good deal of pink & very little paint has been used & in a strong light the figures are hardly discernible, much blue in the tracery. The vicar said he liked our window in the North aisle very & he seems well disposed towards us in regard to further windows. He thought however that if we were to undertake E W [sic] of the chapel we must keep it bright and luminous so that it will not be out of harmony with Whall's window as the two must necessarily be seen together from the West end – The verger told me that many of the congregation did not like the East window at all & that our work in the North wall was most admired in the church.[49]

A. E. Hunt's suspicion was motivated by the very real threat from the new philosophy – he obviously did not sympathise with the new colours – 'a good deal of pink' and 'much blue' – and at a time when orders were growing less he suspected Shrigley and Hunt might become outmoded. Christopher Whall was meanwhile completely changing contemporary views, about not only the colour of glass but the actual substance, quality and density of the glass he used.

Jewitt and Almquist had provided the majority of designs for the firm from the 1880s. After 1909, with George Hunt gone and Almquist calling for free time, there was an urgent need for fresh talent. John C. N. Bewsey (d.1940), a pupil of C. E. Kempe, was first employed by Shrigley and Hunt in September 1908. His style stemmed from a different tradition, based on the fifteenth-century idiom, and was unlike that of his new firm, but nonetheless their partnership produced some fine windows, especially those at Hornby in Lancashire (three-light west window) and Burton-in-Lonsdale (three-light, south wall) (Fig. 23). There was an attempt to hire Bewsey

Fig. 23 All Saints, Burton-in-Lonsdale, Yorkshire, West Riding, detail of a three-light window on the south wall (J. C. Bewsey, 1908). Arthur Hunt commissioned two artists, George Frampton and Bewsey, to design the same window, resulting in some acrimony and Bewsey obtaining the job.

Fig. 24 The Hunt family on the steps of Longlands, Christmas 1918. Arthur Edward, now head of the firm, stands third from the left, and Oliver second from the left. Mrs Hunt is in mourning for her late husband.

on a permanent footing but the parties were unable to settle terms and the short-lived association remained loose. So too did the connection with Edward Frampton (1846–1929) who already had a business in London. His three-light design (of St. Martin, St. Gabriel and St. Augustine), and also for the south wall at Burton-in-Lonsdale church, are most powerful. Their partnership became acrimonious through misunderstandings over money and difficulties that arose from working apart. Very few windows exist as witness to their joint venture.

A more lasting relationship was made with Alfred Charles Weatherstone (d.1945), whose name first crops up in the account book for 1898. He became a close friend of Almquist, who made him an executor and benefactor in his will. Like Bewsey, he worked for lengths of time in the London studio, but he stayed on with the firm after the deaths of Almquist and Jewitt. He supplied the more important commissions for oil paintings, including the reredos at Starbeck Church, Harrogate in 1932 and at St James's Church, Daisy Hill, near Manchester in 1924. He also designed windows for Palm Grove Wesleyan Church, Birkenhead in 1919, now demolished, and a seven-light window at Belton Church near Loughborough.

It is not too surprising that Henry Wilson (1864–1934), an Arts and Crafts polymath, who was a pupil of J. D. Sedding (1838–91) and a friend of Morris and Burne-Jones, should choose to collaborate with Shrigley and Hunt, since he shared their artistic philosophy. Wilson was the most visionary and dramatic of architects but the designs he made for Shrigley and Hunt are mostly of a more traditional nature. Those figures of St Tydfil and St David, made in 1890 for Merthyr Tydfil Church, were mere sketches from which he allowed Almquist to construct the cartoons. Later joint work was more characteristic of the man himself, as he was not only the draughtsman of the cartoons but also journeyed to Lancaster to oversee the whole production process. Commissioned by the Trask family, the three-light window in Norton-sub-Hamden in Somerset is most idiosyncratic in a developed post-Burne-Jones manner (Plate 41). The monumental sculptural figures express a strong sense of devotion whilst the Latin texts, esoteric imagery, innovatory leading and delicate colour impart a symbolist intensity. Lynton Church, Devon, possesses a further but less dramatic example of the collaboration on figure work. The colourful yet conservative four-light window showing four Roman male saints is striking, but the feature that most arrests the eye in the church is the clear glazing of the other windows in the nave. Here Wilson, at his most original, has used the leads alone to draw with, restricting himself to clear glass. He created within such limited means a set of exciting images, evoking the contemporaneous Art Nouveau style, whilst allowing maximum light into an otherwise dark interior, a technique not found elsewhere in the output of the firm.

CHANGES OF OWNERSHIP: CHARLES FREDERICK TURNER AND JOSEPH FISHER

Arthur Hunt died in 1917, much mourned by the town, and was interred in Lancaster cemetery. Arthur Edward succeeded him as head of the firm (Fig. 24). Initially there was plenty of work designing and installing memorial windows to the fallen of World War I. These tended to be repetitive in design, favourite themes being the English patrons St. George (of which both Jewitt and Almquist made convincing designs), St Michael and St Alban. Few windows broke away from the late Pre-Raphaelite image of an armour-clad noble knight, but a remarkable exception exists in St. Nicholas, Wallasey, in which a dead soldier clasps the nail that pierces Christ's feet at the base of the Cross (Plate 43). Such realism was unusual. It was also rare for complex or innovatory designs to occur as war memorials but Weatherstone made two, each showing ancient battle scenes, one mediaeval (Palm Grove Wesleyan Church, Birkenhead), and the other Egyptian (tower window, Clayton Church near Bradford).

There were no great changes in policy under Arthur Edward's direction. From the experience obtained during the time he was articled to Bodley, Arthur Edward was able to converse

Fig. 25   St. Bartholomew, Wilmslow, Cheshire, four-light window on the south wall, Musicians and angels praising God (Jewitt and Turner, 1925): see also Gazetteer.

Fig. 26 The Lancaster Photographic Society, a group photograph taken on a visit to Wyreside in 1892, with Charles F. Turner seated third from the right. His enthusiasm for photographic art resulted in his being commissioned by A. W. Hunt to take portraits of the family and to assume responsibility for photography within the firm.

with architectural clients on their terms. He oversaw and was very proud of the cleaning of many ancient and modern wall paintings, including those in the Houses of Parliament. Not being an artist and only having experience in the mechanical parts of production he, like his father, left the inventive areas to his artists and apprentices. Almquist continued to supply designs up to the mid-1920s. As he gradually lost his sight, however, his later work was paid for but not used. Jewitt carried on designing, sometimes producing outstanding work such as the Boddington Memorial window at Wilmslow Church in 1925 (Fig. 25), and when he died in 1929 he was still working for the firm.

One apprentice, Charles Frederick Turner (1870–1943), was given more authority than the others during the war years when some of the older apprentices had either left to form their own companies or were on war service. Turner had first entered the firm's service aged fourteen in 1884 and had developed a passionate interest in photography which proved very useful (Fig. 26).[50] From the late 1890s he was given responsibility for dealing with Illingworth's, the photographers who reproduced sketches and cartoons for use by the firm. It was most probably he who took the photographs of the model in the workshop to aid the murals in St George's Church, Preston. On the death of Arthur Edward, quickly followed by that of Jewitt in 1929, there was something of a power struggle. Arthur's son Kenneth seemed the most likely successor but he was inexperienced and not wholly committed, whilst the man who was longest connected by his forty-six years' experience with the firm was Turner. Kenneth proved no match for his adversary and left to farm in New Zealand. Turner stayed on, running the firm from 1929 until his death in 1943.

During this time, however, there were no imaginative artists resident; Weatherstone was called in to cater for the more prestigious clients who grew fewer with the years. Because of reliance on the large supply of stock cartoons, the workshop's output became uninventive, merely adjusting existing designs to suit new commissions on many occasions. The colour also deteriorated. Turner had little of Jewitt's genius in that area and his best windows show a taste for sweetly coloured undramatic effects with a strange preference for streaky green glass.

When Turner died, his daughter Barbara Nevison, who had been associated with the firm as a secretary for some fifteen years, took over. At this point connection with the Hunt family finally came to an end. Four directors were now in charge, and the London office, now at 4a Bloomsbury Square, was closed. Lacking leadership and direction, the firm reached its nadir. The windows produced at this point were undistinguished in all aspects. To survive at all it needed a severe reappraisal and new blood.

One of the directors, J. T. Alexander, acted as an art adviser. Anticipating the dire future position of Shrigley and Hunt, he contacted the Dean of York, Eric Milner-White (1864–1963), who had a considerable reputation in stained glass circles because he had overseen the restoration of the windows at King's College Chapel, Cambridge, and who had been brought to York to supervise the post-war work on the cathedral glass. Alexander asked the Dean to recommend some new designers for the firm, since Shrigley and Hunt's designs were being constantly rejected by fabric advisory boards, and by committees who supervised alteration and additions to churches and advised on artistic matters, appointed by the various dioceses. The Dean replied:

> I shall be glad to do my utmost to help you and your firm to re-establish the high standard of design that distinguished it for so many years.[51]

His advice was sought on various commissions over the following decade, and this contact with such an influential figure of the stained glass world proved advantageous.

Another of the four directors was Ray Gardner, owner of Mansergh Carpets in Lancaster. On his design team was a young, gifted trainee, Joseph Fisher (1911–82), who had studied at the local Storey Institute. Gardner facilitated his move from the carpet factory to Shrigley and Hunt's studio, where his talents were greatly needed. Joseph (Jo) was posted to a factory in Chester during World War II but on his return he quickly sensed that the firm was in dire need of re-organisation. In 1948 he was elected on to the board of directors. Later, sensing his own indispensability, he offered an ultimatum; either he would be allowed sole ownership of the firm or he would leave. Since without him it seemed that the firm would falter, and accepting the logic of his argument, the board capitulated, allowing him to purchase the business for a nominal sum. Shrigley and Hunt entered its new and final phase.

JOSEPH FISHER AND MODERNITY

Stained glass had undergone significant changes since the turn of the century. Under the influence of Cubism, flowing lines and figurative images had been broken up and fragmented. Windows were preferred that gave the effect of 'light mosaics', and these suited the new architectural style that was emerging with the 'international movement'. This movement had begun on the Continent, and spread into Britain, making Gothic building obsolete and demanding stained glass that paralleled its angular modernity.

Not all firms responded well to these changes. Morris and Co. failed to integrate the new trends into its production, but Powell's had continued to adapt by recruiting designers who were young and enthusiastic. James Hogan (1883–1940) was the most important, and his work integrated ideas found in early mediaeval glass without being antiquarian. He eliminated extraneous detailing and the 'realism' of his immediate forebears. His work had a profound impact upon the new generation rising between the wars, as did that of Martin Travers (1888–1948), who taught stained glass at the Royal College of Art and actively disseminated the new ideas. In Scotland Douglas Strachan (1875–1950), whose individual mosaic technique developed independently, was responsible for revitalising native talents.

One of the reasons for Shrigley and Hunt's difficulties had been its failure to secure a continuous stream of new blood and its reliance upon its trainees to mature into designers of national stature. Even Arthur Hunt had failed to spot this weakness. Jo Fisher was to develop as a designer himself but he also relied heavily upon other artists to sustain a business beyond the demands of a provincial market. The firm had only one other resident designer, Edward (Ted) Ellis, who had been an apprentice with Shrigley and Hunt. Scaling down the firm to a manageable size, Jo met the changed circumstances of the post-war years by employing rising freelance artists to undertake the designs.

The first of these was John Blyth (1915–99), son of a Scottish stained glass worker, who had attended Edinburgh School of Art and studied stained glass under Herbert Hendrie (1887–1946). After war service he set up his own workshop in which he took on work for other firms, most notably Bowmans of Fulham Road, London, and Shrigley and Hunt. Important examples of his work with Shrigley and Hunt are at St. John's Presbytery, Warrington and Brindle Parish Church, Lancashire (Plate 45). His preference was for angular figures, which fully occupy their section of the window with plain diamond shaped quarries in clear glass surrounding them. The firm followed closely his instructions regarding colour and leading, as can be seen when comparing the windows with his sketches. Jo Fisher's keenness to modernise the firm is shown by the backing he gave to this innovatory artist, who worked for them well into the 1950s. As Jo himself progressed as an artist and advanced his own principles of design he sought out even more radical young artists, although with mixed success. Keith New's (b.1926) design of 1969 was too abstract for the clients and they rejected it in favour of a more figurative window. But pleasingly the experimental design of R. Hayes, a young artist from Preston, was installed that year in St. Barnabas' Church, Heapey, Lancashire (Plate 47).

The 1960s witnessed yet more change in stained glass design. 'The medium is the message' was the credo adopted by the protagonists of pure abstraction. Glass itself was considered as interesting as any subject matter it could represent; in fact some went so far as to suggest that subject matter was a pollution of the purity of the medium. Jo Fisher's development did not take him that far, but he gradually began to reduce the darkening effect of overpainting with enamels. His encounter with Dean Milner-White of York proved salutary in this respect. The Dean was initially unsympathetic to Jo's work and became an obstacle to the firm executing commissions in the diocese of York. Neighbouring Blackburn was within the jurisdiction of York and Jo needed to overcome this problem. He neatly sidestepped the issue by employing Harry Harvey (b.1922), an artist working in York under Harry Stammers (1902–69). Stammers had his own workshop but had worked for many years with Powell's, passing on their ideas regarding stained glass design to his pupil. Harry Harvey maintained a working relationship with Jo which lasted for over twenty years from the 1950s (Fig. 27). It was the custom for Harvey to create a small one-inch-to-one-foot sketch which was then drawn up to a full-sized cartoon in the Lancaster studio. On arrival at the workshop it became the property of Shrigley and Hunt to re-use and adapt as the occasion arose. The fortunate result of Jo Fisher's manoeuvrings was that the Dean became an enthusiastic client:

No. 5725 this is far the most original and interesting. Indeed it is the first rendering of the Ascension in modern glass that I have seen which is purely decorative [*in*] treatment and there is nothing more horrible than a pseudo-realistic Ascension window; the mediaeval painters knew better than to attempt it.[52]

Fig. 27 Harry Harvey in his garden at Haxeby, York, in 1998. He replaced John Blyth as the outside designer for the firm and continued supplying designs into the 1970s.

Dean Milner-White's genuine appreciation was confirmed when, in 1956, he and John Blyth supported Jo Fisher's and Ted Ellis' membership of the Master Glass Painters' Association.

Working with the much reduced team, Jo Fisher created a workshop which had much in common with the Arts and Crafts ethics of total supervision from design inception to completed window. He, Ted Ellis and Tom Mashiter (an experienced glass painter) were personally involved in all stages, although Fisher and Ellis were responsible in the main for the design. At first the windows show continuity with the previous work produced under C. F. Turner, with pictorial scenes that use naturalistic backgrounds and perspective. Confidence grew with experience, however, and Fisher's designs freed themselves from the dictates of realism and took the glass and architectural settings into consideration. They became more decorative and architectonic with a logical two-dimensionality. By the 1960s, through association with John Blyth and possibly under the influence of Harold Harvey, he significantly reduced his subject matter and, accompanied by his own free use of leading, his windows took on a vital abstract energy. The underlying reasoning in the evolution of his style becomes apparent when viewing the sequence of windows made in the 1950s and 1960s. He articulated his underlying philosophy in numerous interviews that he had with journalists, of which the following is typical:

> To be successful his [the artist's] inspirations must satisfy the intellectual and [must be] one which derives satisfaction from the sheer beauty and craftsmanship [of the glass].[53]

His intention was to convey an idea clearly within a contemporary aesthetic. Elsewhere he stated that he wanted to break away from conventional imagery.

Following the lead given by the freelance abstract designers he employed, and in spite of opposition expressed by his conservative clerical clients, Jo Fisher continued with his exploratory designs. Concerns for light interiors led him to isolate some of his figures amongst broad fields of clear glass, within which the leading activated the design and led the eye to the more realistic elements. The lead lines were the first elements that pointed the way towards his abstraction. Never really content with realism alone, Jo was obliged to supply figurative windows all his working life, but he always encouraged his clients to allow him to innovate. One of his common devices when designing a two-light window was to balance a full-length figure with a companion that contained related symbols, and then tying the two lights together by means of expressive leading.

From the early 1970s Fisher began a period of liberated design. The virtually abstract sketches he made in thick gouache are works of art in themselves. Lead lines took on a life of their own; geometric or flowing, they form an architectural basis around which the subsidiary images are conjured into life. Inspired by the windows in Coventry Cathedral designed by Geoffrey Clarke, Lawrence Lee (b.1909) and Keith New, whom Fisher had commissioned a design from in 1969, he, like Arthur Hunt before him, brought the *avant garde* into the northern counties. Paradoxically, however, his most progressive abstract project, for the baptistery of St. Gregory's Catholic Church in Ruislip (Plate 46), for which a stunning series of sketches were made, possibly by R. Hayes, was never executed. It was rejected in favour of a design by Patrick Reyntiens (b.1925).

THE END OF THE FIRM

By the 1950s it was already clear that Shrigley and Hunt's existing premises on Castle Hill had become too large for the reduced business of the post-war years. Jo Fisher vacated them in 1959 in favour of 43 West Road, Lancaster, a small semi-detached building that brought overheads in line with productivity. Part of the re-shuffle included letting the third floor to the Vehicle Licensing Office. As a consequence the building suffered a number of break-ins. The last one caused a fire which almost destroyed the building and incinerated the majority of Shrigley and Hunt's cartoons, sketches and records which stretched back over the entire history of the firm. So in 1973 Jo Fisher moved once again, this time using part of his own home, Lowwood, as a studio/workshop, to run a one-man operation but retaining the name Shrigley and Hunt (Fig. 28). On his death notice of voluntary liquidation was given on 5 August 1982 by his son, Stuart. A firm that had produced stained glass windows for over 100 years finally came to an end, but leaving a legacy of wonderful windows for future generations to enjoy.

Fig. 28 Jo Fisher at work on a window of the Annunciation for St. James, Chorley (c.1978).

Notes

[46] Arthur Hunt to Almquist 2 November 1903 Letter Book, LRO, DDSR 1/6. The connection between Almquist and Burlison and Grylls requires confirmation.

[47] Typically artists and craftsmen worked together in a small studio, produced all the drawings and cartoons, then cut and fired the glass themselves and were supervisors of the installation of the window, the whole process being the responsibility of a single artist. They were also innovatory in the choice of the colour they used, in combination with thicker textured glass, frequently leaving brilliantly white areas. See C. W. Whall, *Stained Glass Work, A Text-Book for Students in Glass* with diagrams by two of his apprentices and other illustrations. With an Introduction by Peter Cormack FSA (Bristol 1999).

[48] Christopher Whall, 1849–1929, an important Arts and Crafts designer.

[49] Letter Book, LRO, DDSR 2/6.

[50] Turner was an early member of the Lancaster Photographic Society.

[51] Letter 10 March 1948. Private family collection in Lancashire.

[52] Letter from Dean Milner White to Joseph Fisher. Private family collection in Lancashire.

[53] *Lancaster Guardian*, 1963, box of cuttings, LRO.

CHRONOLOGY

1719	The firm of plumbers, painters etc. was founded by Jonathan Dunn, Hoddesdon, later taken over by the Hunt family.
1750	Joseph Shrigley formed a firm of 'painters, carvers and gilders' which later occupied the corner of China Lane, Lancaster.
1849	Arthur William Hunt born, second son of John Hunt, builder of Hoddesdon.
c.1866	Arthur Hunt possibly at Morris, Marshall, Faulkner and Co., associated with Burne-Jones.
c.1867	Arthur Hunt began apprenticeship with the stained glass firm of Heaton, Butler and Bayne.
1868	Joseph Shrigley died leaving a wife and eight children.
1869	Death of John Hunt; John Jnr. took over the firm in Hoddesdon.
1870	Carl Almquist moved to London and became a pupil of Henry Holiday.
1873	Contact began between Arthur Hunt and Shrigley's widow for him to take over the firm. Took over new premises on Castle Hill, Lancaster. Beginning of stained glass production: windows assembled and fired in Liverpool and London at Baillie and Mayer's works. Carl Almquist employed as designer and moved to Lancaster. Arthur married Jane Marion Caroline Matthews at St. George's, Kensington, London.
1874	Freelance designers employed – John Milner Allen, Henry Holiday, Alexander Skirving. 1874–8 Payments begun for purchase of firm, name now used: Shrigley and Hunt.
1875	Kilns erected, began making stained glass on site. Began accounts with James Powell, James Hartley and Messrs. Chance for supply of stained glass. Exhibited at The Preston Exhibition.

1876	Represented at The Philadelphia International Exhibition in the display of his father-in-law's – Edward Matthews – stand by tiles and a secular window.
1877	Edward Holmes Jewitt joined as designer. Series of large lucrative commissions from the brewer Henry Boddington begun. The Grosvenor Gallery, Bond Street, London opened, and made Burne-Jones' work easily available for study.
1879	Large illustrated catalogue produced. London studio/office opened at 28 John Street, Bedford Row, Holborn. Edward Jenkins Prest joined the firm as draughtsman aged 22. Alfred Parkinson Bulfield began apprenticeship.
1880	William Tipping joined design team.
1881–1910	Shrigley and Hunt exhibit designs at the Royal Academy regularly until 1910.
1882	New County Offices, Preston, extensively decorated and glazed by firm. Important commissions began from Sir Gilbert Greenall, brewer. Lancaster Amateur Art Exhibitions began; Tipping, Almquist, Prest and Eaton represented. Frederick Alfred Rowarth began apprenticeship.
1884	Charles Frederick Turner began apprenticeship. 'Longlands', the Hunt family home, built to designs by Paley and Austin.
c.1886	Important association with George Faulkner Armitage begun.
1887	Firm exhibited large number of designs and windows at the Manchester Exhibition (Jubilee).
1888	Major contribution to the Glasgow International Exhibition. First of an important series of commissions from the Yorkshire architect Demaine and Brierley. Arts and Crafts Exhibitions began in the New Gallery that became a means of studying contemporary stained glass design.
1889	George Porter employed as designer aged 24. Exhibited at the York Industrial Exhibition, panels of 'Old Masters' by EHJ. Apprenticeships begun – William Cragg Martin, John Bird and James Bibby Wolfendale. Work represented at Paris International Exhibition in Spiers and Pond's Restaurant: figures of the months.
1890	Henry Wilson began period of association with the firm.
1891	William Lambert left firm to establish rival stained glass firm (Lambert and Moore). Eaton and Bulfield, decorative painters and printers, formed by two previous apprentices in Lancaster. Gilbert Gamon began apprenticeship. Arthur Hunt loaned 10 pictures to the 'First Loan Exhibition' at the Storey Institute.

1892	C. F. Turner became member of the Lancaster Photographic Society.
1893	First Annual Exhibition of pictures in oil, at the Storey Institute. Arthur Hunt, Jewitt and Prest on the committee and a number of designers from the firm exhibited work.
1897	Alfred Charles Weatherstone began supplying designs. Arthur Hunt applied for a £2000 overdraft.
1899	Charles Lane and Robert E. Bray agreed contracts to work for the firm. George Jonathan Hunt, Arthur's second son, joins the firm.
1900–02	Austin Jewitt, Edward's son, works temporarily for the firm.
1903	Possible partnership discussed with Ion Pace.
1905	Nominated by G. F. Bodley as suitable firm to supply stained glass for new Anglican Cathedral at Liverpool.
1906	Holman Hunt gave Arthur Hunt permission to use the 'Light of the World' as a stained glass window.
1906–08	Described by Arthur as 'three bad years'. 1907 G. F. Bodley dies, as do hopes of Liverpool Cathedral contract.
1908	John C. Bewsey employed freelance.
1909	G. J. Hunt quarrels with his father and sets up his own stained glass business in London. Archibald Keithley Nicholson (1872–1937) stained glass artist, stays at 'Longlands'. George Frampton employed in a freelance capacity. Patten Wilson (Henry's brother) employed on an occasional basis. Designs prepared for Edmond Sedding rejected. Large commission for T. G. Jackson in St. Luke's Church, Wimbledon.
1911	H. C. Marillier, director of Morris and Co., invites Shrigley and Hunt to exhibit their work at the Church Congress Exhibition at Stoke.
1912	New partnership with A. W. Phillips falls through.
1917	Death of Arthur William Hunt; Arthur Edward takes over.
1922	John Ellis begins apprenticeship.
1924	Death of Carl Almquist.
1925–23	A. Barrowclough apprenticed to the firm.
1929	Deaths of both Arthur Edward Hunt and Edward Holmes Jewitt.
1930	Charles Frederick Turner becomes director of the firm.
1936	'Notes on Stained Glass'. Published a catalogue of all the firm's work (Fig. 29).

1943	Death of C. F. Turner: succeeded for a short period by his daughter, Barbara Nevison, formerly administrative secretary. London office closed.
1948	Joseph Fisher returns to Lancaster to join board of directors with J. T. Alexander, R. Gardner and J. W. Sandham. Employs John Blyth as designer.
c.1950	Fisher ousts other directors to take sole charge.
1956	Represented at the Cambridge Exhibition of recent stained glass. Jo Fisher and Ted Ellis elected members of the Society of Master Glass Painters.
1959	Castle Hill premises sold, business moved to 43 West Road, Lancaster. Death of last member of the Hunt family with any interest in the firm.
c.1960	Harry Harvey recruited to supply designs.
1963	Fisher made recording for BBC programme on craftsmanship in stained glass. John Hughes begins as the firm's last apprentice.
1969	Fisher interested in injecting more abstract design and employs young designers – Keith New and R. Hayes.
1973	Catastrophic fire at West Road premises destroys cartoons and records. Fisher removes and reduces operation to his own home, Lowwood, Haverbreaks, Lancaster.
1982	Death of Joseph Fisher. Shrigley and Hunt go into voluntary liquidation.

Fig. 29 'Notes on Stained Glass' catalogue, 1936.

Plate 30 Kilncroft, Hest Bank, Lancashire (1891–93)

Plate 31 Town Hall, Barrow-in-Furness, Cumbria (1893)

Plate 32 (a) and (b)   St. Catherine, Burbage, Leicestershire (1894)

Plate 33 (a) and (b)   Christ Church, Lancaster, Lancashire (1895)

Plate 34 Christ Church, Lancaster, Lancashire (c.1896)

Plate 35 Christ Church, Lancaster, Lancashire (c.1896)

Plate 36 St. George, Preston, Lancashire (1897)

And suddenly there was with the Angel God, and saying, Glory to God in the

a multitude of the heavenly host praising highest, & on earth peace, good will toward men

Plate 37 Christ Church, Over Wyresdale, Lancashire (c.1897)

Plate 38   St. Anne, St Annes-on-Sea, Lancashire
(c.1899)

Plate 39 St. Mary, Higham Ferrers, Northamptonshire (1899)

APPENDIX B

ARTISTS AND CRAFTSMEN ASSOCIATED WITH SHRIGLEY AND HUNT

ALEXANDER J. T. Apprenticeship begun with Shrigley and Hunt c.1904. Foreman glass painter c.1920–1930s, director/art advisor c.1945–50. His son Reginald John also worked for the firm.

ALLEN John Milner Freelance designer; worked for Lavers and Barraud, Heaton Butler and Bayne (possibly Fouracre and Watson), and with Shrigley and Hunt between 1874 and 1882.

ALMQUIST Carl (1849–1924) Swedish designer; apprenticed to Henry Holiday 1870–73. Designed windows for Powell and Company, Heaton, Butler and Bayne, Burlison and Grylls, and from 1874 exclusively for Shrigley and Hunt until 1924.

BONE Henry (1853–1901) Painter and designer of tapestries at The Royal Windsor Tapestry Manufactory. Worked for Shrigley and Hunt 1876, exhibited at the R.A. 1876–99.

BERRIDGE Arthur Glass painter 1875 until his death c.1931, became foreman glass painter 1891 and is described as an artist from 1910.

BEWSEY John C. (d. 1940) Trained in the studio of Charles Eamer Kempe. Exhibited at the Royal Scottish Academy and R.A. 1906–22; worked for Shrigley and Hunt 1904–09.

BALDWIN Robert Lane Supplied designs for Shrigley and Hunt from 1934 until 1948. His later submissions were repeatedly rejected by commissioners. In partnership with Arthur Lucas in the 1950s. Exhibited at the R.A. 1924–41.

BARROWCLOUGH Allen b. 1880, was a gentleman pupil of A. W. Hunt from 1897, and c.1925 set up his own stained glass firm of B. Sanders at The Greaves, Lancaster.

BLYTH John (1915–99) Scottish designer, pupil of Herbert Hendrie. Worked for Bowmans of

London and Shrigley and Hunt after World War II until 1952. Later worked for Harold Clokey and 'Willie' Wilson.

BRAY Robert E. Joined staff 1899 after having been an apprentice.

BRITTAIN William Head glazier at Shrigley and Hunt in the 1890s. His son George Harry began an apprenticeship with the firm in 1890.

BULFIELD Alfred Parkinson Apprentice with Shrigley and Hunt 1879 and became employed as a 'draughtsman' by 1891. Formed his own company with E. L. Eaton (see below), executing their own windows and mural paintings.

EAVES William (1844–1907) Glasscutter in 1891, who later became head of works.

EATON E. L. (1860–98) Figure designer employed as draughtsman at Shrigley and Hunt. Exhibited paintings in the Lancaster area 1891–95, designed pattern work and figurative tiles, and formed a company in Lancaster with A. P. Bulfield (see above).

ELLIS John Edward (Ted) (1908–c.1980) Apprenticed to Shrigley and Hunt, and became designer under Jo Fisher in the 1950s.

FAGAN Isobel Welsh artist; designed stained glass for Shrigley and Hunt in 1948.

FISHER Joseph (Jo) (1911–82) Designer and owner. Studied at Storey Institute, Lancaster. Joined Shrigley and Hunt after World War II, became a director in 1948, and subsequently the final owner. He promoted a modernist style.

Fig. 30 Thaxted, Essex, St. John the Baptist, detail of Gilbert de Clar from four-light window in Lady Chapel (Gamon and Humphry, c.1915).

FRAMPTON Edward (1846–1929) Trained with Clayton and Bell. c.1870 started his own company in Buckingham Palace Road, London. Supplied designs for Shrigley and Hunt in 1909.

GAMON Gilbert P. (1871–1941) Son of a wealthy Chester solicitor. Apprenticeship with Shrigley and Hunt ended in 1891 and he became a member of design staff. Worked in London office assisting Almquist to reproduce figures from existing cartoons, renewed terms of employment 1896. In partnership with G. W. Humphry c.1903. Invited into partnership with A. W. Hunt 1910 but declined (Fig. 30).

HARVEY Harry William (b.1922) Pupil of Harry Stammers, designed from c.1949 until c.1975 in collaboration with Jo Fisher. Designed and executed windows himself which are signed with initials and an ear of wheat.

HAYES R. A two-light window for Heapey was designed by this Preston artist in 1969, and he may have designed the windows for Ruislip (Plate 46).

HOLIDAY Henry George (1839–1927) Artist and prolific stained glass designer with numerous pupils. Almquist studied with him 1870–73. Worked for Powell and Company; Heaton, Butler and Bayne; and Lavers and Barraud. Set up his own workshop in 1891. The only window made in collaboration with Shrigley and Hunt, in Calder Vale Church, has been removed.

HUNT Arthur William (1849–1917) Founder and director of Shrigley and Hunt: see Chapter 1.

HUNT Arthur Edward (1876–1929) Arthur Snr.'s eldest son, only involved with redrawing cartoons and sketches. After leaving Wadham College Oxford he spent a short time in G. F. Bodley's office. He became director of the firm in 1917 when his father died.

HUNT George Jonathan (1878 – active 1930) Began working in the firm in 1896 copying and redrawing cartoons. In 1900–02 worked in London office under Almquist and studied at South Kensington Schools. Became independent designer but argued with his father and left in 1909 to establish his own business.

HUNT Oliver Grahame (1886–1934) Articled to G. F. Bodley in 1908, spent periods in the studio at Lancaster and London. In 1910 left to become an architect in Canada.

JEWITT Austin Son of Edward Holmes Jewitt, pupil (not apprentice) to A. W. Hunt in 1898, worked in Lancaster and London studios 1900–02 on design projects, and c.1905 went on church visits with his father.

JEWITT Edward Holmes (1849–1929) Joined Shrigley and Hunt September 1876 as joint chief designer. Designed stained glass, tiles, murals, patternwork and also selected glass, for purchasing from the manufacturers. Continued working until the year of his death.

JEWITT Clement W. Sculptor who exhibited at the R.A. 1897–1901. Applied to Shrigley and Hunt for sculptural work in 1909. Executed an alabaster and marble reredos for Penwortham Church in 1908 for the firm.

LAMBERT William Tile painter, worked for Shrigley and Hunt 1875–c.1888. Set up his firm in partnership as Lambert and Moore 'Glass and Tile painters' in 1891.

LAWTON A. L. The artist responsible for lettering. The earliest mention, probably when he was serving an apprenticeship, is in 1892, drawing an illuminated testimonial from a sketch by Eaton. He was responsible for the 1906 list of works. Received promotion to draughtsman and is last mentioned in the wages book in 1931.

Fig. 31   Hollingbourne, Kent, All Saints, detail of St. Catherine from three-light window in south aisle (Edward J. Prest, made in his own workshop, 1904).

NEW Keith C. (b.1926) In 1969 Jo Fisher requested the artist to design windows, but only one was made and this was not executed.

PACE Ion (1846–1928) Trained at Clayton and Bell's works; had his own London firm. In October 1903 discussed with Arthur Hunt the possibility of a partnership, the same year he made a sketch for a window to be executed by Shrigley and Hunt.

PAYNE George Stephen Came from working at Heaton, Butler and Bayne to Shrigley and Hunt in 1903. Assisted Almquist as secretary in the London office until 1905 and returned for a short period in 1909. Almquist thought 'His capacities are not great', but in spite of that he remained his friend and he was made an executor and beneficiary in Almquist's will.

PORTER G. An artist employed from 1889 and 1892 working in the old style. He made copies of details from mediaeval glass. Not many windows were made from his cartoons.

PREST Edward Jenkins Artist draughtsman at Shrigley and Hunt 1883–1892 when he became head draughtsman and manager of the Lancaster works. In 1904 he established his own firm (Fig. 31). In November 1907 when he applied to rejoin the firm, Arthur Hunt replied: 'in the event of engaging you….. [it would be] a pleasure to me to have your services again'. The fact of his re-applying makes it seem his own firm was not a success.

ROWARTH Alfred Apprenticeship with Shrigley and Hunt began February 1882. The records show he was with the firm at least until 1896. He designed figures in a classical style for tiles and domestic glass but undertook very few religious subjects.

SKIRVING Alexander (d.1919) Executed designs for some minor architectural work in 1870–75, including drawings for the works' entrance and the structural framework for the cover of the 1879 catalogue.

TIPPING William (b.1832) Lived in the Birmingham area. Worked for Shrigley and Hunt 1880–82. Arthur Hunt did not like his designs and he left. Subsequently worked in Germany (1895–97). His son, Joseph, also worked for Shrigley and Hunt.

TURNER Charles Federick (1870–1943) His apprenticeship began in 1880 and he remained with the firm until his death. He took over the control of Shrigley and Hunt in 1930. From the 1890s he was responsible for the photographic activities within the firm. He relied heavily on pre-existing designs in his period of directorship.

WEATHERSTONE Alfred Charles (d.1945) Said to have worked for Burlison and Grylls. He exhibited at the R.A. from 1888–1926. He first designed for Shrigley and Hunt in July 1897, but his most active period was from 1919 until 1935 during which Turner relied upon him for original ideas. He worked independently for Almquist who was his friend and benefactor.

WILSON Henry (1864–1934) Arts and Crafts architect pupil of J. D. Sedding, closely associated with the circle of William Morris and Edward Burne-Jones. Intermittently associated with Shrigley and Hunt from 1890 until 1906. Arthur Hunt held his work in high regard; Wilson supervised the production of his windows at Lancaster. His cartoons were purchased by Shrigley and Hunt and used on a number of later occasions.

WILSON Patten (1868–1928) Book illustrator, he designed decorative borders for illuminated addresses and stained glass. He occupied a room at Shrigley and Hunt's London address in 1910. Brother to Henry Wilson.

LIST OF EMPLOYEES IN THE WORKSHOP AT LANCASTER 1884 (Fig. 32)
(job titles given where known)

Atkinson	Apprentice	Jackson	-
Billington	-	Johnson	Glass cutter
Brittain	Glazier	Jolley	-
Casson	Draughtsman	Moon	-
Curtis	-	Preston	-
Dove	-	Redhead	Draughtsman
Eaton	Artist	Seward	-
Gilchrist	-	Stevenson	Draughtsman
Gilich	-	Thompson	-
Hargreaves	-		

Fig. 32 Shrigley and Hunt works supper, c.1890. Arthur Hunt is standing at the top of the table to the left, and Charles Turner is standing second on the right of the table, wearing a white waistcoat. There is no known likeness of E. H. Jewitt extant, but he is most probably amongst the participants in such an important annual event.

STAFF AND EMPLOYEES 1930
(Lancaster Central Library, MS8030)

Arthur Berridge	Artist	James B. Wolfendale	Glass painter
Charles F. Turner	Artist	James Parkinson	Glass painter
Arthur L. Lawton	Draughtsman	W. Edward Eaves	Glazier
Charles T. Armitage	Glass painter	Thomas D. Mashiter	Glazier
Tom Scott Dixon	Glass painter	Arthur Stockdale	Kiln man
John Edward Ellis	Glass painter	John E. Townson	Labourer
R. T. Simpson	Glass painter	Frances Barbara Turner	Secretary
Arthur Whiteside	Glass painter		

APPENDIX C

SELECT BIBLIOGRAPHY

UNPUBLISHED CONTEMPORARY SOURCES

a) Lancashire Record Office:

Letter Books – an incomplete series of letters from 1888 –1933 recording the daily transactions between the firm and its clients and suppliers.

Register of Designs: 1877 –1964 – an incomplete list of designs with locations.

Inventory of Cartoons c.1875 –c.1916, made in 1898 and added to until c.1916.

Notes on Stained Glass, published by Shrigley and Hunt in 1936 for publicity purposes, contains a useful listing of much of their work.

There is a large amount of other material, less collated, which contains the history of the firm's activities from 1860s until the 1960s.

b) Typescript memories of Aileen Hunt made in 1970 – Private collection.

c) Lancaster Central Library: MS8030 Ledger containing letters and details of transactions between clients, staff and the firm. PT 8726, M. Edwards, 'The Studios of Lancaster's artists in stained glass', Lancaster City Museum, n.d. PT 8335 Shrigley and Hunt Catalogue.

d) Orebrö local archive collection, Sweden: Letters from Almquist to Adolf Kjellström.

CONTEMPORARY PUBLISHED WORKS (c.1870–1914)

A few Particulars respecting the Eckstein Family (Privately Printed, 1860).

A. Lys Baldry, *Modern Mural Decoration* (London, George Newnes Limited, 1902).

Georgiana B(urne)-J(ones), *Memorials of Edward Burne-Jones* (London, Macmillan,1904).

Lewis Foreman Day, *Some Principles of Everyday Art* (London, B. T. Batsford, 1882).

T. Goodwin, *The Art of Mural Decoration* (London, Wilson and Newton, 1866).

Anthony Hewitson, *History of Preston*, ('Chronicle Office, Preston', 1883).

H. Holiday, *Stained Glass as an Art* (London, Macmillan and Co., 1896).

H. Holiday, *Reminiscences of my Life* (London, William Heinemann, 1896).

Arthur Heygate Mackmurdo, *Plain Handicrafts* (London, Percival & Co., 1892).

William Morris, 'The Lesser Arts of Life', in *Lectures on Art* (London, Macmillan and Co., 1882).

William Morris, *Hopes and Fears for Art*, 3rd edition (London, Ellis & White, 1883).

John D. Sedding, *Arts and Handicraft* (London, Kegan Paul, Trench, Trübner and Co. Ltd., 1893).

Christopher W. Whall, *Stained Glass Work* (London, John Hogg, 1905).

Gleeson White (ed.), *Practical Designing* (London, George Bell and Sons, 1893).

G. Woolliscroft Rhead, *Modern Practical Design* (London, B. T. Batsford, 1912).

Transactions of the National Association for the Advancement of Art and its Application to Industry, Liverpool Meeting (1888), 22 Albemarle Street, Piccadilly, London.

SELECTED PUBLISHED WORKS

Church Recorders (National Association of Decorative and Fine Arts Societies, 1980), Stained Glass Makers' Marks.

Rosamond Allwood, 'George Faulkner Armitage 1849–1937', *Journal of Furniture History Society,* Vol 23 (1987).

A. Lys Baldry, *Henry Holiday (*Walker's Galleries, Walker's Quarterly, London, 1930).

S. B. M. Bayne, *Heaton, Butler and Bayne: A Hundred years of the Art of Stained Glass* (privately printed, Lausanne, 1986).

F. Broomhead, *The Book Illustrations of Orlando Jewitt* (London, Private Libraries Association, 1995).

H. Carter, *Orlando Jewitt* (Oxford, Oxford University Press, 1962).

G. Christie, *Storeys of Lancaster* (London, Collins, 1964).

Wendy Evans, Catherine Ross and Alex Werner, *Whitefriars Glass, James Powell and Sons of London* (Museum of London, 1995).

Martin Harrison and Bill Waters, *Burne-Jones* (London, Barrie and Jenkins, 1973).

M. Harrison, *Victorian Stained Glass* (London, Barrie and Jenkins, 1980).

B. H. Jackson, *Recollections of Thomas Graham Jackson (1835–1924)* (Oxford, Oxford University Press, 1981).

Norman Kelvin, *The Collected Letters of William Morris* (Princeton, Princeton University Press, 1984–1996).

J. Mordaunt Crook, *William Burges and the High Victorian Dream* (London, John Murray, 1981).

J. Mordaunt Crook and C. A. Lennox-Boyd, *Axel Haig and the Victorian Vision of the Middle Ages* (London, George Allen and Unwin, 1984).

Harry J. Powell, *Glass making in England* (Cambridge, Cambridge University Press, 1923).

B. Rengmyr Lövgren, 'Carl Almquist (1848–1924) His Life and Work', *The Journal of Stained Glass*, Vol. XXI (1997).

J. M. Robinson, *A Guide to the Country Houses of the North West* (London, Constable, 1988).

L. N. S. Smith, *The Stained Glass in the Churches of The Anglican Diocese of Carlisle* (Kendal, CWAAS, Extra Series XXVI, 1994).

M. Stavridi, *Master of Glass, Charles Eamer Kempe (1837–1907) and the work of his firm* (Hatfield, John Taylor Book Ventures, 1988).

Select Gazetteer

Thousands of windows were made by Shrigley and Hunt in the years 1873 to 1982, both secular and sacred, of which only a small proportion are mentioned below, with a particular concentration on the work of 1880 to 1899.

The listing is by county, followed by main town or village, the appellation of the building, in most cases a brief listing of image and location, followed by the name of the artist and a date. The collection of information has taken half a life-time, and hence notification of errors and omissions will be welcome. A complete inventory of all the Shrigley and Hunt output is in the process of compilation.

BEDFORDSHIRE

Bedford: St. Paul, north wall, three lights, Fortitude, Faith and Charity (Almquist, 1884) (Plate 15). Another variation of the aesthetic style, the quarries express a repeated rose pattern above and below the figure areas, whose two-dimensionality is enhanced by means of a blue curtain hung immediately behind. The figures ultimately derive from Holiday and Burne-Jones, but Almquist's maturity has its own distinctive character within the group. E. J. Prest worked with Almquist on the preparatory sketch, and Jewitt worked nineteen hours on the background patterns. In all the window took from 15 August 1884, when the early sketches were begun, until 15 October 1885, when the final guards were fixed in place; a total of fourteen months to complete the work, at a cost of £149.12.2½d.

Shillington: All Saints, east window, five lights, Disputation, Crucifixion, Ascension and Christ blessing little children (Jewitt and Almquist, 1885).

Upper Stondon: All Saints, east window, three lights, Faith, Hope and Charity (Almquist, 1885) (Plate 19). A depiction of Faith, and a masterpiece that places Almquist at the centre of the

Fig. 33 St. Michael, Steeple Claydon, Buckinghamshire, detail of a side panel of the reredos (Jewitt, 1878).

Holiday – Burne-Jones school of design. It puts into question the reasons for his neglect over the past century.

BUCKINGHAMSHIRE

Steeple Claydon: St. Michael, painted reredos (Jewitt and Almquist, 1878). The reredos, now removed from the altar, was a joint work by Almquist and Jewitt. The centre panel depicts the Resurrection and is by Almquist, whilst the two side panels are the work of Jewitt (Fig. 33). Neither artist was most successful as a painter in oil, but this reredos is the most accomplished the firm was to produce.

CAMBRIDGESHIRE

Pampisford: east window, three lights, Crucifixion (Almquist, 1896).

CHESHIRE

Dunham-on-the-Hill: St. Luke's Church, east window, three lights, Annunciation to the Shepherds (Almquist, c.1878) (Plate 4). Almquist has densely packed his figures into a two-dimensional space, creating a tension between the two main protagonists with dramatic effect. This design owes less to his masters, as his own artistic personality forcefully expresses itself. There is also an indication of the direction the colour would take after 1880 in this window, whose darkened palette parallels the artist's narrative intent.

Grappenhall: St. Wilfrid, north wall, four lights, Adoration of the Lamb (scheme and detail) (Almquist, 1887) (Plate 24). A highly complex masterpiece by Almquist, stretched over four lights. The design ingeniously destroys the symmetry by making it pivot off centre. The enamels are applied in a broad painterly fashion, imparting a pleasing overall soft effect, and the leading is unobtrusive around the figures, but actively makes a pattern in the circular void that surrounds the Lamb.

Harthill: All Saints, east window, six lights, Scenes from Life of Christ; detail of Christ before the people (Almquist, 1885–7) (Plate 23). The artist has chosen a Northern European style. Christ is of a type which originates with the 15th century Flemish masters and there is a direct connection with Dürer's 'The suffering Christ before the people', c. 1497–1500 from 'The Great Passion' (see Fig. 9).

Latchford: Christ Church, east window, five lights, Christ in Majesty with Angels (Almquist, 1887) (detail, Plate on front cover). A fine example of the firm's polychromatic glass of their middle period. Almquist's indebtedness to Burne-Jones can be seen by comparing the above with the illustration of his window of 1874 at Easthampstead. A comparison between Almquist's cartoon and the final tracery window gives an idea of the skilled interaction between artist and craftsman and the high quality of the production that came from the workshop.

Thelwall: All Saints, east window, three lights, Good Shepherd, and Nathaniel and Joseph of Arimathea either side (Jewitt). Originally Shrigley and Hunt had painted decoration throughout with mural subjects, of which only St. Christopher and the Last Judgement survive (see original cartoon for the chancel arch: charcoal on paper 83"x27", private collection (Fig. 21)).

Wallasey: St. Nicholas, south wall, two lights, Supreme Sacrifice (1919) (Plate 43). All windows of various dates in church: east window, five lights, Vision of St. John the Divine (Almquist, 1910); south transept, four lights, Christ preaching from a boat (Jewitt, 1915); north transept, St. Nicholas, northern saints (various artists); north chapel, three lights, Guardian Angels (Jewitt). St. Nicholas contains an important and fascinating collection of windows by Shrigley and Hunt. It was built by F. Francis

Doyle from a commission by Mr Harrison, a wealthy shipowner, in 1910. All the windows are by the firm and most contain themes making reference to ships. The War Memorial window is profoundly moving and offers a relief from the hackneyed image of a chivalric knight offering up his noble life.

Warrington: St. John's Presbytery (J. Blyth).

Wilmslow: St. Bartholomew, Prescott Chapel, south wall, four lights, Musicians and angels praising God (Jewitt and Turner, 1925) (Fig. 25). Even at the age of 75 Jewitt was able to produce a beautiful window, though of course by this date Turner had a greater hand in the production. The lyrical colours are typical of the windows made during this period when enough money was available. A special effort was required for this occasion, since the window commemorated Henry Boddington of Pownall Hall, who had been one of their most devoted patrons.

Wilmslow: Pownall Hall, window depicting the Four Winds, of which Eurus is illustrated, c. 1886 (Plate 22). Shrigley and Hunt's most important secular commission was for Henry Boddington, for his house in Wilmslow. Almost every window is filled with their glass and, combined with the furnishings by the Century Guild, it created a most sumptuous interior. Through this commission, Shrigley and Hunt came to the attention of the architects and designers who subsequently proved effective in widening their reputation: for example, George Faulkner Armitage, who was associated with the Century Guild, employed them on numerous occasions. Henry Boddington was a frequent patron, most notably at his retreat in Silverdale, Lancashire, where he again commissioned secular glass as well as the windows at St John (q.v.)

CUMBRIA

Barbon: St. Bartholomew, north aisle, two lights, Fortitude and Peace (H. Wilson after 1914, and attrib. Patten Wilson). Arthur Hunt was so taken with Wilson's designs for Lynton Church that he purchased the cartoons from him for subsequent use at Barbon. He recycled two of them, adding two small episodes above the figures. On stylistic grounds these can be attributed to his brother Patten, who occupied a room in the London studio and supplied designs on request.

Bardsea: Holy Trinity, nave, north wall, two lights, Young men and maidens (Jewitt, 1883); nave, north wall, two lights, Christ in the house of Mary and Martha (Almquist, 1906).

Barrow-in-Furness: Town Hall, staircase window (detail of lion device) (Jewitt and E. L. Eaton, 1893) (Plate 31). Heraldic, secular and municipal stained glass formed an important part of Shrigley and Hunt's repertoire. The staircase at Barrow Town Hall is given a certain gravitas by the addition of this magnificent glass. It would seem that the author of the designs was Eaton, as they are his preferred subject and he was often employed on secular windows.

Broughton-in-Furness: St. Mary Magdalene, south aisle, east wall, symbolic plants (J. M. Allen, 1875); nave, north wall, three lights, Nativity (Almquist, 1896).

Cartmel: Priory, top window, south transept, Adoration of the Magi (Jewitt, 1899); lower window, south transept, four prophets, Annunciation, Nativity, Resurrection and The Last Judgement (Jewitt, 1887) (Plate 26). The mediaeval windows in Fairford Church, Gloucestershire, were the basis for the four prophets in the major part of the window, and in the left panel of four small base subjects, Jewitt has compressed the narrative ingeniously. He subtly indicates heaven (by rays of light) and hell (by flames) above the figures, and humorously contrasts the fate of the saved and the damned (the uplifted hand of the virgin to the left and the hand across the face to the right). He controls all this complex iconography whilst retaining the architectural encasement demanded by the gothic canopies. West end, north wall, Te Deum (Jewitt, 1885); north transept, east window, Saints Aidan, Oswald, Edward and Chad (Jewitt, 1891–92); south transept, Adoration of the Magi (Almquist, 1899); south window, Magnificat (Jewitt, 1886).

Cockermouth, Lorton Hall: (armorial).

Crosby Ravensworth: St. Lawrence, chancel, south wall, three lights, Musical angels (Almquist, 1888).

Finsthwaite: St. Peter, west window, one light, Christ the Good Shepherd (Almquist, 1894); one light, John the Baptist.

Great Strickland: St. Barnabas, east window, three lights, The Crucifixion (detail) (Almquist, 1885) (Plate 17). A moving portrayal of the sorrowing Madonna at the foot of the cross. Almquist has retained the traditional blue draperies in which to clothe her.

Windermere: St. Mary, south aisle, west end, two lights, Moses and Christ (Jewitt, 1879).

DERBYSHIRE

Matlock: Town Hall, previously Smedley's Hydropathic Establishment. Stair window is in three tiers, the upper of floating figures with scrolls by Almquist; the middle tier of the Pool of Bathesda by Tipping (which Arthur Hunt thought 'very poor'), and the lower tier of figures representing Hygeia and Aesculapius by Almquist, all of 1881. Smedley's once boasted numerous rooms with stained glass but much has been flooded. Jewitt was represented by various designs that are now lost, but it was he who designed the fish decoration on the side panels of the staircase (Plate 7).

DEVON

Alverdiscott: All Saints, east window, three lights, figures (Tipping); vine (Jewitt, 1879).

Lynton: St. Mary, south wall, four lights, Wisdom, Labour, Charity and Fortitude and decorative plain glazing (H. Wilson, 1905).

North Bovey: St. John the Baptist, east window, three lights, Angels adoring Christ in Majesty (Jewitt, 1880) (Plate 6). Angels, being the epitome of heavenly beauty, allowed artists to express their ideas relatively unhindered. Both Jewitt and Almquist created angels of an ethereal loveliness. Jewitt in this window displays his indebtedness to Botticelli, no doubt derived from an admiration for Burne-Jones.

DURHAM

Haughton le Skerne: St. Andrew, north chancel, one light, Virgin and Child (G. Porter, 1880s).

Redmarshall: St. Cuthbert, south wall, two lights, Angels with musical instruments (Almquist, c.1905).

Seaton Carew: Holy Trinity, east window, three lights, Cross and symbols (Fisher, 1965).

GLOUCESTERSHIRE

Stanton: St. Michael, two three-light windows, north aisle; first window, St. Anne, St. John and St. Mary Magdalene (Jewitt, 1896); second window, St. Michael and St. Gabriel (Jewitt, 1896); third window, Virgin Mary (Porter, 1896).

HERTFORDSHIRE

Aldenham: St. John the Baptist, south wall, two lights, The Presentation (1906).

Datchworth: All Saints, west wall, two lights, Sower and Reaper (Almquist, 1879).

Hertford: All Saints, east window, south aisle, four lights, detail of St. John as one of the Four Evangelists (Jewitt, 1885) (Plate 21). Jewitt's response to the subject matter of the scriptures is to create the characters as real people. He reaches behind the iconography to present credible beings with a real psychology, unlike Almquist who presents the viewer with a sculptural, generalised and decorative window. Here Jewitt has presented the four evangelists as living beings who have quite distinct personalities.

Hoddesdon: St. Catherine and St. Paul, east window, two lights, Christ preaching to the five thousand, and four evangelists (Tipping, 1880) (Plate 5). The church was built by Arthur Hunt's father, and this window was raised to the memory of his mother. It is therefore surprising that it was designed by Tipping, whose work was not esteemed by Hunt. However, the main part of the design shows Jewitt's controlling influence. The four evangelists (below) are much more characteristic of Tipping's unaffected style.

New Barnet: Trent Church, all the windows in this church are by Shrigley and Hunt, and specifically Almquist (1898–1905), under the supervision of the architect Sir Arthur Blomfield, 1898 onwards. The majority are re-used, except the east wall side lights (mostly Jewitt).

Ware: St. Mary the Virgin, south wall, three lights, Early life of Christ (Almquist, 1885) (detail of St. Joseph, Plate 18). Originally designed for Almquist's home town of Orebrö in central Sweden, these designs were adapted for use in St. Mary's Church. St. Joseph had to be added to adapt the design for the new window and in his new cartoon, Almquist has indicated the precise colours to be used. Once again the firm's skill at adding flowers comes into play. South wall, three lights, Scenes from Christ's later life (Jewitt, 1891).

KENT

Aldington: St. Martin, south transept, two lights, Two angels (Almquist, 1887).

Boxley: All Saints, west end, north aisle, two lights, St. David and St. James Major (Almquist, 1913); bands of Christ Stilling the Tempest (Patten Wilson) (Fig. 34(a)). St. David was first designed for Christ Church, Lancaster in 1895, and St. James was designed for Newton Church, Lancashire in 1899. This is an unusual window for the firm, both in the background patterns and in the insertion of the narrow and incongruous bands by Patten Wilson, possibly linked with an illustration from a book cover by Nora Hopper, *Under Quicken Boughs* (1896) (Fig. 34(b)).

LANCASHIRE

Accrington: St. John, west window, four lights (Christ in Majesty) (Jewitt, 1884). A fine early window by Jewitt, which demonstrates how important it is for the windows to be protected, since the angels in the lower left portion of the window have recently been vandalised by having a brick hurled at them. The artist has chosen a rich golden colour, obtained by repeated firing of the glass with silver salts backpainted, to pervade the window, punctuated with delicate transparent tints throughout. He has ingeniously broken the large window area by contrasting kneeling figures with full length figures above them, and angels with scrolls at the foot of the window with canopy work above. The design does not, however, appear overcomplex because he maintains clarity together with simple stylised canopies.

Aldingham: St. Cuthbert, chancel, north wall, three lights, St. Martin (Almquist, c.1905) (Plate 42). Originally designed as St Alban in 1894, this St Martin shows how stock cartoons were a valuable asset once they were created. Many of the favourite designs were re-used for decades and crop up under several different names.

Plate 40   St. Wilfred, Melling, Lancashire (1905)

Plate 41 (a) and (b)   St. Mary, Norton-sub-Hamdon,
Somerset (1905)

Plate 42   St. Cuthbert, Aldingham, Lancashire (c.1905)

Plate 43   St. Nicholas, Wallasey, Cheshire (1919)

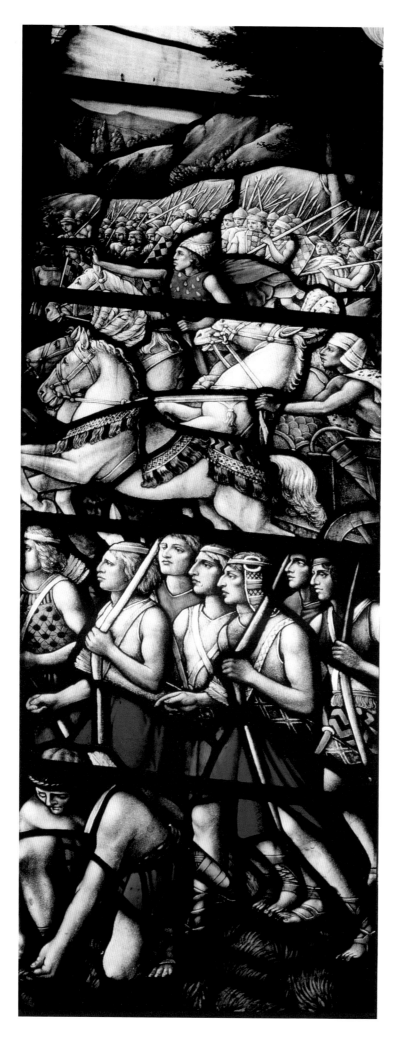

Plate 44 St. John the Baptist,
Clayton near Bradford, Yorkshire,
West Riding (1918)

Plate 45 St. James, Brindle, Lancashire (1950)

Plate 46 (a) and (b) Designs for St. Gregory the Great, Ruislip, Middlesex (1967)

Plate 47   St. Barnabas, Heapey, Lancashire (1969)

Plate 48   St. Oswald, Preesall, Lancashire (c.1972)

Plate 49 (a) and (b)   St. Oswald, Preesall, Lancashire (c.1972)

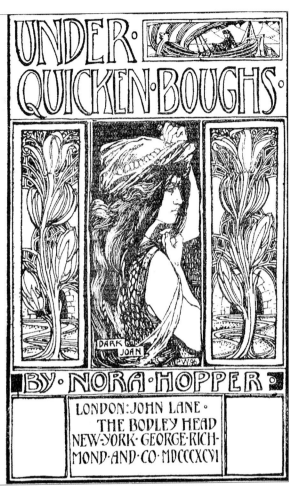

Fig. 34 (a) and (b) Boxley, Kent, All Saints: window of King David and St. James (Almquist, 1913) (a), and underneath a narrow band by Patten Wilson, perhaps drawing on the book cover shown (b).

Blackpool: South Shore Church, Holy Trinity, south wall, two four-light windows, church music and church building (Almquist, 1909). These two superb windows are testament to Shrigley and Hunt's continuing prowess well into the twentieth century, and are perhaps the finest they ever produced.

Bolton-le-Sands: Holy Trinity (formerly St. Michael), west tower window, two lights, guardian angel (Almquist, 1891) (Plate 29). A spectacular window, utilising silver stain to create a golden effect over the whole surface. Almquist's design had also been made the same year for St Nicholas' Church, Aberdeen, but in completely different colours.

Brindle: St. James, two three-light windows, north and south walls, Scenes from Christ's ministry (J. Blyth, 1950) (Plate 45). Brindle Church has two windows by Blyth which are typical of the 1950s – angular drawing, clear glass surrounding and a few suggestive 'props'. Blyth was able to buoy up the firm through a difficult period when it had not yet recreated a distinct character. Also at Brindle are some windows by Abbot and Co., the contemporaneous Lancaster firm which are very similar in style, and may possibly also be by Blyth. Design for a window at Brindle Church, Lancashire. Gouache on paper 14"x16", private collection, John Blyth (Fig. 35).

Copp, near Eccleston: St. Anne, east window, three lights, Crucifixion (Almquist, 1884). This was an unusual window for Shrigley and Hunt in which they used a large amount of decorative foliage most probably inspired by the designs of the Morris firm.

Croft, near Warrington: Christ Church, one light, design for St. Cecilia (T. Ellis, 1952) (Fig. 36).

Daisy Hill near Manchester: St. James, reredos (A. C. Weatherstone, 1924).

Garstang: St. Thomas, east window, three lights, Ascension (Almquist, 1877). This is an early work, showing Almquist's debt to his master, Henry Holiday.

Garston: St. Michael, apse windows, three two-light windows, Dorcas, Last Supper and Moses (Almquist, 1885–6).

Glasson Dock: Christ Church, north wall, three lights Good Shepherd and Angels (Almquist, 1889); south wall, three lights, Christ, St. John and St. Paul (Jewitt, 1893); east window, Christ in Majesty (Fisher, c.1970)

Heapey: St. Barnabas, north transept, two lights (R. Hayes, 1969) (Plate 47). Jo Fisher began looking for new talent in the late 1960s, amongst the younger generation. He contacted Keith New whose work he had encountered at Coventry Cathedral and a young artist, R. Hayes, from Preston. The only completed window produced by Hayes for Shrigley and Hunt was at Heapey.

Hest Bank: private residence named Kilncroft, for which E. L. Eaton designed stained glass windows in 1891 or 1893. Two panels were sold to Lancaster City Museum in January 2003 as part of its permanent collection, one of a Huntsman and the other of a Hawker (Plate 30). E. L. Eaton trained at Shrigley and Hunt with A. P. Bulfield, and in 1884 they set up their own firm in Lancaster at Victoria Buildings, King Street. As well as undertaking painting, engraving and murals, they also produced some stained glass. Since A. W. Hunt normally made an apprenticeship conditional on the person concerned not subsequently setting up a competing business within a hundred miles of Lancaster Town Hall, this firm was unusual. Approval for it to be established may be explained by a compassionate

Fig. 35 Brindle, Lancashire, design for a window, gouache on paper, 14" x 16" (J. Blyth), private collection.

approach to a former apprentice's poor health. E. L. Eaton died of sclerosis of the spine at a young age, and hence working in a third-floor studio may have been out of the question for him.

Higher Walton: All Saints, west window, two lights, scenes from Life of Christ (Almquist, c.1880). These favourite early designs were frequently used; clear in design and easily comprehended, they were popular amongst clients who desired simple, uncluttered designs that appealed to the modern taste. North nave, Parables of good shepherd and sower (H. Harvey, 1970).

Hindley: All Saints, east window, Ascension (Jewitt, 1878) (Plate 3). Jewitt's refined drawing and intricate detail is used with great effect, and his complex design retains its clarity in spite of the proliferation of images. The figure of Christ owes much to Holman Hunt's 'The Shadow of Death' (1873).

Hornby: St. Margaret, Reredos (Jewitt, c.1885) (Plate 20); west window, five lights, Angels and Archangels, Christ in Majesty (Bewsey, 1909). St. Margaret's has an important collection of work by the firm, chiefly through the patronage by the Foster family of Hornby Castle. In the reredos of 1889, painted and closely supervised by Jewitt, his membership of the Pre-Raphaelite movement is clear, and particularly his admiration of Rossetti. Sadly the east windows, a most important early commission, have now deteriorated through borax decay.

Lancaster: Christ Church, numerous windows by Shrigley and Hunt. Christ Church, consecrated in 1857 after funding by the Gregson family, was attended in the later years by the Storey family, local wealthy industrialists who were also benefactors of this church and a related chapel-at-ease. It is arguable that this is the best collection of the firm's work in any one place. Amongst the collection are a west window, Christ and Apostles (Almquist, 1891) and several windows in the south aisle, including River of Paradise (two lights, Jewitt, 1896) (Plate 34); Arrival of the Magi (Almquist, 1905) (detail in Plate 35); and Jairus' Daughter and Raising the Widow's Son (both two lights, Almquist, 1905). As well as the revival in

Fig. 36 Croft, near Warrington, Lancashire, St. Cecilia, watercolour on paper, detail of a design for a three-light window, 12" x 8" (Ted Ellis, 1952). Ted Ellis was apprenticed to Shrigley and Hunt and stayed on to become part of the design team. His work was competent but unimaginative.

taste for elaborate canopy work, there existed an opposite trend for pictorial windows with none at all, of which the River of Paradise is an example. Jewitt has here created a beautiful pictorial window, one of a group funded by the Storey family, for which no expense was spared. In the Baptistry, below the west window, is another important group, dedicated to a vicar of twenty years, Philip Bartlett. Amongst them are Suffer Little Children (one light, Almquist, 1895), an example of the firm's painterly style, in which the glass painters followed Almquist's cartoon literally and recreated his softness of touch. That, together with the reduction in lead lines, results in a modern type of work, unique to the firm. The Good Shepherd (one light, Almquist, 1895) (Plate 33 (a)) was first designed for Oratova Church, Robado, Tenerife in 1890, and proved to be a popular design, used on numerous occasions. Christ at the Door (one light, Jewitt, 1895) (Plate 33 (b)) is the most dramatic and telling of Jewitt's designs and is to be found only in Christ Church. It draws on Holman Hunt's 'Light of the World' but is less passive and challenges the viewer: Jewitt's Christ has opened the door and entered our world, unlike the figure used by Hunt who stands outside and waits to come in.

Lancaster: St. Peter's Roman Catholic Cathedral, Baptistry, St. Peter, Paul, St. Processuss, Martmaeus, St. Philip, St. Augustine and St. Paul (Almquist, 1899); west end, south aisle, Assumption of the Blessed Virgin (Almquist, 1905).

Lancaster: Priory, in The King's Own Memorial Chapel, c. 1903: three-light east window, St. George, St. Michael and St. Alban (Almquist). Two-light east window (to left), King Alfred and St. Oswald; two-light east window (to right), St. Martin and St. Longinus; west wall, four lights, four prophets (Jewitt, c.1910).

Leigh: St. Mary, whole scheme planned for this church (with Paley and Austin) from 1888. It remained incomplete through lack of funds. East window, five lights, Christ and Archangels (Jewitt, 1888); east wall, three lights, St. Mary's chapel, north aisle, Nunc Dimittis (Jewitt, 1882); and many others.

Makerfield, Newton-le-Willows: St. Peter, west window, four lights, Asaph and Solomon (Jewitt, 1898–1901) (Fig. 18). This magnificent church by the Yorkshire architects, Demaine and Brierley, contains numerous windows by Shrigley and Hunt, and an excellent selection of Jewitt's best work in the east and west windows (1892–1901). The architects showed a preference for the firm's work and it frequently shows up in their buildings. The west window at Newton is particularly colourful and was especially designed for the church. Neither window carries canopies but fill the spaces with resplendent musical angels.

Melling: St. Wilfred, north aisle, two lights, detail of David (Almquist, 1887; modified by G. Hunt, 1905) (Plate 40). George Hunt was asked to make the cartoon of David more beautiful to comply with the wishes of the commissioner. Jewitt responded in a letter of 28 February 1905: 'I am awfully pleased with the cartoons. Thanks for the care you have taken in carrying out the little alterations I suggested.'

Oswaldtwistle: St. Paul, east window, five lights, Crucifixion (detail) (Jewitt, 1884) (Plate 14). This extraordinary window is unique in the output of the firm, in its stark, uncompromising idiom. Almost Expressionist both in the treatment of the subject and in the choice of streaky glass, Mary Magdalene is barely distinguishable from the abstract rocks at the foot of the cross and her lost face, buried in her arms, increases the drama. The aesthetic format of figures contrasted with pattern only seems to intensify the experience. One presumes that the architects, Habershon and Fawckner of London, had some hand in the window's appearance, since the east window dates from the time the church was being built. The rigid architectural structure would also tend to support this view.

Over Wyresdale: Christ Church (the Shepherd's church), south wall, two lights, Annunciation to the Shepherds (Almquist, c.1897) (Plate 37). All windows were on the theme of sheep and shepherds, with designs by Almquist from 1891–1903, making a complete set of windows by Shrigley and Hunt. Surrounded by Pennine fells and in the centre of the Earl of Sefton's Abbeystead estate, the Shepherd's church was patronised by the Sefton family. At the end of the nineteenth century they began to fill all the windows with the firm's stained glass, and they chose Biblical stories which in some way concerned sheep. The resultant scheme of windows is thus singular in having a common theme, entirely designed by Almquist. They also share a reduced colour range which is predominantly white/clear and yellow, to compensate for the possibility of an otherwise darkened interior. The windows are entirely pictorial, as insisted upon by Lady Rose Molyneux (the Earl's daughter):

> The shepherd in hat to be bare headed or as hooded as the yellow head-dress in other subjects. St Joseph to be younger, a man of 40 or 45. Annunciation to the Shepherds. Open country, no woodside, shepherds abiding in <u>fields</u>. Col. Wyatt would have liked a vent in clouds & angel appearing, the other angels more distant, see his own sketch…

Pilling: St. John Baptist, north nave wall, St. Margaret (Jewitt, 1911).

Preesall: St. Oswald, north aisle, three lights, Gift of Tongues (H. Harvey, c.1972) (Plate 49 (a) and (b)). Jo Fisher was sufficiently proud of this collaboration that he signed it in person, in addition to the usual Shrigley and Hunt name. The Annunciation (Fisher and H. Harvey, c.1971) (Plate 48). Jo Fisher's eye for colour and the clarity of Harry's design led to a gently dramatic interpretation of the story.

Preston: St. George the Martyr, mural of Exodus (detail) (Almquist, 1897) (Plate 36) and photographic model (Fig. 20). The whole church was decorated by Shrigley and Hunt, beginning in 1885 with the Baptistry window, and was added to continually until 1914. The decoration above the arches on the north and south walls comprises ten panels, illustrating the Exodus of the Israelites and their return. It is interesting to note the use of a photograph (probably taken by C. F. Turner (q.v.)), as an aid to transferring the murals from the drawings by Almquist: he and Waterstone supervised the execution of the work, which was carried out by the painters Casson, Lawton, Stephenson, Bray and Brittain.

Preston: County Hall, murals of Northern Worthies (J. M. Allen, 1878). This building, also known as County Offices, is now demolished.

Quernmore: St. Peter, south wall, two lights, Angels (Jewitt, 1881) (Plate 8). One of Jewitt's most powerful windows. Executed in the aesthetic style – figures set against a patterned background – the impact is made by the angels alone who, rather than terrifying the souls to be judged, suggest the beauties of Paradise that await them. William Garnett of Quernmore Park, who commissioned much secular work from the firm, was responsible for the installation of the window, which is the reason for the high quality of the glass and its design.

Rampside: St. Michael, east window, three lights, Crucifixion (Lambert and Moore, c.1892) (Fig. 14).

St. Anne's-on-Sea: St. Anne, south aisle, three lights, St. Agnes (Jewitt, c.1899) (Plate 38). Specially created for this church, St Agnes was situated between two figures by Almquist.

St. Michael's-on-Wyre: St. Michael, north aisle, west window (Turner, 1936).

Silverdale: St. John, west window, three lights, Nativity (Almquist, 1886) (Fig. 12 (a)); Clerestory windows, Old Testament prophets, (Almquist, 1891). These superb examples by Almquist show how the constant pressure for novelty of design encourages recourse to existing familiar material. In the Nativity Almquist's sources for the angels include Della Robbia (Fig. 12 (b)), while the Holy Family section draws on a Burne-Jones design of 1874 from Castle Howard.

Walton, near Warrington: St. John, east window, four lights, Te Deum (Jewitt, 1883) (Plate 13); west window, four lights, side windows, Angels (Jewitt, 1881). Commissioned by the wealthy brewing magnate Sir Gilbert Greenall, the church was designed by E. G. Paley, and Shrigley and Hunt were commissioned to execute a complete decoration of the interior. Jewitt was responsible for most of the figures and produced a complex and sophisticated body of work. Below the Last Supper he portrayed the noble army of martyrs and angels praising God.

Warton: St. Paul, south wall, two lights, St. Eunice instructing Timothy (G. Porter, 1889) (Fig. 37). Porter was employed by the firm for a period of three to four years around 1890. He was engaged for some time in copying mediaeval detailing in surviving windows. His own designs tend to be mediaeval costume pieces, competently drawn.

West Derby: St. James, transept, three lights, Sermon on the Mount (adapted from Thornton) (Tipping, 1883); north chapel, three lights, Martyrs worshipping the Lamb (Almquist, 1883) (Plate 11); west window, north transept, two one-light windows, Angels (Jewitt, 1883) (Plate 10). This church has one of the most important collections of the firm's windows and was originally decorated throughout (the walls are now whitewashed). Interestingly, the colours of the windows were conceived according to an overall design, one area being predominantly blue, and another red. Annunciation and Nativity (Almquist, 1888); west wall, Scenes from Christ's Life, (Almquist, 1898);

north chapel, Martyrs Worshipping the Holy Lamb (and detail of poppies) (Almquist, 1883). Shrigley and Hunt's glass had a reputation for its beauty. Here poppies, normally used as symbols of sleep, are used ornamentally, and their realistic portrayal provides an interesting contrast with the mediaevally-inspired diapers below.

Winwick: St. Oswald, west wall, four lights, Tree of Jesse (with detail of King David and cartoon) (Almquist, c.1887) (Plate 27 (a) and (b)). Tree of Jesse windows are rare in nineteenth century stained glass. Morris and Co. made only two, while Powell's made one at Waltham Abbey in 1861 from designs by Burne-Jones. They were thought to be archaic and out of line with most Victorian Christian thought. Almquist took a late mediaeval precedent by using a vine as the tree. The purpose was to show the pedigree of Christ through the Kings of Israel from Jesse and David onwards, using as their biblical source the prophecy of Isaiah: 'There shall come forth a rod out of the stem of Jesse, and a branch shall grow out of his roots'. In his example, Almquist has taken liberties with the convention by including Adam and Eve and not putting the kings in chronological order.

Fig. 37 Warton, Lancashire, St. Paul, St. Eunice instructing Timothy (G. Porter, 1889).

Yealand Conyers: St. John, south wall, one light, The Good Shepherd (Almquist, 1889).

LEICESTERSHIRE

Burbage: St. Catherine, south wall, three lights, including Life of Hezekiah (detail) (Jewitt, 1894) (Plate 32 (a) and (b)). Hezekiah's life has here been told by Jewitt in an almost surreal fashion. The king's story is so bizarre that, however it was told, it would seem strange. He returned the Israelites to the righteous path, was healed from a plague of boils, defeated the Assyrians by means of an angel, improved his army and redirected the water supply, all with the aid of various prophets. Jewitt allowed his imagination free rein to produce a minor masterpiece.

Castle Donington: St. Edward, south aisle, Raising of Lazarus (Tipping, 1882).

Gilmorton: All Saints, east window, three lights, Ascension of Christ (Jewitt, 1896).

LINCOLNSHIRE

Belton: All Saints, east end, five lights, Christ healing the sick (Weatherstone, 1925).

Epworth: St. Andrew, south chancel, three lights, After the Resurrection (Almquist, c.1909). Arthur Hunt described the cartoon, when it was made for the east window in Gerrards Cross Church in 1891, as 'excellent' and it was re-used on a number of occasions, never repeating the same colours; north wall, Christ blessing little children (Almquist); Raising Jairus' daughter (Jewitt, 1884). As in many other locations, the parishioners of Epworth stayed with Shrigley and Hunt when they commissioned new windows, their first being erected in 1884. Once a parish had decided it liked the glass of a particular workshop, they often kept to the same firm with the intention of creating a continuity throughout the building. When the commissions survived for more than a generation, on the other hand, the style could change and the continuity was lost.

LONDON

Westminster: St. Matthew, east window, three lights, military chapel, Crucifixion (Almquist, 1904).

MIDDLESEX

Ruislip: St. Gregory the Great: designs for the Baptistry window, 8"×12" (private collection) (possibly by R. Hayes, 1967) (Plate 46). These two variants represent the most abstract of Jo Fisher's ambitions and were probably stimulated by the interior of Coventry Cathedral. The competition for the Baptistry windows was however won by Patrick Reyntious and so these designs were never executed.

NORFOLK

East Bilney: St. Mary, north chancel, Christ healing little children (Jewitt); north chancel, Resurrection (Almquist, 1886).

NORTHAMPTONSHIRE

Higham Ferrers: St. Mary, south aisle, Hymn of the Last Supper (Jewitt, 1897); south chancel, three lights, Seraphim (Almquist, 1899) (Plate 39). The Seraphim was designed by Almquist for the clerestory of Trent Church, New Barnet, which in itself was an adaptation from a cartoon made for Heaviley Church, Stockport in 1895. In addition, the Archangel Gabriel by Jewitt, was designed especially for this window. It is typical of many in the 1890s, when there was a return to the use of canopies in clear glass, thus allowing more light through while at the same time creating an heiratic effect.

NOTTINGHAMSHIRE

Holme Pierrepont: St. Edmund, tiled reredos of emblematic plants (vine leaves and cob on either side of an inscription) (1877) (Fig. 17); south aisle, three lights, Holy Matrons (Jewitt); and Angels in tracery (Almquist, 1891).

OXFORDSHIRE

Oxford: Mansfield College Chapel, west window, Scenes in Life of Christ (Almquist, 1889) (Plate 28). The large six-light window, divided into two parts of three lights, deals with scenes in the ministry of Christ, including The Call of the First Disciples and The Feeding of the Multitude. George Faulkner Armitage was responsible for the interior decoration of the Chapel, and it was he who chose Shrigley and Hunt. Almquist responded to this important university location by creating a strong architectural design which, because of the decorated Gothic style chosen by the architect Basil Champneys, includes canopies. The side walls contain figure windows by Brown of Powell and Co. and the east window is filled by Bell of Bristol, all of which blend into a most impressive whole.

SOMERSET

Norton-sub-Hamdon: St. Mary, east window, three lights, south chapel, Our Lady of Pity, Labour, Love and Life (H. Wilson, 1904–05) (Plate 41). The Trask family commissioned Wilson to execute this window, the strongest design of those he made for Shrigley and Hunt. He was also responsible for the woodwork in the Arts and Crafts style found in the church. Wilson's symbolism and decoration in the window is quite unlike any other made by the firm, and it is not surprising that he later turned to Christopher Whall to execute his designs, as they were both more committed to an Arts and Crafts philosophy. The finished window was despatched on 6 October 1904 and cost £101.10.0d.

SURREY

Grayswood, near Haslemere: All Saints, east window, five lights, Ascension and Resurrection (Almquist, 1905); embroideries and paintings (Almquist, 1905). Almquist worked here for the Swedish artist and his friend, Axel Herman Haig, who designed the church.

SUSSEX (EAST)

East Hoathly: Parish Church, numerous windows of 1884, 1892, 1897 and 1905, including Christ and his disciples (Almquist) (Plate 12). The east window is a curious mixture and indicates the difficulties of identifying the designer behind each window. It shows the emergence of the 'house style', with elements of Almquist (Christ), Jewitt (tracery angels and the disciple with his back to the viewer), and Tipping (the figure in the foreground of the right hand panel apparently running). On either side of the window are opus sectile 'mosaics' by Powell and Co., designed by J. W. Brown – a pupil of Burne-Jones – which harmonise perfectly, clearly showing how close the firms were in their aims. South wall, two lights, Raising of Lazarus (Tipping, c.1890).

WARWICKSHIRE

Lapworth: St. Mary's, St. John and the Virgin Mary. Panel from a three-light east window, designed by H. E. Wooldridge and made by Powell's of Whitefriars, 1872 (Fig. 8).

WORCESTERSHIRE

Evesham: All Saints, two four-light windows, Saints and Prophets (Almquist, 1899).

YORKSHIRE, EAST RIDING

Pocklington: All Saints, south transept, west wall, Annunciation and Crucifixion (Almquist, 1896); transept, four lights, Four Archangels (Almquist, c.1891). Originally designed for St. Augustine's Church, Haggerston, London earlier in 1891, the four archangels here have become significant since St. Augustine's has altered its function and the majority of its fittings, including the stained glass, have been removed, making the Pocklington windows the earliest use of the design. The designs although reduced by Gamon to fit into the windows at Pocklington, are close to Almquist's cartoons.

York: St. Olave, two three-light windows, north wall, Saints (Jewitt, 1889–91); St. John, Andrew and Gabriel (Almquist, c.1905); Transfiguration (Almquist, c.1905); Christ, St. Luke and Tabitha (Almquist, 1902).

YORKSHIRE, NORTH RIDING

Pickering: St. Peter and St. Paul, north transept, two lights, Sower and Reaper (Jewitt, 1878). In two, almost secular windows, of the sower and the reaper, Jewitt has demonstrated his decorative talent. His enthusiasm for the colour of the glass is conveyed to the viewer through his use of red and yellow, and the contrasting light and dark areas. Leading is used to emphasise the pictorial qualities of the window by following the lines his drawing dictates (Plate of Sower, back cover). Jewitt also restored the damaged mediaeval wall paintings during the restoration of the church that took place in the 1870s and 1880s.

Queensbury: Holy Trinity, east window, five lights, Ascension and Resurrection (Jewitt, 1884); north wall, two-light windows, Good Shepherd and Parable of the Talents (Almquist, 1884).

Scarborough: St. James, south wall, four lights (detail), St Alban (Jewitt, 1901) (Fig. 38). The church was begun in 1900 by Paley, Austin and Paley and was intended to have had a set of windows by Shrigley and Hunt, for which Almquist planned a whole scheme in 1894. Unfortunately the scheme – for which windows were being supplied until 1910 – was never completed, and the unfilled windows strike a glaring blow to the eye. Those that were executed are of a high quality, including the St Alban. Particularly notable is the window depicting martyrs on the south wall, with its attractive ruby halos.

Sheffield: (Ranmore), St. John the Evangelist, Baptistry, three lights, Faith, Hope and Charity (Almquist, 1888).

Silkstone: All Saints Church, north wall, centre light of three, Christ as light of the world (Almquist, 1875–76) (Plate 1). One of the earliest designs by Almquist and one that has suffered from borax decay. Its formal frontal presentation and simply stated neoclassicism recalls the work of his recent master, Henry Holiday.

Fig. 38   Scarborough, Yorkshire, North Riding, St. James, detail of St. Alban (Jewitt, 1901).

YORKSHIRE, WEST RIDING

Burton-in-Lonsdale: All Saints, south wall, three lights (J. C. Bewsey, 1908) (Figure 23). A fraught situation arose through the commission at Burton. Arthur Hunt requested two freelance designers to submit work for the same window. There was a lot of acrimony, resulting in angry threats by one, George Frampton, and Bewsey, the other, who was temperamental, obtaining the job.

Clayton, near Bradford: St. John the Baptist, tower window, west end, three lights, Ancient and modern warfare (Weatherstone, 1918) (Plate 44). Weatherstone was a close friend of Almquist and assisted him occasionally in the London studio. He had a preference for war scenes and was called upon when they were required, as here, and also at Palm Grove Wesleyan Church, Birkenhead (now demolished), where he designed a mediaeval battle.

Bolton, near Bradford: St. James, east window, five lights, scenes from Life of Christ; detail of Resurrection (Almquist, 1876) (Plate 2). Almquist here shows himself a product of the Aesthetic Movement in his selection of delicate colours and the elimination of all gothicisms, preferring scrolls and leaf patterns as motifs. Below the window there is a contemporary reredos by Heaton, Butler and Bayne, showing that in 1876 there was a possible link existing between Arthur Hunt's masters and his new business.

Great Ouseburn: St. Mary, west window, one light, Good Shepherd (Jewitt, c.1884).

Halifax: St. John, window above porch, three lights, Elijah in the Wilderness (Jewitt, 1883); clerestory, Twelve Apostles (Jewitt, 1883). Fig. 10 shows a wood engraving of the church by Orlando Jewitt in the 1840s.

Harrogate: Starbeck, St. Andrew, reredos, Christ and his Disciples (A. C. Weatherstone, 1932).

Ledsham: All Saints, east window, five lights, After the Resurrection (Almquist, 1899).

SCOTLAND

Aberdeen, Aberdeenshire: St. Nicholas Church, the East Kirk, south wall, three lights, Three archangels (Almquist, 1891).

Aberfoyle, Perthshire: St. Mary's Episcopal Church, east window, four lights, scenes of life of Christ (Almquist, 1896). This window is typical of its date in having a predominant yellow tone with a relief given by touches of ruby. The Nativity was again used soon afterwards in St Mary Magdalen's church at Broughton-in-Furness.

Aberfoyle, Perthshire: parish church, west window, two lights, The Good Shepherd and Moses (Almquist, 1895).

Dumbarton, Dunbartonshire: Town Hall, Council Chamber, secular figures (Almquist, 1906) (Fig. 19). Termed their Renaissance style, the Council Chamber windows typify one of Shrigley and Hunt's secular formats, and has the virtue of incorporating figures whilst allowing light into the room. Almquist supplied the emblematic female figures set amidst the heraldry and patterns designed by Jewitt and his team.

Glasgow, Lanarkshire: Pollockshaws, Eastwood Church of Scotland Parish Church, south aisle, one light, Mary of Bethany (Almquist, 1884–85) (Plate 16). A richly coloured window commissioned through Campbell Douglas and Sellars. The firm had a productive relationship with this Scottish architectural practice which led to their important contribution to the International Exhibition at

Glasgow in 1888. Shrigley and Hunt owed a great deal to this contact with Scotland, not least the rich colours that they saw the Glasgow stained glass companies using.

Glasgow, Lanarkshire: University Gardens Sick Children's Hospital, now St. Aloysius R.C. School, stair window (1893).

Penicuik, Midlothian: Episcopal Church, one light, St. George (1896); one light, St. Alban (1900); one light, St. Patrick (c.1903), all by Jewitt.

WALES

Bettws, Derry Ormond, Cardiganshire: east window, three lights, Crucifixion (Almquist, 1886); one light, St. Michael (Almquist, 1887) (Plate 25); six one-light windows, six angels (Almquist, 1886); angels in porch (Almquist, 1887).

Colwyn Bay, Caernarfonshire: Queens' Lodge (now a private nursing home), dancing garland weavers on landing above the entrance hall (Almquist, c.1893); Perseus and Andromeda on hearth tiles in drawing room (Almquist, 1893).

Llanbedr Dyffryn, near Ruthin, Denbighshire: St. Peter, north wall, one light, Angel of martyrs (Almquist, 1887).

Merthyr Tydfil, Glamorgan: St. David, south wall, two lights, St. Tydfil and St. David of Wales (H. Wilson and Almquist, 1890). Wilson supplied the sketch of this window from which Almquist made the cartoons, and thus the colour, layout and poses are Wilson's. The collaboration began a productive relationship between the young architect and the firm which lasted for over twenty years.

Pen y Lan, near Ruabon, Denbighshire: all windows in the apse, Christ, St. John, Blessed Virgin Mary, St. Peter, St. Paul, St. Stephen, John the Baptist, St. Ambrose Augustine, St. David of Wales, and St Alban and King David (Almquist, 1888).

SWEDEN

Orebrö: St. Nikolai, north wall, three lights, central panel, Musical angel (Almquist, 1881) (Plate 9). Almquist here has allowed the criterion of beauty to influence his design. The figure of the angel is the only image in the window and it is surrounded by clear glass, with telling effect. The model chosen resembles those of Burne-Jones, and even has similarities to his mistress Maria Zambacco. Almquist designed the east window, the south transept window and various other windows in this mediaeval church of his home town. He remained in touch with his old partner and sponsor, Adolph Hjellstöm, who was responsible for the numerous commissions Almquist received for this church.

INDEX OF PEOPLE AND PLACES

Abbott & Co., Lancaster, 73
Aberdeen, Aberdeenshire, 84
Aberfoyle, Perthshire, 32, 84
Accrington, Lancashire, 72
Adams, Maurice B., 35
Aldenham, Hertfordshire, 39, 71
Aldingham, Lancashire, 72
Aldington, Kent, 72
Alexander, J. T., 47, 56, 57
Alexander, R., 35
All Saints, Silkstone, 83, Pl 1
All Saints, Alverdiscott, 70
All Saints, Barnacre, 38–39
All Saints, Belton, 80
All Saints, Boxley, 72, 73, **Fig. 34**
All Saints, Burton-in-Lonsdale, 43, 83, **Fig. 23**
All Saints, Castle Donnington, Leicestershire, 80
All Saints, Datchworth, 71
All Saints, Evesham, 82
All Saints, Gilmorton, 79
All Saints, Grayswood, near Haslemere, 81
All Saints, Harthill, 19, 68, **Fig. 8, Pl 23**
All Saints, Hertford, 7, 71, **Pl 21**
All Saints, Higher Walton, 75
All Saints, Hindley, 75, **Pl 3**
All Saints, Hollingbourne, 60, **Fig. 31**
All Saints, Ledsham, 84
All Saints, Pocklington, 30, 82
All Saints, Shillington, 66
All Saints, Thelwall, 37–38, 68, **Fig. 21**
All Saints, Upper Stondon, 66, **Pl 19**
Allen, John Milner, 16, 24, 26, 27, 31, 34, 53, 57, 78
Almquist, Carl, 1, 10, 17–20, 32, 40–41, 44, 53, 57, 60, 66, 73, 74, 76, 80, **Pls 1, 4, 9, 11, 12, 15, 16, 17, 19, 23, 24, 25, 27, 28, 33, 35, 37**; blindness of, 46; death of, 55; at London office, 19, 21–23, 40–41; pupil of Henry Holiday, 17, 34, 57; reliance on by Hunt, A. W., 18; style of, 20; work with Jewitt, E. H., 2–3, 21–23
Alverdiscott, Devon, 70
Anderson, Robert, 36
Anglican Cathedral, Liverpool, 33, 55
Armitage, Charles T., 62
Armitage, G. F., 16, 30, 54, 69
Aultshellach, near Inverness, 35
Austin, Herbert, 29

Baillie and Mayer, Wardour Street, London, 10, 53

Baldwin, Robert Lane, 57
Barbon, Cumbria, 69
Bardsea, Cumbria, 69
Barrow-in-Furness, Cumbria, 69, **Pl 31**
Barrowclough, Allen, 55, 57
Bayne, R. T., 34
Bedford Park Estate, London, 35
Bedford, Bedfordshire, 66, **Pl 15**
Belton, Lincolnshire, 44, 80
Berridge, Arthur, 57, 62
Bettws, Derry Ormond, Cardiganshire, 32, 85, **Pl 25**
Bewsey, John C. N., 43, 55, 57, 83
Bird, John, 54
Bishop's Stortford, 7
Blackpool, Lancashire, 73
Blomfield, Sir Arthur, 2, 16, 30, 36
Blyth, John, 48, 49, 50, 56, 57, 69, 73, **Fig. 35**
Boddington, Henry, 2, 30, 35, 54, 64; *see also* Pownall Hall, Silverdale, Wilmslow
Bodley, George Frederick, 2, 33, 41, 55, 59
Bolton, Bradford, 19, 27, 84
Bolton-le-Sands, Lancashire, 73
Bone, Henry, 16, 53
Boxley, Kent, 72, 73
Bray, Robert E., 55, 58
Brindle, Lancashire, 48, 73
Brittain, William, 58
Bromley, Albert, 35
Brown, J. W., 42, 82
Broughton-in-Furness, Cumbria, 69
Broxbourne, Hertfordshire, 7
Bulfield, Alfred Parkinson, 54, 58
Burbage, Leicestershire, 79
Bures, Suffolk, 7
Burges, William, 8, 17
Burlison and Grylls of Langham Place, 18, 29, 33, 41, 57
Burne-Jones, Edward, 1, 3, 14, 22, 24, 34, 42, 54, **Fig. 11**; influence on Almquist, C. and Jewitt, E.H., 24, 68, 78
Burton-in-Lonsdale, Yorkshire, 83

Campbell Douglas and Sellars, 32, 35
Cartmel Priory, Cumbria, 70, **Pl 26**
Castle Hill, Lancaster, 9, 53
Christ Church, Croft, near Warrington, 74–75, **Fig. 36**
Christ Church, Glasson Dock, 74
Christ Church, Lancaster, 38, 42, 75–76, **Pls 33, 34, 35**
Christ Church, Latchford, 68, front cover

Christ Church, Over Wyresdale, 42, 77, **Pl 37**
Christ Church, Oxford, 24
Clarke, Geoffrey, 50
Clayton, near Bradford, 45, 83
Cockermouth, Cumbria, 70
Colwyn Bay, 35, 85
Combe, Thomas, 21
Copp, near Eccleston, 38, 74
Cottier, Daniel, 34
Croft, Warrington, Lancashire, 74
Crosby Ravensworth, Cumbria, 70

Daisy Hill, Manchester, 74
Datchworth, Hertfordshire, 71
De Morgan, William, 12, 25
Della Robbia (at St. John, Silverdale), 23
Demaine Brierley, 29, 36, 54, 76
Dixon, Tom Scott, 62
Doyle, F. Francis, 69
Dumbarton Town Hall, 32, 84, **Fig. 19**
Dunham-on-the-Hill, Cheshire, 68
Dunn, Jonathan, 5, 53
Dürer, 'Suffering Christ', 19, 25, 68, **Fig. 9, Pl 23**

East Bilney, Norfolk, 80
East Hoathly, Sussex, 81, **Pl 12**
Eastwood, Glasgow, 32, 84
Eaton, E. L., 54, 58, 69, 74–75, **Pl 30**
Eaton and Bulfield, 54, 74–75
Eaves, W. Edward, 10, 58, 62
Edinburgh, 35
Egley, Maw, 15
Ellis, John Edward (Ted), 48, 50, 55, 56, 58, 62, 75
Episcopal Church, Penicuik, Midlothian, 85
Epworth, Lincolnshire, 80
Evesham, Worcestershire, 82

Fagan, Isobel, 58
Felsted School, 7
Finlay, J. R., 35
Finsthwaite, Cumbria, 3, 70
Fisher, Joseph (Jo), 3, 47–51, 56, 58, 71, 80, **Fig. 28; Pls 46, 49**; death of, 51, 56; in charge of firm, 56, 58; Lowwood, Haverbreaks, 51, 56; style of, 50, 58
Fisher, Stuart, 51
Foster, W. Jnr., 35
Frampton, Edward, 44, 58
Frampton, George, 43, 55, 83

Gamon, Gilbert P., 3, 19, 40, 54, 58
Gardner, Ray, 47, 56
Garnett, William, 78
Garstang, Lancashire, 19, 74
Garstin, Norman, 15
Garston, Lancashire, 74
Glasgow, 32, 35, 84
Glasgow International Exhibition, 54, 84
Glasson Dock, Lancashire, 74
Grappenhall, Cheshire, 68
Grayswood, Surrey, 81
Great Ouseburn, Yorkshire, 84
Great Strickland, Cumbria, 70
Greenall, Sir Gilbert, 2, 54, 78
Gregory and Co., London, 34
Grosvenor Gallery, Bond Street, 24

Haig, Axel Herman, 17, 81
Haileybury School, 7
Halifax, Yorkshire, 84
Halton Green Farm, 12
Harthill, Cheshire, 68
Hartley Wood and Chance, 53
Harvey, Harold (Harry), 49, 56, 59, 77, **Fig. 27**, **Pl 49**
Haughton-le-Skerne, Durham, 71
Hayes, R., 49, 50, 56, 59, 74, 80
Heapey, Lancashire, 74
Hearts Convalescent Home, St. Leonards, 7
Heaton, Butler and Bayne, Cardington Street, Hampstead Road, 8, 16, 17, 25, 27, 53, 57, 59, 84
Hendrie, Herbert, 48, 57
Herman, R. W., 8
Hertford, Hertfordshire, 7, 71
Hest Bank, near Lancaster, 21, 74
Higham Ferrers, Northamptonshire, 80
Highgate School, 7
Hindley, Lancashire, 75
Hoddesdon, Hertfordshire, 5, 7, 53, 71
Hoddesdon Gas Company, 5
Hogan, James, 48
Hogges Hall, 7, **Fig. 2**
Holiday, Henry, 1, 3, 8, 14–15, 16, 53, 59; tutor to Almquist, C., 17, 34, 57, 74
Holme Pierrepont, Nottinghamshire, 81
Holy Trinity, Bardsea, 69
Holy Trinity, Blackpool, 73
Holy Trinity, Bolton-le-Sands, 73, **Pl 29**
Holy Trinity, Queensbury, 83
Holy Trinity, Seaton Carew, 71
Hornby, Lancashire, 75
Hudson and Shrigley, 9
Hughes, John, 56
Humphrey, G. W., 58
Hunt, Arthur Edward, 41, 42, 45, 47, 55, 59, **Fig. 24**
Hunt, Arthur William, 1, 3, 8–13, 59, **Figs. 1, 5, 24**; and Almquist, C., 18, 19, 21–23, 40–41; clients of, 36–39; death of, 45, 55; early years, 53; family of, 9–12, 41, 44; overdraft for, 40, 55
Hunt, George Jonathan, 2, 19, 41, 42, 55, 59, 76, **Fig. 22**
Hunt, Holman, 55, 76

Hunt, Jane, 9, 44
Hunt, John, 5, 7, 53, 71
Hunt, Kenneth, 47
Hunt, Oliver Grahame, 41, 42, 59
Hunt, Samuel, 7
Hunt, Thomas, 7
Hunt, William, 5

Jackson, Thomas Graham, 15, 55
Jesus College Chapel, Cambridge, 22, **Fig. 11**
Jewitt, Austin, 19, 55, 59
Jewitt, Clement W., 59
Jewitt, Edward Holmes, 1, 20–21, 42, 54, 59, 70, 72, 76, 82, 83, **Figs. 18, 38, Pls, 3, 6, 7, 8, 10, 14, 20, 21, 26, 34**; death of, 46, 55; style of, 21, 71; work with Almquist, C., 2–3, 21–23
Jewitt, Orlando, 20, 21, 84, **Fig. 10**

Kempe, Charles Eamer, 10, 43, 57
Kilncroft, Hest Bank, 74, **Pl 30**
King's College Chapel, Cambridge, 47
Knellström, A., 85

Lambert, William, 25, 27, 54, 59
Lambert and Moore, 54, 59, 78
Lancaster: Castle Hill premises, 9, 10, 53, 56, **Fig. 3**; China Lane, 53; Christ Church, 75–76; Longlands (residence), 10, 15, 44, 54, **Figs. 4, 5, 6**; Priory Church, 12, 76; St. Peter's Cathedral, 76; West Road, 9, 51, 56; *see also* London
Lancaster Amateur Art Exhibition, 54
Lancaster City Museums, 74
Lancaster Photographic Society, 46, 55
Lane, Charles, 55
Lapworth, Warwickshire, 82
Latchford, Cheshire, 68
Lavers and Barraud, 57, 59
Lawton, Arthur L., 59, 62
Ledsham, Yorkshire, 84
Lee, Lawrence, 50
Leigh, Lancashire, 76
Leyland, F., 35
Liberty and Co., London, 34
London, Shrigley and Hunt office: at Bedford Row, 10, 19, 21–23, 34, 40–41, 42, 54, 58; at Bloomsbury Square, 47, 56
Longlands: *see* Lancaster
Lorton Hall, Cockermouth, 35, 70
Lucas, Arthur, 57
Lynton, Devon, 70

Makerfield, Newton-le-Willows, Lancashire, 76
Manchester Exhibition (Jubilee), 54
Mansergh Carpets, Lancaster, 47
Mansfield College Chapel, Oxford, 16, 30, 81, **Pl 28**
Marillier, H. C., 55
Martin, William Cragg, 54
Mashiter, Thomas D., 50, 62
Master Glass Painters, Society of, 56
Matlock, Derbyshire, 70
Matthews E. and Sons, 8, 31, 54

Matthews, Jane Marion Caroline, 8, 53: *see also* Hunt, Jane
Maxwell and Tuke, Manchester, 32
Mayer of Munich, 29
Meade King, H. W., 35
Melling, Lancashire, 76
Menai Bridge, Anglesey, 19
Merthyr Tydfil, Dyfed, 85
Milner-White, Eric, 47, 49–50
Morris and Co., 1, 22, 25, 33, 34, 48, 55
Morris, Marshall, Faulkner and Company, 8, 14, 33, 53
Morris, William, 8, 33
Morton, W. S. and Sons, 32

Nevison, Barbara (neé Turner), 47, 56, 62
New Barnet, Hertfordshire, 30, 36, 72
New, Keith, 49, 50, 56, 60
Nicholson, Archibald Keithley, 55
North Bovey, Devon, 71
Norton-sub-Hamdon, Somerset, 81

Oaks, Millom, 35
Oakhurst, Colwyn Bay, 35
Orebrö, Sweden, 72, 85
Oswaldtwistle, Lancashire, 77
Over Wyresdale, Lancashire, 77
Oxford, Oxfordshire, 81

Pace, Ion, 40, 55, 60
Paley and Austin, 2, 3, 10, 16, 29, 36, 54, 76
Paley, E. G., 29, 78
Palm Grove Wesleyan Church, Birkenhead, 44, 45
Pampisford, near Cambridge, 68
Paris International Exhibition, 54
Parkinson, James, 62
Payne, G. S., 19, 60
Pen y Lan, near Ruabon, Denbighshire, 85
Penicuik, Midlothian, 85
Philadelphia International Exhibition, 53
Phillips, A. W., 55
Pickard, G. S., 15
Pickering, Yorkshire, 82
Pilling, Lancashire, 29, 77
Plymouth Guildhall, 16
Pocklington, Yorkshire, 82
Pollockshaws, Eastwood, Glasgow, 84
Porter, George, 7, 54, 60, 71, 78
Powell of Whitefriars, 1, 14, 15, 17, 18, 33, 42, 48, 53, 57, 59, 79, 82
Pownall Hall, Wilmslow, 30, 35, 69, **Pl 22**
Preesall, Lancashire, 77
Prest, E.J., 3, 54, 60, 66, **Fig. 31**
Preston, Lancashire, 36–37, 47, 77, 78; **Fig. 20**
Preston County Offices, 16, 54, 78
Pugin, A. W. N., 21

Queensbury, Yorkshire, 83
Queen's Lodge, Colwyn Bay, Caernarfonshire, 85
Quernmore, Lancashire, 78

Rampside, Lancashire, 78

Red House, Bexley Heath, 33–34
Redmarshall, Durham, 71
Reyntiens, Patrick, 50
Rochdale Town Hall, 34
Rowarth, Frederick Alfred, 54, 60
Royal Academy, London, 31, 54, 57
Royal Chamber of Commerce, Stockholm, 17
Royal College of Art, 48
Royal Scottish Academy, 57
Royal Windsor Tapestry Factory, 57
Ruislip, Middlesex, 80

St. Andrew, Epworth, 80
St. Andrew, Haughton le Skerne, 71
St. Andrew, Starbeck, Harrogate, 84
St. Anne, Copp, 74
St. Anne, St. Anne's-on-Sea, 78, **Pl 38**
St. Barnabas, Great Strickland, 70, **Pl 17**
St. Barnabas, Heapey, 49, 74, **Pl 47**
St. Bartholomew, Barbon, 69
St. Bartholomew, Wilmslow, 45, 46, 69,
    Fig. 25
St. Catherine and St. Paul, Hoddesdon, 71,
    Pl 5
St. Catherine, Burbage, 24, 79, **Pl 32**
St. Cuthbert, Aldingham, 72, **Pl 42**
St. Cuthbert, Redmarshall, 71
St. David, Merthyr Tydfil, Glamorgan, 85
St. Edmund, Holme Pierrepont, 26, 27, 81,
    Fig. 17
St. Edward, Castle Donington, 79
St. George the Martyr, Preston, 36–37, 47,
    77, **Fig. 20, Pl 36**
St. Gregory the Great, Ruislip, 50, 80, **Pl 46**
St. James, Bolton near Bradford, 84, **Pl 44**
St. James, Brindle, 48, 73, **Pl 45**
St. James, Daisy Hill, Manchester, 44, 74
St. James, Scarborough, 36, 83, **Fig. 38**
St. James, West Derby, 24, 78–79, **Pls 10, 11**
St. John the Baptist, Pilling, 77
St. John the Baptist, Aldenham, 71
St. John the Baptist, Clayton near Bradford,
    84, **Pl 44**
St. John the Baptist, North Bovey, 71, **Pl 6**
St. John the Baptist, Thaxted, Essex, 58,
    Fig. 30
St. John the Evangelist, Sheffield, 83
St. John, Accrington, 72
St. John, Halifax, 20, 84, **Fig. 10**
St. John, Lapworth, 82
St. John, Silverdale, 23, 78, **Fig. 12**
St. John, Walton near Warrington, 78
St. John, Yealand Conyers, 79
St. John, Calder Vale, 16
St. John's Presbytery, Warrington, 48, 69,
    Fig. 25
St. John, Stansted, 7
St. Lawrence, Crosby Ravensworth, 70
St. Luke, Dunham-on-the-Hill, 68, **Pl 4**
St. Luke, Wimbledon, 55
St. Margaret, Hornby, 75, **Pl 20**
St. Margaret, Rochester, 42
St. Martin, Aldington, 72
St. Mary Magdalene, Broughton-in-Furness,
    16, 69

St. Mary the Virgin, Ware, 72, **Pl 18**
St. Mary, East Bilney, 80
St. Mary, Great Ouseburn, 84
St. Mary, Higham Ferrers, 80, **Pl 39**
St. Mary, Lapworth, 82, **Fig. 8**
St. Mary, Leigh, 16
St. Mary, Lynton, 45, 70
St. Mary, Norton-sub-Hamdon, 44, 81
St. Mary, Windermere, 70
St. Mary Episcopal Church, Aberfoyle,
    Perthshire, 24, 84
St. Mary, Leigh, 36, 76
St. Matthew, Westminster, 33, 80
St. Michael, Garston, 74
St. Michael, Rampside, 25, 78, **Fig. 14**
St. Michael, St. Michael's-on-Wyre, 78
St. Michael, Stanton, 71
St. Michael, Steeple Claydon, 67, **Fig. 33**
St. Nicholas, Aberdeen, Aberdeenshire, 73, 84
St. Nicholas, Wallasey, 45, 68, **Pl 43**
St. Nikolai, Orebrö, 85, **Pl 9**
St. Olave, York, 30, 82
St. Oswald, Preesall, 77, **Pl 49**
St. Oswald, Winwick, 79, **Pl 27**
St. Paul, Bedford, 24, 66, **Pl 15**
St. Paul, Oswaldtwistle, 77, **Pl 15**
St. Paul, Warton, 78, **Fig. 37**
St. Paul, Scotforth, Lancaster, 25
St. Peter, Finsthwaite, 70
St. Peter, Llanbedr Dyffryn, near Ruthin,
    Denbighshire, 85
St. Peter, Makerfield, Newton-le-Willows,
    30, 36, 76, **Fig. 18**
St. Peter and St. Paul, Pickering, 82
St. Peter, Quernmore, 78, **Pl 8**
St. Peter's Roman Catholic Cathedral,
    Lancaster, 76
St. Thomas, Garstang, 74
St. Tydfil, Merthyr Tydfil, 44
St. Wilfred, Melling, 76, **Pl 40**
St. Wilfrid, Grappenhall, 68, **Pl 24**
Sandham, J. W., 56
Scarborough, Yorkshire, 83
Seaton Carew, Durham, 71
Sedbergh School, 12
Sedding, Edmond, 55
Sedding, John D., 44, 61
Sefton, Earl of, 77
Shaw, Richard Norman, 2, 33
Shepherd's Church: *see* Christ Church,
    Over Wyresdale
Shillington, Bedfordshire, 66
Shrigley and Hunt: art tiles, 25–27, **Figs.
    15, 16, 17**; at Castle Hill, 9, 53; 1879
    Catalogue of designs, 24, 25, 31, 54, **Fig.
    13**; clients of, 36–39; commissions, archi-
    tectural, 29–30; establishment of, 9–10,
    53; exhibitions, 31–33; liquidation of, 57,
    56; London office: *see* London; at
    Lowwood, Haverbreaks, 51, 56; nadir of,
    47; revival of, 50; secular and domestic,
    33–35; at West Road, 51, 56
Shrigley, Eliza, 9, 53
Shrigley, Ellen, 9
Shrigley, Joseph, 8, 53

Sick Children's Hospital, Glasgow, 32, 85
Silkstone, Yorkshire, 19, 83
Silverdale, Lancashire, 69, 78
Simpson, R. T., 62
Skirving, Alexander, 16, 24, 31, 53, 60
Smedley's Hydropathic Establishment,
    Matlock, 35, 70, **Pl 7**
South Kensington Schools, 59
South Kensington Museum, 34
Stammers, Harry, 49, 59
Stanton, Gloucestershire, 16, 71
Starbeck, Harrogate, 44, 84
Steeple Claydon, Buckinghamshire, 67
Stockdale, Arthur, 62
Storey Institute, Lancaster, 12, 47, 54, 55, 58
Storeys of Lancaster, 75
Storrs Hall, near Lancaster, 18
Strachan, Douglas, 48
Street, G. E., 21

Thelwall, Cheshire, 68
Thompson, Reginald, 15
Thurland Castle, near Lancaster, 35
Tipping, William J., 17, 27, 54, 61, 71, 79,
    Pl 5
Tonbridge Chapel, 7
Townson, John E., 62
Travers, Martin, 48
Trent Church, New Barnet, 30, 36, 72, 80
Trinity College, Cambridge, 15, **Fig. 7**
Tullamore, Central Ireland, 18
Turner, Charles Frederick, 46–47, 50, 54,
    55, 56, 61, 62, 77, 78, **Fig. 26**

University Gardens, Glasgow, 35, 85
Upper Stondon, Bedfordshire, 66

Wadham College, Oxford, 12, 59
Wales, Prince and Princess of, 32
Wallasey, Cheshire, 68
Waltham Abbey, 8, 15
Walton, near Warrington, 35, 78
Walton, Issak, 5
Ware, Hertfordshire, 72
Warrington, Cheshire, 69, 78
Warton, Lancashire, 78
Waterhouse, Alfred, 2
Weatherstone, Alfred Charles, 36, 44, 45,
    47, 55, 61, 74, 80, 83
Webb, Philip, 34
West Derby, Lancashire, 78
Whall, Christopher, 43, 52, 81
Whiteside, Arthur, 62
Williamson, James, 8
Wilmslow Church, 46
Wilson, Henry, 44–45, 54, 61, 69, 70, 81,
    85, **Pl 41**
Wilson, Patten, 55, 61, 72
Windermere, Cumbria, 70
Winwick, Lancashire, 79
Wolfendale, James Bibby, 54, 62
Wooldridge, Henry Ellis, 17, 18, 34

York Industrial Exhibition, 54
York, Yorkshire, 30, 82

SOCCER
THE WORLD GAME

SOCCER
THE WORLD GAME

St. Martin's Press   New York

Endpapers: *Martin Peters trapped in a Forest sandwich; Kenny Burns and Archie Gemmill, with Peter Withe and Peter Shilton looking anxiously on, defend the Forest goal against Norwich City during the 1977/78 season. Forest became League Champions for the first time in their history, although drawing this game 3–3. It was one of only two occasions during the season that a team scored more than two goals against Forest.*
Half title page: *The greatest name of them all, Pele.*
Title page: *Kenny Dalglish and Gordon McQueen with the rain and sweat spraying during an attack on the Welsh goal at Anfield. This was the final qualifying game for the 1978 World Cup and Scotland won 2–0.*
Right: *Johan Cruyff, the Dutch master who led his side to the 1974 World Cup final.*
Page 6: *Kevin Keegan during what many consider to be his greatest individual performance, in the 1977 European Cup final, which Liverpool won 3–1 against Borussia Monchengladbach.*

Written and edited by Phil Soar and Martin Tyler

Copyright © 1978 by Marshall Cavendish Limited
All rights reserved. For information write;
St. Martin's Press Inc.,175 Fifth Avenue, New York, New York 10010.
Printed in Great Britain.
First published in the United States of America in 1978.

Library of Congress Cataloging in Publication Data
Tyler, Martin
    Soccer : the world game

    1. Soccer. 2. Soccer—History 3. Soccer
players—Biography. 4. Soccer—Rules. I. Title.
GV943.T93   796.33'4'09   78-2982
ISBN 0-312-73134-5

Introduction

The 1978 World Cup in Buenos Aires was watched by a television audience of over one thousand million people. Not only is this the greatest audience for any single event in the history of mankind, it was an event that also generated more column inches, more emotion, more excitement, more commitment, and more widespread interest than any other sporting event ever. Such is the role of soccer in the world today.

From its clumsy origins in the public (meaning private) schools of Great Britain in the 19th Century, soccer became codified as Association Football and then, from the start of the 20th Century onwards, spread throughout the world. And there were very few parts of the world which did not take it to their hearts. Only North America held out, but in the last decade even that bastion seems to have fallen with the great stars of Europe and South America travelling to New York, Florida and Chicago to compete during the summer season in the world's richest country.

It is a game which can unite nations, a common currency from Chile to Finland to China to Tahiti. All over the world men and women know the names of Pele, Cruyff, Beckenbauer and Best. Soccer is a universal language, perhaps the single most universal language; it is a game for today, it is a game that the whole world can play. Beyond all doubt, it is *the* World Game.

Contents

The History of Soccer   9

Techniques And Tactics   15

The Rules of Soccer   25

The World Game   39

1930 World Cup   40

1934 World Cup   41

1938 World Cup   42

1950 World Cup   44

1954 World Cup   46

1958 World Cup   48

1962 World Cup   50

1966 World Cup   54

1970 World Cup   58

1974 World Cup   66

1978 World Cup   72

The European Game   77

The European Cup   77

The European Cup Winners Cup   80

The UEFA Cup   81

The European Championship   82

U.S. Soccer   85

Soccer Superstars

Gordon Banks   95

Franz Beckenbauer   99

George Best   104

Bobby Charlton   110

Giorgio Chinaglia   117

Charlie Cooke   120

Johan Cruyff   123

Alfredo di Stefano   126

Eusebio   129

Geoff Hurst   132

Kevin Keegan   139

Stanley Matthews   142

Rinus Michels   146

Bobby Moore   148

Gerd Muller   154

Pele   161

Ferenc Puskas   170

Kyle Rote Jr.   175

Helmut Schoen   180

EVERYING as it should be
PRACTICAL from a Practical Man

FOOTBALLS—
Round, Sound, and Durable
The Football King, **9/6**
Used England v. Scotland (5 times)
English Cup Final (6 times), every
event in the world of Football.
The League Ball..............**8/6**
Centre-Half   ,, ...**7/6**
Klynker   ,, ...**6/6**
Junior League,, ...**5/-**

KNICKERS—
Wide-fitting but not Baggy.
Navy or White, **1/6, 1/11, 2/6, 3/6**

SHIRTS—
Well Sewn and Comfortable
Flannelette, **2/3, 25/-** per doz.
Matting Cloth, **2/9, 30/-** per doz.
Untearable, **3/6, 40/-** per doz

BOOTS—
*With Permanent Toes, on Good
Lasts, Easy yet Tight-fitting.*

Scot **10/6**	Junior League **6/9**
League **10/6**	Don **6/-**
S.C. **7/9**	Marvel **5/-**

SHIN GUARDS, 10d, 1/6, 2/6
BAGS - **3/6, 4/6, 5/6, 7/6**
GOAL NETS—**30/-, 35/-, 48/-**
HOCKEY BALLS—
          3/6, 4/6, 5/-
BOXING GLOVES—Per Set of 4, **4/9.**

HOCKEY STICKS,
  Bulger Pattern.
Lanc. Witch ..**7/6**
Cork Grip......**6/-**
Special........**5/-**
Klynker......**4/6**

Gold Cape **6/6 8/9, 11/6, 14/6**

The History of Soccer

The origins of soccer are confusing in that they are both accessible and obscure. Accessible, because we know very well how it began in the late nineteenth century, when the various English Public Schools, all playing their own different codes, eventually formulated a unified set of rules, splitting with the handling devotees who went on to form rugby. But speculation on the origin of the game can be protracted indefinitely. Since kicking a ball, even if it be the wicker-work ball that was favoured in ancient China, is a simple human activity, claims can be made for its origins throughout the ancient world.

It may well be that the first international matches were played between the Chinese and Japanese. The Munich

Ethnological Museum in West Germany contains a text written by Li Ju, who lived about 50 BC, which mentions games between Chinese and Japanese, playing their respective codes. There are records indicating that in 1004 BC the Japanese played a game similar to soccer on a tiny field, delineated by trees at each corner. The Chinese had a game in which a leather ball (filled, allegedly, with female hair) was kicked, and it is certain that in the ancient Japanese capital of Kyoto a soccer game was played in AD 611.

Among the Ancient Greeks, the ball game of *episciro* was very popular. The Romans adapted it, calling it *harpastum*. Caesar is said to have played it, once winning 50 talents in a contest with Cecilius; Virgil and Horace knew and disapproved of it; Ovid advised women against playing it. It was, in fact, a robust sport, in which the object was to win the ball from all one's opponents. The Roman legions may well have brought it to Britain, and legend has it that a British team beat a legionary one in a famous victory of AD 276.

Above left: An advertisement for soccer uniform and equipment in the early 1900's; the price of the ball being nine shillings and sixpence (about $1.50)!
Left: Amateur Cup winners in 1904, the only honour for Sheffield F.C. Founded in 1857 they are the oldest club in the world.

Certainly a rough kind of soccer had taken root by the Middle Ages – much to the displeasure of a succession of English kings, who wanted the peasantry to apply itself to the martial arts. There is abundant documentation of this. There is a record by Fitz-Stephen to the effect that London boys would play soccer after dinner on Shrove Tuesday. In 1314, King Edward II issued his famous proclamation banning the game, with its 'hustling over large balls', in the city, with prison as the punishment for disobedience. Richard II had cause to issue a further proclamation in 1389, so clearly the game's popularity was such as to make it resilient. His complaint was that it interfered with archery practice. This Act was con-

firmed by Henry IV in 1401 and Henry VIII in the following century. In Scotland, the situation was much the same when King James I condemned the game, but in 1497 James IV's High Treasurer is known to have purchased two soccer balls, so that the King might play soccer at Stirling that April. In 1572, however, it was the turn of Queen Elizabeth I of England to condemn the game.

A contemporary scribe, Sir Thomas Elyot, complained that it was 'a pastime to be utterly objected by all noble men, the game giving no pleasure, but beastlie furie and violence'. Those who deplore these qualities in the game today may note that it was in it from the beginning. Stubbs,

the antiquarian, was still less enamoured of it, dismissing it as 'a friendlie kind of fighting', rather than recreation, while another Elizabethan coined the memorable phrase, 'a bloody and murthering practice' in describing the soccer played by apprentices in the Crooked Lane, Cheapside, and Covent Garden areas of London.

The tradition of the Shrove Tuesday soccer match grew up in the North and Midlands of England, where large groups roamed and raged through the town or village, playing against one another, the goal being set up each end of the village. In 1829, an account of such a match in Derbyshire spoke of 'broken shins, broken heads, torn coats and lost hats'. The Industrial Revolution gave a great impetus to the game but the pitch, ball, and rules continued to vary from place to place.

It was the English Public Schools – the top establishments of private education – that domesticated this rough sport, as they did so much else. Eton, Harrow, Winchester, Charterhouse, Rugby and Cheltenham all had their own special codes which blended when their boys went to Oxford and Cambridge Universities. Eton gave the game its conception of offside – which they called 'sneaking' – and also initiated the practice of changing ends at half-time rather than at every goal; at Harrow, the goals stood 150 yards apart, the forerunner of rugby's try line; Cheltenham originated the throw-in from touch, the word 'offside' and the crossbar – although for many years soccer goals made do with tapes.

Far left: An Italian forerunner of soccer – 'Calcio', played in Florence between two teams sponsored by royalty.

Left: The brawling, sprawling inter-village games played in England in the Middle Ages and the Tudor era. At times the violence led to the sport being banned by order of Parliament.

Below left: Getting ready for the game – here in Italy in the seventeenth century.

Right: The first international game, when England met Scotland in 1872. The match took place in Glasgow and finished goalless. Since then England against Scotland has developed into an annual fixture of great traditional rivalry, with Scotland having the edge over the years.

Below: A newspaper drawing from March 1883 of a Cup tie in Scotland between Dumbarton and Queen's Park, the two leading Scottish teams of that decade, later to be completely superseded by the Celtic and Rangers clubs of Glasgow. Queen's Park had beaten Dumbarton in the two previous Scottish Cup finals but this time the tables were turned and Dumbarton won 3–1 in front of 10,000 spectators to go on to their third successive final and their one and only success. In modern times Celtic and Rangers have been supreme in Scottish soccer.

✄ MANCHESTER CITY FOOTBALL CLUB. ✄

WINNERS OF ENGLISH CUP, 1903-4.
RUNNERS-UP, FOOTBALL LEAGUE, 1903-4. ◆ JOINT HOLDERS MANCHESTER CUP, 1903-4.

| T. E. MALEY,
Secretary and Manager. | S. FROST. | W. GILLESPIE. | J. McMAHON. | T. HYNDS. | J. HILLMAN. | S. B. ASHWORTH. | J. BROAD,
Trainer. |
| H. BURGESS. | | G. LIVINGSTONE. | W. MEREDITH,
Captain. | | A. .TURNBULL. | F. BOOTH. | |

Above: The Manchester City team that won the F A Cup and finished second in the First Division in 1904.
Right: The excitement of an F A Cup final with Milburn scoring for Newcastle against Arsenal in 1952.

In 1862, matters almost came to a head when a Mr. J. C. Thring, from Uppingham School, drew up a code of 10 rules called '*The Simplest Game*', which was believed to have had its origins at Cambridge University. Hands could still be used, but only to stop the ball; goals were scored when forced between the posts and under the bar or tape, but not when thrown; when the ball was kicked out of play, the 'offender' had to return it into play, in an undeviatingly straight line. But one rule at least had more to do with rugby – a player in front of the ball was 'out of play'.

The following year soccer and rugby split, soccer gaining its name when a famous centre-half, Charles Wreford-Brown, was asked in his Oxford rooms whether he was that day playing rugger. No, he replied facetiously, he was playing 'soccer', an evident play on the word 'association' – in Britain the game is formally known as 'association football'.

The rugby men wanted to retain hacking (the unpleasant habit of kicking an opponent's shins) the soccer people did not. So, in a meeting at the Freemasons'

Tavern in Great Queen Street, London, England's 'Football Association' was born.

Under the early rules the field could be 200 yards long, but there was no minimum width. Goalposts already stood 8 yards apart, although there was no provision for tape or bar. There was to be no hacking and no running whilst holding the ball.

By 1871 the maximum length of the pitch had been fixed at 200 yards, the maximum width at 100 yards and the goals had tapes. Emphasis was on dribbling, possession

and individualism. However, it was the Scots who, led by the fine Queen's Park amateur team from Glasgow, initiated the passing game and changed the whole pattern of soccer.

It was from Scotland too, that most of the first disguised professionals, traditionally finding their money in their boots, went south in the 1880s. In 1885, after intense debate, professionalism was finally legalized. In 1888

England's Football League was founded by William McGregor, a Scot transplanted to Birmingham, and the professional clubs had an economic context in which to operate.

From that time the game never looked back. Europe soon followed Britain – Austria played Hungary in 1902 – and in 1904 Belgium, France, the Netherlands, Spain, Sweden, and Switzerland founded FIFA, still soccer's international governing body. By World War I many European countries had national league competitions, and soccer was firmly established in South America. Since then the story has been one of constant growth, both as a spectator and as a participant sport with the United States the latest, and potentially the greatest, converts.

13

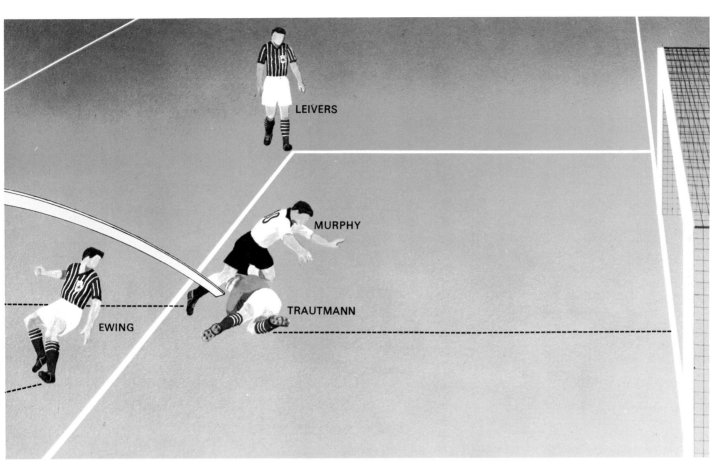

LEIVERS

MURPHY

EWING

TRAUTMANN

Techniques And Tactics

Soccer is a team game, the basic object being to both initiate and execute attacks with passing movements until a player is in a position to shoot or head at goal. The days of dribbling – in the 1870s, when each player held onto the ball with the intention of beating as many opponents as possible – were soon overtaken by the passing game. Every generation includes its individualists, but it is in the nature of soccer that each player is ultimately dependent on the other members of his side.

Goalkeeping

Goalkeeping is in a category of its own. Although the goalkeeper will probably be a useful sort of player in any position, and may well have started his career in another spot, he is less of a soccer player than a gymnast with superb reflexes, a keen eye, safe hands – and courage. He has three main ways of saving the ball: catching it cleanly, tipping it around the posts or over the crossbar (when it is unsafe to try to catch it, when he is under

Goalkeepers have to be brave to dive at opponents' feet.
Top left: Bert Trautmann of Manchester City collected the ball and a broken neck in this incident at the feet of Murphy of Birmingham City in the 1956 FA Cup final.
Centre: Peter Bonetti saves from Liverpool's Graham.
Left inset: John Hope dives to save Sheffield United.
Right inset: Bobby Graham is foiled again, this time by the courage of Manchester United's Alex Stepney.

pressure, or when he cannot reach it to hold) and punching it (also when he is under pressure or unable to hold the ball). If all else fails, goalkeepers are expected to come off the line to block shots with any part of the body. Although the goalkeeper has the advantage of arms' length and a certain amount of protection from the laws, he is expected to put himself in situations that expose him to great risk, such as diving at an opponent's feet.

A goalkeeper must learn timing and positioning (for corners, free-kicks, etc.) and be particularly adept at 'narrowing the angle' – coming out of his goal to reduce the effective area at which an oncoming opponent can aim. Goalkeepers must be decisive. Hesitation can cost goals.

Despite the skills in contact with the ball, it is, by the law of averages, highly unlikely that any player will be in possession for more than a few minutes during a match. Thus the vast majority of a player's time on the field is taken up with movements and actions that do not necessitate possession: running off the ball, running into space and taking up positions for a pass, covering defending colleagues when they are committed to an opponent or a tackle and marking opponents throughout varying phases of the play. Because the spectator follows the ball, he is normally unaware of what each player does for 95 per cent of a match. He merely expects him to be in the right place, at the right time, and do the right thing when he receives the ball.

Passing and shooting

The basic skills, however, are inherently individual. The first and most obvious is kicking the ball – passing and shooting. Three main parts of the foot are usually employed: the instep (where the boot or shoe laces up), more often than not for power and shooting; the inside of the foot, with which a player can obtain accuracy and spin; and the outside of the foot, particularly useful for a pass that can curve round an opponent to a colleague. Good players can use either side of the foot to bend a powerful kick – the 'banana' shot perfected by the Brazilians. In exceptional circumstances players use the heel (for a back-pass) or, if unable to reach the ball for full control, the toe or even the sole.

There are several guidelines to kicking a ball. In most cases it is important, for the sake of balance, to have the non-kicking foot alongside the ball and keep the weight of the body above it. But the primary rule is the one that applies to all ball games: to keep the eye on the ball while it is being played.

The basic pass of soccer is to place the ball in front of a colleague so that he does not have to alter his pace or direction drastically when running onto it. But the occasions when there is sufficient space or time, except when moving out of defence, are few and a player is expected to control passes that arrive at all speeds, heights and angles. Trapping a ball is the basic method of bringing it under control before deciding how to utilize it. One way is with the sole, or sole and inside, of the foot, used for killing a ball that arrives on the bounce; another is

with the side of the foot which can be used to control a low pass. There are also several other parts of the body commonly used: the head, the chest (taking a high ball and dropping it down to the feet), the stomach (hunched over for a rising ball), and the thigh.

Running with the ball – dribbling – is usually associated with the feet, although on occasions a player finds it necessary to take the ball on the chest, thigh, and so on. Dribbling has come back into the limelight in the era of packed defences: first, through players attacking frontally and trying to beat several opponents, and second, through the return to favour of wingers who can beat a man, get round the back of a square defence, and cross the ball, or centre. But whether in vogue or not, dribbling has always been an integral part of soccer.

So too has heading, which is unique to the game among major sports. It is done with the forehead where the thickness of the bone precludes the chance of injury or brain damage and the ball can be propelled with great accuracy and force – provided the timing is correct and the muscles of the neck are properly utilized. Eyes must be kept fixed on the ball and timing is something that comes, to the majority of players anyway, only with constant practice.

Right: Perfect technique from Martin Peters, a member of England's 1966 World Cup winning side. Note the eye on the ball, the balance and the follow-through.
Far right: Among major sports heading is unique to soccer, propelling the ball with force and accuracy.

Right: Soccer requires a high level of physical fitness – a combination of strength, agility and stamina.
Centre right: George Best, in the red shirt of Manchester United, had all these qualities to go with his mastery of skills and techniques. Best's phenomenal ability made him a target for cynical defensive play, and in the end his disenchantment with that type of treatment was a major factor in his early departure from the British game. Europe's loss became the gain of the United States when he re-emerged with the Los Angeles Aztecs in the NASL.
Far right: Best in high-kicking action for Manchester United against Dave Mackay of Derby County.

Tactical Systems

The development of soccer tactics has in essence been the story of a gradual reduction in the number of forwards in favour of the number of midfield players and defenders. In 1870 there would have been as many as eight forwards; a century later there might well be as few as one.

The early forwards were expected to dribble past man after man until they scored – or, more likely, lost the ball. It was in Scotland where they first evolved the passing game and, with their progress and superiority, it quickly became the norm. The basic configuration of 2–3–5 (which is still often used for line-ups on paper and which gives the positions their traditional names of right-half, inside-left, and so on) then held sway for about 40 years.

It was the change in the offside law in 1925, made

Left: The dribbling game of 1870.
Below: Brazil won the 1958 World Cup with the 4-2-4 system, which was copied by England in the early 60's.
Right: Beckenbauer's sweeper role allows him to cover defensively and to move forward to start attacks.
Below right: England's 1966 World Cup winning 4-3-3.

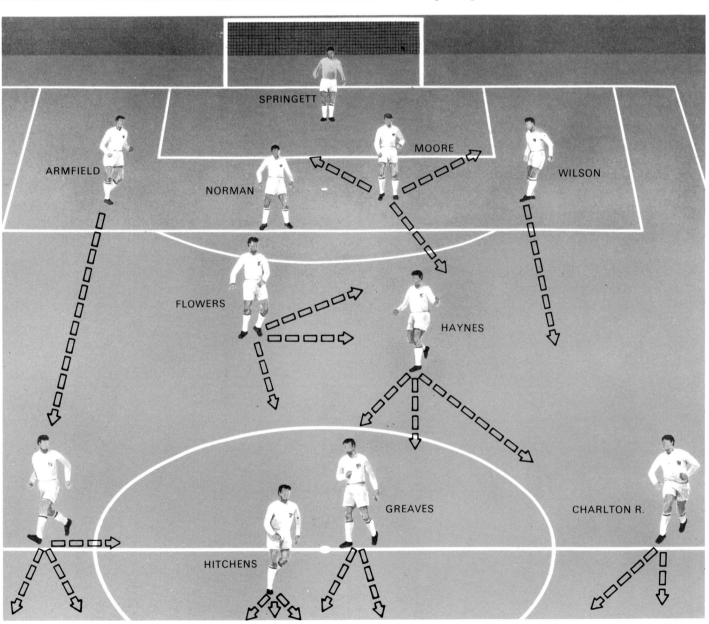

SPRINGETT

ARMFIELD

NORMAN

MOORE

WILSON

FLOWERS

HAYNES

HITCHENS

GREAVES

CHARLTON R.

necessary by the extravagant use of an offside trap, that sparked off the next major change. The new rule stipulated that only two players, and not three, had to be between the player and the goal-line when the ball was played, and it resulted in a steep increase in the number of goals being scored. In the first season with the change (1925–26) the number in the English Football League rose by almost a third and it was inevitable that it would provoke tactical reorganization. The centre-half, previously the midfield 'general', was moved back between the full-backs to become a third- or centre-back and the area he vacated was filled by the two inside-forwards, who retreated behind the wingers and centre-forward to produce the configuration descriptively called the 'W'.

Although some European and South American countries persisted with the attacking centre-half – Austria were still using him in the early 1950s – the third-back game was the basic structure in soccer for a quarter of a century. It was, of course, like all systems, merely a model and each team had its own variation moulded round the players it possessed.

Despite some successful developments – Karl Rappan's 'bolt' defence in Switzerland (the forerunner of *catenaccio*) and Hungary's use of the deep-lying centre-forward, copied by Manchester City – it was not until the 1958 World Cup and Brazil's spectacular performances with their 4-2-4 system that the game took its next big tactical turn.

It was almost universally imitated, but by 1962 the Brazilians had refined it to 4-3-3, with Zagalo, their left-winger in 1958, dropping back to midfield. Some European and South American countries took the process a stage farther in the mid-1960s with *catenaccio* (in effect 1-4-3-2- or 1-4-2-3) which was epitomized by Inter-Milan under Helenio Herrera. This system depended on a rigid man-for-man marking discipline with each defender deputed to follow a specified attacker all over the field; behind them a sweeper, with no marking responsibilities, would be free to quell any danger. The marked drop in the size of scores at European club matches illustrated the grip that the system, with its use of defensive absorption and quick breakaways, took on the game.

Inter-Milan's progress to the 1966–67 European Cup final is typical: 1–0, 0–0, 2–1, 2–0, 1–0, 2–0, 1–1, 1–1 and 1–0.

England team manager Alf Ramsey, after persevering with wingers for some time, eventually discarded them and his side won the 1966 World Cup with what was in effect 4-3-3 system. Ramsey opted for even greater midfield strength. Later in the 1970s the pendulum swung back to more attacking philosophies led at world level by West Germany and the exhilarating Dutch who gave defenders freer roles to supplement the offense.

There are, of course, qualifications in talking of tactical systems. They are only simplified models, useful frameworks, and are open to numerous permutations and refinements. This is governed not only by the players available – it is easier and more profitable to adapt a system to suit the talents and shortcomings of a team, than expect players to tailor their styles to fit a plan – but also by the type of match being played. Soccer tactics, like the game itself, are the source of infinite variety.

Referees

The referee and his art are the subject of endless controversy and it needs only one bad decision in an important match to set the old debate rolling.

Far left: England opted to defend the World Cup in 1970 with four midfield players but lost in the last eight.
Left and below: Referees in aggressive mood. So often a thankless task, carried out by amateurs in the world of professional soccer. The best go unnoticed.

21

The referee in Europe is in some ways an anomaly in soccer. In an era of intense professionalism and specialization, at least at the top levels, he remains the unglamorous part-timer who once or twice a week dons his black gear and takes complete control of a match, perhaps a vital one, for its whole duration.

His job is thankless; good decisions (using the advantage where applicable) and quietly firm control (well-chosen words to a player off the ball) go largely unnoticed – that is what makes them good. A bad or controversial decision gives a referee a stigma that takes a long time to lose. The abuse and comments – some funny, some unnecessary, some cruel – are probably an occupational hazard he soon learns to tolerate or ignore.

In the early days of soccer the game was controlled by two umpires, one from each club. But the increased and keener competition made it imperative that the men in charge be neutral and a referee was added to the number of match officials with the task of settling any disputes between the umpires.

The referee gained complete control in 1891, when the umpires were converted to linesmen. He moved from his place on the touchline to the field of play and was given the power to make decisions without consulting his colleagues. In Britain referees were sufficiently established by 1893 to form their own association.

The problems of the referee were accentuated in the 1960s. The trends of the modern game – speed, the crowded defences, the tactical foul – and the increased rewards for success, have all helped to heighten the difficulty of his task. Television, too, with its sterile and unemotional 'instant replays' and slow-motion analysis has often proved a necessarily quick decision on the field to be wrong and the 'man in the middle' has come under criticism. The pressures of the game have discouraged many potential referees from joining the ranks and the number of referees with character who exercise a grip on the game and earn the respect of the players is dwindling throughout the advanced soccer nations.

Referees in top-class soccer are under more pressures than the players they control. Whereas a player can make up for a human error later in the game, one refereeing mistake cannot be compensated for and can decide the destiny of a match.

Top left: Positional play is an art in itself for the referee who must give himself the very best view of the play. Here the referee takes up a position on the goal-line beside the near post as he waits for a corner.

Centre left: Size sometimes makes it easy to administer discipline. Scottish referee 'Tiny' Wharton seems to have a psychological advantage as he hands out a lecture to the former England midfield player Alan Ball.

Left: Problems afoot here for referee Ray Tinkler as he awards a free-kick against Leeds United in an English First Division match. One white-shirted Leeds player is already making his feelings known and two others are on their way to add weight to his argument. It's at times like these that referees can seem lonely, small figures in the tough conflicts between professionals.

Glossary of Terms

Blind side The side of a player or defence away from the play or ball.

Catenaccio Literally, 'big chain'. Very defensive tactics first evolved in Switzerland in the early 1950s and later employed with great success, particularly by Italian clubs. Consists of a sweeper behind the four defenders, with three midfield players and two strikers.

Centre or cross A pass, most often in the air, played from the area of the pitch near the touchline into the penalty or goal area.

Chip A short-range lob with backspin; a skill used to lift the ball into the air from the ground.

Containing When a defending player prevents an opponent from attacking at speed by slowly retreating.

Covering When a player fills a position vacated by a colleague who has committed himself to a tackle or when he forms a second line of defence behind him.

Cross See Centre.

Crossfield pass/ball A pass made from one side of the field to the other with the intention of changing the direction of the attack.

Dead ball When the ball is kicked from a stationary position (corner, free-kick, etc).

Dribbling Moving the ball past opponents by a series of contacts with the ball with one or both feet.

Extra-time (overtime) A period of play usually of two halves of 15 minutes each, played when games are tied at the end of normal time. In Europe extra-time (overtime) is only used to decide a match in a knock-out competition. N.B. All tied games in the NASL are decided this way using a "sudden death" format.

Far post The goalpost, or side of the goal, farther away from the player in possession.

Four-four-two (4-4-2) Defensive formation with four defenders, four midfield players, and only two permanent strikers.

Four-three-three (4-3-3) Formation first illustrated by Brazil in the 1962 World Cup and employed by England in 1966. Uses one more midfield man (and thus one fewer striker) than 4-2-4.

Four-two-four (4-2-4) Formation used by Brazil in the 1958 World Cup, an evolution from Hungary's style in 1953. It comprises four defenders, two midfield players, and four strikers.

Funnelling When a defence retreats, converging on their own goal.

Killing the ball See Trapping.

Linkman See Midfield player.

Lob A volley of the ball over opponents.

Marking Keeping within playing distance of an opponent, particularly at set pieces, to discourage his colleagues from passing to him and to hamper or tackle him quickly if he does receive a pass.

Midfield player or Linkman A player operating for the most part in the central areas of the pitch, whose job it is to connect defence and attack.

Near post The goal post, or side of the goal, nearer the player in possession.

Overlapping When a player, often a full-back, goes outside his winger or fills the area where his winger would normally operate.

Over the top Going into a tackle over the ball and kicking the opponents legs; a serious foul.

Pitch The field of play.

Reverse pass When a player runs one way and passes the other.

Running off the ball The movement into 'space' of players not in possession in order to be available for a pass from a colleague who has the ball.

Selling a dummy Feinting to dribble or pass one way and then going another in order to beat an opponent.

Set piece A predetermined situation (corners, free-kicks, throw-ins, etc) from which practised moves can be executed.

Shoot out Used in the North American Soccer League after extra-time (overtime) has been played and no decisive result achieved. Five players from each team alternately take the ball from the 35 yard line and shoot within 5 seconds. If there is still no decisive result, the teams continue to take alternate kicks until one team has scored more from the same number of kicks.

Shoulder charge A legal charge, shoulder to shoulder, in competition for the ball.

Sliding tackle Sliding into a tackle on one leg, to attempt to take the ball with that leg.

Square pass A pass made laterally. A square defence is one all of whose members are in a line at right-angles to the touch-line.

Stopper One or other of the two centre backs in a defensive line, originally used to denote the centre-half of the third-back game.

Striker Forward players who stay upfield with the intention of scoring. An all-out attacking player.

Sweeper or *libero* The player operating behind the defensive line of four in a *catenaccio* system. He 'sweeps up' loose balls.

Trapping Controlling (or killing) the ball so that it stays close to the player. The feet, head, chest and thighs can be used to trap the ball.

Third-back game Initiated as a response to the change of the offside law in 1925. The centre-half was converted from a midfield attacker to a centre- or third back.

Through pass A pass to a colleague running through that splits the opposing defence.

W formation Another facet of, and name for, the third-back game, deriving its name from the 'W' formed by the disposition of the five forwards, with the two inside-forwards playing behind a spearhead (centre-forward) and the two wingers.

Wall pass or one-two: When a player receives a quick return from a colleague, using him like a wall, in order to beat an opponent.

Wing The area of the field near to the touchlines. Wingers are players who operate in these areas in offence.

Work-rate A term that emerged in the 1960s to assess and describe a player's capacity for running, chasing etc.

The Rules of Soccer

The Laws governing how soccer is played stem from a code laid down by the English Football Association as far back as December 1863. Since that time there have been regular up-dating and amendments, mostly on minor points, One major change came in 1925 concerning the offside law, making a player onside when two opponents, instead of the previous three, were between himself and the opposing goal-line. FIFA, the world controlling body, has added other riders to the laws concerning international matches and has also permitted certain countries to conduct experiments of their own; hence the NASL's use of the shoot-out and the offside line 35-yards from goal – rulings that are not in regular use elsewhere in the soccer playing world. Yet by and large the law-makers are conservative and the main tenets of the game rarely change, which is a sign of the appeal of soccer.

The laws are reproduced by permission of the Football Association.

Left: The whole of the ball must cross the line to be out of play, so Peter McCloy of Glasgow Rangers still has a couple of inches to spare as he leaps to prevent his side from conceding a corner.

The Ball

The ball shall be spherical; the outer casing shall be of leather or other approved materials. No materials shall be used in its construction which might prove dangerous to the players.

The circumference of the ball shall not be more than 28 inches and not less than 27 inches. The weight of the ball at the start of the game shall not be more than 16 ounces nor less than 14 ounces. The pressure shall be equal to atmospheric pressure ($9-10\frac{1}{2}$ pounds per square inch, ie 600–700 grams per square centimetre at sea level). The ball shall not be changed during the game unless authorized by the referee.

The International Board has also made the following clarifications over the years:

a: The ball shall always be returned to the referee at the end of a game.

b: If the ball bursts during the game play shall be stopped and restarted by dropping the new ball where the incident happened, unless the game has already stopped for a goal-kick, free-kick, corner kick, penalty-kick or throw-in etc.

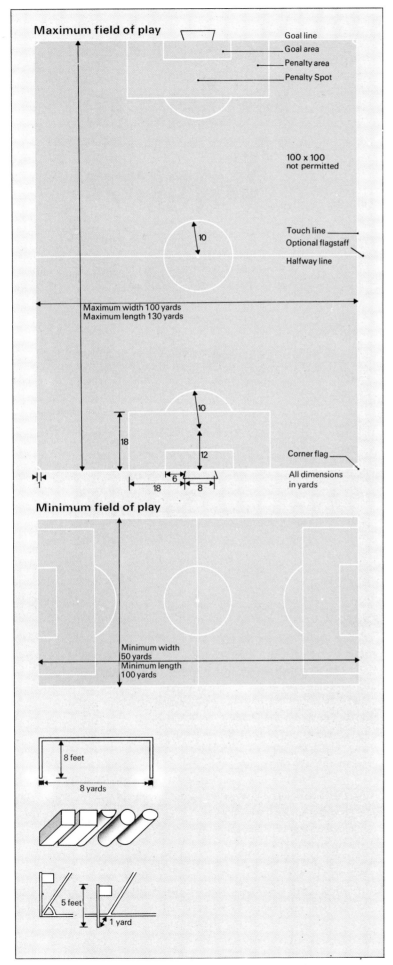

Maximum field of play

Goal line
Goal area
Penalty area
Penalty Spot

100 x 100
not permitted

10

Touch line
Optional flagstaff
Halfway line

Maximum width 100 yards
Maximum length 130 yards

10

18

10

12

Corner flag

All dimensions
in yards

1

18   6   8

Minimum field of play

Minimum width
50 yards
Minimum length
100 yards

8 feet

8 yards

5 feet

1 yard

The field of play

1 Dimensions: The field of play shall be rectangular, its length being not more than 130 yards nor less than 100 yards and its breadth not more than 100 yds nor less than 50 yards. (In International Matches the length shall be not more than 120 yards nor less than 110 yards and the breadth not more than 80 yards nor less than 70 yards.) The length shall in all cases exceed the breadth.

2 Marking: The field of play shall be marked with distinctive lines, not more than 5 inches in width (not by a V-shaped rut), in accordance with the plan, the longer boundary lines being called the touch-lines and the shorter the goal-lines. A flag on a post not less than 5 feet high and having a non-pointed top shall be placed at each corner; a similar flag-post may be placed opposite the halfway-line on each side of the field of play, not less than 1 yard outside the touch-line. A halfway-line shall be marked out across the field of play. The centre of the field of play shall be indicated by a suitable mark and a circle with a 10 yards radius shall be marked.

3 The Goal-Area: At each end of the field of play two lines shall be drawn at right-angles to the goal-line, 6 yards from each goal-post. These shall extend into the field of play for a distance of 6 yards and shall be joined by a line drawn parallel with the goal-line. Each of the spaces enclosed by these lines and the goal-line shall be called a goal-area.

4 Penalty-Area: At each end of the field of play two lines shall be drawn at right-angles to the goal-line, 18 yards from each goal-post. These shall extend into the field of play for a distance of 18 yards and shall be joined by a line drawn parallel with the goal-line. Each of the spaces enclosed by these lines and the goal-line shall be called a penalty-area. A suitable mark shall be made within each penalty area, 12 yards from the mid-point of the goal-line, measured along an undrawn line at right-angles thereto. These shall be the penalty-kick marks. From each penalty-kick mark an arc of a circle, having a radius of 10 yards, shall be drawn outside the penalty-area.

5 The 35-Yard Line: FIFA have given the NASL permission to add a line in each half across the field and 35 yards from each goal-line (see Offside Law).

6 The Corner-Area: From each corner-flag post a quarter circle, having a radius of 1 yard, shall be drawn inside the field of play.

7 The Goals: The goals shall be placed on the centre of each goal-line and shall consist of two upright posts, equidistant from the corner-flags and 8 yards apart (inside measurement), joined by a horizontal crossbar the lower edge of which shall be 8 feet from the ground. The width and depth of the goal-posts and the width and depth of the crossbars shall not exceed 5 inches (12 cm). The goal-posts and the crossbars shall have the same width.

Nets may be attached to the posts, crossbars and ground behind the goal. They should be appropriately supported and be so placed as to allow the goalkeeper ample room.

Number of players

A match shall be played by two teams, each consisting of not more than 11 players, one of whom shall be the goalkeeper.

Substitutes may be used, the number of which depends on the rules of the particular competition (in international matches two substitutes from five nominated players are allowed).

The referee shall be informed of the names of the substitutes before the start of the match.

One of the other players, or a named substitute, may change places with the goalkeeper, provided that notice is given to the referee before the change is made.

Punishment: If, without the referee being notified, a player or a named substitute, changes places with the goalkeeper during the game, at the half-time interval, or at any other interval in a game in which extra time (overtime) is played, and then handles the ball within the penalty area, a penalty-kick shall be awarded.

The International Board has also made the following clarifications over the years:

a: The *minimum* number of players shall be left to national associations, but should not be less than seven.

b: The referee should be informed of the names of any possible substitutes before the game. The number who can be called shall be left to the national association but should not be more than two from five.

c: A player who has been ejected from the game *before* the match begins can only be replaced by a named substitute. A player ordered off *during* the match cannot be replaced.

d: Substitutes may only enter the field with the permission of the referee and when the ball is out of play.

Equipment

A player shall not wear anything which is dangerous to another player. Footwear must conform to the following standard:

a: Bars shall be made of leather or rubber and shall be transverse and flat, not less than half an inch in width and shall extend the total width of the boot or soccer shoe and be rounded at the corners.

b: Studs (cleats) shall be made of leather, rubber, aluminium, plastic or similar material and shall be solid. With the exception of that part of the stud forming the base, which shall not protrude from the sole more than one-quarter of an inch, studs shall be round in plan and not less than half an inch in diameter. Where studs are tapered, the minimum diameter of any section of the stud must not be less than half an inch. Where metal seating for the screw type is used, this seating must be embedded in the sole of the boot or soccer shoe and any attachment screw shall be part of the stud. Other than the metal seating for the screw type of stud, no metal plates even though covered with leather or rubber shall be worn, neither studs which are threaded to allow them to be screwed onto a base screw that is fixed by nails or otherwise to the soles of shoes, nor studs which, apart from the base, have any form of protruding edge, rim, or relief marking, or ornament, should be allowed.

c: Studs (cleats) which are moulded to the sole shall be made of rubber, plastic, polyurethane or similar soft materials.

d: Combined bars and studs (cleats) may be worn, provided the whole conforms to the general requirements of this law. Neither bars nor studs on the soles or heels shall project more than three-quarters of an inch. If nails are used they shall be driven in flush with the surface. (NB The usual equipment of a player consists of a jersey or shirt, shorts, stockings and boots or soccer shoes. A goalkeeper shall wear colours which distinguish him from other players.)

Below left: The relief of a stand-in goalkeeper. Arsenal striker Radford needed the referee's permission before he could take over from his injured team-mate.
Below right: Spectacles as used by Belgian winger Jurion can be worn if they do not endanger other players.

pencil

in pocket: spare pencil, spare whistle, stop-watch yellow and red warning cards

wrist-watch

note-pad, including team-sheet

whistle

coin

football

for use in dressing-room: pressure gauge and tape measure†

†for testing the ball before the match

Above: When the posts are broken, as here when the winger ran into one, the referee stops the game and restarts with a dropped ball.

Punishment: For any infringement of this Law, the player at fault shall be sent off the field of play to adjust his equipment and he shall not return without first reporting to the referee, who shall satisfy himself that the player's equipment is in order; the player shall only re-enter the game at a moment when the ball has ceased to be in play.

The International Board has also made the following clarifications over the years:

a: Players may take the field without shoes, though the Board prefers referees not to allow this when other players are wearing them.

b: Referees shall inspect players' equipment before the game and can order a player to change his equipment at any time during a match.

c: Players who have been ordered to change their equipment shall not return to the game until the referee has examined their new equipment and approved it.

Referees

A referee shall be appointed to officiate in each game. He shall:

Enforce the Laws and decide any disputed point. His decision on points of fact connected with the play shall be final so far as the result of the game is concerned. His jurisdiction begins from the time he signals for the kick-off, and his power of penalizing shall extend to offences committed when play has been temporarily suspended or when the ball is out of play. He shall, however, refrain from penalizing in cases where he is satisfied that by doing so he would be giving an advantage to the offending team.

Keep a record of the game; act as timekeeper and allow the full or agreed time, adding thereto all time lost through accident or other cause.

Have discretionary power to stop the game for any infringement of the Laws and to suspend or terminate the game whenever, by reason of the elements, interference by spectators, or other cause, he deems such stoppage necessary. In such a case he shall submit a detailed report to the competent authority, within the stipulated time, and in accordance with the provisions set up by the National Association under whose jurisdiction the match was played. Reports will be deemed to be made when received in the ordinary course of post.

Have discretionary power, from the time he enters the field of play, to caution any player guilty of misconduct or ungentlemanly behaviour and, if he persists, to suspend him from further participation in the game. In such cases the referee shall send the name of the offender to the competent authority, within the stipulated time and in accordance with the provisions set up by the National Association under whose jurisdiction the match was played. Reports will be deemed to be made when received in the ordinary course of post.

Allow no person other than the players and linesmen to enter the field of play without his permission.

Stop the game if, in his opinion, a player has been seriously injured; have the player removed as soon as possible from the field of play and immediately resume the game. If a player is slightly injured, the game shall not be stopped until the ball has ceased to be in play. A player who is able to go to the touch- or goal-line for attention of any kind, shall not be treated on the field of play.

Have discretionary power to suspend from further participation in the game, without previous caution, a player guilty of violent conduct.

Signal for recommencement of the game after all stoppages.

Decide that the ball provided for a match meets with the requirements of Law 2.

The International Board has also made the following clarifications over the years:

a: Referees in international matches shall wear a colour distinctive from the teams, be selected from a neutral country (unless otherwise agreed by the countries concerned) and be chosen from the official list of international referees.

b: The authority of the referee starts as soon as he enters the field of play, and he should report to the appropriate authority any misconduct on the part of spectators, officials, players and so on which takes place prior to, during, or after the match.

c: Linesmen are the *assistants* of the referee. He should not consider the intervention of the linesmen if he has been in a better position to assess events except during that phase of play immediately before a goal. He may then cancel the goal if he thinks fit, but only if he has not restarted play.

d: The referee cannot revoke his decision after allowing advantage if that advantage is not realized.

e: In order to provide games as free from interference as possible it is the *duty* of referees to penalize only deliberate breaches of the law.

f: Though a referee can terminate a match in the event of grave disorder, he has no right to decide that either team is disqualified and therefore the loser of the match. He must send a detailed report to the proper authority.

g: If a player commits two infringements at the same time, the referee shall punish the more serious offence.

h: It is the duty of the referee to act on the information of linesmen about incidents that do not come under his notice.

i: The referee must not allow trainers or anyone else on the field of play during the game unless they receive a signal from him, and he must also prevent coaching from trainers and club officials from the touchlines.

Linesmen

Two linesmen shall be appointed, whose duty (subject to the decision of the referee) shall be to indicate when the ball is out of play and which side is entitled to the corner-kick, goal-kick or throw-in. They shall also assist the referee to control the game in accordance with the Laws. In the event of undue interference or improper conduct by a linesman, the referee shall dispense with his services and arrange for a substitute to be appointed. (The matter shall be reported by the referee to the competent authority.) The linesmen should be equipped with flags by the club on whose ground the match is actually being played.

The International Board has also made the following clarifications over the years:

a: The linesmen shall draw the referee's attention to any breach of the Laws they consider that he may not have seen, but the referee shall always be the judge of the decision to be taken.

b: National associations are advised to appoint official referees of neutral nationality to be linesmen in international matches, and their flags shall be of a vivid colour – bright red or yellow.

c: A linesman may be subject to disciplinary action only on a report of the referee for unjustified interference or insufficient assistance.

Duration of the game

The duration of the game shall be two equal periods of 45 minutes, unless otherwise mutually agreed upon, subject to the following:

a: Allowance shall be made in either period for all time lost through accident or other cause, the amount of which shall be a matter for the discretion of the referee.

b: Time shall be extended to permit a penalty-kick being taken at or after the expiration of the normal period in either half.

At half-time the interval shall not exceed five minutes except by consent of the referee.

The International Board has also made the following clarifications over the years:

a: If a match has been stopped by the referee before the completion of the time specified in the rules (for any reason stated in Law 5, which relates to referees) it must be replayed in full unless the rules of the competition concerned provide for the result of the match at the time of such a stoppage to stand as the final result.

b: Players have a right to an interval at half-time. The duration shall be at the referee's discretion.

NB In the North American Soccer League all games which are tied at the end of regulation play will be extended by 15 minutes overtime play (two halves of $7\frac{1}{2}$ minutes) This is sudden death and the first team to score a goal is the winner. If there is no score the match is decided by the Shootout. Five players from each team, going in alternate order, will in turn take the ball from the 35-yard line and must shoot within five seconds; the goalkeeper may move freely. The kicks shall finish when one team has achieved a winning position. If the teams remain tied, they continue to take alternate kicks until one team has scored more from the same number of attempts. Only players still in the game at the end of the overtime period are eligible to take part in the Shootout. No player may take a second kick until all other members of his team still in the game have taken one attempt.

The start of play

a: At the beginning of the game, choice of ends and the kick-off shall be decided by the toss of a coin. The team winning the toss shall have the option of choice of ends or the kick-off.

The referee having given a signal, the game shall be started by a player taking a place-kick (ie a kick at the ball while it is stationary on the ground in the centre of the field of play) into his opponents' half of the field of play'. Every player shall be in his own half of the field and every player of the team opposing that of the kicker shall remain not less than 10 yards from the ball until it is kicked-off; it shall not be deemed in play until it has travelled the distance of its own circumference. The kicker shall not play the ball a second time until it has been touched or played by another player.

b: After a goal has been scored, the game shall be re-started in like manner by a player of the team losing the goal.

Left: Of all the examples in the diagram the ball is only out of play at point A when it has swung out and then come into play again, and at point B. On both occasions it has totally crossed the line and the linesman will signal for a throw-in.
Below: Perhaps the most fiercely contested goal in the history of the FA Cup. In the 1932 Final the Arsenal players stopped, thinking the ball had crossed the line before Newcastle's Richardson reached it. But Allen scored from the centre; the goal stood and Newcastle won.

c: After half-time; when restarting after half-time, ends shall be changed and the kick-off shall be taken by a player of the opposite team to that of the player who started the game.

Punishment: For any infringement of this Law, the kick-off shall be retaken, except in the case of the kicker playing the ball again before it has been touched or played by another player; for this offence an indirect free-kick shall be taken by a player of the opposing team from the place where the infringement occurred. A goal shall not be scored direct from a kick-off.

d: After any other temporary suspension; when restarting the game after a temporary suspension of play from any cause not mentioned elsewhere in these Laws, provided that immediately prior to the suspension the ball has not passed over the touch- or goal-lines, the referee shall drop the ball at the place where it was when play was suspended and it shall be deemed in play when it has touched the ground; if, however, it goes over the touch- or goal-lines after it has been dropped by the referee, but before it is touched by a player, the referee shall again drop it. A player shall not play the ball until it has touched the ground. If this section of the Law is not complied with the referee shall again drop the ball.

The International Board has also made the following clarifications over the years:

a: A player infringing the Laws at a dropped ball shall be dealt with by the referee according to the seriousness of the offence. If the ball has not touched the ground, however, a free-kick cannot be awarded as the ball was not in play at the time of the offence. There is nothing in the Laws which insists that a drop-ball must be contested by players of opposing sides.

b: Kicking-off by anyone but one of the players competing in the match is not allowed.

Ball in and out of play

The ball is out of play: –

a: When it has wholly crossed the goal-line or touch-line, whether on the ground or in the air.

ALLEN

RICHARDSON

b: When the game has been stopped by the referee. The ball is in play at all other times from the start of the match to the finish including: –

a: If it rebounds from a goal-post, cross-bar or corner-flag into the field of play.

b: If it rebounds off either the referee or linesman when they are in the field of play.

c: In the event of a supposed infringement of the Laws, until a decision is given.

The International Board has also made the following decision:

The lines belong to the areas of which they are the boundaries, ie the touch- and goal-lines, are in play.

Offside

A player is offside if he is nearer his opponents' goal-line than the ball at the moment the ball is played unless:

a: He is in his own half of the field of play. (NB In the NASL the player cannot be offside if he is more than 35 yards from his opponents' goal-line.)

b: There are two of his opponents nearer to their own goal line than he is.

c: The ball last touched an opponent or was last played by him.

d: He receives the ball direct from a goal-kick, a corner-kick, a throw-in, or when it was dropped by the referee.

Punishment: For an infringement of this Law, an indirect free-kick shall be taken by a player of the opposing team from the place where the infringement occurred.

A player in an offside position shall not be penalized unless, in the opinion of the referee, he is interfering with the play or with an opponent or is seeking to gain an advantage by being in an offside position.

The International Board has made the following clarification:

Offside shall not be judged at the moment the player in question receives the ball, but at the moment when the ball is passed to him by one of his own side. A player who is not in an offside-position when one of his colleagues passes the ball to him or takes a free-kick does not therefore become offside if he goes forward during the flight of the ball, although he might appear to be offside when he receives it.

Top centre: The drawing shows a defender appealing for offside as a forward moves clear. The eleven diagrams show how he could have been onside. 1 There are two defenders between him and the goal. 2 When the ball was last played he was in an onside position. 3 He is behind a team-mate who was the last player to touch the ball. 4 He has dribbled through on his own. 5 The ball has been last played by an opponent. 6 He has received the ball direct from a bounce-up by the referee. 7 He has gained possession inside his own half and broken through. 8 He has got the ball straight from a corner, 9, a throw-in or, 10, a goal-kick from his own goalkeeper. In diagram 11, he can be onside if the referee decides that, although he is standing in an offside position, he is not interfering with play or seeking to gain an advantage while his colleagues build-up an attack. Several attempts have been made recently to alter the offside law – the most permanent being the NASL's 35 yard ruling.

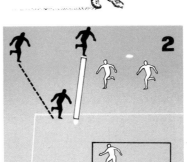

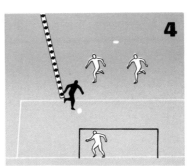

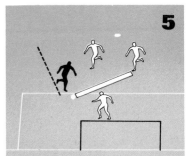

Method of scoring

Except as otherwise provided by these Laws, a goal is scored when the whole of the ball has passed over the goal-line, between the goal-posts and under the cross-bar, provided it has not been thrown, carried or propelled by hand or arm, by a player of the attacking side, except in the case of a goalkeeper who is within his own penalty area.

The team scoring the greater number of goals during a game shall be the winner; if no goals, or an equal number of goals are scored, the game shall be termed a 'draw'.
NB In the NASL there are no drawn or tied games (see Shootout).

The International Board has also made the following decisions over the years: –

a: This Law defines the *only* way a match is won or drawn.
b: A goal cannot be allowed if the ball has been prevented from crossing the goal-line by some outside interference. If this happens (except in the case of a penalty-kick) the game must be restarted by a dropped ball.
c: If a spectator tries to prevent a score when the ball is heading for the goal, the goal shall be allowed only if the spectator does not make contact with it or interfere with play. If he does, the game must be restarted by a dropped ball at the place where the interference with play occurred.

Fouls and misconduct

A player who intentionally commits one of nine specified offences (or fouls) shall be penalized by the award of a direct free-kick to be taken by the opposing side from the place where the offence occurred.

Should a player of the defending side intentionally commit one of the same nine offences within the penalty area he shall be penalized by a penalty-kick. A penalty-kick can be awarded irrespective of the position of the ball, if in play, at the time an offence within the penalty area is committed.

A player committing any of a number of other offences (or fouls) shall be penalized by the award of an indirect free-kick to be taken by the opposing side from the place where the infringement occurred.

A player shall be cautioned if:
a: He enters or re-enters the field of play to join or re-join his team after the game has commenced, or leaves the field of play during the progress of the game (except through accident, without, in either case, having first received a signal from the referee showing him that he may do so. If the referee stops the game to administer the caution the game shall be re-started by an indirect free-kick taken by a player of the opposing team from the place where the offending player was when the referee stopped the game. If, however, the offending player has committed a more serious offence, he shall be penalized according to the section of the Law he infringed.

Inset far left: Violence flares in a match in Greece.
Inset above left: Gang warfare in England's First Division.
Left: A spot of furtive and illegal shirt-pulling.
Right: In criticising the referee players risk being cautioned for dissent. Here Billy Bremner makes his point.

b: He persistently infringes the Laws of the game.
c: He shows by word or action dissent from any decision given by the referee.
d: He is guilty of ungentlemanly conduct.

A player shall be sent off the field of play if:
a: In the opinion of the referee he is guilty of violent conduct or serious foul play.
b: He uses foul or abusive language.
c: He persists in misconduct after having received a caution.

The International Board has also made the following clarifications over the years:
a: If the goalkeeper throws the ball at an opponent in the penalty area the referee shall award a penalty kick.
b: A player deliberately turning his back on an opponent to avoid a tackle may be charged.
c: If the goalkeeper is intentionally impeded inside the goal area by an opponent even though he is not in possession of the ball, the referee should award an indirect free-kick.
d: The referee does not have to stop the game to administer a caution. He may apply the advantage clause and then caution an offender when play does stop.
e: A player joining or re-joining play after the start of the match must attract the attention of the referee. The referee does not have to wait for play to stop to wave him on (except in the case of a substitution).
f: A player already in possession of the ball cannot be penalized for obstructing an opponent.
g: A player shall be cautioned for ungentlemanly conduct if he stretches his arms or moves from side to side to obstruct an opponent, even if he does not make bodily contact.
h: Intentional obstruction of the goalkeeper shall be dealt with by the award of an indirect free-kick.
i: If a player strikes an opponent during the half-time interval he shall still be dealt with according to the Laws.
j: The referee shall award an indirect free-kick against a goalkeeper if he lies on the ball intentionally longer than is necessary.
k: Spitting at opponents, officials or any other person shall be considered as violent conduct.

Indirect free-kicks

An indirect free-kick can be given against a player in any of the following circumstances, all of which are somewhere written into the Laws or covered by International Board decisions:

1: Playing in a manner considered by the referee to be dangerous; eg attempting to kick a ball held by the goalkeeper.

2: Charging fairly, ie with the shoulder, when the ball is not within playing distance of the players concerned and they are definitely not trying to play it.

3: When not playing the ball, intentionally obstructing an opponent; ie running between the opponent and the ball, or interposing the body so as to form an obstacle to an opponent. There need not be physical contact between the players.

4: Charging the goalkeeper except when he is holding the ball, obstructing an opponent or has passed outside his goal-area.

5: When playing as goalkeeper he takes more than four steps while holding, bouncing or throwing the ball in the air and catching it again without releasing it so that it is played by another player.

6: When playing as goalkeeper he indulges in tactics which, in the opinion of the referee, are designed merely to hold up the game and thus waste time.

7: Showing by word or action dissent from any decision given by the referee.

8: Being guilty of ungentlemanly conduct.

9: If a player is ordered from the field for an offence for which no specific provision is made in the Laws (eg swearing at the referee) the game shall be restarted by an indirect free-kick against his side.

10: Entering, re-entering or leaving the field of play without the referee's permission.

11: Touching the ball twice in succession at a kick-off.

12: If he is adjudged to have been offside.

13: Using a team-mate to assist in gaining height to head the ball.

14: Touching the ball twice in succession at a free-kick.

15: Touching the ball twice in succession at a corner-kick.

16: Touching the ball twice in succession at a penalty-kick.

17: Playing the ball backwards at a penalty-kick.

18: Encroaching into the penalty area at a penalty-kick. (This is only applicable if the kick is missed, when the referee may award an indirect free-kick against any player of the *attacking* team who was encroaching. If a player of the defending team was encroaching the kick would be retaken. If the kick is successful, and a member of the attacking team was encroaching the kick would be retaken. If a member of the defending side was encroaching the referee would apply the advantage clause.)

19: Playing the ball after taking a throw-in *without* any other player touching the ball.

20: Playing the ball a second time *outside the penalty area* after taking a goal-kick without another player touching it. If the ball has not left the penalty area when it is played a second time the goal-kick has to be re-taken.

21: Not placing the whole of the ball in the quadrant at a corner-kick. The referee, at his discretion, may order the kick to be retaken.

(There may be other offences, nowhere specified, which can be punished under the blanket 'ungentlemanly conduct' clause.)

Free-kick

Free-kicks shall be classified under two heads: 'Direct' (from which a goal can be scored direct against the offending side), and 'Indirect' (from which a goal cannot be scored unless the ball has been played or touched by a player other than the kicker before passing through the goal).

When a player is taking a direct or an indirect free-kick inside his own penalty-area, all of the opposing players shall remain outside the area, and shall be at least ten yards from the ball whilst the kick is being taken. The ball shall be in play immediately it has travelled the distance of its own circumference and is beyond the penalty area. The goal keeper shall not receive the ball into his hands, in order that he may thereafter kick it into play. If the ball is not kicked direct into play, beyond the penalty-area, the kick shall be re-taken. ·

When a player is taking a direct or indirect free-kick outside his own penalty area, all of the opposing players shall be at least ten yards from the ball, until it is in play, unless they are standing on their own goal-line, between the goal-posts. The ball shall be in play when it has travelled the distance of its own circumference.

If a player of the opposing side encroaches into the penalty-area, or within ten yards of the ball, as the case may be, before a free-kick is taken, the referee shall delay the taking of the kick, until the Law is complied with.

The ball must be stationary when a free-kick is taken, and the kicker shall not play the ball a second time, until it has been touched or played by another player.

Punishment: If the kicker, after taking the free-kick, plays the ball a second time before it has been touched or played by another player, an indirect free-kick shall be taken by a player of the opposing team from the spot where the infringement occurred.

The International Board has also made the following clarifications over the years:

a: The referee must signal an indirect free-kick by raising his arm, and this must be done before he blows the whistle for the kick to be taken. No signal is required for a direct free-kick.

b: Players who do not retire the proper distance must be cautioned and, if they do it again, be ordered off. Attempts to delay the taking of free-kicks by encroaching should be treated as serious misconduct.

c: It is ungentlemanly conduct to distract the taker of a free-kick, and the offender should be cautioned.

Penalty-kick

A penalty-kick shall be taken from the penalty-mark and, when it is being taken, all players with the exception of the player taking the kick, and the opposing goalkeeper, shall be within the field of play but outside the penalty-area, and at least 10 yards from the penalty-mark. The opposing goalkeeper must stand (without moving his feet) on his own goal-line, between the goal-posts, until the ball is kicked. The player taking the kick must kick the ball forward; he shall not play the ball a second time until it has been touched or played by another player. The ball shall be deemed in play directly it is kicked, ie

Above: Players must retreat 10 yards at a free-kick except when it is less than 10 yards from their goal.

travelled the distance of its circumference, and a goal may be scored direct from such a penalty-kick. If the ball touches the goalkeeper before passing between the posts, when a penalty-kick is being taken at or after the expiration of half-time or full-time, it does not nullify a goal. If necessary, time of play shall be extended at half-time or full-time to allow a penalty-kick to be taken.

Punishment: For any infringement of this Law:

a: by the defending team, the kick shall be retaken if a goal has not resulted;

b: by the attacking team other than by the player taking the kick, if a goal is scored it shall be disallowed and the kick retaken;

c: by the player taking the penalty-kick, committed after the ball is in play, a player of the opposing team shall take an indirect free-kick from the spot where the infringement occurred.

The International Board has made the following clarifications over the years:

a: The referee must not signal the taking of the kick until the players have taken up the position ordered by the Law. If, after giving the signal, the referees sees that the 'keeper is not correctly placed on the goal-line between the goal posts he must await the outcome of the kick. If the 'keeper moves his feet after the blowing of the whistle but before the kick is taken and no goal is scored, the kick must be retaken.

b: If either an attacker or defender enters the penalty area before the ball has been kicked, he shall be cautioned, as shall the player taking the kick if he is guilty of ungentlemanly conduct.

c: When a match is extended, at half-time or full-time to allow a penalty to be taken, the extension ends the moment the kick is completed, ie when the ball goes directly into the goal, goes in off the goalposts or crossbar, goes directly out of play, rebounds off the goalposts, crossbar or the 'keeper into play, or goes into the goal off the goalkeeper unless he drops it well after making a save.

d: If any outside agent interferes with the course of the penalty, the kick shall be retaken. If the match has already been extended to allow the kick to be taken, the referee shall extend the extra period further so that the penalty can be properly completed.

Direct free-kicks

A direct free-kick can be given against a player who commits any of the following nine offences:

1: Kicks or attempts to kick an opponent.
2: Trips an opponent; ie throwing or attempting to throw him by the use of the legs or by stooping in front of or behind him.
3: Jumps at an opponent.
4: Charges an opponent in a violent or dangerous manner.
5: Charges an opponent from behind unless the latter be obstructing.
6: Strikes or attempts to strike an opponent.
7: Holds an opponent with his hand or any part of his arm.
8: Pushes an opponent with his hand or any part of his arm.
9: Handles the ball; ie carries, strikes or propels the ball with his hand or arm. (This does not apply to the goalkeeper within his own penalty-area.)

Above: In pushing Derby County's Colin Todd to the ground, Derek Jeffries of Manchester City conceded a direct free-kick. Rodney Marsh, centre, acted out the role of accomplice.
Below: At a penalty kick all players except the goalkeeper and the taker of the penalty must be outside the area. Players must NOT stand behind the goal-line, so the players indicated doing so here would be penalized by the referee.

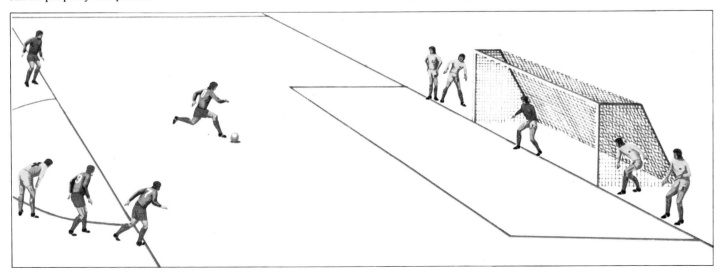

Corner-kick

When the whole of the ball passes over the goal-line, excluding that portion between the goal-posts, either in the air or on the ground, having last been played by one of the defending team, a member of the attacking team shall take a corner kick, ie the whole of the ball shall be placed within the quarter-circle at the nearest corner flag-post, which must not be moved, and it shall be kicked from that position. A goal may be scored direct from such a kick. Players of the team opposing that of the player taking the corner-kick shall not approach within ten yards of the ball until it is in play, ie it has travelled the distance of its own circumference, nor shall the kicker play the ball a second time until it has been touched or played by another player.

Punishment: For an infringement of this Law, an indirect free-kick shall be awarded to the opposing team, to be taken from the place where the infringement occurred.

Goal-kick

When the whole of the ball passes over the goal-line, excluding that portion between the goal-posts, either in the air or on the ground, having last been played by one of the attacking team, it shall be kicked directly into play beyond the penalty-area from a point within that half of the goal-area nearest to where it crossed the line, by a player of the defending team. A goalkeeper shall not receive the ball into his hands from a goal-kick in order that he may thereafter kick it into play. If the ball is not kicked beyond the penalty-area ie direct into play, the kick shall be retaken. The kicker shall not play the ball a second time until it has touched or been played by another player. A goal shall not be scored direct from such a kick. Players of the team opposing that of the player taking the goal-kick shall remain outside the penalty-area whilst the kick is being taken.

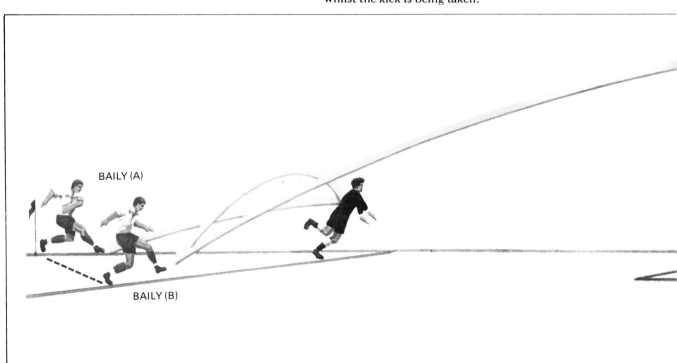

BAILY (A)

BAILY (B)

Punishment: If a player taking a goal-kick plays the ball a second time after it has passed beyond the penalty-area, but before it has touched or been played by another player, an indirect free-kick shall be awarded to the opposing team, to be taken from the place where the infringement occurred.

International Board decision:

a: The kick must be retaken if the taker touches the ball again before it has left the penalty-area.

Throw-in

When the whole of the ball passes over a touch-line, either on the ground or in the air, it shall be thrown in from the point where it crossed the line, in any direction, by a player of the team opposite to that of the player who last touched it. The thrower at the moment of delivering the ball must face the field of play and part of each foot shall be either on the touch-line or on the ground outside the touch-line. The thrower shall use both hands and shall deliver the ball from behind and over his head. The ball shall be in play immediately it enters the field of play, but the thrower shall not again play the ball until it has been touched or played by another player. A goal shall not be scored direct from a throw-in.

Punishment: a: If the ball is improperly thrown in the throw-in shall be taken by a player of the opposing team.

b: If the thrower plays the ball a second time before it has been touched or played by another player, an indirect free-kick shall be taken by a player of the opposing team from the place where the infringement occurred.

The International Board has also made the following clarifications:

a: The referee will award a direct free-kick if the thrower plays the ball a second time by handling it.

b: A player taking a throw-in must face the field of play

with some part of his body.

c: If an opposing player acts in a way calculated to impede or distract the thrower the offender will be cautioned.

Below: The right and the wrong way to take a throw-in. The player on the left has one foot in play and one in the air when the law states that part of both feet must be on the touch-line or on the ground behind the touchline. He would also be penalized for not delivering the ball correctly from behind and over his head. The player on the right has obeyed these rules and his throw-in would be deemed perfectly fair. There is little excuse, in fact, for an incorrect throw-in.

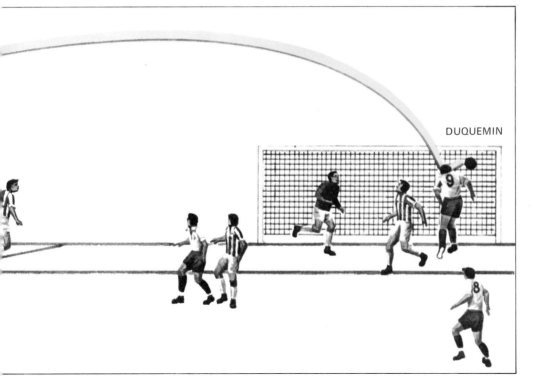

DUQUEMIN

Top left: George Armstrong taking a corner-kick for Arsenal.
Left: Diagram of a celebrated and totally illegal goal that was allowed to stand after a corner-kick. In 1952 Eddie Baily of Tottenham Hotspur took a corner against Huddersfield when the referee was running away from him. The ball hit the official on the back and dropped for Baily to cross it to Duquemin who scored. Baily should not have played the ball a second time because it had not touched another player. But the unsighted referee gave the goal. Huddersfield were relegated at the season's end.

The World Game

On 21 June, 1970, the soccer elevens of Brazil and Italy emerged from the subterranean dressing-rooms of the Aztec Stadium in Mexico City and prepared to battle for 90 minutes, or perhaps more, to decide who were the soccer champions of the world. They were also competing for an additional honour – that of securing the Jules Rimet Trophy for good. Both nations had already won the championship on two occasions and any country winning it three times were to become the permanent owners.

Thus the ninth World Cup was the last to be played under the official title of the Jules Rimet Trophy. Brazil won the final in spectacularly convincing fashion and for 1974 FIFA presented a new trophy, the FIFA World Cup, which cannot be won outright.

For all its present status and popularity, the World Cup had a laboured beginning. At the first meeting of FIFA in Paris in 1904 the seven member countries – Switzerland, Belgium, Denmark, France and Netherlands, Spain and Sweden – did include a provision in the constitution stating that only FIFA had the right to organize such a tournament. Yet it was not until 1920, at the Antwerp Congress, that the principle of the cup was agreed. It was at this meeting that Jules Rimet, President of the French Football Federation, was elected President, a position he was to hold until 1954. No person did more to gain support for the idea of a world championship and it was appropriate that the cup was named after him.

At the 1926 Congress, the secretary of the French Federation, Henri Delaunay, maintained that the Olympic Games no longer represented the best (ie the professionals) from many nations. And two years later, at the FIFA

Left: Mario Kempes, the man who won the 1978 World Cup, celebrates his first goal against the unlucky Dutch, twice runners-up in the 1970s.

meeting during the Amsterdam Olympics, it was decided to hold a world championship every fourth year – only the Scandinavian countries opposing the motion. The following year, at Barcelona, Uruguay won approval to stage the initial tournament in 1930 against mild opposition from Italy, Hungary, the Netherlands, Spain and Sweden.

The Uruguayans had several claims to be the hosts: they had won the Olympic gold medals of 1924 and 1928, they celebrated their centenary in 1930, and they promised to pay every team's full expenses and install a crash programme to build a new stadium with a capacity of 100,000.

As the competition approached, however, European enthusiasm evaporated, and with only eight weeks to go, no country had entered. The prominent soccer powers – Austria, Czechoslavakia, Germany, Hungary, Italy, Spain and Switzerland – all declined, and the British contingent were ineligible, having withdrawn from FIFA in 1928 over the question of broken-time payments. France, with their personal participation and after the visit of the Uruguayans to the Paris Olympics in 1924, had a moral obligation to go, as did Belgium, whose Rodolphe Seeldrayers was a prominent member of FIFA in its early days. The Romanians had the unusual asset of royal influence, King Carol selecting the players himself and arranging release from their jobs. With Yugoslavia making a late decision, Europe was represented by four nations, though none could be rated as a major force in continental soccer.

The South Americans, on the other hand, provided seven entries, with Argentina, Bolivia, Brazil, Chile, Peru and Paraguay joining the hosts. The United States, who were to do surprisingly well, and Mexico made up the thirteen, on their way to the first of a seemingly permanent set of places in the World Cup finals.

39

Top: Jules Rimet, centre, the instigator of the World Cup.
Centre: Dorado gives Uruguay the lead in the 1930 final.
Above: Castro's shot beats a defender for Uruguay's 4th goal.
Right: Guaita's goal that took Italy to victory over Austria in
the semi-final of the 1934 World Cup.

1930 – SOUTH AMERICAN WALKOVER

As the tournament lacked the number of sides necessary for the planned knock-out system, the organizers seeded the teams and grouped them in four sections, with four in one and three in each of the others. The Centenary Stadium was not ready in time and the opening matches were played on the club grounds of Penarol and Nacional, both in Montevideo.

The competition proved an exercise for the South Americans, Uruguay and Argentina repeating their 1928 Olympic final, though Yugoslavia and the United States were losing semi-finalists. The Americans were the surprise of the series. Nicknamed 'the shot-putters' by the French because of their size, the side included six British ex-professionals.

The first ever World Cup match saw France beat Mexico 4–1 in Group 1 on Sunday 13 July 1930. The French triumphed despite losing goalkeeper Thépot, but they failed to keep up that standard, and subsequently lost to Argentina and Chile, on both occasions by a single goal scored in the second half. The seeded Argentinians, with Stabile scoring five, comfortably removed Mexico and Chile to lead the group.

In Group 2 Yugoslavia surprised Brazil, the seeds, by 2–1, and then qualified for the last four by beating Bolivia 4–0. Uruguay scraped home 1–0 against Peru in the hurriedly completed Centenary Stadium, and then beat Romania 4–0 to head Group 3. Meanwhile, the United States lived up to their unexpected seed rating in Group 4 by producing 3–0 wins over both Belgium and Paraguay.

These sectional games were not without incident, particularly in Group 1. In the Argentina-France match, Brazilian referee Rego blew for time six minutes early, and the Uruguayan crowd, who were supporting the French, invaded the pitch; it was 15 minutes before the contest could be resumed. Trouble seemed to follow the Argentinians: their 6–3 win over Mexico produced five penalties, and the game with Chile included a fight that had to be broken up by the police.

The semi-finals proved illuminating. An experienced Argentina exposed the brave but limited qualities of the Americans and won 6–1 with five of their goals coming in the second half. Uruguay dealt with Yugoslavia by the same score, Cea getting three, even though the Europeans took an early lead through Seculic.

Thus the final, played in front of 100,000 people on 30 July, involved traditional and bitter rivals. Uruguay had beaten Argentina 2–1 in the replayed Olympic final of 1928 and there were 11 survivors of that game.

It was expected to be a tough, explosive game, with temperament a key factor. Boatloads of Argentinians crossed the River Plate and were searched for arms. The rivalry of the two sides was such that, after an argument, the two halves of the match were played with different balls – one manufactured in Uruguay, the other in Argentina.

Uruguay, who started without their young centre-forward Pelegrin Anselmo, won 4–2.

Outside-right Pablo Dorado put them ahead in the 12th minute, but the Argentinians equalized through

Carlos Peucelle and then took the lead with a disputed goal by Stabile, his eighth of the series. In the second half, however, Uruguay began to capitalize on their technical superiority, especially at half-back. Cea made it 2–2 after a fine dribble, Iriarte gave them a lead with a fine opportunist goal, and then Castro, deputizing for Anselmo, put the issue virtually beyond doubt with a long-range drive.

Montevideo went wild, and the following day was declared a national holiday. The Argentinians demonstrated in the streets of Buenos Aires, slated Uruguay in their press, and finally broke off relations with the Football Association in Montevideo.

With its limited European entry, violent play and indifferent refereeing, the initial competition for the Jules Rimet Trophy could hardly be described as an unqualified success. It had, nevertheless, made the long-awaited break into intercontinental national competition, and adequately laid the basis for the contests of the future.

1934 – EUROPEAN REASSERTION

Impressed by the first series, but more enticed by the decision to hold the tournament in their continent, the European nations responded well in 1934. The entry list rose to 34, grouped in 10 sections to produce 16 finalists.

Unlike 1930 there was no outstanding nomination for host country, but it was obvious that the World Cup would have to be staged by one with several large cities and the financial resources to cope. It took FIFA eight meetings before they made their decision and it was Italy, anxious to make political capital out of the situation, who eventually secured the vote.

The composition of the final series was very different from that of 1930. The United States were present again, but only Argentina, Brazil, Belgium and France of the other teams of the initial tournament joined them and the Argentinians, frightened of losing more players to Italian clubs, did not compete at full strength. The most notable absentee was Uruguay, no doubt annoyed by the European reaction four years earlier but also troubled by domestic matters. It meant that, for the only time in its history, the Jules Rimet Trophy was not defended by the holders.

The Italians had the most improved team in Europe.

Team manager Vittorio Pozzo had brought in three Argentinians of Italian extraction – Guaita, Orsi and Luisito Monti, who played in the 1930 final; he had a splendid goalkeeper in Combi, and a fine striking inside-forward in Guiseppe Meazza.

Italy's great rivals were Hugo Meisl's Austria. Although the *wunderteam* was now past its peak, the Austrians, led by the elusive Mattias Sindelar at centre-forward, still posed a great threat and enjoyed the psychological advantage of having beaten Italy 4–2 in Turin the previous February.

A simple knock-out system was employed, with half the 16 sides seeded. Italy started proceedings on May 27 by beating the United States, who had only three of their 1930 team left, 7–1 in Rome, one of eight venues used for the series. At Florence the Germans, thorough as ever in preparation but somewhat uninspired, took Belgium 5–2, with a hat-trick from Conen, after being 1–2 down at half-time. Austria made heavy weather of beating France at Turin. The French made all the running, despite an injury to centre-forward and captain Nicolas and a lethargic Austria required an allegedly off-side goal to get through in extra time by 3–2.

A workmanlike Swedish team overcame Argentina (with none of the 1930 final side present) by the same margin at Bologna and, with Brazil missing a penalty in their 3–1 defeat by Spain in Genoa, the South American challenge came to an early end.

The Czechs needed two fine saves from Frantisek Planicka to help them past Romania at Trieste, and in Naples, Egypt put up a spirited fight against Hungary before going down 4–2. Switzerland were aided by a freak goal against Holland at Milan and got through 3–2.

On the whole the first round had been free from incident but the quarter-finals were to provide a different story. The worst, perhaps, was at Florence, where a splendid display by Zamora enabled Spain to hold Italy to a 1–1 draw. For the replay the following day seven Spaniards, including the roughly handled Zamora, and four Italians were non-starters because of injury. The hosts got through with a Meazza goal in a game even more badly refereed than the first – so much so that the Swiss official, M. Mercet, was suspended by his national federation.

At Bologna, what promised to be a classic duel between neighbours Austria and Hungary degenerated to an ill-tempered scramble. Hungary's outside-right, Markos, was sent off after a fight and Austria held on to win 2–1.

Germany beat a Swedish side reduced for much of the game at Milan to 10 men. By far the best match of the round was in Turin, where Czechoslovakia played Switzerland. The Swiss swarmed all over their opponents but the Czechs, with Planicka again superb in goal, kept their heads and won 3–2 with a Nejedly goal seven minutes from time.

One semi-final saw the favourites clash. The Italians had Schiavio and Ferrari back after the debacle against Spain, but Austria lacked Horwath, who had come into the side against Hungary and scored in the opening minutes. The traditional game of the Austrians was, however, lost in a sea of mud at Milan and Italy, showing considerable staying power only two days after their replay with Spain, won with a first-half goal from Guaita.

In Rome, the improving Czechs were too clever for the Germans and won with two goals from Nejedly and one from Krcil. In the third place match at Naples a dejected Austria lost 3–2 to Germany, who took the lead through Lehner after only 24 seconds.

Three days later, in a final remarkable for its two goalkeeper-captains, Czechoslovakia surprised Italy with the standard of their neat, short-passing game. With Antonin Puc causing havoc on the left and Planicka supreme in goal, they had slightly the better of a goalless first-half. The 55,000 spectators saw Puc score from a corner 20 minutes from time, and the Czechs should then have clinched it, Sobotka missing a good chance and Svoboda hitting a post. But with Schiavio and Guaita changing positions the Italians came more into the game, and Orsi equalized eight minutes from time with a goal that was either genius or fluke, his swerving shot curling over the hands of a groping Planicka (in practice the next day he could not repeat it). After seven minutes of extra time the ball went from the injured Meazza, on the wing, to Guaita and on to Schiavio, who scored the winner. The hosts had again secured the Jules Rimet Trophy.

Like the 1930 contest, the second series emanated mixed feelings. It was a financial success and Europe regained some lost reputation. But it also proved that violent play, poor refereeing and fervent nationalism in soccer were by no means confined to South America.

1938 – ITALY RETAIN THE CUP

Argentina wished to stage the 1938 World Cup but, in spite of the mounting political tension in Europe, France was chosen. The competition attracted 36 entries with 16 of these qualifying for the finals. Uruguay, still worried by the crisis of professionalism, again refused to participate, as did a peeved Argentina. Spain was in the throes of Civil War, and Austria, having qualified, were forcibly withdrawn when that mid-European state was swallowed up by an increasingly belligerent Germany. No less than 11 of the countries who competed four years earlier were present, and the newcomers were Poland, Norway, Cuba and the Dutch East Indies. The United States failed to qualify.

Italy, the champions, were thought by manager Pozzo to have a stronger side than in 1934. Only Meazza and Ferrari survived from that eleven and between them Schiavio had been replaced by the tall and powerful Silvio Piola. At centre-half, Monti had given way to another South American, Andreolo from Uruguay.

A much-changed Hungary, conquerors of Czechoslovakia by 8–3 the previous September, had an in-form Sarosi getting good support from the young inside-left Szengeller. Planicka, Kostalek, Nejedly and Puc survived from the Czech side of 1934, and they were well fancied, but Germany, now under Sepp Herberger, were smarting from the 6–3 defeat by England in Berlin only weeks before – their first loss in 15 matches. Brazil, South America's sole representative, were a younger and better side, but still had the old head of Leonidas at centre-forward.

The straight elimination system was again employed, but after England had refused a generous offer to take Austria's place, Sweden won a bye through to the quarter-finals. The first round was close fought, with two matches requiring replays and three being decided in extra time (overtime).

Only France, who beat Belgium 3–1 at the Stade Colombes in Paris with the help of two goals from Nicolas, and Hungary went through immediately.

Three fancied countries were extended to extra time by less endowed sides. At Le Havre, Czechoslovakia, who scored all three of their goals against the Netherlands in the extra period, were perhaps lucky that the Dutch lacked their leading scorer Bakhuijs. Italy were almost upset by gallant Norway at Marseille. Ferrari gave the holders the lead after two minutes, but Norway fought back and levelled after the interval through outside-left Brustad; he scored again but was ruled off-side. Piola, bottled up for most of the game, grabbed the winner in extra time (overtime).

Poland really surprised Brazil in a remarkable game at Strasbourg. In recent years the Poles had enjoyed wins over some fine teams, including Austria, Sweden and Yugoslavia (in a World Cup qualifier) and Ernest Willimowski was among Europe's best inside-forwards. Brazil, with six players winning their first cap, took a 3–1 half-time lead, but at the end of 90 minutes Poland had pulled back to 4–4. In extra time both Leonidas and Willimowski took their personal tallies to four goals each but another by Romeu was decisive: 6–5. Poland's brief appearance in the World Cup had been an exciting one.

Two matches went to a replay. Germany, fielding four Austrians, took a half-time lead at the Parc des Princes in Paris against Switzerland, but André Abegglen headed an equalizer. Germany's outside-left, Pesser, was sent off in a goalless extra time (overtime). For the replay five days later Herberger introduced six new men, including the 1934 captain, Szepan, and his team were two up by the interval. The Swiss, however, made a spirited come-back and, despite losing left-winger Aebi for a time, won the match 4–2 with Abegglen scoring the third and fourth goals.

The greatest surprise of the first round was Cuba's elimination of Romania in Toulouse. Five of the Romanians had previous World Cup experience, but the unknown Cubans were ahead in extra time before Dobai levelled at 3–3. Cuba surprisingly dropped their excellent goalkeeper Carvajales for the replay, but Ayra deputized superbly and they won 2–1.

In the quarter-finals, Italy, with three changes looked more like champions in beating France 3–1 in front of 58,000 at the Stade Colombes. Delfour and Mattler were playing in their third World Cup for France, but it was Piola, with two goals, who stole the limelight. Sweden aligned freshness with experience to end the Cuban dream 8–0 at Antibes, with Gustav Wetterstroem accounting for half the score. Switzerland also seemed tired after their replay and went down to two goals from Szengeller of Hungary, at Lille.

At the new municipal stadium in Bordeaux, Czechoslovakia took on Brazil in what proved to be the one large blot on the 1938 copybook. Two Brazilians and a Czech were sent off by referee von Hertzka, while Planicka with a broken arm and Nejedly with a broken leg ended in hospital – the latter after he had equalized Leonidas' goal from a penalty. The match finished at 1–1 after extra time (overtime). The replay, under M. Capdeville of France, was remarkably well tempered, with only seven players remaining from the first encounter. Leonidas, one of the two surviving Brazilians, and Roberto erased Kopecky's half-time lead.

For the semi-final against Italy at Marseille two days later, Brazil unaccountably omitted Leonidas and Tim, and paid the price. Colaussi gave the holders the lead and Meazza made it 2–0 from a penalty after the clever

but rash Domingas had brought down Piola – who feigned injury and started trouble. By the time Romeau had grabbed a consolation goal in the second-half, play was being dictated more by temper than by skill. In the other game, Hungary exposed Sweden 5–1 at the Stade Colombes. Nyberg scored inside a minute, but the Hungarians were unruffled and led 3–1 at half-time through Szengeller (2) and Titkos. Sarosi and Szengeller added goals after the interval, and it was obvious that they would be difficult to beat. In the third-place match, at Bordeaux, Brazil won 4–2 after Sweden had twice forged ahead.

The final, watched by 65,000 at the Stade Colombes on 19 June was a good one, the Italians playing with speed and energy, the Hungarians with grace and precision. Ill-feeling against Italy had grown among the French, particularly after their quarter-final defeat, and the crowd were behind Hungary. Colaussi, for the third successive match, put Italy ahead, but a tremendous cheer went up when Titkos equalized less than a minute later. Meazza, given too much space, then made two goals – one for Piola and a second for Colaussi – and the holders went in 3–1 up at half-time. Sarosi scrambled one in after the break to raise hopes of a revival, but the Italian defence remained tight. Piola restored the two-goal difference and fast, hard Italy had retained the Jules Rimet Trophy.

Pozzo's team had reached their peak at the right time – the final – and the side, though by no means delicate, was more cultured than the over-physical one of 1934.

Meanwhile Brazil had given warning that with better team selection and control of temper, their players would win the prize in the future.

Left: The Italy team which retained the World Cup in 1938. Once again they were managed by Vittorio Pozzo but this time they were a more skilful side. Only Meazza and Ferrari survived from four years earlier and two new goalscorers proved to be key men, Silvio Piola and Colaussi. Both netted twice in the final in the Stades Colombes in Paris in the 4–2 victory over Hungary. Their skill on the day was too much for the Hungarians even though the many French in the crowd supported them because Italy had beaten France in the quarter-finals.

1950 — URUGUAY ROB BRAZIL

No country had a greater impact on the 1950 World Cup than the United States. When news of their 1–0 victory over mighty England was wired around the globe, sports editors accepted the scoreline as an error and printed 10–1 to England. Only later did they receive confirmation that one of the favourites to win the Jules Rimet trophy had been toppled by a country with no real soccer tradition.

England were, in fact, entering for the first time. Britain had rejoined FIFA in 1946 and the 1949–50 Home International Championship was generously designed as a qualifying group with two teams going through. Scotland, with inexplicable narrow-mindedness, stated they would go to Brazil only as champions, so after England beat them 1–0 at Hampden Park they stayed at home.

The playing arrangements were unsatisfactory, but the Brazilian authorities, like the Uruguayans in 1930, were left with 13 sides. India had qualified and then withdrawn, Portugal declined to take Scotland's place, and France, having replaced Turkey, backed out when told of their travel programme – not such a petty excuse in a country of Brazil's size.

The groups were left as one of four, two of three, and one of two sides, Uruguay and Bolivia (France having withdrawn). For the first and, so far, only time the cup was to be decided on a league basis and won by the country finishing top of a final pool. Four sides – Brazil, England, Italy and Uruguay were seeded.

Above: Larry Gaetjens is chaired off the field in Belo Horizonte after scoring the goal that brought about one of the most sensational World Cup results: United States 1 England 0 in the 1950 competition.

Below: Gaetjens moves in for the kill again as an anxious Bert Williams, in the England goal, watches the ball this time drop over the bar. Though England dominated the game they could not fashion an equaliser.

The first two of these were favourites – Brazil for a combination of talent and home advantage and England (presumably) for historical reasons, though they had won 22 of their 29 games since the war and scored 100 goals. They had lost centre-half Neil Franklin to the Colombian League, but Swift, Ramsey, Wright, Matthews, Mortensen Mannion and Finney seemed to form a fair backbone. Brazil approached the finals with monastic dedication, hibernating outside Rio under manager Flavio Costa. With Barbosa in goal, the magnificent inside trio of Zizinho–Ademir–Jair, a heap of reserve strength and an easy travelling schedule, they would be *the* team to beat.

The giant Maracana Stadium in Rio, with a capacity of 200,000, was not ready when the teams arrived and still uncompleted when they left, though the final was played there.

In this shell, Brazil kicked off against Mexico on 24 June preceded by a 21-gun salute, fire-crackers, balloons, and pigeons. Mexico's 'keeper Carbajal, playing in what proved to be the first of five consecutive World Cups, let in four goals, including two from Ademir, and Brazil had an easy passage. It was a different story, however, when the Brazilians travelled to Sao Paulo to play Switzerland. Costa included several local players to please the crowd, but Switzerland proved no easy opponents and Brazil were booed off after the Swiss had squared the match at 2–2 a few minutes before time.

With an in-form Yugoslavia having produced two convincing wins – 3–0 over Switzerland in Belo Horizonte and 4–1 over Mexico at Porto Alegre – Brazil had to win in Rio to qualify. Zizinho played his first match, but perhaps more significant was the accident to Rajko Mitic, the Yugoslav inside-right. He cut his head on a girder outside the dressing-room, missed the start, and Ademir scored in the third minute. Zizinho added a second after the interval to see Brazil through.

Then came those sensations in Group 2. In their opening game at Maracana, England had a laboured win over a Chile side that included George Robledo, the Newcastle United star, at centre-forward; Mortensen and Mannion got the goals. At Curitiba the Americans aroused memories of 1930 by taking the lead against Spain and holding it until 10 minutes from time before going down to goals from Basora (2) and Zarra. The same players then scored one each against Chile in Rio to give Spain maximum points from two games.

Meanwhile, at Belo Horizonte came that biggest upset in the history of international football. The Americans, captained from right-half by Eddie McIlvenny (given a free transfer by Wrexham of the English Third Division 18 months earlier), knew they had little hope and had stayed up till the small hours at a party. But on a small, bumpy pitch England never settled down, missed chance after chance, hit the bar and the posts and then after 37 minutes fell behind. Goalkeeper Bert Williams seemed to have Bahr's cross covered, but Haitian-born centre-forward Larry Gaetjens headed past him. Anxiety, frustration and then panic gripped England, and for all their second-half pressure they could not equalize. Borghi in goal, Colombo at centre-half and McIlvenny

were outstanding in a besieged defence. A header from left-winger Mullen may have crossed the line, but the Americans deserved their win for sheer courage.

Spain then beat England 1–0 to win the Group while in Recife the gallant American side scored twice against Chile but conceeded five.

Giant-killers emerged from Group 3 in the shape of Sweden. English coach George Raynor had rebuilt the 1948 Olympic winning side – one which had lost Gunnar and Bertil Nordahl, Gunnar Gren, Nils Liedholm and Henry Carlsson to Italian soccer – with players such as Hasse Jeppson and Nacka Skoglund. Italy, with managerial and selection rows and still suffering from the loss of several key players when a plane carrying the Torino team crashed in 1949, were unsettled, but managed to take the lead through their captain, Carapallese, in front of a Sao Paulo crowd full of Italo-Brazilians. The Swedes retaliated with three goals, two of them by Jeppson and, although Muccinelli pulled one back, Italy had lost. Eight of the Swedish side later went to play in the Italian League. Sweden could only draw 2–2 with Paraguay at Curitiba, but Italy's 2–0 win over the South Americans at Sao Paulo three days later put Sweden through.

In the fourth group, if that was what it was, Uruguay humbled Bolivia 8–0 at Belo Horizonte, with four coming from Juan Schiaffino. The final pool thus comprised two seeds, Brazil and Uruguay, with Sweden and Spain.

Brazil opened at Rio by swamping Sweden 7–1, and received a bonus the same day when Uruguay, their obvious rivals, were held to a 2–2 draw by Spain.

Spain travelled up to Rio to face Brazil and were beaten 6–1, Jair and Chico both scoring twice. But it was Zizinho's goal that typified Brazil – he beat Spanish 'keeper Eizaguirre, waited for him to get up, and then dribbled round him again before slipping the ball home. At Sao Paulo, Uruguay had to come from behind twice to beat Sweden but having won through with goals from Ghiggia and Miguez (2), they had to beat Brazil to win the World Cup.

For the 'final' on 16 July, 200,000 squeezed into the unfinished Maracana Stadium, despite only 150,000 tickets being sold. Brazil were 1–10 favourites but they knew as well as anyone that Uruguay were their 'bogey' team. And so it proved. Yet early on it was all Brazil, who for 45 minutes pounded an iron Uruguayan defence superbly controlled by Varela and with Maspoli in remarkable form in goal. Two minutes after half-time it cracked, Friaca scored, and 200,000 passionate fans waited for the deluge. It did not come. Uruguay with Varela moving up, came more into the play. After 65 minutes he sent Ghiggia down the right, and the tiny winger crossed to an unmarked Schiaffino, who beat Barbosa with his shot. With 11 minutes to go Ghiggia took a return pass from Perez and ran on to score the winner.

The Uruguayans obviously knew Brazil. They absorbed the pressure, stayed cool and, when the moment arrived, took the initiative with clinical precision. Brazil had been robbed, but legally. They had to wait eight years for compensation and 20 years for revenge.

1954 – HUNGARY'S TOURNAMENT, WEST GERMANY'S CUP

If Brazil had been favourites in 1950, Hungary were virtual certainties in 1954. They were unbeaten in four years, during which they had played the cream of Europe, scoring 104 goals against 25 in 25 matches. They had thrashed England 6–3 at Wembley in November 1953 and 7–1 in Budapest the following May – three weeks before the World Cup. They had produced players who will always rank with the game's finest and their side has few competitors for the title of the world's best ever international team.

In addition, there seemed to be no outstanding rival from Europe, though the European contingent had risen from 6 in 1950 to 11. West Germany and Yugoslavia were perhaps the best outside bets.

The Latin American representation dwindled from six to three – Brazil, Uruguay and Mexico. The Brazilians had Bauer and Baltazar from 1950 and three of the players who were later to gain two World Cup winners medals – Djalma and Nilton Santos and Didi – were already established in the team. Uruguay, twice winners and yet to lose a match, at last entered a European World Cup. The United States, after their moment of glory four years earlier, again failed to qualify for the final stages.

The tournament was in many ways badly organized. Switzerland had got the vote largely because it was the 50th anniversary of FIFA, whose headquarters were in Zurich. The small grounds were to a large extent compensated for by high admission charges, good crowds (encouraged by the success of neighbour West Germany),

and the advent of television. The system adopted had two vital differences from 1958: first, two teams in each group of four were seeded and did not meet (and nor, of course, did the other two) and second, extra time (over-time) was to be played whenever teams were level at 90 minutes

The tournament opened on 16 June with seeded France losing to the 1952 Olympic finalists Yugoslavia by a single goal in Lausanne. Brazil strolled to a 5–0 win over Mexico in Geneva, but found Yugoslavia more difficult in a splendid tied game at Lausanne.

In Group 2, which was to provide both finalists, Hungary started by swallowing South Korea 9–0 at Zurich and West Germany beat Turkey 4–1 in Berne. Then came the match which, in its subtle way, was to decide the series: Germany against Hungary at Basle.

Hungary, apart from Toth for Budai at outside-right,

Below: Action from the Group game in which Hungary beat Germany 8–3 in the 1954 World Cup finals with Kocsis in the dark shirt on the hunt for goals. He scored four but Germany were to have the last laugh when the two teams met again to contest the final. Sepp Herberger, the German manager, had fielded several reserves in the first match and in the final the quality of Germany's play took Hungary by surprise. The favourites raced into a two-goal lead but with Puskas, their captain and key forward, carrying an injury Germany were level by half-time. Hungary had not lost for four years, and were the current Olympic Champions, but five minutes from time Germany's Rahn hit the winner for the most unexpected final result in the competition's history.

were at full strength, but Sepp Herberger fielded a side that included at least six reserves. His reasoning seems to have been that Germany would easily dispose of Turkey in the play-off, and then, if the Hungarians met his side again in the final, they would know little of them. As it was, it worked, but he had an unexpected piece of fortune. Ferenc Puskas, after a clash with Werner Liebrich, had to go off with an injury that was to keep him out until the final, when against medical orders Hungary's captain and key forward decided to play. Hungary won the initial encounter 8–3 (four from Kocsis, whose heading was superb) and in fact scored three after Puskas had left the field. Turkey, as expected, beat South Korea (7–0), and West Germany, as planned, beat Turkey in the play-off, by 7–2.

Austria and Uruguay were the seeds in Group 3. Uruguay found Czechoslovakia difficult to master in the Berne mud and were seen through only by two late goals, while at Zurich Austria were a little fortunate to beat Scotland 1–0. Team manager Andy Beattie then resigned following criticism, and the Scots were in no mental state to face Uruguay at Basle. An unchanged side crashed 7–0 giving away five in the second-half. Meanwhile Austria showed their class against Czechoslovakia in Zurich winning 5–0 with a hat-trick by Probst.

In Group 4, seeded England – with only Wright, Dickinson and Finney surviving from their fiasco against the United States – drew a fluctuating game with Belgium at Basle. Anoul put the Belgians ahead after five minutes, but a Matthews-inspired England were 3–1 up with only a quarter of an hour left. The Belgians, however, took advantage of their complacency and the match went to extra time (overtime). Lofthouse crowned a fine Broadis-Tommy Taylor move to make it 4–3, but two minutes later Jimmy Dickinson headed into his own net for an unfortunate equalizer.

At the same time, Italy were being upset 2–1 by Switzerland at Lausanne. Poor refereeing by Viana of Brazil led to a plethora of fouls and the Italians chased him off the field after he had ruled a goal offside.

England's game with Switzerland at Berne three days later was a dull encounter, a 2–0 win enabling England to qualify . At Lugano, Italy beat Belgium 4–1 to secure a play-off with Switzerland in Basle, but lost the chance to reassert themselves when they went down 4–1 in a cleaner game than the first.

The first two quarter-finals, played on 26 June, were Uruguay v England at Basle and Austria v Switzerland at Lausanne, and the two games produced no less than 18 goals. England, with Matthews and Lofthouse back, lost 4–2 after a well-fought game. It is true that at least two of the goals could have been saved by Gil Merrick (it proved to be his last international) but Uruguay had three players injured and did very well to win.

At the same time Austria and Switzerland were involved in a record 12-goal classic at Lausanne. The Swiss took a 3–0 lead, but Austria, prompted by Ocwirk and using the speed of the Koerners down the wings, produced some magnificent soccer to win 7–5 despite a missed penalty. The next day, a full-strength West Germany beat Yugoslavia 2–0 at Geneva, but they were hard-pressed until the closing minutes.

In the meantime the fourth quarter-final provided the most violent World Cup scenes since the Brazil-Czechoslovakia affair of 1938. Brazil were again involved, this time with Hungary, in what became known as the 'Battle of Berne'. With heavy rain falling and Hungary leading 2–0, the tackling became over-zealous and Djalma Santos scored from the spot after Buzansky had bundled over Indio. After 60 minutes Lantos made it 3–1 from a penalty following a disputed Pinheiro handling and the trouble really started. Brazil got angry, a brawl between Nilton Santos and Boszik resulted in both being ejected by English referee Arthur Ellis, who then repeated the order to Humberto Tozzi of Brazil for kicking an opponent. Between the frequent melees Julinho scored to give Brazil hope, but the irrepressible head of Kocsis made it 4–2. The battle was continued in the dressing-rooms.

For Hungary's semi-final against Uruguay, steel-helmeted police ringed the Lausanne pitch. The game, however, proved not a brawl but a delight, rich in the skills of soccer, and all in pouring rain. Hungary stole a first-half lead with a goal from Czibor, increased it through Hidegkuti and held it until the 75th minute. Schiaffino put Hohberg through to score and repeated the sequence with only three minutes left. Hohberg, later to be the Uruguayan manager in 1970, was put through a third time in the extra period, but he hit the post and Hungary won the game with two headers from Kocsis, who took his tally to 11.

In the other semi-final, at Basle, the Austrian defence, with goalkeeper Zeman unusually off-form, collapsed against a West German attack superbly generalled by Fritz Walter, and lost 6–1. Austria gained some compensation when they beat Uruguay 3–1 in the third place match at Zurich.

The final, played at Berne on 14 July, again in rain, proved a dramatic match. Puskas insisted on playing and Hungary opened in traditional style, Puskas following up to score from Kocsis' blocked shot in the sixth minute and Czibor adding a second two minutes later. But the Germans replied first through Morlock, within a minute and then through Rahn, after 18 minutes and the game was wide open. In the second-half Hungary put the pressure on: Hidegkuti hit the bar, Kocsis the post and Turek made some tremendous saves. Eckel and Mai eventually got the measure of the Hungarian attack and the German forwards came more into it, with Fritz Walter feeding his wingers well. With five minutes to go Boszik untypically mispassed; Schaefer found Walter, his cross was cleared, but Rahn cracked the ball home. A revived Puskas put the ball in the net, and it looked like extra-time (overtime) but Welsh linesman Mervyn Griffiths had his flag up for off-side – and Hungary had lost. West Germany, unseeded, had beaten Hungary, undefeated in four years, and demonstrated a resilience and courage that was to appear again in subsequent World Cups.

1958 – BRAZIL EDUCATES THE WORLD

In many ways 1958 proved the watershed between the old and the new World Cup tournaments; the arrangements of grouping and quarter-finals were adopted; Brazil, with a 4-2-4 system, became the first country to win outside its own continent; Russia entered for the first time and television and commercialism in world soccer really came into their own as we know them.

In their sixth consecutive series, and after the anticlimax of 1950, Brazil at last won the cup, and in a style that secured them a place at the peak of world soccer history. The Brazilians, under Vicente Feola, had learned from their mediocre tour of Europe in 1956 and only Djalma and Nilton Santos (not related) and Didi remained from the battle with Hungary at Berne. The Hungarians, too, had only three players left from that game in 1954 – Groscis, Boszik and Hidegkuti.

Hungary's conquerors in Switzerland, West Germany, had a rough passage after their success (winning only 4 out of 17 matches), but had improved greatly over the previous 18 months. With Hans Schaefer (now an inside-forward), Helmut Rahn and Fritz Walter, from Berne and some fine new players including Szymaniak, they had a good chance.

England, like Italy earlier, were suffering from the Manchester United air disaster in Munich in February 1958 when Roger Byrne, Duncan Edwards and Tommy Taylor, all certain choices, had perished. Although they had beaten Scotland 4–0 in Glasgow in the April, they then crashed 5–0 to Yugoslavia in Belgrade. Scotland had done well in a strong group, but on the whole their record was a poor one.

For the first, and so far only, time all the British

Top left: The seventeen-year-old Pele is overwhelmed after his first taste of success – the 5–2 victory over Sweden in the 1958 World Cup final in which he scored twice and established himself internationally.

Left: Garrincha, Brazil's mesmeric right-winger is foiled by the French goalkeeper Abbes in the semi-final of the 1958 World Cup.

Right: France again on the receiving end – this time from Northern Ireland's inside-forward Jimmy McIlroy in the quarter-finals. France won 4–0 to end a gallant effort from the Irish who had been given no chance of making any impact on the only World Cup to date to have all four British nations in the finals. With McIlroy and Danny Blanchflower the orchestrators they battled their way into the last eight after winning a play-off with Czechoslovakia.

countries were competing, but Wales and Northern Ireland arrived by rather different routes. The Welsh had qualified by beating Israel in a play-off following East Germany's withdrawal from the group headed by Czechoslovakia (who beat Wales twice). The Irish, by contrast, won a strong group with Portugal and Italy. In the final match – after the scheduled one was refereeless, made a friendly, and then drawn – they beat Italy 2–1 in Belfast, inspired by Danny Blanchflower, later a commentator in the United States in 1967.

The Olympic champions, Russia, had eliminated Poland only after a play-off, but their recent record was excellent. Sweden, the hosts, were now professionals and they had Gren and Liedholm of their 1948 Olympic side back from Italy. Team manager George Raynor could also recall from Italy Julli Gustavsson, a commanding centre-half, and Kurt Hamrin dazzling at outside-right, while on the other wing was 1950 veteran Skoglund.

In South America, Ireland's performance was emulated by Paraguay, who beat Uruguay 5–0 in Asunción, while Argentina were making their first appearance in the finals since 1934.

Although there was no seeding, the 16 finalists (whittled down from an original 53) fell into an arrangement of one team from Britain, one from Western Europe, one from Eastern Europe and one from Latin America in each group.

All teams played each other, with those level on points playing off.

After the opening ceremony in Stockholm, Sweden beat Mexico 3–0 in Group 3. At Sandviken, John Charles equalized for Wales after Boszik had given the lead to a Hungary lacking Puskas, Czibor and Kocsis (who had all stayed in the West after the 1956 uprising). Jack Kelsey was in great form in goal, but it was the attack that let them down in the next match, when they could only draw with Mexico in the Rasunda Stadium at Stockholm, the Mexican equalizer coming minutes before half-time. The following day, on the same ground, goals from Hamrin took an unimpressive Sweden past Hungary 2–1, but against Mexico at Sandviken the Hungarians came to Life. Lajos Tichy, who had played well and scored against Sweden, started a 4–0 drubbing with two good goals. Meanwhile, in the capital, Sweden fielded five reserves against Wales and were quite content with a goalless draw – one that gave the Welshmen a play-off with Hungary.

Play-offs for second place also resulted in Groups 1 and 4. In the former, Northern Ireland started in spirited style by beating Czechoslovakia at Halmstad with a goal from Wilbur Cush. The Germans also kicked off well, beating Argentina 3–1 at Malmo. Rahn, star of the 1954 final, scored two of the goals, and he was again on target with another to secure a draw for West Germany against Czechoslovakia at Halsingborg. The Irish, meantime, had the wind taken out of their sails at Halmstad with a 3–1 defeat by Argentina, who had recalled the 40-year-old Angel Labruna at inside-left.

That glory was short-lived. At Halsingborg Argentina crashed 6–1 to Czechoslovakia and, had Germany then beaten Ireland at Malmo, the Czechs would have been safe. But Peter McParland twice put the Irish ahead, twice the Germans equalized, through Rahn and Uwe Seeler, and Czechoslovakia had to play-off with Ireland.

The strongest section, Group 4, saw Brazil, without Pele (injured) or Garrincha, beat Austria 3–0 at Boras. Team manager Feola preferred Mazzola (real name Altafini) to Vava at centre-forward, and he scored twice. England and Russia, who had drawn 1–1 in Moscow three weeks before, drew 2–2 at Gothenburg. The Russians took a 2–0 lead, but then Derek Kevan and Tom Finney, from a penalty, beat Lev Yachin to square it.

On the same field England then produced a fine defensive display against Brazil, who had Vava back, but in place of Dida. Colin McDonald was cool in goal, while Bill Slater virtually erased Didi from the game. Meanwhile, at Boras, Russia had a comfortable 2–0 win over a dull Austria.

Assuming Brazil beat Russia at Gothenburg, England had to beat Austria at Boras to be sure of qualifying. But, they stumbled to a 2–2 draw. Brazil, with Zito, Garrincha and Pele replacing Dino, Joel and Mazzola, duly beat Russia with two goals from Vava to give England a play-off.

It was left to Group 2 to come up with two clear qualifiers, and it was apparent from the first match, when France beat Paraguay 7–3 at Norrkoping, who would be one. Just Fontaine, whose 13 goals (many stemming from his fine understanding with Raymond Kopa) were to be a record, started with three. At Vasteras, Scotland, with Eddie Turnbull a fine right-half, pulled their game with Yugoslavia out of the fire to draw 1–1, but in their next game at Norrkoping they went down 3–2 to Paraguay.

Yugoslavia, remaining at Vasteras, beat France, 3–2 against the run of play, with Fontaine scoring both French goals. Scotland brought in new cap Bill Brown in goal and had Dave Mackay at left-half for the game with France at Orebo, but first-half goals by Kopa and Fontaine put them out of the competition.

The three play-offs, held on June 17, all involved British teams. At Malmo in Group 1, Northern Ireland repeated their earlier win over Czechoslovakia with two McParland goals, the second coming in extra time, while in Group 3 at Stockholm, Wales beat Hungary.

The Group 4 play-off saw England and Russia meet for the third time within a month. Brabrook hit the post twice and had a goal disallowed, but when Ilyin hit the post, the ball went in and England went out.

In the quarter-finals, Northern Ireland, with goal-keeper Gregg not really fit, were beaten 4–0 at Norr-koping by France – the unstoppable Fontaine adding two more to his total. Wales, too, went out, but not before giving Brazil (without Vava) a real defensive fight at Gothenburg. The only goal came in the second-half from Pele. At Malmo, West Germany repeated their 1954 quarter-final win over Yugoslavia and again it was Rahn who scored the all-important goal. As in Switzer-land, the Slavs dominated the game but just could not score. Sweden beat Russia 2–0 in Stockholm, with Hamrin heading the first goal and making the second for Simonsson.

At Stockholm in the semi-final, Fontaine became the first player to score against Brazil when, after a superb move with Kopa, he equalized Vava's first-minute goal. But after France lost centre-half Robert Jonquet in the 37th minute Didi got number two, and Pele scored a hat-trick in the second-half. In Gothenburg, official cheerleaders whipped up a national fervour rarely associated with Scandinavia but nonetheless it was Germany's Schaefer who scored first. Skoglund equalized before half-time, though Liedholm had obviously handled; Juskowiak was sent off just after the break for kicking an opponent and Sweden took full advantage through Gren and Hamrin.

On the same ground four days later France beat West Germany 6–3 for third place. The inevitable Rahn scored again but it was the four from Fontaine (taking him past Kocsis' World Cup finals record) that formed the star turn.

In the final the following day in the Rasunda Stadium, Sweden, seeking revenge for the 7–1 defeat in 1950, seemed to have a great start, with rain affecting the pitch and Liedholm picking his way through to score after five minutes. The Brazilians, to the surprise of many, remained unflustered and Garrincha, after a lovely dribble, made the equalizer for Vava. With their full-backs (Djalma Santos replacing De Sordi for his first match of the series) bottling up Hamrin and Skoglund, and Zagalo dropping back to assist Zito and Didi in midfield, Brazil got on top. In the 32nd minute Garrincha repeated his act and Vava once again beat Svensson. In the second-half the precocious Pele produced a marvellous goal to seal Brazil's superiority, juggling the ball with his back to the goal before twisting to score.

Zagalo added a fourth before Simonsson reminded the crowd of Sweden's attack. Pele made it five right on time with a brilliant header. Brazil, at their sixth attempt, had won the Jules Rimet Trophy with a scintillating display of soccer.

1962 – NEGATIVITY INVADES THE WORLD

The 1962 competition, in Chile, is remembered as the one everyone wants to forget. Poor standards, defensive soccer, vicious tackling and rampant commercialism made it the most disappointing of all the World Cups.

The selection of Chile, hardly a major soccer nation, was in itself surprising, particularly as the country was just recovering from a disastrous earthquake. Nevertheless, Chile organized the series well, constructing several new stadias and making money from high admission fees (which tended to exclude the enthusiastic poorer classes) and advertising.

A general air of second-best and anticlimax, sur-rounded the tournament. In a field that had several teams on the wane, Brazil and Russia stood out as favourites. Brazil started with nine of their 1958 side and Mauro in place of Bellini and Zozimo for Orlando.

England were the only British representatives, Scotland having been eliminated by Czechoslovakia, Wales by Spain and Northern Ireland by West Germany. But England, without a settled centre-forward, looked apprehensive.

Chile started well enough in Group 2 by beating Switzerland 3–1 in the new stadium at Santiago. The next match on the ground, between West Germany and Italy, produced an early example of the typical 1962 match: a defensive goalless tie.

Group 2 was then host to the most violent game in the series, between Chile and Italy. The trouble had started with inflammatory articles written by Italian journalists in Chile, and a hostile atmosphere existed before the match began. Early on, Leonel Sanchez, the Chilian left-winger, and Ferrini, the Italian inside-forward, had a kicking match that the English referee, Ken Aston, did not see; Ferrini was kicked again by Landa, retaliated, and

was ordered off. He refused to go and it took eight minutes and the police to get him away. Some of the ensuing acting was worthy of a bad western: Sanchez, after a foul by David, leapt to his feet and 'knocked out' his opponent with a superb left-hook – an incident seen by the 66,000 spectators but not, apparently, by any of the three officials. Minutes later David was sent off for kicking. Italy, reduced to nine men, concentrated on defence and time-wasting, but Chile eventually scored through Ramirez and Toro. After seeing a film of the game, FIFA suspended Ferrini for one match and merely cautioned Sanchez and David. Chile qualified with West Germany, who beat Switzerland and the host nation.

In Group 1, at waterless Arica in the far north, Uruguay began with a narrow scrape against Colombia, winning the odd goal in three. Russia then won a violent game with Yugoslavia, who sent Mujic home because he had been responsible for breaking Dubinsky's leg. Yugoslavia were involved in another bad-tempered game against Uruguay. They led 3–1 with 20 minutes to go, when Popovic was sent off along with Cabrera of Uruguay. Ironically the Uruguayans paid tribute to Sekularac, the architect of their defeat, carrying him off at the end of the game. The following day Russia were surprised by Colombia, who fought back from 1–4 to draw 4–4.

Russia beat Uruguay 2–1, but the South Americans lost right-half Elisio Alvarez with an injury, hit the woodwork three times and let Ivanov score in the last minute. Thus Yugoslavia had only to draw with Colombia to qualify with Russia and duly won 5–0.

At Vina del Mar, in Group 3, Brazil opened (as they had in 1950 and 1954) by beating Mexico, this time by 2–0. But they were not in form, and Pele, making the first and scoring the second, was the only spark. The next day Czechoslovakia had a good win over a Spanish side that included Puskas now a 'Spaniard', but missed an injured di Stefano. The Czechs, with goalkeeper Shcroiff and Popluhar outstanding, then held Brazil to a goalless draw, but in the 25th minute, tragedy struck for the champions who lost Pele for the rest of the game – and the tournament – with a severely pulled muscle.

Spain, despite their talented line-up, only squeezed through against Mexico with a last-minute goal by Peiro. Then Brazil and Spain drew the largest crowd of the group (18,715), and Amarildo, Pele's teenage deputy, scored twice in the last 10 minutes to wipe out Spain's early lead.

Group 4, at Rancagua, started with Argentina scoring the only goal of a mundane encounter with Bulgaria. The following day Hungary beat a pedestrian England side 2–1. The best crowd of the group – but still under 10,000 – turned up to see an improved England beat Argentina 3–1. The Hungarians then trounced Bulgaria 6–1, Tichy scoring two and Albert a brilliant hat-trick, but the last two games were both goalless. Hungary secured top place against Argentina, while a cautious England played out a tedious game with Bulgaria and qualified above Argentina on goal average.

Of the quarter-finals the highest scoring was at Vina del Mar, where England met a Brazil side playing 'at home'. Garrincha, springing to life after a quiet time in the qualifiers, headed a 31st minute lead. Hitchens, replacing the injured Peacock, equalized after Greaves hit the bar, but Garrincha won the game in the second-half: first Springett failed to hold his shot and Vava followed up to score, and then he scored the third with a long, swerving shot.

Below left: West Germany's Seeler heads for goal in Chile.
Below: Where's the ball? Action from the 1962 World Cup

At Arica, Chile caught Yachin on a bad day and he should have saved both goals, from Sanchez and Rojas. Hungary had Czechoslovakia pinned down at Rancagua, but the Czechs held on tenaciously to Scherer's 13th minute goal to go through. In Santiago, Yugoslavia at last beat Germany in a quarter-final, Radakovic scoring from Galic's pass with only four minutes left.

Garrincha again inspired Brazil in the semi-final against Chile, played in front of 76,594 (the biggest crowd of the series) at Santiago. He scored from 20 yards after nine minutes and then headed another from a corner. Brazil ran out 4–2 winners, but the match was spoilt when Landa and Garrincha were sent off.

The cat-and-mouse tactics of the Czechs came off again against Yugoslavia at Vina del Mar, and they won 3–1 against the general run of play. In a dreary game at Santiago, Chile beat Yugoslavia 1–0 with a goal by half-back Rojas to capture third place.

In the final, Czechoslovakia took on Brazil for the second time in the competition. With Kvasnak dictating a steady pace in mid-field, the Czechs took a lead when Josef Masopust (later voted European Footballer of the Year) scored after Scherer had made the opening. They then broke down in the position they least expected – goalkeeper. Amarildo equalized with an amazing shot from the goal-line; Zito headed in Amarildo's cross from close-in 13 minutes from time and Schroiff dropped Djalma Santos' high cross into the sun to present Vava with number three. It was a disappointing end to a disappointing competition.

Above: Amarildo, left, was an inspired deputy for Pele in Brazil's World Cup triumph in Chile in 1962.
Right: The Golden moment for England's 'Golden Boy'. Bobby Moore receives the World Cup from Queen Elizabeth after England had beaten West Germany 4–2 in the thrilling World Cup final of 1966.

1966 – AND ALL THAT

England staged the 1966 World Cup, and became the first hosts to win it since Italy in 1934. They did so by team spirit on and off the field, by faith in themselves and their manager, and by calculated, hard-working, stereotyped soccer. The panache and virtuosity of previous post-war winners were absent.

The tournament left mixed feelings. On the credit side there were the record figures for gates and receipts, the success of, and support for, the little North Koreans, the prowess of Eusebio, the Portuguese genius, and a nail-biting final. But as an overall spectacle it was poor. As in 1962, 89 goals were scored in 32 matches, but soccer had become even more negative and defensive, with most teams employing a 'sweeper' behind the defence. Five players were sent off, four of them against West Germany.

The competition was host to 13 of the nations who had played in Chile. The absentees were Czechoslovakia, Yugoslavia and Colombia. The Czechs, second four years before, were beaten by Portugal, who at their seventh attempt made it to the finals.

England, as hosts, were a good bet in a field with no obvious favourite other than Brazil. Alf Ramsey had taken over as manager in 1963 and had predicted his side would win in 1966. His record had been a good one, and England showed promising form on the pre-World Cup tour of Scandinavia and Poland. Once again they were the only British representative.

West Germany had eliminated Sweden and, despite an unsettled side, were recording some good wins while Hungary had beaten Austria and East Germany in their section. Brazil, the champions, were still under Feola but plagued by selection problems. Argentina had eliminated Paraguay and Bolivia. North Korea qualified in Group 16 by beating Australia.

Group One of the finals was scheduled for London, with England playing all three games at 'home' at Wembley Stadium. After Queen Elizabeth had opened the tournament, it started on 11 July, with an archetypal match – a goalless draw between England and Uruguay. The Uruguayans employed a mass defence throughout, with Troche sweeping-up, and though England worked hard they lacked any real penetration.

Mexico, somewhat surprisingly, then took a point off a disappointing France. Two days later, in the only game played at London's White City Stadium, Uruguay beat France 2-1.

The following day, England, with Paine and Peters coming in for Ball and Connelly, beat Mexico 2-0. The defensive Mexicans held out until the 37th minute, when Bobby Charlton ended the stalemate with a magnificent individual goal. In the second-half Hunt put in Greaves' blocked shot to score another. Antonio Carbajal replaced Calderon in the Mexico goal for the game with Uruguay at Wembley, and thus appeared in his fifth consecutive World Cup, an unrivalled record. He was not unduly troubled: Uruguay played for a draw and secured it. France, however, had to attack England and it suited Ramsey's tactics well. Herbin, already bandaged about the leg, fell awkwardly and was a passenger from an early

stage (substitutes were not allowed until 1970). Just before the interval Hunt put England ahead after Jack Charlton had headed against the post. The French then produced some fine moves, with Simon prominent. But he was hurt in a nasty clash with Stiles and while he lay injured Hunt scored again with a header.

It was expected that Group 2, played at Sheffield (Hillsborough) and Birmingham (Villa Park), would produce West Germany and Argentina as qualifiers. The Germans, well managed by Helmut Schoen, began in fine style by beating group chopping-block Switzerland 5-0 at Hillsborough, while Argentina took a cautious line against Spain at Villa Park but won 2-1.

The Swiss made wholesale changes against Spain at Sheffield and led after half an hour. With Spain in trouble, full-back Sanchis dribbled through to equalize and then Amancio – one of five Real Madrid players on duty – headed home Gento's cross for the winner. The next day West Germany (who had three Italian League players – Schnellinger, Haller and Brulls) were involved in an untidy 0-0 draw with Argentina at Villa Park. Both teams played defensively, tackling grew fierce and Albrecht, after a knee-high tackle on Weber, was sent off. Three days later, Argentina, without a suspended Albrecht, made heavy work of beating Switzerland 2-0.

For their next game at Villa Park West Germany rested Haller and had Emmerich in for the injured Brulls, while Spain dropped their three Italian exiles – Del Sol, Peiro and Suarez. Spain had to win, and their chances looked good when Fuste scored after 23 minutes. But Emmerich equalized before half-time with a superb shot from a tight angle and Seeler, playing in his third series, scored the winner with six minutes left.

Although Brazil were in the strongest group, they were still favoured; Gylmar, Djalma Santos, Bellini, Garrincha and Pele remained from previous successes, but Zito, Gerson, and Amarildo were all injured and did not face Bulgaria at Goodison Park. Pele scored from a free-kick after 14 minutes (the first goal of the competition) but for most of the match he was policed by Jetchev and took some rough treatment. A jaded Garrincha made it 2-0, while on the other wing there was a promising youngster named Jairzinho.

Hungary, with defenders Matrai and Sipos playing in their third World Cup, lost 3-1 to Portugal at Old Trafford. Goalkeeping errors by Szentmihalyi were responsible for letting Augusto score twice. Against Brazil at Goodison three days later, Hungary with Gelei in goal, produced stirring soccer despite the heavy rain, and Brazil, with Gerson fit but with Tostao replacing the injured Pele, suffered their first World Cup defeat since 1954 when their conquerors had been the very same country. Bene scored after three minutes, Tostao levelled, and then in the second half Hungary, with Albert rampant, exposed the obsolete Brazilians. Farkas hit a quite perfect volley, and then Meszoly made it 3-1 with a penalty after a fine run by Bene had been illegally halted. At Old Trafford, Portugal, with Pereira for Carvalho in goal, were helped through against Bulgaria by an own goal and a mistimed back-pass.

A desperate Brazil brought in nine new players and had an unfit Pele in the line-up for the match with Portugal at Goodison. But with Manga unsafe in goal, Portugal took a 2–0 lead through Simoes and Eusebio. Vincente and Morais felled Pele at every opportunity; eventually he had to limp off, and with him went Brazil's final hopes. Hungary qualified with a 3–1 win over Bulgaria at Old Trafford.

In Group 4 in the North-East, the tiny North Koreans illustrated their boundless enthusiasm and stamina against Russia at Middlesbrough, but still lost 3–0. Italy met Chile at Roker Park, Sunderland, and rain seemed to damp any ardour left over from the disastrous clash of 1962. In fact, only Eyzaguirre and Sanchez of Chile, and Salvadore were present from that game. Italy won 2–0.

North Korea introduced two 'big men' against Chile. Marcos scored a first-half penalty, but Korea kept plugging away and were rewarded two minutes from time, much to the delight of the Ayresome Park crowd who had by now 'adopted' them. Italy left out Gianni Rivera against Russia at Roker Park and went down to a Chislenko goal.

Then came the real surprise of the competition. The North Koreans, who had only booked accommodation for the group matches, beat an Italian side that showed seven changes, including the return of Rivera. Cheered on by the crowd, they worried the Italians, tackled like terriers, and eventually broke what little morale they possessed. Bulgarelli went off, Pak Doo Ik beat Albertosi just before half-time, and they held on to their lead. It was a win to rival the United States' over England in 1950 and the Italians returned home to an early morning reception of rotten tomatoes.

Russia fielded nine reserves against Chile at Sunderland and one of them, Porkujan, scored twice, with Marcos replying for a dejected Chile.

The quarter-finals were played on July 23. England, the only side not to concede a goal, faced Argentina in brilliant sunshine at Wembley. They brought in Geoff Hurst for the injured Greaves, while the Argentinians had Albrecht back after suspension. The match proved to be a microcosm of the tensions that existed between European and South American football. Reports vary: referee Kreitlein of West Germany seemed to penalize England more but took three Argentinian names early on. He gradually lost control, and the crunch came when he blew up for yet another foul. This time Rattin, the tall Argentina captain, argued; as Kreitlein could speak no Spanish, and Rattin no German, the conversation must have been limited, but it resulted in the player, who had already had his name taken, being sent off. After eight minutes of pantomime, with the Argentinians threatening

Above right: Manager Alf Ramsey concedes a goal during a practice match before the 1966 World Cup. Ramsey, a defender himself, always based his sides on a strong defensive formation.

Right: Rattin (right) is ordered off at Wembley in the quarter-final in which England beat Argentina 1–0.

to leave en masse and FIFA committee members intervening, Rattin eventually left.

Almost immediately after play was resumed, Hurst cut down an opponent; the Argentinians appealed for justice, but Hurst stayed on. Forced to open up, Argentina played some good attacking soccer, but in the 78th minute Hurst scored with a well-timed header from a Peters' cross to decide the contest. Rattin was suspended for four matches, Onega and Ferreiro for three.

Above: Geoff Hurst becomes the first player to score a hat-trick in a World Cup final with these three goals which were to make him a household name.

There was drama, too, between West Germany and Uruguay at Hillsborough. Uruguay produced a more attacking line-up and were unlucky early on when first Cortes hit a post and then Schnellinger clearly handled on the line with impunity. Held put Germany ahead after 11 minutes, and the frustrated Uruguayans fell prey to provoking tactics. Troche was sent off by Jim Finney for kicking Emmerich and, five minutes later, Silva followed his captain after fouling Haller, whose acting was superb. Germany had little trouble in increasing their lead against nine men. Cortes kicked referee Finney after the match and received a six-match suspension, three more than Troche and Silva.

Sensations of a different kind were happening at Goodison, where the North Koreans were running rings round Portugal and led 3–0 after only 24 minutes. But instead of closing up, they continued to attack and Eusebio took full advantage. He scored twice before half-time (the second from a penalty) and Augusto scored the fifth.

Hungary's goalkeeper Gelei let his side down against Russia at Sunderland. After five minutes he fumbled Porkujan's shot and Chislenko tapped the ball home, and just after the interval Porkujan capitalized on a misjudged clearance. Bene reduced the deficit soon afterwards, but Rakosi missed an open goal late in the game and Hungary were out.

Russia and West Germany then met in a physical semi-final at Goodison. The first casualty was Sabo – a self-inflicted injury when he tried to foul Beckenbauer and missed. Germany looked enterprising in attack, but Russia, with Shesternev commanding at the back and Yashin in good form, seemed secure. Two minutes before half-time Haller scored; seconds later Chislenko kicked Held and with the German writhing convincingly on the ground, referee Lo Bello ordered Chislenko off. Russia, with Sabo a passenger, fought bravely, but Beckenbauer made it 2–0 before Porkujan scored a consolation goal.

Right: Wolfgang Weber shoots past the lunging Ray Wilson and the diving Gordon Banks for the goal that took the 1966 World Cup final into extra time. Bobby Moore's right arm is raised in protest because there was a suspicion that Schnellinger, second right, had handled before the ball had reached Weber. It was a moment that did not rob England of the World Cup – they scored twice in extra time to win 4–2 – but it took from Martin Peters, the scorer of England's second goal the distinction of scoring the winning goal in a World Cup final and handed that prize to his team-mate Hurst.

In the other semi-final, England met Portugal at Wembley. They kept an unchanged side, while Portugal replaced Vincente and Morais with Festa and Carlos. Portugal played old-style attacking soccer and Bobby Charlton, in his element, distributed with rare subtlety in one of his best ever internationals. In the 30th minute Hunt's shot was blocked by Pereira and Charlton followed up to score. After some delightful play from both sides Hurst rode a tackle and pulled the ball back for Charlton to crack in his second goal nine minutes from time. Seconds after the restart Jack Charlton handled Torres' header and Eusebio sent Gordon Banks the wrong way from the penalty. In the dying minutes Stiles thwarted Simoes in front of goal and Banks saved superbly from the fine Coluna.

The third place match two days later proved a bitter contrast, though 70,000 turned up to see it. An unnecessary handling by Khurtsilava gave Eusebio his fourth penalty and ninth goal of the series. Malafeev equalized, but Torres spared the crowd extra time (overtime) by scoring the winner with two minutes left.

For the final – a dramatic, undulating affair – England and West Germany both fielded unchanged sides, in spite of speculation about the return of a fit Greaves to England's forward line. Germany marked man for man, detailing Beckenbauer to shadow Charlton

Early on, England used their overlapping full-backs to test Tilkowski's alleged weakness in the air, but it was Germany who took the lead. After 13 minutes, Ray Wilson miscued a header to the feet of Haller, who made no mistake. A few minutes later Bobby Moore took a quick free-kick on the left and club-mate Hurst headed past a stationary German defence to equalize. Ball was tireless in midfield, Moore immaculate at the back, while Banks made fine saves from Overath and Emmerich. In the second-half, Germany appeared to tire and England, raised by the crowd, began to dominate. In the 78th minute Peters scored in a packed penalty area.

But Germany counter-attacked and won several free-kicks. In injury time, Emmerich took one 10 yards outside the box, it ricochetted off the defensive wall, Held helped it on and Weber poked the ball past Banks. It was extra time (overtime).

After 10 minutes Ball pulled the ball back to Hurst, whose shot hit the underside of the bar, and then bounced out for Weber to clear. Referee Dienst consulted linesman Bakhramov (who was no better placed to give an opinion), he nodded, and Dienst pointed to the middle. It is unfortunate that the match was decided by what must always be, despite all available evidence, a hotly disputed goal. Hurst's fine goal in the dying seconds, to complete the first hat-trick in a World Cup final, was virtually irrelevant.

The victory was celebrated with remarkable virility in England, but elsewhere the reaction was different. The Germans felt robbed, the Argentinians cheated. Italy and Brazil had been humbled. Yet four years later they were to contest the permanent possession of the Jules Rimet Trophy.

Below: Impassive in triumph, Alf Ramsey, the England manager (sitting left), keeps his head while around him others lose their composure. Geoff Hurst has just settled the destiny of the World Cup with England's fourth goal.

*Top: Brazil, as expected, and unheralded Peru contributed greatly
to the refreshing attacking emphasis that shone through the 1970 World Cup.
Above: England used full-backs like Keith Newton, left, to
add width to their attack as they tried to retain the Cup.*

1970 – A RESTORATION OF FAITH

The ninth competition for the Jules Rimet Trophy
promised so little and produced so much. It was widely
believed that there would be a perpetuation and even an
extension of the tendencies that had bedevilled world
soccer in the 1960s: negative play, low scores, ruthless
tackling and childish infringements leading to frayed
tempers. Defensive play and violence would, it was
thought, be the order of the day in the heat and altitude
of Mexico.

Instead it was an entertaining and intriguing affair.
Brazil, with a forward line rivalled only by its predecessor
in 1958 and Hungary's in 1954, made it perhaps the most
memorable of all World Cups and, at the same time,
restored faith in the idea of international competition.
Supported by Peru and West Germany, they showed that
attacking soccer could once again pay, reminding us that
in soccer the winner is the side that scores the most goals,
no matter how many it lets in at the back. Refereeing
standards were on the whole better; nobody was sent off
and no player was seriously injured. The heat and altitude
proved to be exaggerated worries, mainly because FIFA,
at last, allowed the use of two substitutes in every game.

Mexico, having staged the 1968 Olympic Games with
sense and efficiency, repeated their performance. The
only possible blight on the organization came from FIFA
with their decision to employ a toss-up in the quarter-
and semi-finals if games were still drawn after extra time
(overtime).

A record entry of 71 was grouped in 16 sections, and all
but the South Americans began battling for a place as
early as the autumn of 1968. The United States began
by losing 4–2 in their first group match against Canada,
but they won the return with an Albrecht goal and beat
Bermuda twice to go into the second round; there, two
narrow defeats by Haiti put an end to the dreams of
qualification. After months of struggle, only half the
16 teams who had played in England in 1966 had made
the grade again, and they included the holders and the
hosts, who, as usual, did not have to kick a ball.

The biggest disappointment was Portugal, who had
made such an impressive World Cup debut four years
before. Not only did they fail to qualify, they finished
behind Greece and Switzerland in the group headed by
Romania, winning only one of their six matches. They
still relied on an ageing backbone from the Lisbon Club
Benfica (with Eusebio not fully fit) and realized their
mistake too late. Europe produced two other upsets:
in Group 6, Belgium amassed points early on against
Yugoslavia and Spain and qualified with 4 of the 12
games in the group still to play, while Czechoslovakia
eliminated a talented Hungary. These two sides dominated
Group 2 (with Denmark and the Republic of Ireland),
and the Czechs, taking advantage of a surprise Danish
defeat of Hungary, forced a play-off, which they won 4–1
in Marseille.

Bulgaria held off late challenges from Poland and the
Netherlands to top Group 8, but in the remaining
European groups the favourites won through. Sweden,
able to call on her exiles, beat France and Norway;

Italy removed East Germany and Wales; and Russia were a little lucky to elude Northern Ireland. In Group 7 Scotland's chance went when they lost 3–2 to West Germany in Hamburg.

The major surprise of the qualifying round came from South America. Peru, coached by the former Brazilian star Didi, first beat Argentina in Lima and then drew in the return in Buenos Aires. The Argentinians, in a disastrous summer, also lost to Bolivia. Brazil annihilated the opposition from Paraguay, Colombia and Venezuela, scoring 23 goals and conceding only 2. Tostao scored 9, Pele 6, and Jairzinho 4. Uruguay made heavy weather of surmounting Chile and Ecuador.

While countries such as Spain, Yugoslavia, Portugal, Poland and Scotland were being eliminated (robbing the finals of star players such as Eusebio, Lubanski and Jimmy Johnstone), three nations of lesser quality were winning a place. This remains one of the outstanding faults in a competition based on geographically determined groups. In the final African pool, Morocco beat Nigeria and Sudan. El Salvador beat Haiti in the Central American final with a play-off, but only after their drawn-out win over Honduras had sparked off a war between the two countries. Australia beat South Korea, Japan and Rhodesia before falling to an Israeli side that had beaten New Zealand. North Korea were eliminated by FIFA for refusing to play Israel.

The January draw saw the two favourites (England and Brazil) put in the same group, which meant that if they both qualified for the last eight they could not meet again until the final. But Brazil, for all their talent, were beset by problems. Team manager Joao Saldanha, who had not endeared himself either to the Brazilian soccer authorities or the government, was sacked in March. His team had lost 2–0 to Argentina two weeks before, and the dismissal decision was no doubt hastened by Saldanha's insistence on dropping Pele for the match against Chile. His place as manager was taken by Mario Zagalo, who had played for Brazil in the 1958 and 1962 finals (another criticism of Saldanha was that he had never been a player). A further problem was the fitness of Tostao who, it was rumoured, was suffering from the after-effects of an intricate eye operation. But Zagalo worked hard, and though he did not appear to have an eleven settled by the end of May, the squad of players had enough natural talent to worry any team. Their biggest problem was the lack of an obvious choice for goalkeeper.

England, too, had their problems, not least the infamous 'Bobby Moore Affair'. During England's pre-World Cup visit to Colombia and Ecuador, captain Moore was accused by a Bogota shop assistant of stealing an expensive bracelet and was asked to remain in the capital to give evidence. After three days, during which time he received widespread sympathy in the world's press, he was released and flew to his colleagues in Mexico, arriving at Guadalajara only a few days before England were due to play their first match, against Romania.

Though England had not been impressive in recent months, they looked more than useful playing at altitude in South America. Their squad, which missed only

Cohen, Wilson and Hunt from the 1966 winning side, was reckoned by manager Ramsey (now Sir Alf) to be a stronger one than four years before. Where they fell down, perhaps, was in public relations. Thinking England lucky to win at Wembley, the Mexicans were antagonistic, and Ramsey, whose distant attitude gave the impression of arrogance, was not interested in placating them.

West Germany and Italy, on the other hand, employed public relations personnel and, as the finals approached, both teams grew in favour. But it was not all due to gimmicks: the Germans had scored 20 goals (Gerhard Muller got 10) and conceded only 3 in qualifying. Nevertheless, Helmut Schoen was thought to rely too much on older players: Uwe Seeler was in his fourth World Cup, and Willy Schulz, Karl-Heinz Schnellinger and Helmut Haller in their third. Italy, trying to erase the memory of their defeat by North Korea in 1966 – and usually unsettled away from home – looked surprisingly at home in Mexico. The inevitable centre of attention was Cagliari's Luigi Riva, top scorer in the Italian League and a man who got 7 of Italy's 10 goals against East Germany and Wales.

The challenge to Italy in Group 2 would come from Uruguay and Sweden. Uruguay, as usual, drew their players almost entirely from Penarol and Nacional, and relied on a tight defence. But they had at least two figures who could turn a match: one was Ladislao Mazurkiewicz, second only to Gordon Banks among the world's goalkeepers, and another was Pedro Rocha, their gifted midfield player. The team coach was Juan Hohberg, the Argentina-born player who was at inside-forward for Uruguay in the 1954 World Cup.

In Group 1 Russia were expected to be one of the qualifiers for the quarter-finals. Gavril Kachalin had been recalled as coach and he had developed some fine youngsters to play alongside experienced players such as Albert Shesternev in defence and Anatoli Byshovets in attack. Mexico, with home advantage, were trying to get past the initial hurdle for the first time in seven tournaments and they had six players with previous World Cup experience to help them do it.

Czechoslovakia and Romania joined England and Brazil in Group 3 to form the strongest section. Both were defensive, the Romanians more obviously, but both were capable of upsetting the favourites. Like many sides in the series, they used players from only two or three clubs and so knew each other's play well. In Group 4 Bulgaria were even more defensive, and their major star, Georgi Asparoukhov, had a nagging injury. Peru claimed to have amalgamated the best of Brazilian and Uruguayan methods and as the first games neared they became firm favourites to go forward with West Germany from Group 4.

Finally there were the complete outsiders. El Salvador, in Group 1, would never have made the finals had Mexico not been hosts, and as it turned out were unable to produce a goal; Israel had a fine striker in Mordechai Spiegler and were thought to have a chance of a point in Group 2; and Morocco, though they had recently beaten Bulgaria, were not expected to trouble the bigger sides in Group 4.

The finals started at midday on Sunday 31 May, with Mexico and Russia playing a goalless Group 1 draw in the giant Aztec Stadium in Mexico City. The match was dominated by the zealous refereeing of West Germany's Tschenscher, who was acting to strict instructions from FIFA. It ruined this game, but probably had a beneficial effect in that during subsequent matches there was little trouble when referees relaxed the tight discipline. Mexico did most of the attacking but after Lopez had missed a couple of chances the Russian defence, with Shesternev policing, was rarely worried. Russia, despite some pleasant moves in midfield from Asatiani and Muntian, failed to find a rhythm because of the continual interruptions. Four Russians and one Mexican were booked – an unfair reflection on the European side.

The following Tuesday, the other sections caught up and had the benefit of playing at 4 p.m. (as all non-Sunday matches were). Group 2, playing at Puebla and Toluca, opened with Uruguay finding little difficulty in beating Israel at the Cuauhtemoc Stadium in Puebla. Uruguay were at full strength apart from Morales, and played well within themselves against a side that, although brave, was not in the same class. Vissoker made some good saves but after 22 minutes Maneiro headed in and Jujica added a second just after half-time.

At Guadalajara England took the field against Romania to loud boos from the crowd, whose feelings had not been eased by a remark Ramsey made about the field. The champions played slow, controlled soccer and they might have taken the lead in the first half when Lee, on his 'wrong' foot, could only hit the cross-bar. The Romanians were hard in defence, and two minutes after half-time Newton (who had played exceptionally well) had to go off following a tackle by Mocanu. His substitute, Everton colleague Wright, began the move which ended with Hurst scoring the only goal after 78 minutes. Hurst beat full-back Satmareanu before putting a low left-footer past Adamache.

The game at Leon, between Bulgaria and Peru, made up for the others in both goals and drama and was the first hint of a revival of attacking play in World Cup matches. Bulgaria took the lead after 12 minutes through Dermendjiev from a brilliantly worked free-kick set-piece and, five minutes into the second-half, Rubinos failed to hold one from Bonev. Peru then staged a magnificent recovery, scoring three times in less than half an hour. Gallardo pulled one back and then Chumpitaz equalized from a free-kick after Peruvian players had joined the Bulgarian 'wall'. With Baylon's replacement Sotil pressing hard, Peru were on top and it was Cubillas who scored the third after a solo run.

The next day involved all sections and produced widely varied matches. In Group 1 Belgium beat El Salvador 3–0 (including a late penalty) but should have scored a lot more. Captain Paul van Himst was the main offender, missing chances he would have taken with ease in a league match. Meanwhile Italy, leaving out Rivera, out-classed a ragged Sweden at Toluca in Group 2, but could manage only one goal, and that came from a goal-keeping error. In the 12th minute Domenghini took a short corner on the left, picked up a return from Facchetti and shot from outside the area. Reserve 'keeper Hellstrom dived in plenty of time, but he let the ball go under his body and it squeezed inside the post.

In Group 3 a superb attacking display, full of flair and individualism, gave Brazil a 4–1 win in their game against Czechoslovakia. The Mexican crowd had adopted Brazil as their favourites and their support was fully rewarded. Yet it was the Czechs who scored first, when Petras took advantage of a defensive mistake and surged through to beat Felix. Rivelino equalized with a ferocious free-kick, with Jairzinho making a dummy run, and then it was all Brazil. With half an hour left, Pele chested down a pin-point chip from Gerson and cooly beat Viktor. Three minutes later Jairzinho, again from a splendid Gerson pass, scored number three (though he looked suspiciously offside) and then the same player beat four men before getting the fourth goal.

But the highlight of the afternoon came five minutes before the interval. Pele, inside his own half, saw that Viktor was on the edge of his penalty area; he hit a masterly lob which from 60 yards missed by only inches, with the goalkeeper struggling to get back into position, hopelessly beaten.

The underdogs also scored first in the Group 4 match. A cross from Ghazouani caused panic in the West German defence and Houmane gave Morocco a surprise lead. They held on until past-half time, but after intense German pressure Seeler equalised and then Muller headed the winner 12 minutes from time to relieve a very worried side.

Thus with every team having played one match, only Group 1 had emerged without a clear division of points. The next match was perhaps the vital one: Russia v Belgium. The Russians made four changes, the Belgians only one, strengthening their defence with Jeck and moving Dockx upfield. Russia overpowered their opponents with strong, simple soccer, Byshovets doing most of the damage with two fine goals, and Belgium's reply came only after they had conceded four.

At Puebla, Uruguay and Italy were playing out what was probably the most uninspired match of the competition. The play of both sides was dictated by a fear of defeat, and in soulless, goalless draw what few chances arose were badly wasted. In Group 3 Romania beat a Czech side that showed five changes, including Vencel for Viktor in goal and Kvasnak (who played in the 1962 World Cup final) for Hrdlicka in midfield. Petras again gave the Czechs an early lead, this time with a perfectly executed back-header, but again it was thrown away. Neagu equalized seven minutes after the break, and Dumitrache scored the winner from a penalty. Peru, meantime, beat Morocco 3–0 at Leon to become – barring miracles – the first country to qualify for the quarter-finals. The amateur Moroccans kept them waiting an hour before Cubillas scored, but, with no intentions of resting on their lead, Peru scored two more.

The matches on the following day, Sunday, produced more goals (14) than any other qualifying day, despite being played at noon. In the Aztec Stadium, Mexico scored four against El Salvador. Roared on by a near-hysterical crowd, the hosts still took 44 minutes to break through, and then it came in extraordinary circumstances: El Salvador appeared to have gained a free-kick near the touchline in their own half, but instead Mexico took it and, with the El Salvador defence looking on in disbelief, Valdivia scored. The goal was allowed. El Salvador refused to restart, and after four minutes of heated argument referee Kandil of Egypt judicously blew for an early (or late) half-time. After the break Mexico had few problems in putting three more past a very dejected side.

Sweden were expected to atone for the Italian defeat in the match against Israel at Toluca, but could only draw. They introduced five new players (first choice 'keeper Sven Larsson replaced Hellstrom) and took the lead through Turesson in the 54th minute, but Spiegler equalized with one of the best shots of the tournament. The game was, however, a rough and untidy affair, witnessed, appropriately, by fewer than 3,000 people.

The Jalisco Stadium in Guadalajara, by contrast, was packed to its 75,000 capacity for the much-vaunted encounter between Brazil and England. The game proved a fascinating battle, rich in the skills of soccer. Brazil started in the knowledge that in seven previous meetings they had lost only one – the first, at Wembley in 1956 – and had beaten England 2–1 in Rio in 1969 (14 survivors of that match were on duty, five Brazilians and nine Englishmen).

Without Gerson in midfield, Brazil tended to retreat more than usual but were still essentially an attacking force. England were on top early on (Peters and Lee both missed chances) while Pele from Jairzinho's centre, headed down to produce a phenomenal reflex save from Banks, the best piece of goalkeeping in the competition. In the second-half Brazil asserted themselves, and a goal had to come. When it did it was touched off by the genius of Tostao, who, after 'handing off' Ball and wrong-footing Moore, clipped across goal to Pele. Holding the ball just long enough to draw two defenders, Pele fed Jairzinho with the sort of opportunity he does not fail to take. In the closing minutes Ball hit the woodwork twice and Astle, who had just come on as a substitute for Charlton squandered a ridiculously easy chance leaving Brazil fortunate to have taken both points.

The same could not be said of West Germany against Bulgaria at Leon. They brought in two specialized wingers, Libuda and Lohr, for 1966 men Haller and Held, and it paid dividends. Once again they conceded an early goal against the run of play, but again they came back, two men winning the game for them. Libuda's shot was misjudged by Simeonov; his centre was converted by Muller; he was brought down in the box and Muller scored from the penalty; Muller laid on the fourth for Seeler, and then completed his hat-trick. Kolev scored a second for Bulgaria two minutes from time.

Top right: Mario Zagalo, World Cup winner as a player in 1958 and 1962 coached Brazil to victory in 1970.
Right: Jairzinho gives Banks no chance with Brazil's winning goal against England in 1970.

On the Wednesday a solid performance by Russia took them into the last eight, while El Salvador went out without scoring a goal. The Central Americans did well to hold the Russians until after half-time, but then Byshovets scored two goals, both made by Muntian.

At Puebla, Uruguay were content to take it gently against Sweden, knowing they were almost guaranteed of qualification. The match looked like being another goalless draw when Grahn, who had come on as substitute, headed past Mazurkiewicz to give Sweden a surprise victory in the 89th minute – an event that did not prevent Uruguay celebrating as though they had won by several goals.

In Group 3 Brazil registered maximum points by beating Romania 3–2. They started in scintillating style. Pele scoring direct from a free-kick and Jairzinho getting a second from close in. But then the other side of their character was bared: Romania began to expose their weakness in defence, and the Brazilians started arguing with each other and protesting to the referee about the tackling, particularly from Dinu. Dumitrache scored a fine goal after half-time and Brazil looked brittle. Pele saved the situation, but then Dembrovski beat Felix eight minutes from time to give Romania renewed, if unfulfilled, hope.

At Leon, West Germany and Peru, who were both through, played a game with two advantages for the winners – they would not have to travel for their quarter-final, and they avoided Brazil. With Libuda, Lohr, and substitute Grabowski using old-fashioned wing-play, and with a rejuvenated Seeler combining well with the elegant Beckenbauer and Overath in midfield, West Germany won the benefits by 3–1. Muller, beginning to look as though he might overhaul Just Fontaine's 1958 record of 13 goals, scored another hat-trick before Cubillas replied for Peru.

The next day Mexico, Italy and England joined the qualifiers, but Mexico's success was achieved in a most unsatisfactory way. The Belgians were under almost unbearable pressure in the Aztec Stadium, and so, as it proved, was the Argentine referee. After Belgium had started well he gave a penalty for what appeared to be a legitimate tackle, by Jeck on Valdivia, and Pena scored. It was a decision that demoralized Belgium, who tried hard but found the crowd and referee more difficult opponents than a very ordinary Mexican side. To the fans, however, the method and margin of victory was irrelevant.

A 0–0 draw with Israel at Toluca was enough to give Italy top place in Group 2, but their negative play was reflected in their goal analysis: one for, none against. On paper this result was a good one for the Israelis, but an unchanged Italy rarely attempted to play soccer. The only significant event was the substitution of Rivera for his first game of the series.

England had only to draw with Czechoslovakia at Guadalajara to qualify. If they lost by a goal, they would be equal on goal difference with Romania and draw lots,

while if they lost by two or more goals they would be eliminated. As it was, they won 1–0 with a penalty. Ramsey rested several players, bringing in Jack Charlton for Labone, Clarke and Astle for Lee and Hurst, and Bell for Ball, but the new line-up produced poor, obvious soccer, the only tactic seeming to be high balls into the middle of the Czech defence. England's second-half penalty (it looked like an accidental hand ball but the referee stated afterwards that it was for a foul on Bell) was coolly converted by Allan Clarke, playing in his first full international.

The struggle to avoid the ignominy of bottom place in Group 4 was not resolved. Bulgaria's 1–1 draw with Morocco left the two countries with equal goal differences.

In Group 1 Russia won the draw for top place with Mexico (both teams had the same goal difference) which meant that, much to their understandable annoyance, Mexico had to travel away from the Aztec Stadium to meet Italy at Toluca, while the Russians remained in the capital to face Uruguay.

The quarter-finals were really the turning-point of the competition, producing 17 goals and one magnificent come-back. The highest score came at Guadalajara, where Brazil stayed on to meet Peru. The Brazilians were

Right: On their way to a third World Cup, the Brazilians celebrate a goal against Romania.

elevated by the return of Gerson, and looked dangerous from the kick-off. After 11 minutes Tostao pushed the ball into the path of Rivelino, who hit a low, swerving shot past Rubinos. Four minutes later the same two players worked a short corner on the left and Tostao scored with a deceptive shot from near the goal-line. Gallardo put Peru back in the game from a similar situation, with Felix badly out of position, but Tostao steered home a deflected Pele shot just after the interval to restore the margin. Peru refused to be outpaced, and in the 59th minute Cubillas capped a fine run by substitute Sotil to score from 20 yards for his fifth goal of the series. For an instant it seemed Peru might pull it off, but within minutes Tostao split the defence with a diagonal pass to Jairzinho, who rounded Rubinos with nonchalant ease before slipping the ball into the net.

Brazil were to play Uruguay, who had left it until the 27th minute of extra-time (overtime) before scoring against Russia in Mexico City. Uruguay had Morales in their attack for the first time, but they played their traditional game of absorbing attacks, tackling hard, and then moving forward in the later stages. For three-quarters of an hour Ubinas, Ancheta and the rest dealt with everything the Russians could offer, but when they

began their gradual offensive midway through the second-half Uruguay found that Shesternev, Kaplichny and Afonin were equally capable of stern resistance. The game drifted into extra time (overtime) and Russia began to tire. But the goal that beat them, coming only three minutes away from the drawing of lots, was a disputed one. Cubillas scooped the ball back from the line for Esparrago to head in, but the Russians contended that it was over for a goal-kick before he centred. Linesman 'Tiny' Davidson of Scotland was in no doubt, however, and referee van Ravens pointed to the centre.

Mexico, trailed by thousands of supporters (many of whom could not get into the ground), travelled to Toluca to play the European champions Italy. After early Italian pressure, they took a surprise lead through Gonzales, Albertosi being beaten for the first time in the tournament. In the 27th minute Italy were fortunate to equalize when Domenghini's shot was deflected past the helpless Calderon by a defender. The second-half started even, but it soon became apparent that it would swing Italy's way, with Rivera, the substitute, beginning to make the attack tick. First Riva scored with his much publicized left-foot shot; then Rivera began a move in his own half and, after a bizarre succession of Mexican clearances, finished it off with a goal; and finally Rivera found Riva, who rode two tackles before somewhat luckily prodding it past Calderon. Though it was not exactly a brilliant performance, the Italian attack had at last emerged from its conservative shell.

Meantime at Leon, England and West Germany met in a repeat of the 1966 final and, including the substitutes, there were 11 survivors from that match. Like that game, the team that scored first lost; like that game it went to extra time (overtime); like that game, England changed to red; but unlike that game, West Germany won. While Schoen fielded the side that played so well against Bulgaria and Peru, Ramsey reverted to his initial line-up except that Bonetti was in goal in place of Banks, who had a severe stomach complaint.

The Germans were urged on by the thousands of their countrymen who had made Leon a temporary home, but it was England who went in front. After half an hour of undulating fortunes, Mullery found Newton, picked up the return, and beat Maier to score his first goal, a classic, for England in 30 internationals. Four minutes into the second-half Peters, again from a Newton cross, put England two up. It looked all over. Ramsey substituted Hunter and Bell for Peters and Charlton, neither of whom had been in form in any of England's matches. But Germany pulled one back with a 20-yard shot from Beckenbauer in the 70th minute and then, summoning all their stamina and spirit, began to take control. The equalizer came eight minutes from time, when Schnellinger's lobbed pass was spectacularly if luckily back-headed over the hands of Bonetti by Seeler. In extra time (overtime) it was Germany who threatened to score, and they did: five minutes into the second period Grabowski crossed to the far post, Lohr nodded back square and Muller hit a waist-high winner from point-blank range. It was fitting recompense for 1966.

When Brazil and Uruguay clashed (in more ways than one) in the semi-finals at Guadalajara on 17 June, it was the first time the two countries had met in a World Cup match since Uruguay snatched the championship from the hosts, and favourites, in 1950. There was still no country that knew the Brazilians so intimately.

And so it seemed. Uruguay were in command, early on, their hard defence deterring the ball-playing Brazilian forwards, and in the 18th minute they went ahead. Brito made a present of a mispass to Morales, who found Cubilla; the chunky player put a shot across the face of the goal, and a hopelessly positioned Felix watched the ball squeeze over the line. The old tenet that a team cannot win the World Cup without a top-flight goal-keeper appeared close to being borne out. The match became rougher, two players from each side being booked by referee de Mendibil before half-time, and Brazil looked sadly out of touch. They were rescued, however, during the first-half injury time, when Clodoaldo ran onto a perfect return pass from Tostao and beat Mazurkiewicz.

Brazil started the second-half in better style, and in the 75th minute they went ahead after a superb move: Jairzinho, inside his own half, passed to Pele, who flicked onto Tostao; he held the ball for a second, and then sent a raking pass into the path of Jairzinho, who beat Matosas for speed and put a good shot past Mazurkiewicz. Felix atoned with a reflex save from Cubilla's header and, in the dying seconds, Pele set up a third for Rivelino. Brazil were through to their fourth final.

The Aztec Stadium meanwhile, played hosts to Italy and West Germany. The Italians were unchanged, but Germany included the two substitutes who had played so well against England, Schulz and Grabowski, and also had Patzke in for Fichtel. Italy took the lead after nine minutes through Boninsegna (who had come to Mexico only as replacement for Anastasi, the most expensive player in the world), who was immediately immersed in an orgy of celebration. The Germans, however, began to reassert themselves as only they can. Despite an injury to Beckenbauer – he had to remain on the field with an arm in a sling because Held and Libuda had already come on as substitutes – they pressed continually for the last 20 minutes, and only Albertosi's fine goalkeeping and some desperate kicks off the line prevented their scoring. Their reward came in the second minute of injury time, when full-back Schnellinger volleyed in Held's cross with the precision and aplomb of an experienced striker.

Extra-time (overtime) produced five goals in a tense and exciting climax. Muller put Germany in front with his ninth goal of the competition; Burgnich equalized following a German error, and Riva put the Italians in front before the interval; just after the break Muller levelled the scores yet again. It was left to Rivera – on for his third match as substitute – to decide the game, capitalizing on an opening made by Boninsegna straight from the kick-off. A match that had looked like finishing at 1–0 had ended 4–3. Not the best soccer of the tournament, but certainly the most entertaining.

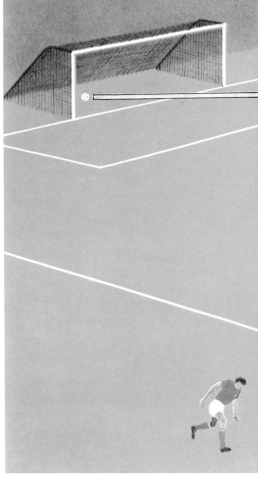

The match for third place on the same ground the following Saturday was expected to be an inevitable anticlimax. But with Uruguay attacking more and tackling less than usual, and West Germany surprisingly fresh after two successive extra-time (overtime) matches, it produced some of the most skilful and polished soccer of the 1970 World Cup. With Beckenbauer absent, more duties fell on Wolfgang Overath in midfield and he shouldered them supremely well. He had enjoyed a fine tournament, and it was fitting that it was he who scored the goal that gave his country third place, though on this display alone, Uruguay deserved the honour.

In the final, played on Sunday, 21 June, in a surprisingly cool Aztec Stadium, Brazil did not let down those whose sympathies lie with adventurous soccer. After testing attacks by both sides, Brazil forged ahead in the 18th minute. Tostao's throw-in on the left was lobbed across by Rivelino, and up went Pele to head past Albertosi. The only question left was how many goals this remarkable forward line would amass. With Jairzinho taking the Italian left-back and captain Facchetti into the middle, the way was clear for Carlos Alberto to exploit the right flank in overlapping runs, while Gerson and Clodoaldo controlled events in midfield. But the match did not quite run like that; Mazzola matched Gerson in midfield, and the Italians looked capable of an early reply, particularly if they could take advantage of Brazil's combined weaknesses – complacency and lack of depth in defence. And that is what they did. In the 37th minute Clodoaldo

casually tried a clever back-pass, failed, and Boninsegna pounced on the chance, urging Riva out of the way and picking his spot to shoot past the oncoming Felix.

The sun came out for the second half, and the crowd grew restless. Italy, hard at the back and using the breakaway, continued to hold a side trying to hit its true form. It was a Gerson goal in the 65th minute – a left-footer from the edge of the box that no goalkeeper in the world would have saved – which triggered off a display of Brazil's real talents. Five minutes later Gerson sent a high diagonal cross to the right-hand post and Pele (lesser men would have tried to score) nodded down for Jairzinho to scramble the ball home. In doing so he became the first player ever to score in every round of a World Cup including the final. From then on it was exhibition soccer. Carlos Alberto's goal three minutes from time – a thundering shot after Pele, apparently without even looking, had pushed the ball into his stride – was of only statistical interest.

The scenes that followed were unprecedented at a World Cup final, or anywhere else, with the Brazilians being mobbed (dangerously at times) as if they had won in Rio. The way they had played soccer – with artistry and skill, virtuosity and grace – they would have received a standing ovation in Rome, Reykjavik or Rochester.

Far left: Jairzinho, a scorer in every round in 1970.
Centre and below: Carlos Alberto's magnificent fourth goal in the final and the joy of icing the victory cake.

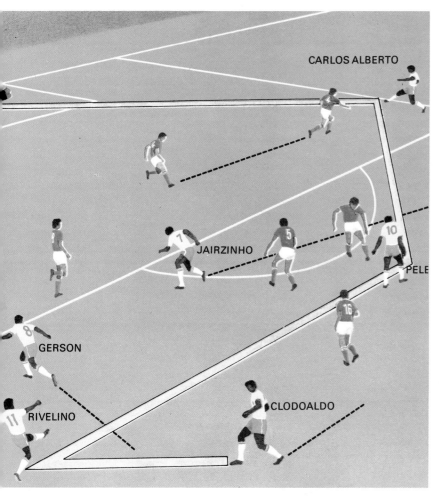

1974 – A TIME OF CHANGES

A new trophy, a new-look competition, a new superstar. No Pele, no sudden-death quarter- and semi-finals to raise the tournament above the defensive attitudes of the group matches, no England. Sadly, too, the Brazil of 1970 had gone, and in its place, to defend the world title if not the trophy, was a side more reliant on solid, uncompromising defence than the explosive sambas of Pele, Gerson, and Tostao. Rivelino and Jairzinho at times excited, yet rarely displayed the verve and panache of Mexico. Had Clodoaldo, injured on the eve of the World Cup, been there to rule the midfield, there may have been a different ending. As it was, Brazil's challenge for the new FIFA World Cup ended in ignominy, with the talented but crunching Luis Pereira being sent from the field in the decisive match against the Netherlands for the right to meet West Germany in the final.

But if Brazil's demise came with regret, it came nonetheless on the world stage. England, for the first time since entering the competition in 1950, failed to qualify; a failure that ultimately brought the downfall of Sir Alf Ramsey who, eight years earlier, had taken England to the pinnacle. His opposite number then, Helmut Schoen, in his unpredictable, often controversial manner, welded together a team which, having begun the tournament as European champions and favourites had threatened to disintegrate in the early rounds as rumours of internal strife abounded.

Led by the dynamic Billy Bremner, Scotland were certainly a more interesting proposition than England, who failed to overcome Poland in the qualifying group. The 33-year-old Denis Law was enjoying a remarkable Indian summer; Hay, Bremner, Willie Morgan and Dalglish could control the midfield and, up front, Jordan and Lorimer benefited from their Leeds United partnership. In addition, manager Willie Ormond's introduction of the long-legged winger Tommy Hutchison gave Scotland a possible matchwinner with his willingness to take on and beat defenders in the classical manner. Certainly, the Scots, though in a difficult group, had a chance of reaching the second round of matches.

This World Cup was to have two further four-team groups following the initial four groups, instead of quarter-finals and semi-finals. The winners of the two groups were to meet in the final; the runners-up playing a somewhat meaningless third-place match. It was feared that additional group matches would further increase the number of defensive games, but fortunately this was not the case and, in the event, the final groups threw up matches that were virtual semi-finals. At the same time, though, it did mean there were two other group matches of little significance.

Franz Beckenbauer dominating the field in the 1974 World Cup final against Holland. The West Germans won 2-1 before a home crowd in Munich. Indeed over half the team came from the local club Bayern Munich, which was also to win the European Cup three years running. Beckenbauer did not play in Argentina in '78.

The decision to do away with the knockout rounds was, however, the least controversial of FIFA's major decisions on the 1974 World Cup. Because the 16-finalists system had been retained, there were places for only 14 teams, plus the holders (Brazil) and the hosts (West Germany). And with the Europeans insisting on having no less than 10 finalists, the South Americans four, and at least one place each going to Central and North America, Asia, and Africa, there was obviously one country too many. FIFA, in its decision was hardly fair, but no one could have foreseen the rumpus that was to follow.

Europe's Group 9 was won by Russia who beat the Republic of Ireland twice and France once after losing in Paris. In South America Group 3 went to Chile, who contested the group solely with Peru after Venezuela withdrew. Both sides won their home matches 2–0 which meant a play-off in Montevideo, which Chile won 2–1, and so another of the 1970 quarter-finalists was out.

Chile, still recovering from the traumas of the military coup that toppled President Allende's left-wing government, next travelled to Moscow, where they played dourly for a goalless draw, obviously hoping to win the return at Santiago's National Stadium. But the National Stadium was, at that time, a virtual concentration camp holding supporters of Allende, and the Russians refused to play there – or anywhere else in Chile – and insisted on a neutral ground. FIFA, ruling that the game should be played in Santiago, had no alternative but to disqualify the Russians when they failed to turn up.

Elsewhere around the world, a qualifying competition which had begun in 1971 with a record 95 entries in 23 preliminary groups, was drawing to a close. In the first preliminary round of the North American Group 1, the United States and Canada both found the opposition from Mexico, quarter finalists in 1970, too strong – though the Mexicans were not to survive the next round when they could only draw with Guatemala and Honduras, and were sensationally beaten 4–0 by Trinidad.

In Europe, Sweden qualified at the expense of Austria and Hungary, the latter going out on goal difference as Sweden and Austria went on to a play-off which the Swedes won at Gelsenkirchen. With the elegant Ralf Edstrom lethal in front of goal, the busy Sandberg to provide him with the chances and a solid defence built around Nordqvist and 'keeper Hellstrom, the Swedes were not to be discounted, despite their permutations of age and youth, professional and part-timer. Italy – surviving a shaky 0–0 draw with Turkey in Naples – had little trouble emerging unbeaten from their group, and goalkeeper Dino Zoff went to West Germany unbeaten in 12 internationals. Their rating was high, but there was an ominous dependence on ageing players and the beloved *catenaccio*. East Germany, Yugoslavia, and Bulgaria made up the Eastern European bloc, the latter putting paid to Portugal and Northern Ireland, while Yugoslavia had to beat Spain in a play-off.

If there was a consolation prize, the Belgians must surely have been the outstanding candidates. Unbeaten, without even conceding a goal, they were eliminated more by goal difference than by the Dutch, whose 24–2 tally eclipsed Belgium's 12–0. However, the Dutch had problems, despite possessing the world's most valuable player in Johan Cruyff, and such stars as Neeskens, Van Hanegem, Haan, Krol and the promising Rensenbrink. Payment, inter-club rivalry and jealousy all raised their ugly heads, and it needed the advent of the former Ajax manager, Rinus Michels – back again with Cruyff at Barcelona – to commit the players to a united effort.

From South America, holders Brazil were joined by Uruguay and Argentina, as well as Chile. The Uruguayans, having drawn and then lost to Colombia, found themselves having to beat Ecuador by two goals in their last game, which they did with two to spare. But by the time Uruguay left for the finals, half their stars had accepted offers from foreign clubs and left the country. Back came Mazurkiewicz, Rocha and Montero-Castillo, but the graces had gone. In their place was a cynicism; ugly, unnecessary, and amply illustrated by the karate chop which paralyzed Australia's Ray Baartz in a friendly *en route* to West Germany. Argentina were another story, building a side that would still be available to contest as host nation in 1978. With Babington, cool and elegant, and Brindisi in midfield to direct the way for such gifted ball-players as Ayala and, later, Houseman, the Argentinians were to prove entertaining, if defensively suspect, qualifiers.

Which leaves the three total long shots – Haiti, Zaire and Australia. Haiti won their passage by topping that final group which included Mexico. Trinidad might have qualified but for the referee's decisions in their match with Haiti; they had four goals disallowed and Haiti won 2–1!

Zaire, managed by Blagoie Vidinic, who took Morocco to the 1970 finals, qualified after three preliminary rounds and some controversy – Morocco refused to play a return match after a penalty dispute. They brought great promise of enormous natural talent in Bwanga, Kazadi and Kakoko.

The Australians, an amalgam of nationalities coached by a Yugoslav, were unbeaten in their sub-group, then beat Iran before finally contesting a three-match eliminator with South Korea – a match which was decided by Jim Mackay's 25-yard shot in Hong Kong.

So the scene was set. The 16 qualifiers came together, bringing with them the world press, radio and television. Around the world many millions were drawn to West Germany by these media as the finals of the tenth World Cup kicked off at Frankfurt on Thursday, 13 June.

For the third successive World Cup finals, the opening match produced a goalless draw, Brazil and Yugoslavia sharing 90 minutes of dominance and missed chances. In the first half, Maric was in brilliant form to frustrate the blond, overlapping full-back Francisco Marinho, and Rivelino; and Jairzinho should have scored after a typically Brazilian set-piece completely deceived the defence. Then it was Yugoslavia's turn: Petkovic missed an easy chance, Oblak hit a post, Katalinski and Acimovic were thwarted.

This draw did not help the Scots, who were in the same Group 2, especially when, the next day, they could put no more than two past an exhilarating but disorganized Zaire. Lorimer, with a magnificent volley, and Jordan, with a header that slipped through the 'keeper's hands, scored in the first half. Their failure to exploit the Zairean weaknesses was to cost them dear, and there can be no excuses for the possession soccer the Scots indulged in late in the match.

Earlier in the day, in Group 1, the West German challenge had begun with a 1–0 victory over Chile in Berlin. The goal was a beauty, a long-range drive by the Bohemian Breitner, but by no means was this the West Germany that won the European Championship in 1972. Overath had returned in place of the injured, out-of-form Netzer; Beckenbauer's cultured detachment seemed to permeate the side; and Chile, with Figueroa and Quintano strong in defence, and Reinoso and Caszely sharp in attack, looked good value.

Sadly, as well as bringing the first goal of the tournament, this match also saw the first dismissal, Caszely going for retaliating when Vogts fouled him. Four others were to suffer the same fate during the tournament: Ndaye (Zaire), Richards (Australia), Montero Castillo (Uruguay) and Luis Pereira (Brazil), the last two against the Dutch. In all, 84 players were cautioned, and but for some hesitant and lenient refereeing, the number could have reached three figures – an indictment of the cynical attitudes that pervaded many of the matches.

East Germany, ironically drawn in the same group as West Germany, beat Australia in a physical game at Hamburg, and so the day ended with both Germanys on top of Group 1, and Scotland leading Group 2.

Saturday saw Groups 3 and 4 in action and introduced the Dutch . . . plus Cruyff; inspired, inspirational and infuriating. Against Uruguay he was at his majestic best; seemingly indifferent to the scything tackles that were intended to maim, always prompting, stamping his personality on the match and the competition. Rijsbergen, young in age and experience, promised much at the heart of the defence, Rep scored twice, and there could have been more. The sending-off of Castillo for punching Rensenbrink in the stomach reflected the Uruguayan approach.

In the other Group 3 match, Sweden and Bulgaria contented themselves with a goalless draw, but life was much more lively in Group 4, where Poland beat Argentina 3–2 in a highly entertaining match, and Haiti's Sanon put paid to Zoff's unbeaten record. Two mistakes by goalkeeper Carnevali gave Poland two of their three goals, both to the excellent Lato, whose defence-splitting pass gave Szarmach the second goal. Heredia had reduced the leeway to 2–1 after half-time, but Babington's goal was of little consequence.

In Munich, Haiti looked like doing a North Korea to Italy before Rivera, Benetti and the substitute, Anastasi, gave the scoreline due respectability. Troubles however, were to follow for Haiti on Sunday, when centre-half Jean Joseph was found guilty of taking a stimulant – and then was ominously whisked off home despite the protests of the German hosts.

After three days rest it was again the turn of Groups 1

and 2 to hold the world's attention – and especially of Scotland, who met world champions Brazil in Frankfurt Willie Ormond bravely brought back Martin Buchan to police Jairzinho, but it was to take some truly brilliant goalkeeping by Harvey before the Scots found their feet – and their confidence. Bremner grew in stature every time he touched the ball, but the Brazilians – Rivelino and Pereira in particular – were not without recourse to violent methods and body checking and for all Jordan's bravery, there was no breaking the deadlock. Brazil, still to meet Zaire, could afford the draw, Scotland could not. The news of Yugoslavia's record-equalling 9–0 thrashing of the Africans meant Scotland had to beat Yugoslavia to qualify for the next round – or draw and hope Zaire could hold Brazil to two goals.

On the Saturday, the respective dramas unfolded simultaneously. In Frankfurt, Scotland opened with the same side that drew with Brazil and again found goals hard to come by against a side that knew a draw was sufficient. At half-time, however, the news from Gelsenkirchen was a little encouraging: Brazil 1 Zaire 0. In the second half, Lorimer, in world-class form, hooked over Maric, but Buljan cleared off the line. Then the feared happened. The Yugoslavs broke, Dzajic beat his man and the substitute Karasi was there to head the cross home. Back Scotland came, and it was their substitute, Hutchison, on for the disappointing Dalglish, who took the ball up the left and pulled it back for Jordan to tuck it, left-footed, inside the far post.

But to no avail. A draw was not enough. In Gelsenkirchen, Kazadi had allowed Valdomiro's tame shot to pass him and the post for the vital third goal, and Scotland, ultimately the only unbeaten side, were out of the World Cup on goal difference.

In Group 1, the two Germanys, as expected, went through: the East convincingly, the West less so after a morale-sapping 1–0 defeat in the first-ever international between the two sides. Earlier in the week, West Germany had beaten Australia 3–0 beginning impressively then falling away as the Hamburg crowd whistled their derision, and there was the unusual sight of Beckenbauer losing his cool at their treatment. Chile approached East Germany more physically than they had the West and held them to a 1–1 draw in Berlin, only to find themselves held 0–0 by Australia five days later at the same venue.

Consequently, by the time West and East Germany met, national pride was the important issue. Defensively strong around the captain Bransch, superbly fit, and possessing hard-running forwards, the East Germans were well-equipped to take full advantage of West Germany's problems, and did so late in the match when Sparwasser forced his way past Vogts to beat Maier. West Germany, dominant for periods, had their chances, but the inability to translate control into goals was worrying. Netzer, coming on for Overath with 20 minutes remaining, was a sad shadow of his former self; Hoeness seemed to have lost his appetite; the defence was too shaky under pressure. Yet, in retrospect, the defeat was advantageous for it put West Germany in the weaker of the two final groups and brought back memories of 1954. Yet again

West Germany had tactically gained by losing a qualifying match. They remained the only eventual winners to have lost a game in the final rounds.

The Dutch, as expected, qualified, but their group contained one of the two real surprises of the tournament. Sweden, after enjoying a goalless draw with the Dutch in Dortmund, hit three second-half goals past the Uruguayans in Dusseldorf to take the second qualifying place. Bo Larsson and Grahn did the prompting and Sandberg and Edstrom made full use of their opportunities. That same day, the Bulgarians scored against the Dutch – albeit through an own goal by Krol past the amazing Jongbloed, the 33-year-old recall whose sorties off his line would take him 20 to 30 yarads into his half when the frequently used off-side trap looked in danger. His goalkeeping brought back memories of Brazil's Felix in 1970; he was said to be a sweeper rather than a goalkeeper. Nevertheless, Krol was the only person to beat him until the final. That goal, however, was little comfort to Bulgaria as Cruyff and Co. rattled up four in a lively display.

The other surprise was Italy's failure to qualify. An own goal by Perfumo gave the Italians a 1–1 draw with Argentina in Stuttgart; Houseman and Babington excelled and delighted, and Telch prevented Rivera from exerting influence. Both Rivera and Riva were dropped for the vital match against Poland, who earlier in the week had scored seven against Haiti. A draw would have kept Italy in West Germany, but the Poles, over-brimming with confidence and full of running, had a taste for goals. Kasperczak sent over the crosses that Szarmach, with his head, and Deyna, with a volley, gloriously converted. The Italians thought they should have had an early penalty, and when Capello did score in the 86th minute it was too late.

Argentina, meanwhile, had beaten Haiti 4–1 to win a place in Group A along with the Netherlands, Brazil and East Germany. West Germany, in Group B with Poland, Sweden and Yugoslavia, had a much easier assignment.

If the Dutch thought they were in the harder group, it did not seem to worry them. They opened in Gelsenkirchen with a 4–0 win over an Argentinian side deprived of Babington – suspended after three yellow cards. Cruyff and Krol emphasized their first-half superiority, and though torrential rain slowed them in the second half, there were further goals from Rep and Cruyff again. In Hanover, Brazil beat East Germany 1–0 with a Rivelino free-kick, while in Group B, Lato added to his tally to produce a similar scoreline against Sweden. The Poles were pressed, though, and Tomaszewski had to save a penalty.

In Dusseldorf, playing Yugoslavia, the West Germans showed they were getting it together at last. The introduction of the strong young Bonhof added fire to the midfield, and Hoeness, out of the starting line-up showed true form when brought on as a substitute. It was he who pulled the ball back for Muller to score their second. Another Breitner spectacular had produced the first.

Next to fall to the West German revival were Sweden, but not before they had shown talents of their own and exposed the fallibility of the German defence. Edstrom's perfect, looping volley gave Maier no chance and Sweden a half-time lead. Despite the rain – a feature of these group matches – both sides played some of the best soccer of the tournament, and a flurry of second-half goals did nothing to slow the tempo. First, Muller laid on goals for Overath, and, immediately afterwards, for Bonhof. Two minutes later, Sandberg equalised. Then it was Muller again, setting up Grabowski's goal and winning a penalty that Hoeness put away

Poland's 2–1 win over Yugoslavia in Frankfurt meant their match against West Germany was a virtual semi-final; winner take all Unfortunately for Poland, the rain followed West Germany to Frankfurt – to such an extent that the start was delayed – and a saturated pitch 'held' the long, diagonal through-balls meant for the flying Lato and Gadocha Maier pulled off a superlative double save to stop these two from scoring, and in the second half it was Tomaszewski's turn for the applause, saving Hoeness's poor penalty. Finally, Muller ended Germany's agony, scoring after aggressive running from the ever-improving Bonhof.

In Group A, the East Germans were no match for the ebbulient Dutch, Neeskens getting an early goal at the end of a brilliant opening phase and Rensenbrink finishing off a beautiful move involving Cruyff, Neeskens and Van Hanegem. And Brazil suddenly flowered against Argentina in a thrilling, skilful game. With Ze Maria back again and Paulo Cesar Carpegiani in midfield, the Brazilians looked an entirely different proposition. Rivelino opened the scoring with one of his swerving specialities, but four minutes later Brindisi's clever free-kick lobbed over Leao for the equaliser. It was the first goal Brazil had conceded and they quickly made amends. Shortly after half-time Ze Maria burst to the goal-line, crossed and Jairzinho headed the winner.

Brazil against the Netherlands in Dortmund for the right to meet West Germany, a game that promised so much, produced two magnificent goals by Neeskens and Cruyff, and saw soccer at its worst. The Dutch, niggling, were by no means blameless, but Brazil's conduct was indefensible. Ze Maria upended Cruyff with a rugby tackle; Mario Marinho knocked out Neeskens when the ball – and referee – was in another part of the field; and finally, crudely and brutally Luis Pereira scythed Neeskens and thus himself, out of the game.

The third-place match, the day before the final, was the inevitable anticlimax and had gone 76 minutes before Lato scored his seventh goal of the World Cup finals to win it for Poland. He missed an easier chance in the last minutes, but perhaps Brazil did not deserve that final ignominy. The former world champions had been humiliated enough by their own behaviour and fourth place had little meaning for them.

Right: Johan Cruyff, the Dutch Master, was the outstanding individual in the 1974 finals. His inspiration to his side led Holland into the Final as favourites, but their temperament did not match their talent.

THE FINAL

Other World Cup finals have been more entertaining; none has begun so dramatically. From the Dutch kick-off, the ball was moved to Cruyff, whose burst into the penalty area ended when he was brought down by Hoeness. Penalty! The first ever in a World Cup final. English referee Jack Taylor's decision was as immediate as it was brave, in front of a Munich crowd with six of their own Bayern Munich men in the German team. Neeskens' shot from the spot flashed to the centre of the goal as Maier dived to his right: 1–0, and no West German had yet touched the ball.

Now the Dutch took charge, spraying passes left and right across the field with Cruyff directing operations in magisterial style. But, for all their monopoly of possession, the Dutch did not score and the West Germans, with Beckenbauer fully committed, recovered. With 25 minutes gone, Holzenbein, one of the wingers so essential to Schoen, took the ball down the left as the Dutch defence retreated. Into the penalty area, where Jansen, at last trying to stop him, possibly mistimed his tackle. Holzenbein seemed happier to fall, when perhaps he could have evaded the tackle. But down he went and Jack Taylor awarded his second penalty. This time it was highly debatable but Breitner made no mistake.

With West Germany back in the game, and Vogts forcing Jongbloed to give his best, the Dutch attacked with more vigour. Cruyff, seemingly satisfied to wander deep to take his marker Vogts out of the game, suddenly flowed forward to escape the defence with only Beckenbauer and Maier to beat. But Rep squandered the chance. It was an expensive miss, and soon Muller would show Rep how it should be done. Grabowski sent the powerful Bonhof up the right where he tore past Krol and turned the ball back – just too far back for the advancing Muller. Unperturbed, Muller turned, controlled the ball and, pivoting, shot through the Dutch defence to give West Germany the lead, and the World Cup.

The second half was goalless, though the Dutch pressured. Maier spectacularly saved a Neeskens volley; Van der Kerkhof, on for the unfit Rensenbrink, shot wide; Rijsbergen went off injured. The Dutch were frustrated.

For Helmut Schoen, runner-up in 1966, third in 1970, winner of the European Championship in 1972, it was the ultimate achievement. Experimenting throughout the tournament, on the day that mattered he produced the right blend. The Dutch might have been more adventurous, more attractive, but Schoen had a team with character to fight back from the shock of the early penalty. And he had Gerd Muller.

1978 – SOUTH AMERICAN STYLE

And so to Argentina. It was always likely to be a different, if not strange, World Cup. The game's major prize was returning to South America for the first time in 16 years – but they had been a hard 16 years. Most of South America was under military rule and both Chile, the last South American hosts, and Argentina had received a particularly vitriolic press in Europe for the brutality of their more recent rulers.

In Argentina, a near civil war against urban guerilla groups, known generically in Europe as the Montoneros had been going on since the final collapse of Peronism. Prices were doubling annually, foreign businessmen were kidnapped, and Argentinian businessmen just left; numerous people disappeared, no-one seemed safe. Until 1977 there was considerable doubt whether to hold the World Cup in Argentina at all, and on the footballing front several performances – particularly against England and Scotland – cast the old doubts over the Argentinians' intense desire to win at all costs, and new doubts about whether referees would have the courage to disallow Argentinian goals or send off over-cynical home players.

In the end FIFA, now with a South American president in Joao Havelange, decided to go ahead but Europe remained doubtful. There were serious, if helpless, movements in France, Holland and Sweden to organise boycotts of the event. The French even decided to take their own snipers, in addition to doctors, cooks and physios. The Argentinians wouldn't allow it – but did accept security teams and the Germans were to take several of the special unit which had rescued passengers from the highjacked jet at Mogadishu.

Group matches were not played at a single venue, or at a pair of venues, as in previous years, but most grounds would stage games from different groups. Two groups shared Buenos Aires and Mar del Plata and, in all, nine of the 16 teams – Argentina, France, Italy, West Germany, Poland, Spain, Sweden, Austria and Hungary – were scheduled to play group games in the capital.

This was no hardship for the teams, with relatively short air journeys, but it rendered the competition less clean-cut to its television viewers. No longer was there a single victor from a single group in a single venue, nor were there any quarter- and semi-finals. For European viewers, at least, the groupings began to matter rather less than the impressions of who was playing well, and who was likely to be a force to be reckoned with.

So, just as it soon became obvious in 1974 that West Germany were the team that had to be beaten, Holland were the team likely to do it, and that the most promising outsiders were Poland, so the 1978 World Cup was to settle down to a similar pattern.

To make it more complicated, there were no really clear-cut favourites. England, knocked out on a very tight goal-difference by Italy because of their inability to score sufficient goals against Finland and Luxembourg, and Russia knocked out by Hungary, were the most obvious absentees. East Germany, eliminated by Austria but not losing once in their six qualifying games, Czechoslovakia, 1976 European Champions, beaten by Scotland, and

Uruguay also had cause to argue that they were superior to some of the countries represented.

Of the teams that were to compete, Argentina had to be counted among the most likely winners, particularly when taking account of the uncertainties about their style of play and worrying refereeing habits. But the European challenge had faded. West Germany, having lost Beckenbauer, whom the New York Cosmos refused to release, and Gerd Muller, then also went and lost to Brazil and Sweden. But then they had been in the last four six times and had never failed (when they entered at all) to reach the last eight. The Dutch seemed over the hill, with Cruyff refusing to leave Spain amid dark rumours around the real story behind the strange break-in to his Barcelona flat. Brazil had completed a relatively successful – if physical – European tour and were probably the most fancied of all. Italy made up the heavyweights. The dark horses were Poland, a new and little known Spanish side, who would at least be at home linguistically, and France. Elsewhere both Sweden and Scotland were not to be discounted.

The Scots arrived very unhappy, having left behind Andy Gray, Aston Villa's leading goalscorer and the man who looked certain to lead the side a year earlier, but took an unfit Gordon McQueen (the most expensive player in British football) and thus had real worries about the key to their aerial defence. They had undergone a traumatic lead-in to Argentina in the British Home Championship, which they had expected to win relatively easily. They drew at home to Ireland and Wales in not only unsatisfactory but occasionally comical fashion, and then lost 1–0 to the old enemy England via a Steve Coppell goal. Considering that all three games had been played at Hampden Park, their home ground, these results could be counted little better than disastrous. The only possible consolation was that players were afraid to risk injury before the finals began. But then the vital engine room, which had been the key to success for the previous two years, appeared to be firing on very few cylinders indeed. Rather than having a problem on who out of the six contenders to leave out, manager Ally MacLeod was more concerned with having three playing well enough to even be considered.

Although Gemmill and Souness appeared to have had the best of the home internationals, MacLeod seemed committed to his established trio of Rioch, Masson and Hartford – though the first two of those had just been put on the transfer list by Derby County. Up front Johnstone – who had scored both Scotland's home international goals – was clearly disappointed by MacLeod's apparent preference for Jordan – though both seemed worried by recurrent injuries and there was no doubt that Scotland would rely heavily on Kenny Dalglish, scorer of the goal which had given Liverpool the European Cup three weeks earlier.

And so at 3 p.m. Buenos Aires time on Friday 1st June, West Germany and Poland began the eleventh World Cup. Not since 1962 had the opening game provided a goal, and this was to be no exception. It was a poor match – much criticised in the world's press, and there were already mutterings that the Germans were seeking tactical results. They had a weak group, could afford to drop a point and seek to choose whether they finished first or second in the group, and were, of course, the only side ever to have lost a group game (which they did in both 1954 and 1974) and then gone on to win the Cup. This time they were lucky to draw – Poland were clearly the better side and Szarmach was unlucky to be denied two penalties.

The first goal of the competition was to come the following day in Mar del Plata after just 31 seconds of the game between France and Italy. Lacombe scored with a clever header for the fastest goal in a World Cup game since 1934. But it wasn't to be enough and Italy came back with goals from Rossi and Zaccarelli. Vicenza had just valued Rossi at £3,300,000 by buying out Juventus' half share in the player for an astonishing 2,500,000,000 lira. It made him easily the most highly valued player of all time. Group 1 was the hardest of the four and later that evening the other two sides – Argentina and Hungary – took the field before a fanatic 80,000 Buenos Aires crowd.

'This was the game that the host country had been waiting for, but within nine minutes they were one down to a goal from Csapo. Six minutes later Argentina were level through Luque and in the last few minutes went ahead through substitute Bertoni. Hungary then had Torocsik and Nyilasi sent off and effectively kissed goodbye to their World Cup chances. Elsewhere Tunisia sprang the first surprise – beating Mexico 3–1 and serving a warning to Germany and Poland. It was the first time an African country had ever won a game in the World Cup finals.

Group 3 was also to spring some surprises. Austria beat fancied Spain 2–1 and Brazil were the more fortunate side in a 1–1 draw with Sweden. Even so, they were to suffer a strange misfortune when referee Clive Thomas blew his whistle just as a header from Zico was about to enter the net – it was a split second that all present realised might cost the favourites dear.

So two groups were now headed by outsiders – Tunisia and Austria – but it was Group 4 that was to spring the biggest surprise. Holland beat Iran easily, with Robbie Rensenbrink scoring a hat-trick that included two penalties. But in Cordoba, Scotland virtually eliminated themselves from the competition with a disastrous display against Peru. The turning point came, with the score at 1–1, when Masson missed a penalty, or, rather, Quiroga saved it. Cubillas then scored two marvellous goals which Rough could do nothing about. It was a game in which Ally MacLeod's chickens came home to roost. It became clear that the home internationals – and what had gone before – had not produced a settled team. Andy Gray was at home as a television commentator, Gordon McQueen was in Cordoba but couldn't play. There was no experienced international full-back. Johnston and Dalglish did virtually nothing. But after all that, it was in midfield that the side failed. MacLeod's decision to stick with Masson and Rioch, though the latter had made Jordan's goal, was clearly a

Above: 'El Loco', Peruvian goalkeeper Quiroga, humbly receives the yellow card after he had rugby tackled Lato in the Polish half.

failure. Both came off with a quarter of an hour to go, but it was far too late by then – just as it was for Scotland. The following day MacLeod was to be subjected to a barrage of press criticism unparalleled even in the days of Alf Ramsey. He had said that he would return to Scotland a hero or a villain. Now he knew which.

Group 1 was quickly settled. Italy beat Hungary 3–1 and Argentina disposed of France. This put them both through and rendered the last two games academic. This was sad for France, who had looked the third best side in the whole tournament. Group 2 was similarly straightforward, West Germany and Poland qualifying as expected. Germany crushed the tournament weaklings Mexico 6–0 but struggled against Tunisia for a goalless draw. They were not showing their real form, but many observers remained slightly suspicious of Schoen and expected far better things in the second round.

Group 3 was poor fare compared with Argentina, France and Italy. Without Rivelino, the Brazilians could only draw with Spain and then just managed to squeeze

Above: Willie Johnston turns his back on the cameras and his international career in Alta Gracia.

test on winger Willy Johnston proved positive, he admitted taking some banned pills which probably had no effect on his performance at all, was banned for life by the Scottish FA and returned home in ignominy. The team then played even worse against Iran, being lucky to draw 1–1 through an own goal. The British press attacked MacLeod for his lack of preparation, their arrival in Argentina without a settled side, his faith in Masson, Rioch and Jordan, his refusal to play Souness and Derek Johnstone, his excessive optimism and just about everything else they could think of. Morale in the Scottish camp virtually disintegrated, only to be suddenly revived and followed by a fine performance against Holland. The Scots won 3–2, with one great goal from Archie Gemmill, but they went out on goal difference for the second consecutive World Cup. Peru, meanwhile, beat Iran 4–1, with Cubillas getting a hat-trick and went through on top of the group.

That left the two groups as follows: Austria, Italy, West Germany and Holland; Argentina, Brazil, Peru and Poland.

Italy and Argentina remained favourites.

The European group, Group A, had Italy as favourites from the start. But West Germany immediately held them to a 0–0 draw while Holland were crushing the Austrians 5–1. Dutch manager Ernst Happel was, of course, an ex-Austrian international. Doubts grew. In the second game Italy only managed a 1–0 win over Austria, while Holland and Germany drew 2–2. The Dutch, who needed a draw to stay in the tournament, equalised just six minutes from time through Rene van der Kerkhof. So the scene was set for a tense decider between Italy and Holland. The Dutch needed just a point, the Italians needed to win – though if it had been a draw the Dutch would have gone through having won only two games out of six and having been beaten by Scotland. The Italians, on the other hand, would have won four and drawn two – an odd system indeed.

The Italians took a first half lead with an own goal by Brandts, and Dutch keeper Schrijvers was carried off after the incident – to be replaced by the 37-year-old Jongbloed. But Happel knew the Italians. All but Zaccarelli and Rossi played for Juventus, and the Belgian club that Happel also managed, Bruges, had knocked Juventus out of the European Cup just a few weeks earlier. Gradually the Dutch came back into the game – probably helped by the fact that Benetti had received his second yellow card and was seemingly affected by the fact that he now couldn't play in the final if Italy won. Brandts made up for his error by scoring the equaliser from 20 yards. Then Arie Haan, restored to the team as playmaker, capped his 30-yard goal against Germany with another glorious effort, this time from all of 35 yards, off the post and past Dino Zoff. That sort of goal even an Italian defence cannot legislate for. So Holland were through, only the third side ever to reach consecutive World Cup finals. In Cordoba, Germany had given up their crown in losing 3–2 to Austria, for whom Krankl scored another two.

Group B also reached a remarkable climax. Brazil had

through with a 1–0 defeat of Austria. By then Claudio Coutinho had effectively been relieved of his responsibilities as manager. Austria looked reasonably competent, Krankl beating Sweden with a penalty and taking his side through. Austria then finished top of the group by virtue of having scored more goals than Brazil (who shared the same goal difference).

The tragedy was played out in Group 4, where Scotland just disintegrated after their defeat by Peru. First a dope beaten Peru 3–0 and drawn with Argentina. The hosts had bettered Poland 2–0, as Deyna missed a penalty in his 100th international. So the Argentinians and the Brazilians were level on points and goal difference would probably decide it on the final day. Brazil kicked off first and defeated Poland 3–1. That left the Argentinians to knock four past Peru if they were to reach the final for the first time since 1930. In an enormously enjoyable and highly emotional game in Rosario, they actually went two better than that – with two from Kempes, two from Luque and one each from Tarantini and House-man. It was a famous victory that set Argentina against Holland in a final that was bound to add a new name to the list of holders.

The third-place match was thus between Brazil and Italy. Italy were ahead at half-time, but Brazil finally won it 2–1. Rivelino, the only player in either squad remaining from the 1970 final came on as sub in what must have been his swansong appearance. Brazil thus finished the competition as the only undefeated team.

Argentina and Holland had never won the World Cup, though both had been runners-up to the host country –

Argentina in 1930 and Holland in 1974. Form indicated the Dutch, coming good at the right time, but emotion, the crowd and good fortune appeared to favour the Argentinians. The game started ten minutes late after the Argentinians had protested about a plaster cast worn by Rene van der Kerkhof.

The hosts scored the only goal of the first half after Kempes burst through the middle of the Dutch defence. The Dutch, suffering from some poor refereeing, equalised seven minutes from time through Nanninga, and then Rensenbrink hit the post just on the final whistle. But extra-time, against the run of play, belonged to Argentina. Twice more Kempes burst through, once to score himself, once to give an easy chance to Bertoni. So, for the third time in four World Cups, the hosts had won through. The Argentinians had succeeded for two major reasons – one was home advantage, the more important was Mario Kempes.

Below: Bertoni runs to collect the ball after he had put Argentina 3–1 up in extra-time of the 1978 World Cup final. Kempes scored the other two.

The European Game

If the French had shown as much flair for the playing of soccer as they have for organizing it they would always be world champions. The country whose international reputation on the field is no more than ordinary has produced a succession of soccer philosophers whose vision has shaped the development of the game.

Jules Rimet, whose persistence finally established the World Cup, was a Frenchman. So were the two men who paved the way for the international competitions which have become the focal point of the European season – Gabriel Hanot, who foresaw the European Cup, a tournament involving the club champions of each country, and Henri Delaunay whose brain child was the European Championship, a mini-World Cup involving national teams.

Left: Kneib of Borussia Monchengladbach holds on to a cross in the 1977 European Cup final when the Germans were beaten 3–1 by Liverpool. Liverpool provided England's second only success in the competition which began in 1955, following Manchester United's win ten years earlier. The European Cup had developed from a brainchild of a French journalist Gabriel Hanot through early disinterest among many strong European nations into the top club tournament in Europe and probably in world soccer.

The European Cup

Hanot, an ex-international player, influenced the European Football Union (UEFA) from his platform as editor of the French sports newspaper *L'Equipe*. Encouraged by the increase in the number of friendly fixtures between teams from different countries through the development of floodlighting and better means of travel, Hanot published plans for a tournament. Although UEFA were initially unenthusiastic, the French journalist persisted; in September 1955 the dream became reality when Sporting Club of Lisbon met Partizan of Belgrade in the first match of a novel competition involving 16 clubs.

The concept disturbed a number of traditionalists in soccer administration, like those in England who feared that there would be too many fixtures and, initially, teams were refused permission to enter. But once clubs realized that participation 'in Europe' was a profitable exercise there was no stopping the spread of interest. The European Cup's success led to the development of two other competitions at club level, the European Cup Winners Cup, for the winners of each country's knock-out tournament, and the Inter-Cities Fairs Cup, for teams in cities staging industrial or trade fairs. Delaunay's European Championship, first contested in 1958, fitted perfectly into this trend.

Yet much of the European gospel was spread by one team. Real Madrid won the first five European Cups (1956–60) with such panache that those who doubted the validity of European competition had their misgivings dispelled by a club which played scintillating soccer. The first final exceeded all expectations. Staged in Paris, in honour of the efforts of the French in setting up the tournament, the venue was to the advantage of Rheims, the French champions, who had reached the final. But in a game of dramatic fluctuation and splendid skill, Real Madrid won the new trophy 4–3.

With Alfredo di Stefano pulling the strings for Real they began a run of invincibility. Their attack had a cutting edge that defenders throughout the continent could not blunt and, later, di Stefano would have support from Ferenc Puskas, the Hungarian maestro whose exile from his homeland brought together the two best players in Europe.

In 1957, Real retained the Cup by beating Fiorentina from Italy; in 1958 with the aid of extra-time (overtime) they overcame AC Milan, and the following year they repeated their triumph over Rheims, the margin of their success this time 2–0. Yet their most conclusive triumph was the last of this phenomenal run. With entrants now more than doubled from the first year and almost every European country represented, Real still reached the 1960 final, played in the vast Hampden Park stadium in Glasgow.

Below: Kocsis' first goal for Barcelona in the classic 1961 European Cup final. Benfica won 3–2. Below right: Gento, a six-times winner !

What followed was a soccer classic. In front of 130,000 fans, Eintracht from Frankfurt, the champions of West Germany, took a shock lead, and played their part in a memorable occasion by scoring twice more. But Real got seven goals, four to Puskas, three to di Stefano, one a solo thrust from the man they called the Golden Arrow in which he surged forward with the ball from inside his own half. Although Real were to be champions again in 1966, this was the perfect epitaph for one of the great teams in soccer history. In the first round of the next year's tournament they were beaten by Barcelona, who had qualified as a second representative for Spain as champions of the Spanish League.

Although no one club could dominate like Real, the European Cup nevertheless continued in clearly defined eras. After Real the Latin influence remained for several years. Benfica, from Lisbon, won in 1961 and 1962, the second success coming over Real for whom Puskas scored a first-half hat-trick. But the Portuguese club had the younger talent in the precocious Eusebio from Mozambique and he inspired a 5–3 win on another memorable night for European soccer.

Benfica missed their chance of a hat-trick by losing in the 1963 final to AC Milan, the first of three successive Italian triumphs. AC's bitter rivals, Internazionale from Milan won the following two seasons, beating first Real and then Benfica to emphasize yet again the domination of the first ten years of this new style of tournament by a very few clubs. Real's 1966 triumph came over Partizan Belgrade, the only club from Eastern Europe ever to reach the final of the European Cup.

Then followed a brief spell of British supremacy.

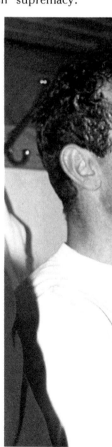

Celtic from Glasgow beat Inter-Milan in the 1967 final, a clear case of the good guys beating the bad guys; Inter had based their success on a grudging defensive style which hardly set the rest of the continent a good example. Celtic's praiseworthy philosophy was to go for goals. Manchester United kept the trophy in Britain the following year in a match of great emotion. Ten years earlier eight United stars had been killed in an air crash on their way home from a European Cup tie in Belgrade. Inspired by a virtuoso performance from the young George Best and Bobby Charlton, a survivor of the crash, United swept aside Benfica 4–1 in extra-time (overtime).

Meanwhile one of the continent's less heralded nations, Holland, began to make a surprising mark. Ajax from Amsterdam, rank outsiders at the outset, reached the 1969 final only to be betrayed by their inexperience when they were trounced 4–1 by AC Milan, including three goals from striker Prati. But the Dutch did not have to wait very much longer. In 1970 Feyenoord from Rotterdam exhibited the quality of the very top clubs in the Netherlands by beating Celtic 2–1 in the final in Milan's San Siro stadium. And the next three years belonged to Ajax.

Like Real had their di Stefano, Ajax had their orchestrator in Johan Cruyff, a brilliant attacking general in a side capable of attacking play from every outfield player. While many European experts could not understand how the Dutch, whose national League had no real strength, could produce such virtuosos, Ajax conquered the continent. In 1971 they beat Panathinaikos from Athens, now managed by Ferenc Puskas; the following year Cruyff scored twice to beat Inter Milan; in 1973 they overcame more Italian opposition in Juventus from Turin.

But now other teams on the horizon had learnt from the Dutch approach. Incredibly, one of soccer's strongest nations, West Germany, had produced no champions and only one finalist in the first 19 years of the European Cup. But by marrying off their traditional competitive strengths with a fluent pattern of soccer in the Dutch style, Bayern Munich, under Franz Beckenbauer, emulated Ajax. Their own hat-trick of successes began against Atletico Madrid when after a tied first game they scored four times in the replay, two of them from Gerd Muller, that cold-eyed taker of half-chances. Muller scored again in the 1975 final in which Beckenbauer once more collected the giant trophy, a 2–0 success over England's Leeds United. St. Etienne, France's first representative in a final since the days of Rheims, could not stop the hat-trick though Bayern had only the margin of a solitary goal.

England, like the Germans, had not made the impact on the European Cup that had been expected, but in 1977 Liverpool brought the founders of soccer their second success. Once again the match itself produced the style of soccer that gave further vindication, if that were necessary, of the success of Hanot's plan, Liverpool took the trophy away from the Germans with a magnificent 3–1 win over Borussia Monchengladbach.

Below: Bobby Lennox of Celtic has a shot deflected by Facchetti of Inter Milan during the 1967 European Cup Final in Lisbon. The occasion provided a triumph for the attacking skills of the Glasgow side who came from behind to defeat the undisputed masters of a grudging defensive system of play.

The European Cup Winners Cup

The European Cup Winners Cup was not the natural offspring from the European Cup. England was one of very few nations which took their Cup competition seriously; for many other countries it was an end of season knock-about with little real commitment. When the idea of the Cup Winners Cup was first mooted in 1958 only six countries showed any interest; Hungary and Belgium were among those who revived their Cup competition when the tournament finally got under way in 1960.

Because of their Cup tradition, it is not surprising that British clubs have revelled in the Cup Winners Cup. After Fiorentina and Atletico Madrid had been the first two winners, Tottenham Hotspur pummelled Atletico 5–1 in the 1963 final. Two years later Bobby Moore climbed the winners steps at Wembley Stadium to collect the trophy for West Ham United, 13 months before he would collect the World Cup for England from the same platform. Other British successes came in 1970 when Manchester City beat Gornik Zabrze from Poland in Vienna, in 1971 when Chelsea needed two matches in Athens to overcome Real Madrid and in 1972 when Glasgow Rangers proved too strong for Moscow Dynamo, though the Scottish club had their great night spoilt by the violent behaviour of their followers which led to Rangers being banned for a year from European competition.

West Germany, too, has been represented with success by Borussia Dortmund in 1966, Bayern Munich the following season, and SV Hamburg in 1977. Though the clubs from the Eastern bloc have made little impact on the European Cup they too have found the Cup Winners Cup more accessible. In 1969 Slovan Bratislava were the winners, their victory coming at a most appropriate time.

Because of Russia's invasion of Czechoslovakia in 1968, the 1968–69 European competitions, including the European Cup, were re-drawn to keep clubs from Eastern and Western Europe apart – a decision which led to most of the Communist countries withdrawing their clubs. But Slovan remained and their victory – 3–2 in the final over Barcelona – provided a popular success for the Czech club at a time of crisis for their country. Later, FC Magdeburg, from East Germany, won the Cup Winners Cup in 1974 while Dynamo Kiev, whose players comprised the entire Russian national team at the time, succeeded them in 1975.

Sporting Club of Lisbon in 1964 provided Portugal with their solitary success, while Anderlecht of Brussels were the first Belgian winners in 1977. The Italian influence has remained with AC Milan carrying off the trophy in 1968 and 1973. In general, however, the Cup Winners Cup has been a poor relation of the European Cup and attendances all over the continent are always lower than those for the premier competition.

Below: The blue-shirted Rangers defenders held Bayern Munich to extra time in the 1967 final of the European Cup Winners Cup. Then they conceded the winning goal to Franz Roth.

The UEFA Cup

More interest has been stimulated by the UEFA Cup which has grown out of the former Inter-Cities Fairs Cup. Today it has the largest number of entrants of the three European club competitions with each country allowed more than one representative. Yet throughout its formative years there seemed no way that it would ever reach such an established place on the soccer calendar. All its headlines came for the wrong reasons; the Fairs' Cup was nicknamed the 'Fouls Cup'.

Even in its muddled beginning when the trade fair qualification was upheld and players from a number of League clubs were chosen to represent 'London', the soccer had an unnerving violence to it. In the early days a difference in playing styles and in interpretations by referees was partly to blame – after three seasons in the Fairs' Cup, Birmingham City had eight players sent from the field against foreign opposition – but the cynicism remained long after that excuse had become invalid.

In 1965, Chelsea arrived in Rome for the second leg of a Fairs Cup tie with Roma, leading 4-1 from the first match but labelled by the Italian press as 'killers'. When the players went out to inspect the pitch they were pelted with fruit and garbage; the club provided no practice balls for the pre-match warm-up and sarcastically the Chelsea players kicked piles of rubbish to each other. Bottles and pieces of metal were hurled at the players during the match; the windows on the team coach were shattered by stones as it left the ground. Roma were subsequently banned from European competition for two years.

Below: It's all Greek to the neutrals in London's Wembley Stadium as supporters from Panathinaikos of the Greek First Division arrive for the 1971 European Cup final. Managed by the great Hungarian forward Ferenc Puskas, the Athens club had exceeded expectations in reaching the final, where they met their match in Ajax Amsterdam.

Another London–Italian clash in 1970 had even less dignity; after a provocative first leg of a Fairs Cup tie in Italy, players of Arsenal and Lazio dined together but neither side would forgive or forget what had taken place on the field. The end product was a street brawl between the players and officials of both teams.

The International Inter-Cities Industrial Fairs Cup (its full title which eventually became the UEFA Cup in 1971) began in 1955 and took three years to produce its first winner – Barcelona who beat London 8–2 over two matches. The second tournament lasted two years with Barcelona triumphing again, but from 1961 onwards it has been an annual affair. After Roma had won for Italy that year, the next five seasons were a Spanish extravaganza with four victories, three of them in all Spanish finals. Valencia, twice, Real Zaragoza, and Barcelona were the Spanish clubs who laid their hands on the trophy.

The intervening year, 1965, saw Ferencvaros from Hungary beat Juventus, and Eastern Europe fashioned another success in 1967 when Dynamo Zagreb beat Leeds United. It was only to be a temporary set-back for England who then produced the next six winners. Leeds themselves won the Fairs Cup in 1968 and 1971; Newcastle succeeded them in 1969 and were superceded by Arsenal in 1970. In 1972 Tottenham won the first competition under the UEFA Cup heading in an all-English final over Wolverhampton Wanderers, while Liverpool reigned supreme in 1973, a feat they repeated three years later.

Above: Mick Jones heading Leeds United to victory over Juventus in the 1971 Fairs Cup.

Feyenoord finally loosened the English grip in 1974, beating Tottenham Hotspur in another match where the tag of violence stayed with the competition – this time on the terraces where the Spurs fans damaged the stadium and then ran up against the Dutch police. The trophy should have remained in Holland when FC Twente from Enschede survived the away leg of the 1975 final against Borussia Monchengladbach in a goalless tie; yet unaccountably in their own stadium they were beaten 5–1 by the German side.

The UEFA Cup remains the only one of the three European club competitions to play out its final over two games, on a home and away basis, rather than the one match on a neutral ground. If the scores are level on aggregate the result can be decided on the principle of away goals counting double. In the 1977 final Juventus beat Atletico Bilbao 1–0 in Turin but lost 2–1 in Spain. However the goal in their away game counted double and Juventus won the trophy.

The European Championship

Henri Delaunay, the instigator of the European Championship (its official title from 1966 after being called the European Nations Cup) did not live to see a match played in the competition he had done so much to institute. From humble beginnings, it has taken its place as a renowned four-yearly event with the final played at the mid-point between World Cups. Like the World Cup it has a history of favouring the nation which stages the finals; Spain in 1964 and Italy in 1968 winning on home soil.

The competition began in 1958 with the finals set for France two years later. Italy, West Germany and the British nations chose not to compete which rather devalued Russia's eventual victory; less than 18,000 spectators saw them beat Yugoslavia 2–1 in the final. Spain might have prevented the Russian march but when the draw paired the two countries, the Spanish government ordered the soccer administrators to withdraw from the fixture as a protest against Russian involvement in the Spanish Civil War 25 years earlier.

Ironically both countries battled through to earn places in the final in 1964. This time politics cast no interfering net and Spain won 2–1 in Madrid. It had been a much more representative competition with 29 countries taking part, England's first effort being aborted when France came up with a crushing 5–2 defeat in Paris. Spain reached the final by beating Romania, Northern Ireland, the Republic of Ireland and Hungary. The gallantry came from Denmark, with a totally amateur side, who reached the semi-final before going down to the steam-rollering Russians.

Russia remained unbeaten in the 1968 competition, but did not win it; they didn't even reach the final because of a ridiculous decision to decide a tied semi-final on the toss of a coin. Russia's match with Italy, the host nation, finished 0–0 and they lost the toss. Italy then met Yugoslavia who had beaten England in an unsavoury match in which Alan Mullery became the first Englishman to be sent off while representing his country in a full international. Italy came from behind to equalize in the final but this time the coin was not flipped. In the replay the Italians won comfortably with first-half goals from Riva and Anastasi.

Russia continued their run in 1972 when they reached the final for the third time in four tournaments. They were joined in the last four by Belgium, the host nation, who had eliminated the holders; West Germany who had put out England with a devastating 3–1 win at Wembley; and Hungary who had needed three games to beat Romania.

The perfect final would have been West Germany against Belgium, but the two nations were paired in the semi-final and the Germans overcame territorial disadvantage to win 2–1. Russia carried too much experience for Hungary but were devastated in the final by West Germany who were not flattered by a three-goal victory. Gunter Netzer, their tall, blond midfield man, created all the goals just as he had done in the semi-final, and for all the play-making skills of Netzer, it was the opportunism of the extraordinary goalgetter, Gerd Muller, which set Germany apart from their rivals.

Four years later West Germany reached the final again; by now they were world champions and they were strong favourites to retain their European crown. Gerd Muller had retired but Dieter Muller, from FC Cologne, had staked a claim to be his successor by coming on as substitute in the semi-final against Yugoslavia and turning the game upside down in extra-time (overtime) with three goals.

Form favoured a repeat of the 1974 World Cup final with Holland fancied to beat Czechoslavakia in the other semi-final. But the Dutch fell from grace, again in extra-time (overtime), both by conceding two goals and by having Van Hanegem sent off for arguing with the referee. The Czechs who had eliminated England and Portugal in their qualifying matches still remained long shots to win the championship. But they gave the final a magnificent opening with early goals from Svehlik and Dobias before the new Muller pulled one back for the holders. In a fluctuating second-half both sides squandered opportunities until with the very last moment of normal time Holzenbein, their smallest attacker, headed West Germany level from a corner.

In extra-time (overtime) neither side could score the winning goal, so for the first time in the history of soccer a major tournament was to be settled in a sudden death battle of penalty-kicks. Eventually Hoeness missed for West Germany leaving Panenka to stroke in the winning goal and make Czechoslovakia champions of Europe.

The drama of the final brought a perfect end to a week of competition full of thrilling soccer – a perfect example of what Henri Delaunay had envisaged. The European club competitions, too, continued to flourish giving total justification to the dreams of Gabriel Hanot. Yet none of the tournaments has provided France with a winner; the innovatory French are still waiting for their virtue to be rewarded.

Below: A memorable goal for a memorable occasion. Terry McDermott races away in triumph after putting Liverpool into the lead in the 1977 European Cup final, in which his side beat Borussia Monchengladbach 3–1.

U.S. Soccer

Until the mid-seventies the United States held little credibility in the world of big-time professional soccer. Except for an occasional appearance in the World Cup finals – and in particular one sensational result, the 1–0 defeat of England in the 1950 Cup – the national side had no status. The professional league, the NASL, was seen from afar as a rest-home for journeymen professionals from major soccer nations, a chance for one last big pay cheque. Yet through the persistence of a few visionaries, notably Welshman Phil Woosnam and Englishman Clive Toye, those days are long gone. Once Pele had been lured out of retirement to play in New York, no professional in the world could turn his nose up at a career in the United States. At the same time a policy of acquiring the best players in the world has been matched by an 'Americanization' theme designed to cultivate home-grown players of top-class ability. Soccer is on its way to major-league status and could even become the top sport in the United States.

Left: Pele, the catalyst. The acquisition of the legendary Brazilian by New York Cosmos in 1975 gave the NASL the highest credibility and heralded a US soccer boom.

Soccer – for so long an ethnic pastime played out on the back-lots of big cities – broke into the big-time in 1977. Regular season games in the North American Soccer League showed a 31 per cent improvement to average more than 13,500 spectators per game. On one significant night in New York, the Cosmos outdrew the Yankees. In the play-off, the same club pulled in a massive 77,691 attendance against Fort Lauderdale Strikers. After ten years, mainly of survival, the NASL set out on an expansion programme.

To many observers the reasons behind this boom could be spelt out in four letters . . . Pele. The simplification is unfair because it was the foresight of the Cosmos which enticed the world's number one soccer star out of retirement in his native Brazil. However his arrival gave a focal point to a strong and sensible marketing campaign to sell soccer – not to ethnic groups but to the new American spectator. Moreover Pele's acceptance of a contract in the NASL immediately gave world stature to a league which had previously been regarded throughout Europe and South America as a rest home for ageing journeymen professionals.

Yet for so long it seemed that the world's number one ball game would take no roots in the United States. Baseball and football, both home-grown products, dominated sports. With so much immigration, soccer naturally had its supporters but insular thinking kept it from spreading. For thousands of Poles, Hungarians, Italians and Yugoslavs the game represented a reminder of home; they named their own teams after the great clubs of Europe and their semi-pro and amateur leagues were sporting ghettos.

Not surprisingly there was hardly unanimity in the quest for a governing body to administer soccer through the country. As long ago as 1884, an organization was set up with the confusing title of American Football Association, co-ordinating the activities of clubs, mainly semi-professional and mainly in the East. This preference for clubs who paid their players led to the formation of a breakaway body, the American Amateur Football Association. In 1912 both units looked to FIFA for recognition on an international level only to be told to go away and sort out their domestic dispute before any application could be considered.

The domestic fight was won by the AAFA and in 1913 FIFA granted their renewed request for membership, now as the United States Football Association. (Thirty years later they became the United States Soccer Football Association and more recently the United States Soccer Federation.) But the prestige of FIFA's backing did not guarantee popularity for the game. Far from it.

Baseball and football sunk their roots even more firmly into the culture. At about the time Babe Ruth was giving up pitching to become 'Sultan of Swat', the American Soccer League did attract isolated pockets of support, Scottish immigrants supplementing American-born soccer players. But no-one or no team produced the charisma needed to lift the game above its minor-league status.

Even a flutter of success from the United States national team could not capture the public imagination. When Jules Rimet finally introduced the World Cup in 1930, the United States went to Uruguay as one of 13 contestants for that initial trophy. And they did not just go along for the ride. With three-quarters of the squad home-grown players, they began with a handsome 3–0 win over Belgium, with the follow-up of a triumph over Paraguay by the same margin. This took the side – nicknamed the 'Shot-putters' because of the formidable physique of some of its members – into the semi-final.

Even though the first staging of the World Cup was devalued by the withdrawal of a number of leading countries and even though the occasion was hardly the focal point for the media that it is today, had the United States become world champions in 1930 soccer might not have had to wait for its popularity. But against Argentina the 'Shot-putters' found themselves out of their class, in terms of physical play as well as skill. Beaten 6–1, they limped out of the competition in more ways than one.

After competing less successfully in subsequent World Cups, arguably the greatest sensation in the competition's history featured another US triumph. Brazil

staged the 1950 competition, the first to include mighty England whose Association had finally settled a long-standing and petty dispute with FIFA. England had spread soccer's gospel throughout the world and they expected to win the World Cup.

They began with a win over Chile in Rio; their second fixture was scheduled in the town of Belo Horizonte and it was to be against United States, who fielded a hybrid side, captained by Eddie McIlvenny, a Scot, and with other players of varying nationalities. On paper hardly a contest, but the American players, all from humble soccer backgrounds, were better equipped to meet the sight that greeted the teams when they arrived at the stadium. The locker-rooms were filthy – England opted for alternative changing accomodation at an athletic club nearby; the field was riddled with stones and bumps.

England still began confidently but the elements cancelled out their superiority in skill. Two shots which beat goalkeeper Borghi but rebounded from the post added to their frustration, as did the denial of one genuine claim for a penalty. Naturally these incidents had the opposite effect on the Americans who grew in stature as every minute passed with the game still tied. And then fortune favoured their brave efforts. Bahr drove the ball into the goalmouth where centre-forward Larry Gaetjens glanced it with his head into the back of the net. Newspaper editors back in England did not believe the wireflash

Bombshell for our World

And win is a 'must'

England's defeat has led to a tense situation in Group "B" of the World Cup competition.

Spain now head the Group with two wins from two games, and they meet England on Sunday. Spain need only to avoid defeat in that game to shatter all hope of England going forward to the final pool. United States, by beating Chile could, in the event of an English win, force a triple tie in this pool.

Italy, holders of the Jules Rimet World Cup, have failed to survive for the final because of Sweden's draw yesterday with Paraguay. Sweden top Group C with one game to be played

ENGLAND
U.S. AM

From JOHN

ENGLISH Soccer was humbled as stadium here today, when Americ The Americans, who entered the comp and completely unfancied, were the victory.

England

24

86

of the final score, amended in the Stop Press to England 10 United States 1.

Yet such an achievement had no appreciable effect on the domestic game which continued along its well-worn ethnic, unpublicized lines; soccer remained a minority sport with the majority of Americans totally unexposed to the appeal of a game which on most other fronts was still increasing in popularity. Even when greater sophistication in transportation encouraged South American and European clubs to undertake off-season tours in the United States, the response was only lukewarm. Like an Englishman watching baseball, American audiences could not appreciate the subtleties of the game: enormous ballooned headed clearances would be greeted with rapturous applause while intelligent movement by a player off the ball would be misunderstood.

But in 1960 the relative success of the International Soccer League – staffed by touring club sides like Everton from England and Dukla Prague – captured the attention of the sort of entrepreneurs who back major-league sport. Television showed an interest, another major-league prerequisite. Crowds were no longer confined to groups watching teams simply because they came from 'back home'.

Unfortunately those who saw a sudden surge of soccer to major-league status and a resultant fast buck were undone by their own speed. What followed was a sad series of events which, but for the persistence of a few dedicated visionaries, very nearly proved conclusively that America did not want soccer. The mid- and late-60s became the time of the 'Great American Soccer Disaster'.

In 1965 three quite separate groups of businessmen approached the United States Soccer Football Association, each hoping to start *the* pro soccer league. By tradition soccer's governing bodies are steeped in conservatism and the USSFA was no exception. Their executive committee was hardly convinced that the public would support one league let alone three. They also decided to test the commitment of the businessmen; whereas each American Soccer League member paid a token $25 to be registered with their governing body, each group wishing to support a pro league team were told, to their own shock, that every franchise would cost $25,000! A percentage of television rights and admission fees would also find its way into the coffers of the USSFA.

Whether the executives of the Association thought that in setting out this structure they would kill off all three attempts and preserve the status quo is not clear, but it does seem possible. In fact all they did was reduce the number of business groups from three to two by dint of one voluntary amalgamation. Unfortunately for the Association they could not persuade the two groups to join together, so a choice had to be made.

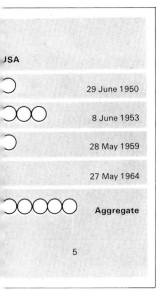

Above left: How the English press reacted to England's defeat by the United States in 1950.
Left: The record between the two sides in official international matches.
Above: Larry Gaetjens, the scorer of the goal that beat England at Belo Horizonte.

In 1966 after due deliberation the USSFA opted for the combine led by Lamar Hunt, Jack Kent Cooke and Judge Roy Hofheinz who, as a now official group, gave themselves time to co-ordinate their venture with an announcement that they would not start the league until the 1968 season; they also gave themselves the name of the United Soccer Association – USA of the USA! But their rival syndicate refused to admit defeat.

In August 1966 came their announcement that they would start their unratified National Professional Soccer League a year earlier i.e. April 1967. Moreover, the NPSL produced an ace from the pack in the shape of a network television contract with CBS. As a result the USA immediately brought forward their inaugural date to the 1967 season. For all its efforts the USSFA found themselves with two pro leagues, one unofficial, due to start inside a few months. Worse still, neither league had any players – since the part-time performers in the American Soccer League were immediately written off as not good enough – nor any real knowledge of how to get them. In short it was a shambles induced by business opportunism which had no real interest in the good of soccer.

The two organisations started to recruit with different approaches. The USA followed the pattern of the International Soccer League and planted European and South American clubs in the twelve cities granted franchises; Washington were represented by Aberdeen of the Scottish League, Boston by Shamrock Rovers from the League of Ireland, Chicago by Cagliari from the Italian League.

The NPSL opted to attract individuals and created ten brand-new teams like the Chicago Spurs and the New York Generals. Each signing was greeted by

Above: Phil Woosnam, seated, now Commissioner of the North American Soccer League.
Below: After years of effort from Woosnam crowds like these watching football are now filling soccer stadia across the United States.
Right: The banner advertises its support for Portland Timbers.

rapturous handouts from press and publicity officers with minimal soccer knowledge; many imported 'stars' were poor quality professionals who could not make their way in their own country. The untutored American spectator could be fooled but the immigrant with a soccer background spotted the charade and a large area of potential support was immediately lost.

Five cities – Chicago, Los Angeles, New York, San Francisco and Toronto – had foisted upon them teams from both leagues, a saturation of the market. Nevertheless both leagues began on time and fulfilled their fixtures. Wolverhampton Wanderers from England won the USA championship, which had the bonus of a splendid final won 6–5 after two bouts of extra-time (overtime); the crowd average of almost 8,000 was reasonably satisfactory. The NPSL, despite the advantage of the sales pitch of television, could only average around half that amount over a much longer season.

In fact television probably worked against the NPSL. Soccer, unlike most American sports, is not full of time-outs and stoppages; indeed much of its world-wide appeal is because it is a free-flowing game in which the ball is in play for much of the time. Live coverage of the game posed a dilemma for producers who had to fit in regular commercials; the end product bordered on farce when players were ordered to feign injury or delay over the taking of a free-kick so that the commercial break could be inserted. (Even as late as 1975 Pele's first goal in the NASL was missed live because of a commercial break though it was recorded and immediately shown once the break had finished.)

Yet neither the USA nor the NPSL had come up with the right soccer product for the American market. When the two finally merged for the 1968 season – after FIFA had ordered a settlement following the NPSL's attempt to sue them – worse was to follow. The new league, the NASL, now had 17 teams. By the end of a disastrous season for attendances – some games attracting just a few hundred loyalists – only five of those 17 remained. Pro-soccer in America had finally come to the end of the road. Or so it seemed.

Three men refused to lie down. Two were Britons, Clive Toye, formerly a soccer correspondant on the London Daily Express, and Welshman Phil Woosnam, a rare combination of university graduate and soccer international. But even their resolution could not have survived without the continual backing of Lamar Hunt, whose track record included successful support of football and tennis. Hunt's money gave the NASL the financial credibility it needed to pick itself up from the darkest hours when Toye and Woosnam ran their administration from the visitors' locker room in Atlanta Stadium.

They began to stimulate new ventures even though many clubs who had given up the battle in 1968 had sustained losses in excess of half a million dollars. Most important they learned from their mistakes and attempted a total development of the game down to grass roots level. They recognized that they had been wrong to aim their selling of the game at the adult male immigrant, who preferred to read newspapers sent from the old country or even use a short-wave radio to check the scores in Europe or South America. The theme of the new regime was to make soccer an attractive sport for the entire family.

The very nature of the game had an immediate appeal. Unlike football, baseball or hockey it is not known for a high risk of serious injury. Soccer equipment is very cheap. Soccer players don't have to weigh in excess of 200 lbs and have the physique of a Mr. Universe. Three good reasons for the American parent to encourage children to take up the game.

Toye and Woosnam also recognized that the media posed a problem. Newspapers were committed to support the traditional sports; if ever soccer was given some space reporters showed little enthusiasm and usually a total lack of knowledge. How could a television network be persuaded to add its support to the NASL (CBS had opted out in 1968) if the large newspapers gave little more than the results of their matches. High on the list of priorities at each franchise was to wipe out the apathy of the press.

By 1974 a number of significant corners had been turned. The NASL expanded from a membership of nine clubs, mostly in the eastern area of the country, to 15 all over the nation. Attendances improved too, with certain clubs drawing crowds in excess of 10,000. But still the League lacked the real personality on the field with which those potential converts to the game could identify. For all the efforts of Americans like Kyle Rote Jnr., Bobby Smith, Shep Messing and Bobby Rigby, there were not enough home-produced players to break down the prevailing impression that soccer was a foreigner's game. Rosters were still full of Europeans and South Americans, many of only average talent and some who used the season as a vacation in the sunshine.

Though the game continued to spread in the schools, the NASL officers realized that an injection was needed to speed up the process of conversion. The young soccer lovers needed a hero; the League itself needed a focal point. Fortunately there was enough money and power of persuasion to capture the only man who could fulfil the role of catalyst – Pele.

The great Brazilian goalscorer had retired after a career of sustained brilliance unique in the modern game – a premature decision, perhaps, hastened by the overwhelming pressure put upon him in every match for his club Santos and for Brazil. When New York Cosmos persuaded him to change his mind and sign a three-year contract to play in the NASL, the League came of age. No player in the world, from that point on, could dismiss the possibility of a career in American soccer. What was good enough for Pele would certainly be good enough for anyone else.

His presence brought an immediate positive response. It awakened the media, who were now forced to acknowledge that serious attempts were being made to sell soccer. Television provided live coverage for his first match, against Dallas. Most important of all Pele, now 34, was equal to the challenge both off the field and on it. His

Right: George Best gets a close look at the master as Pele plays the ball off to a team-mate.

appearance at every stadium in the League guaranteed record attendances, and he responded in scintillating style with goals and tricks of skill that did more than influence the course of a particular match; he spread soccer's gospel. Moreover, his sunny personality, at first grappling with the English language, added another endearing aspect to his arrival. Very quickly the United States discovered what the rest of the world already knew: that everybody loves Pele.

The NASL was not above tinkering with the way the game was played in order to tailor-make it for the American

market. In this respect they trod a tight-rope, because getting out of step with the other soccer playing countries could have meant a fall in international competition. But two innovations, approved by FIFA, worked splendidly. The introduction of a 35-yard offside line stretched play in midfield so that the players were given more room to create goals; hence higher scoring which was also given the encouragement of a points for goals system.

The second major amendment had to be introduced because of the American's dislike of a game that can produce a tied result – all of the major soccer leagues in the world accept tied games. After establishing a sudden death extra-time (overtime) period the NASL added first of all a penalty-kick competition to bring a definite result. When this became a little stereo-typed, it was further amended by borrowing a principle from hockey. Now games still tied at the end of the extra-time (overtime) period are settled by the 'shootout', in which players in turn are given the ball on the 35-yard line and then have five seconds in which to hit a scoring shot.

With Pele taking an emotional and final second retirement at the end of the 1977 season, American soccer has lost the one man who has really brought the game alive. But he has left it in a remarkable state of health. Clubs are now making profits, a fact which will encourage further investment and expansion. The NASL has publicly committed itself to an eventual structure of 32 teams; franchises in the end may be worth 30 million dollars and more. Pele may be unique but he is not irreplaceable and already German World Cup star Franz Beckenbauer, the NASL MVP in 1977, is taking over his mantle along with the likes of Giorgio Chinaglia, the Italian international striker, and George Best. The imported players are no longer the journeymen looking for a paid vacation; better quality players all over Europe are clamouring for the chance to pursue a lucrative career in the United States.

If the grass-roots policy continues as it should – and hundreds of soccer clinics around the country are safeguarding the supply of local talent – there will be fewer and fewer places for the European and South American. The NASL has pledged to Americanize the League by a sliding-scale policy which year by year will reduce the numbers of foreigners allowed on each roster; eventually there will only be room for the cream.

That, in effect, remains the one key problem to be solved. As yet the newly established production line has not fashioned American-born soccer players of true international class. Though that class gap is narrowing it still has to be bridged, and until it is, the long-term future of soccer in the United States, though now stable, will not be totally secure.

The achievements of the mid-70s have been remarkable. If more converts are still needed in areas like Chicago and Los Angeles, the magnificent successes in places like Tampa, Minnesota and San Jose shine out. Soccer has become a white-collar sport for Americans – watched by the family unit and played enthusiastically by girls as well as boys. Survival is no longer the key word for the NASL. Now there are new ambitions – like staging the World Cup finals and providing an American team to win it, and like developing the United States into the soccer centre of the world.

In 1967 these were just pipe dreams. Yet inside ten years the Great American Soccer Disaster was well on its way to becoming the Greatest Show in town.

Far left: Giorgio Chinaglia, Cosmos' Italian international.
Left: The end of an era. A tearful Pele prepares to address the crowd before his second, and final, retirement at the end of the 1977 season in the United States.

Soccer Superstars

'Great' or 'Superstar' are the most overused terms in all sports. Soccer is of course no exception. But in the following section there is a close analysis of a number of players of exceptional talents, who have each in their own way made a major contribution to the development of the game. Kyle Rote Jr, for example, would be the first to admit that in sheer skill he cannot compare with George Best and Franz Beckenbauer from the present or Alfredo di Stefano and Sir Stanley Matthews from the past. Yet Rote's own considerable achievements have done so much to make the game come alive in his home country when there were so many doubters about whether an American could play soccer at high levels. Many of our chosen names have played internationally and contributed to the games reputation, others may be fresh names to the reader. Each has created his own niche in soccer history.

Opposite: Gordon Banks, voted best keeper of the 1966 World Cup finals in England.
Top: One of the many injuries he sustained.
Inset: Playing for England against Greece in 1971. He had conceded 53 goals in 69 internationals.
Bottom: One that got away at Crystal Palace.

Gordon Banks

On October 22, 1972, an automobile accident in a quiet country lane in England appeared to have ended the career of the greatest goalkeeper in the world. Gordon Banks, 73 times an international for England, lost the sight of his right eye in the crash.

Bravely, the man whose mastery of his profession had been a key factor in England's World Cup success in 1966, tried a comeback. But in vain, and even his closest friends feared for his reputation when in 1977 he was persuaded by Ron Newman to join the Fort Lauderdale Strikers four and a half years after his accident.

Though he had kept fit, the absence of regular competition would surely be a handicap. At 39, even for a goalkeeper, he seemed too old, and surely, in the end, his impaired vision would be an insuperable drawback.

But, just as he had done for years in the goal areas of the world, Gordon Banks refused to be beaten. His inspiring agility lit a fuse under the Strikers; unheralded they raced to the Eastern Division title with a run of six successive wins on the road. A superb career had taken another remarkable turn.

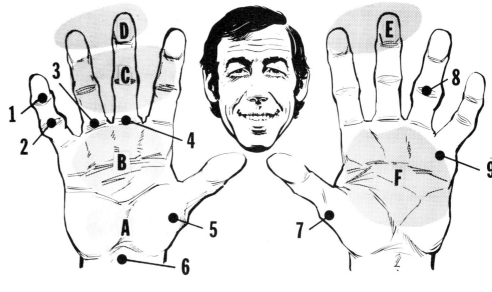

Top and column left: Banks' brilliant save that thwarted Pele, England v. Brazil 1970. Above: The injuries. 1 broken right little finger, 2 broken middle joint, 3 and 4 dislocations, broken and dislocated thumb, 5 and wrist, 6 and 7 a torn and dislocated left thumb, 8 and break and 9 a mysterious knuckle injury. The letters key the part used to make his six most memorable saves from A Pele, B George Best, C Francis Lee, D Wyn Davies, E Martin Peters and F Bobby Charlton.

In 1956, when he was 18 and just starting on a career in professional football with the first of his unfashionable clubs, Chesterfield, Banks used to imagine he was Bert Trautmann, the German ex-prisoner of war who stayed to become the first goalkeeper to be named Player of the Year for his skill for Manchester City. When, in 1972, Banks became the second to be honoured, he was 34. He had been at the top for nearly ten years and, like all immortals, he looked as good as new. In a country where the standard of goalkeeping in the First Division is probably higher than anywhere in the world, Banks was number one – even to the ambitious young men burning their hearts out to take his place in the England side.

'He's brilliantly professional,' said Chelsea's Peter Bonetti at the time, 'a model goalkeeper'. 'I've watched him on television at every opportunity and he's always been my idol,' said his future successor with England, Ray Clemence of Liverpool; 'He's the best goalkeeper in the world and he could have played for England for years,' said Leicester City's Peter Shilton.

For a decade from 1963 Banks kept the international appearances of some fine keepers down to a handful. Ron Springett, Tony Waiters, Alex Stepney, Gordon West, Bonetti and Shilton were players who, in most countries, would have been regular choices.

It was ironic that Shilton should have replaced Banks in the Leicester City side in 1967. The door opened when Leicester transferred Banks to Stoke City for £52,000 ($93,600) on 17 April – a move described as 'the bargain buy of the century.'

People are paying £200,000 ($360,000) for strikers in 1972,' commented Stoke chairman Albert Henshall, 'yet this fellow destroys strikers with saves that are out of this world.'

Why, then, did Leicester sell? Their manager at the time was Matt Gillies: 'I was placed in a most unenviable situation,' he explained. 'Banks was firmly established as England's number one, but Leicester also had Shilton a local boy with tremendous potential and ambition. Shilton was 17 and Banks 28. One had to go.

'Arsenal were keen on Shilton and he wanted first-team soccer. With the future, in mind I decided to keep the younger man. I didn't want an auction, so I decided on what I thought was a fair price and Stoke were the first club to put that price in writing.' The interest of Bill Shankly had not been shared in the Liverpool boardroom, so Banks went to the Victoria Ground and not to Anfield.

Although Banks and Leicester had not seen eye to eye on more than one occasion, the goalkeeper was not exactly enthralled about the move. 'I was hurt that Leicester were ready to part with me and keep Shilton. It was all too soon after the World Cup.'

Banks had been voted the best goalkeeper in the 1966 World Cup finals in England when he conceded only three goals in six games, including one penalty.

'I worried about my career at that point in 1967', he said. 'But then I recalled that three of the world's best goalkeepers, Russia's Yashin, Scotland's Simpson and Mexico's Carbajal, were all older men.'

Stoke manager Tony Waddington had no inhibitions. 'We had tried to buy Gordon 18 months before when Leicester wouldn't sell at any price. He'd always played brilliantly against us.'

The Stoke players were soon to become the observers of Banks' amazing pre-match loosening-up ritual: a combination of ballet movements and the stretching actions of a cat. The effect is not only a relaxation of the nervous system but a toning up of every muscle in readiness for the action ahead.

Banks has always believed in practice, and more practice. The young Shilton, studying him at Leicester, was amazed at his dedication and the hours he put into perfecting some facet of his game. Shilton admits he was fortunate. 'If you've got the England goalkeeper at your club you know how good you have to be to get to the top.'

Though his position invites exhibitionism, Banks has never been showy. The continentals may play to the gallery with tumbling routines and exaggerated gestures. It is easy to give the illusion of greatness; it is not easy to maintain it. Yet the two really memorable saves of the many Banks had made needed no artificial dressing. They needed only genius.

The first was against Brazil in the blazing heat and high altitude of Mexico and the 1970 World Cup. England, the holders, and Brazil, the favourites, had been playing for 18 minutes in Guadalajara when the South Americans launched an attack on the right.

Jairzinho sped down the wing and cut inside; his cross seemed to hang in the air as Pele climbed to meet it. Banks takes up the story: 'I'd been covering the near post but as Jairzinho chipped the ball over I started back across the goal. Halfway across I was sure the ball was too high for anyone to reach but then I saw Pele. He seemed to climb higher and higher until he got the ball on his forehead, putting everything behind it. The ball landed just in front of me and to be sure of saving it I flicked it away. Never at any point did I think I was beaten, but I'm prepared to admit it was the save of my career.'

Pele was aghast. 'At that moment I hated Banks more than any man in soccer. I just couldn't believe it. But when I cooled down I had to applaud him with my heart. It was the greatest save I had ever seen.'

Pele's comments conveyed the greatness of that save more so than Banks' modest recollections. The header was low and fast, heading for the corner, the bounce was awkward; Banks, sprinting across his line, still had to stretch full-length and, as the ball was almost over the line, scoop it up; and up it went, in a tense parabola over the bar. The whole stadium, on its feet in anticipation of a goal, sat down in disbelief.

The other really great save could easily have been over-dramatized for the simple reason that it changed history. Whereas Brazil went on to win against England, Stoke, who had won nothing in 109 years until they triumphed in the Football League Cup final of 1972, would have had to wait at least another season if Banks had been beaten by a Geoff Hurst penalty three minutes from the end of extra time (overtime) during the second leg of the semi-final against West Ham at Upton Park.

Stoke had lost the first leg 2–1 but had drawn level on aggregate with a goal from John Ritchie after 72 minutes of the return. But the hearts of their supporters sank when Banks impeded West Ham's Harry Redknapp in a furious scramble for the ball in the goalmouth. Hurst had beaten Banks from the spot in the first leg and there was no surer striker of a ball.

The two England men faced each other, enemies now. Hurst shot fiercely to Banks' right – just as he had done at Stoke. Banks followed the right way, but his anticipation was almost too good: the shot was straighter than at Stoke. Banks, at full stretch, wrenched himself in mid-air, got his two arms up in line – and, as in Mexico, the ball curved up over the bar.

Hurst just stood there gaping in disbelief; the Stoke players ran at Banks and smothered him in gratitude. He came out of the clinch bawling and gesticulating angrily in that nervous fashion of all goalkeepers when they are trying to hide the embarrassment of having achieved something extraordinary.

What does Banks remember of that save? 'I was concentrating so much that the rest of the field was completely shut out of my mind. All I could see was the ball and Geoff. I decided to go right but I'm not prepared to say why. It was certainly the most vital penalty I've ever saved.'

'Of course I like to make special saves,' he continues, 'but the greatest compliment I can be paid is when a player says, "that was an easy game, Gordon." I may know differently.'

Banks talked to himself during matches, coaxing and cajoling himself to maintain his concentration. But he was not invincible.

Banks was once criticized by their manager Harry Catterick. 'He seems a bit susceptible to the ball crossed to the near post', was one criticism. This is a weakness of most goalkeepers. 'You can't be everywhere at once,' retorted Banks. 'I don't make a habit of conceding these kind of goals.'

That was the thing about Banks. He had lapses, like anyone else; but he had no *consistent* weakness, though his distribution, sometimes erratic, was suspect.

His temperament is good – though he gets irritable when he knows he is in the right and is penalized. He was cautioned against Crystal Palace for showing dissent after he had been penalized for handling outside the area. Banks claimed that 'for ten years I've cleared balls from the edge of the area by throwing the ball up inside the area and kicking it outside. This way I can use the area to the full.' On occasions like this the famous Fernandel grin disappears and Banks stands with feet rooted to the spot and his arm beating up and down like a railway signal. But these occasions are few and far between.

Right: Banks in the familiar yellow goalkeepers jersey that he wore with distinction for England until a car crash ended his career.

With the attendant physical risks of keeping goal, it was ironic as well as tragic that it should appear to end for Banks in that off-the-field accident. An accident which would not have happened but for his professionalism.

He elected to drive to a friend's house to watch the televised highlights of Stoke's game at Liverpool the previous afternoon – a match that was not being broadcast in his home television region. He didn't have to go, but a foul awarded against him had cost Stoke a goal, and he badly wanted to see if he had transgressed.

He never got there, and glass from the shattered windscreen reached his eyes. For Stoke, for England, for soccer, it was a stunning blow.

In August 1973 he actually announced his retirement, but he never entirely lost hope. That is why in 1977, away from some of the spotlight, he tried again at Fort Lauderdale. The NASL could have been witness to a sad failure; thankfully it became part of a soccer fairytale.

Franz Beckenbauer

In 1977, during his first season in the United States, Franz Beckenbauer was voted 'Most Valuable Player' by the North American Soccer League – yet another triumph for this supremely gifted player who cost the Cosmos a reported $2.8 million (over £1½ million) for a four-year contract. Even at that price the deal represented good business. At 31, Beckenbauer still had plenty to offer. After a glittering career in which he made 103 appearances for West Germany, including captaining them to the European Championship in 1972 and the World Cup in 1974, he relished the new challenge.

Perhaps the key to understanding Franz Beckenbauer is to know that he is a Bavarian. Bavarians are different from other Germans. They are more akin to the Austrians than their compatriots to the North, and their carefree ways are far removed from the image of the stereotyped German. Given that he is a German, Beckenbauer's style, with all its elegance and seeming nonchalance, could only be that of a Southerner.

His manner may be that of his race, but his talents are unique. Beckenbauer's skills have allowed him to play in any of the outfield positions at international level. He is as capable of leading the attack as directing the defence, but his preference is for the role of sweeper.

Practically all his past and present coaches recognize that this is the position which suits Beckenbauer best. In Italian football, where its roots lie, the role of the sweeper is entirely defensive. Beckenbauer has turned it into a kind of launching pad for attack. He is, perhaps, as much the first line in attack as the last line in defence. His remarkable playing intelligence and range of vision enable him to select exactly the right moment for a counter-attack. With either a long, accurate pass to a colleague already running into space through the middle, or by using a crossfield ball to start a movement along the wings, Beckenbauer will at a stroke direct the attack where his opponents suspect it least. Combining and inter-changing with Gunter Netzer in the 1972 European Championship, Beckenbauer seemed to hold the reins of a near unstoppable soccer force.

No sweeper can ever have been so adventurous as Beckenbauer. At every opportunity he will move forward into attack. His skill on the ball and the inventiveness of his quick reverse and return passes would do credit to any South American virtuoso.

Beckenbauer's ability was clear from the start, but perhaps the most interesting facet of his early career is the number of positions he has played in. Then, as now, he was astonishingly versatile. It was his exploits as a centre-forward in his school team, for whom he once scored 100 goals in a season, that convinced Bayern Munich of his potential. He played regularly in the Bayern youth teams as a centre-forward, but it was on the left-wing that he made his first-team debut in 1964.

Right: Cool and composed as ever, Franz Beckenbauer takes time to assess the situation during one of his 103 appearances for West Germany.

99

Beckenbauer's family background did much to help him in these early days. His father, a postal worker, had been a soccer player and his older brother played for and later managed 1860 Munich. Soccer in Germany was then still largely amateur so, after leaving school, Beckenbauer had to learn a profession.

He first trained as an insurance salesman and later spent 18 months as a supervisor of a clothing store. In February 1964, a year after the formation of the professional Bundesliga, the national league of West Germany, Beckenbauer signed a professional contract with Bayern Munich at the age of 18. Now able to devote himself entirely to soccer he completed his apprenticeship under the guidance of junior coach Rudi Weiss, then with Bayern managers Zlatko Cajkovski, Branco Zebec and Udo Lattek.

Just three months after taking over from Sepp Herberger as the manager of the national team, Helmut Schoen called up the 19-year-old Beckenbauer for the preparations for the 1966 World Cup. He gained his first full cap in a vital World Cup qualifying game in Stockholm against Sweden. In March he scored his first goal for the national team, getting two in a 4–2 win over Holland at Rotterdam, and by June he was a certainty for a place in the World Cup team.

In England, he faced the first truly great test of his career, when West Germany met England in the World Cup final at Wembley. Beckenbauer, whose role in the previous matches had always been a creative one, was now detailed to the restrictive task of closemarking Bobby Charlton. Years later Schoen still insisted that his decision to make Beckenbauer do this was correct, that Germany's best chance of victory lay in cutting Bobby Charlton out of the game, but for many it seemed a cruel waste of so much talent. Beckenbauer prevented his adversary from scoring, but even he was powerless as Germany went down to the disputed third goal credited to Geoff Hurst. Beckenbauer is emphatic that the goal should never have been allowed: 'I was 12 yards away, and that ball never crossed the line. Even Bobby Charlton patted me on the back, saying "Sorry Franz". He too, must have known that it was not a goal.'

While England were content to rest on the laurels of their triumph, the Germans were reappraising their whole attitude to the game. The emphasis came to be placed on skill on the ball rather than hard running off it, and where skill was at a premium, Beckenbauer was in his element.

The culmination of this development was not to come until the 1972 European Championship, but in the meantime Germany got their revenge for that defeat in 1966, winning a friendly in Hanover by the only goal and eliminating England from the World Cup in Mexico. In both games Beckenbauer scored an excellent and crucial goal.

Right: Another problem solved for Franz Beckenbauer as West Germany goalkeeper Sepp Maier collects at the feet of Johan Cruyff during the 1974 World Cup final, which West Germany won by two goals to one against Holland.

Despite his ability, Beckenbauer, like all great players, has his critics. They point to his often lazy-looking, casual approach and nonchalance, sometimes even depicted as arrogance. Perhaps the best answer to this came from Sepp Herberger, Schoen's predeccessor as national team manager: 'Franz is so smart, intelligent and mature that he could be playing for Germany when he's 40. So many players today are like clockwork toys. They run themselves silly and then stop. But Franz knows how to conserve his energy, and that is vital for anyone who is going to have a long playing career.' In fact Beckenbauer is far from a lazy player. As Herberger says he is simply intelligent enough to avoid the senseless expenditure of energy that cuts short the careers of so many others.

In Munich, where they still enjoy royal titles in nostalgic reminiscences of the nineteenth century, they call Beckenbauer 'Kaiser Franz'.

Off the field Beckenbauer is always co-operative and diplomatic. On his visit to Britain for the 1972 European Championship he wanted to be rid of an English journalist but, rather than be rude to the man, Beckenbauer declined the interview by saying that he was on an exclusive contract to a German paper. It was a white lie, but one which avoided creating any ill-feeling.

Before deciding to leave his homeland, after 103 internationals, Beckenbauer had long been pursued by numerous foreign clubs ready to offer fabulous fees and fringe benefits for his services. As far back as 1966, AC Milan reputedly offered $450,000 (£250,000) to Bayern. However, because of the ban on imports of foreign players, the deal fell through.

Throughout the soccer world, Beckenbauer is recognized as no ordinary defender. For comparisons one has to turn to the past. In some respects he is in the tradition of the great attacking centre-halves of an earlier era, especially the last of that exclusive breed, the unforgettable Ernst Ocwirk of the Austrian side of the late forties and fifties.

Beckenbauer's boyhood idol was another of the great players of those times, Fritz Walter, captain of the German side that won the World Cup in 1954. In Munich, twenty years later, 'Kaiser Franz' emulated his idol, captaining West Germany to World Cup success in the final against Holland.

Under Beckenbauer, Bayern Munich, too, scaled the heights. From 1974–76 they were Europe's champion club, winners of three successive European Cups. Their fluid soccer was based on a core of players who had helped West Germany to the World Cup – Sepp Maier, George Schwarzenbeck, Uli Hoeness and Gerd Muller. But the dominating influence was that of Beckenbauer.

With nothing else to win in Europe, Beckenbauer was ready for the overtures of the Cosmos and their president Clive Toye. The United States provided new battle-fields for the 'Kaiser' and there was never any doubt that on them he would be a winner.

Left: Franz Beckenbauer becomes one of the privileged few as he collects the World Cup in 1974.
Right: Beckenbauer in action for New York Cosmos.

George Best

Like most Britons, George Best loves California. Of course he enjoys the sunshine; until his marriage in 1978 he showed a passing interest in the beauties of the Golden State. But most of all he appreciates being allowed to play soccer away from the pressure of his lifestyle in England.

George Best became the first player with a pop star image. Handsome and long-haired, he appeared in the English First Division as an impressionable seventeen year old at the same time as the Beatles ruled the airwaves. His impish brilliance on the field ensured that he would always be noticed had he been given less charisma. But the combination made him a cult figure and in the end that almost ruined his career.

'Almost' because with the Los Angeles Aztecs – at the age of 30 – he regained a love for soccer which had been destroyed by his inability to cope with the unrelenting demands of being a celebrity. His downfall on the field had been caused by a number of sensational disappearances from his club, Manchester United; by a late-night social round with hangers-on and a self-confessed sex life that would make even the movie gossips blush.

In his prime there were even greater pressures on the field. English soccer entered a cynical age. Best would have won a place in any side for his dribbling skills, but to that you could add pace, vision, a sense for goals and a tigerish ability to reclaim the ball when he lost it. Few players had more gifts, but there were plenty who were set the task of denying their expression.

'I know six players in the First Division', he once said, 'who are going to trip and kick me. They're told to do it, usually. Some of them laugh about it, they think it's clever. With these players you have to watch two things; the ball, and someone coming to chop you. There aren't many cowards in soccer. If you think about getting hurt, you're a loser before you start out.' He also said that there were two full backs in the First Division who deliberately set out to break his leg, adding sombrely, 'I think you have got to say that I hate these men.'

Best began as an outside-right but prefers to be in the middle of the pitch, directing play, and looking for chances to score. Often he will beat a man simply with a sudden and remarkable turn, as he did when he ran through to score a vital goal for Manchester United early in extra time (overtime) in the European Cup final of 1968 against Benfica, at Wembley.

Two years later, on the same ground but down the other end, a similar, extraordinary pivot took him round his United colleague Nobby Stiles, to score a memorable goal against England. That was four days after he had been sent off the field at Windsor Park, Belfast, for throwing mud at the referee and spitting during an international against Scotland.

His quarrel with referees over the years has been a bitter one, which has led to such incidents as the one in Belfast, and to a two-month suspension which followed a piece of unnecessary petulance after a televised floodlit game against Manchester City.

'Do they seriously think I don't want to change?' he cried at the time. 'Of course I do. But I can't change. I know myself well enough to realise I can't promise to change. I can only try and go on trying. I can get whacked from the back or hit when the ball has gone past 28 times in a row and do nothing or say nothing. I don't know why it should boil, the 29th time, which has been no different. It just happens'.

Best was brought up in one of the ugly, red-brick streets of Belfast, born in that city on 22 May 1946, the son of a shipyard worker, and he has paid tribute to his father in these words: 'I might have missed everything I'm enjoying now if my father had not pointed me in the right direction. But then he had me kicking a ball from the time I could toddle, before I can even remember.'

It was his father, too, who insisted that he return to Old Trafford when, as a homesick 15-year-old, he left Manchester to return home to Belfast within 48 hours of starting his new career. This time Best settled down, thanks largely to a kindly landlady. At 17 he was in the Manchester United League team, despite his fragility. He had weighed just seven and a half stone on his arrival in Manchester, and it was only the insistence of United's Irish scout which took him there in the first place, after others had passed him over.

His keenness on the game had led him to give up the chance of going to a grammar school, because he wanted to go on playing soccer. Soccer, rather than the Protestantism in which he was brought up, was his virtual 'religion'; and he has always been amiably free from bias. 'Even when I was a kid,' he has said, 'religion didn't bother me. I was a Protestant and I went to school in a Catholic district, and when I was walking home the Catholics would start fighting, so I've got as good a reason as any to hate them, but I don't.'

Among the first to marvel at his talents at Old Trafford was a fellow Ulsterman, Harry Gregg, then the international goalkeeper. Gregg had been injured, and took part in a practice game with the juniors. 'Well, this kid from Belfast came at me with the ball,' he has said. 'I went out to meet him; and he done me. In those days, I could usually dictate what League players should do, never mind youngsters. But with this boy, I'd gone one way and the ball the other. For the sake of my ego, I tried to believe that I'd sold myself, but it happened again shortly afterwards.'

At Old Trafford, too, Best came under the benign, paternalist influence of United's manager, Matt Busby, the most significant figure in his career. Busby was always one who let his gifted players play, rather than put them in a tactical straightjacket, which was greatly to Best's advantage; though Busby himself was often exasperated at times. He speaks, particularly, of one of Best's most brilliant performances; a quarter-final away tie in the European Cup, in 1966 against Benfica, in Lisbon. 'We planned to contain them for the opening 20 minutes or so, let them come at us hold them, then strike back suddenly. That was the plan.

'But George must have had cotton wool in his ears. He didn't hear. Within the first quarter of an hour he destroyed them on his own with two goals and another made. It was fantastic, and I was almost angry.'

This was complemented by the remark of another United player when Best, in sensational circumstances, dropped out of the team to play Chelsea in London early in 1971, and United, after a long, bad run, won the game. 'The reason we went so well today was that George wasn't there hogging the ball. We all got a chance to play with it.'

Which was basically unfair since Best, all that season, had been taking risks and knocks, going it alone, precisely because he was getting so little support; though he himself has admitted that his besetting fault is to hang on so long.

This Chelsea episode was in some sense the turning point of Best's career, the incident which showed just how astonishingly prominent a national figure he had become. Never before had so much newspaper space and television time been devoted to the escapades of a professional soccer player.

Best, who had been missing more and more team trips to London, and who had recently obliged Busby to eat humble pie after turning up late for a meeting of a disciplinary committee at the Football Association, now missed another train. United arrived in London on the Friday without him, and although Best followed them down, he went to ground in the Islington flat of a talented young actress.

The flat was besieged by television and newspaper reporters, and there was buzzing speculation as to whether the immense pressures of Best's life, on the field, where he was maltreated, and off it, where he lived in an illuminated goldfish bowl, had finally proved too much.

The following Monday, Busby, 'the Boss', waited in his office for Best to come to see him. Best didn't come. Sympathy swung away from him. But soon come he did, apologizing, promising to be good, and receiving a light two-week suspension. The liaison came, like so many of Best's much publicized amours, to a quick conclusion, and Best, on his return, lobbed a spectacular goal against Tottenham.

'If there are three of four people I can regard as real friends', he has admitted, 'that's the lot. I don't find it easy to get really close to people, or maybe I should say I don't find it easy to let them get really close to me. A lot of the other people I come in contact with I've learned to suspect, because I know how little their friendship means. But I'm not suggesting that's the full explanation of why I can count my friends on one hand. The thing is I don't really need other people all that much. I don't have to lean on them emotionally.

In this connection, a revealing anecdote concerns the girl Best was once seeing in London, whom, originally he had long cherished from afar. One morning, in Best's words, 'She was coming round to pick me up at the place where I was staying, but suddenly I got out of bed, packed and took off for Manchester. I left a note on the door for her. It said, "Nobody knows me".'

Right: Much praised for his skills on the ground, George Best emphasises his considerable talent in the air.

At this time Best's character seemed to be a compound of loneliness and immaturity; yet how many young men could, with so sketchy an educational and worldly background, at so early an age, have coped with such adulation? Best has complained of the negative attention he often has to put up with. 'I can take stick,' he said, 'I don't mind that. I know when I'm not playing well and I don't care who tells me so. But sometimes, just sometimes, the pressures of it all can become just too much, particularly when it's criticism all the way. I'm not a machine you know; I have feelings like everyone else. I don't always show them, but they are there. What upsets me is the way people can say what they like about me, and I can say nothing back . . . I would be lying if I said I didn't like all the fuss when I first started – I did. In the beginning, I liked it. Then suddenly it all started to go sour. Suddenly I could go nowhere, do nothing, without people staring, trying to pick fights, or telling me how to do my job. Men would come up and try to pick a fight because a friend of a friend had told them that I was looking at their wife in some club or another. They will jostle me in bars and then accuse me of trying to cause trouble. They come and look at my house and say it looks like a public lavatory . . . They wait for me to make a mistake on the field and they start. My God, do they start.'

The first signs that the pressure was really beginning to tell came in January 1972, two months after he was forced to withdraw from an international in Belfast because of death threats.

On 7 January it was announced from Old Trafford that Best had gone missing, that he had not reported for training for a week. He was consequently dropped from the Saturday match against Wolverhampton Wanderers.

United were by now being managed by Frank O'Farrell. Busby had assumed the stature of a father figure at Old Trafford. On the following Monday Best was interviewed by O'Farrell and the upshot was that the prodigal was ordered to leave his luxury bachelor home and move back into digs for the rest of the season. He was also fined two weeks wages and told to report for extra training, morning and afternoons, to get fit for a forthcoming Cup tie.

The match was at Southampton and United drew, their goal coming from a Bobby Charlton shot after a magical Best dummy had set up the chance. In the replay at Old Trafford, Best gave a virtuoso performance to win the game in extra time (overtime).

He saw out the season to finish at the top of the club's scoring lists, but in May he failed to report to the Northern Ireland training camp for the Home International Championship. He was reported to be holidaying in Spain. Understandably the team manager Terry Neill had to drop Best from the squad, and while the team were losing 2–0 at Hampden Park, their reluctant star was preparing a sensational announcement.

On 20 May George Best proclaimed that he was retiring from soccer: 'I am a physical and mental wreck,' he explained. 'I have been drinking too much because of the pressures particularly over the last four months.'

At the news Terry Neill generously offered to take Best back into the international squad, but he refused to talk to anybody – even his past mentor Matt Busby.

But Busby was a significant figure in eventually persuading Best to retract, and he lined up for the first match of the new season. But it was an uneasy peace, not only for Best but also for Frank O'Farrell and the rest of the United players, who were far from happy with the tolerant attitude shown to Best's aberrations by the board of directors.

On the field the tension within the club began to show. The Best affair could not be solely blamed for the fact that United were bottom of the First Division, without a win until their tenth League match, but their failure was relevant.

Best lasted until 25 November 1972 when United beat Southampton to lift themselves to 19th in the table, but the following week he missed further training sessions. O'Farrell, already under immense pressure, dropped him and, after talks, Best not only walked out on United but on Manchester itself, without the club's permission. The most persistent of London journalists located him in a London night club.

The following day United and O'Farrell took a stand, and George Best, for so long the hottest property in British soccer, was put on the transfer list. It was a testimony to the extent of Best's unreliability that only one manager expressed any interest in purchasing him.

Ten days later came a staggering announcement from Old Trafford that Best would start training again, and that presumably he would not be available for transfer. But the news did not come from Frank O'Farrell but from the United chairman Louis Edwards.

What the players thought of the apparent total reprieve of a man who had from their point of view abandoned the club in a crisis never reached beyond the dressing-room door. What Frank O'Farrell thought about the matter being taken out of his hands he was too gentlemanly to reveal.

But the performance of the team in their next fixture spoke volumes about the state of morale. United, away to fellow strugglers Crystal Palace, were not only beaten, they were totally destroyed as the Palace players, unable to believe their good fortune, scored five times without the hint of a reply.

Three days later, O'Farrell, his coach Malcolm Musgrove and the chief scout John Aston were sacked. 'The team is bottom of the table,' was O'Farrell's only reason as he explained his dismissal to the Press. The same day a letter arrived at Old Trafford from George Best in which he once more stated that he was retiring from soccer. It was a sorry epitaph to O'Farrell's stay with United. During his period in charge he had rarely shown publicly that he could control Best. Or even if he had been able to do so, the events at board room level had impaired his control.

Right: George Best in action in the famous red shirt of Manchester United, the club that saw his flowering and his controversial series of 'retirements'.

The managerial chair went to Tommy Docherty, who imported Scottish internationals in large enough numbers to keep United in the First Division. Best flitted around the world, refusing at that time an offer to play in North America, turning his back on soccer. To his critics it was an irresponsible joy-ride. To his supporters it was a detailed, detached period of self-analysis.

The events of the summer of 1973 illustrate the complexities and the contradictions of the man. Television personality and sports journalist Michael Parkinson had approached Best about compiling a book telling the story of his final disenchantment with soccer. It was to be a serious work, unlike so many of the cheaply contrived souvenirs that typified much of the Best image propagated by the hangers-on that had surrounded him in droves.

Best accepted the offer, and in close collaboration much of the book was written. Suddenly late in the summer, with the season a couple of matches old, a press conference was called at Old Trafford. George Best had been forgiven once more; he was back.

The news came as a surprise to Parkinson who had dined with Best an evening or two earlier. He had told him not to let the work stand in his way if he seriously wanted to return to soccer. All Parkinson asked, a reasonable request, was a quick telephone call to put him in the picture before the story broke. As he admitted with some humility he is still waiting for that call.

Best returned a stone overweight, an almost chubby caricature of himself. But with United again in the grips of a fight for survival, there was a premium on a quick return – provided the magic remained.

Two testimonial appearances, one for Denis Law against Ajax, only emphasised the physical problems he faced. But within two months of his return he won a place in the League side. The saga had taken yet another twist.

Below: The goal touch of George Best, scoring in the English First Division against West Ham United, a match in which he registered a hat-trick.

But on New Years Day 1974, his final comeback with Manchester United ended in a drab performance in London against Queens Park Rangers. Now it was back to the hangers-on and the nightlife, concentrated around his own club in Manchester. His book, full of jaundiced comments about the state of the English game and revelations about his social life, sold well, but only gave further impressions that he had joined the has-beens.

But his disillusionment could not totally stifle his love for playing. In the fall of 1975 he flirted with another return . . . now freed by Manchester United. He took up residence at a health clinic while playing occasionally for Stockport in England's Fourth Division and Cork Hibernians in the League of Ireland.

Then the Aztecs brought about a renaissance. In 1976 he totalled 37 points from 23 games; away from the spotlights of home, he relaxed, lost his chubbiness and recaptured much of his magic. At the end of the season, Fulham, now with Bobby Moore in their line-up, brought Rodney Marsh from Tampa Bay Rowdies and

Best back to the English game.

If Best had lost anything from his repertoire, it was not his sense of occasion. He scored within 90 seconds in his comeback match. He inspired the friendly London Second Division club to a number of stirring performances, but again couldn't keep out of controversy. His very registration became a test case between the Football League and the NASL; he was sent off for arguing with a referee; later he was to crash his car at four a.m. one morning. But before that he had reached a level of performance that saw him recalled to play for Northern Ireland after an absence of several years.

Another dispute between Fulham and the Aztecs arose in the fall of 1977. He left the English club in mid-season to return to Los Angeles, but now he was not running away. And wherever you met him . . . in a London night club or on Redondo Beach . . . he would speak lovingly of California. There George Best had come to terms with himself and there a great career had been saved from an early grave.

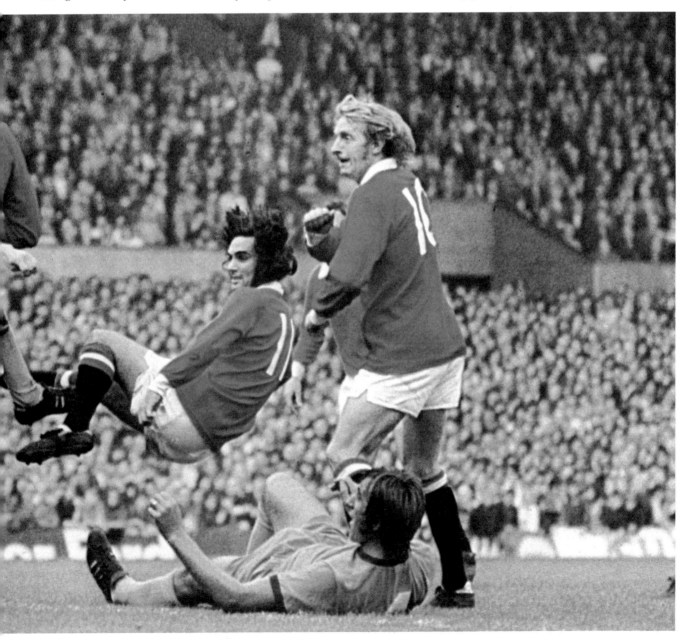

Bobby Charlton

Joe Armstrong knew Manchester Victoria railway station only too well. He lost count of the number of times early morning trains have carried him to some remote part of the British Isles in search of that elusive goal – the great soccer player – for his employer, Manchester United. He had no reason to believe that 9 February 1953 would be different from most other days as his train pulled out.

Armstrong's destination was Newcastle; his object to watch East Northumberland Schoolboys play Hebburn and Jarrow Schoolboys. Someone had given Matt Busby, Manchester United's manager, a tip. Occasionally something came of these trips, usually they were a waste of time. Perhaps once in a lifetime, if he was lucky, a soccer scout would find what Joe Armstrong found that cold winter's day.

Mrs. Cissie Charlton tells of the United scout's reactions: 'Joe came up and said, "I don't want to butter you up, but your boy Bobby will play for England before he's 21." And he did'.

And he did much more. Not only did Bobby Charlton play for England more than any other man in the history of the country (later superseded by Bobby Moore) he also undisputably took the mantle of the best-loved player of his time. It's no surprise to learn that within 24 hours Armstrong was telling Busby that he had made the find of his career.

This is how Joe recalled his first sight of Charlton: 'It was one of those thin February days, with frost on the ground. In fact we had to peer through the mist. Bobby didn't do so much at first, but what I saw was enough for me.

'He was like a vision. This kid could run like a gazelle drift past opponents with a shrug of the shoulders. And a shot: well it was unbelievable that a kid of 14 could kick so hard and accurately. I knew we'd just got to have him so of course I made a few enquiries and eventually we got him.'

In July of that year, 1953, the 15-year-old Charlton arrived at Manchester United with his father. Bob Charlton senior, a miner, was not at all convinced that his son should move so far from home. After listening to what Matt Busby and his chief aide Jimmy Murphy had to say, he said abruptly: 'Send for our kid.'

Into Busby's office came Bobby Charlton junior, to be asked by his father: 'What do *you* want to do son?'

'I want to come Dad. This is my type of club.' 18 clubs had wanted his signature – one is said to have offered his father £800 ($2,000) for it. It is one of the greatest tributes to Busby and Armstrong's talents that he went to United. Later, Charlton admitted: 'It was probably the wisest decision I have ever made. I never wanted to leave that

Right: Though Bobby Charlton earned his place on soccer's role of honour with a wide range of skills, it was his power shooting that really thrilled the crowds. Though adept on either foot, his right was the more powerful and brought spectacular goals for Manchester United and England.

club.'

And yet those early years with Manchester United were not easy. The schoolboy wonder was plunged head-first into the realities of the professional game. He was now under the direct control of Bert Whalley, the club coach, and Jimmy Murphy, a tough Welshman who was no respector of schoolboy reputations.

These two men were already busily honing the skills of perhaps the finest group of young soccer players ever assembled at one club . . . the kids who in a few years were to become the 'Busby Babes.' By the time that Charlton joined the club, they had already revealed to a startled soccer public one of those young stars: a boy, by name Duncan Edwards, who on Easter Monday 1953, before Charlton had joined the club, had played his first game in the First Division against Cardiff City aged 16 years 285 days. With a young star like that on the books, who was Bobby Charlton but a very promising young player? Indeed Murphy said of those days: 'A nicer, more genuine kid you couldn't wish to meet. He was loaded with talent, but, oh dear, Bobby was one of the hardest pupils Bert and I ever had to coach at Old Trafford. Even as a 15-year-old he had that thunderbolt shot in his left foot. And has there ever been a more graceful mover with the ball at his feet?

'He had all of that, as a boy. Maybe he had too many talents, because our job was to get them co-ordinated. He would keep hitting these stunning long balls to right or left wing, then standing still, instead of realizing the game was one of continual movement.

'Many a kid would have had his heart broken by our treatment of Bobby. Bert and I would bring him back in the afternoons when the other lads had a free period. We would get behind him, building up triangular short-passing moves screaming at him: "Play it short Bobby . . . play it short son . . . don't give the long ball until it's on." He learned.'

Charlton himself remembers those apprentice years with a tolerant smile now: 'I think if it hadn't been for Jimmy and Bert I might have given up the game. But I used to think that if they could give up their time to coach me, I had to try and improve my game to prove them right. It wasn't easy, but their love of the game was infectious.'

In the youth team and reserve side young Charlton was scoring plenty of goals, and United fans were anxious for Matt Busby to push a teenage shooting star into the first team along with the other youngsters. Busby hesitated, for Charlton was not as mature as the astonishing Duncan Edwards, only a year older and already a fully fledged international becoming, at the age of 18 years and 6 months the youngest soccer player ever to play for England. That was against Scotland at Wembley, April 1955, while Bobby Charlton was still playing in the reserves and was a virtual unknown outside Manchester.

Busby was keeping the boy under wraps but a series of injuries to his regular first-team inside trio – England centre-forward Tommy Taylor, Eire international Bill Whelan and quicksilver Denis Viollet (later a coach in the NASL) – forced the Manchester United manager to

Above: Bobby Charlton on a visit to the family home in Ashington in the North East of England.
Right: Charlton survived the Munich tragedy of 1958 when eight of his team-mates were killed in a plane crash on the way home from a European Cup tie in Belgrade (of those listed as survivors Duncan Edwards died later). Though he was thrown sixty yards clear of the plane he escaped with only a deep cut on his head.

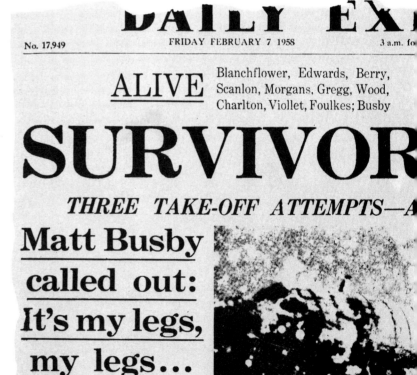

DAILY EX

No. 17,949   FRIDAY FEBRUARY 7 1958   3 a.m. fo

ALIVE   Blanchflower, Edwards, Berry, Scanlon, Morgans, Gregg, Wood, Charlton, Viollet, Foulkes; Busby

SURVIVOR

THREE TAKE-OFF ATTEMPTS—A

Matt Busby called out: It's my legs, my legs...

Express Staff Reporters

MANCHESTER United foot-ballers told last night the stark, dramatic story of how the airliner bringing them home from experiment. He gave Charlton his first chance against, appropriately enough, Charlton Athletic, and the boy responded with two goals. He didn't win a regular first-team place. Busby explained: 'Bobby is going to be great, but at the moment he thinks the game begins and ends 30 yards from the opposing goal. Once he realizes he has the whole pitch to play in . . . he'll be great. Just great.'

Charlton's chance came when Tommy Taylor fractured a small bone in his leg which resulted in Viollet moving to centre-forward with Charlton at inside-left. In the 1957 FA Cup semi-final, Charlton showed his goalscoring prowess with an astonishing acrobatic shot on the half-turn from a corner which helped to put United into the Cup final by beating Birmingham City 2–0.

Now he was in the big time, playing against Real Madrid in the European Cup semi-final that year and at Wembley a month later in the FA Cup final side against Aston Villa. Charlton remembers that match, because in the first few minutes he could so easily have put United one up, but at 19 he was too inexperienced and shot too hurriedly. United lost the game by the odd goal in three.

In that first season, Charlton experienced the happiness and heartbreak of big-time professional soccer, winning a League Championship medal, then ending on the losing side at Wembley. But everything that had gone before paled into insignificance with an event which lay just a few months away.

Charlton was just the 'boy' of that United team, although many of his team-mates such as Duncan

Edwards, Eddie Colman, David Pegg and Bill Whelan, were not so very much older. The side, with an average age of just over 23, had already won the League Championship twice in succession, and had failed only narrowly to achieve a remarkable treble by losing to Aston Villa in the FA Cup final and Real Madrid in the semi-final of the European Cup.

As season 1957–58 dawned Matt Busby said: 'Our matches with Real Madrid were a contest between the two best sides in Europe, one experienced, the other still only youngsters. Our turn will come. My ambition is for this team to win the League three times in three years.

On a wet soggy pitch from which the snow had been swept on the Wednesday afternoon of 5 February 1958, Charlton played for the last time with the young men he idolized. They were already in the last 16 for the FA Cup, and favourites to win it; if they beat Red Star Belgrade they were in the semi-final of the European Cup for the second year running; and they had shown a welcome return to form in the League on the previous Saturday, beating Arsenal 5–4 after taking a 3–0 lead at one point in a non-stop thriller.

By half-time in Belgrade, United were leading 3–0, Charlton scoring two of them and having a third mysteriously disallowed. True, Red Star levelled the scores in the last minute, but United were through on aggregate and a happy party set off home, with a cheery Tommy Taylor saying: 'I find it great playing alongside Bobby. I just nod 'em back and he whacks 'em in.' A few hours later Tommy Taylor, England's centre-forward, was dead, and so too were Roger Byrne, Mark Jones, Eddie Colman, David Pegg, Bill Whelan and Geoff Bent. Duncan Edwards died later. Two other players, Jackie Blanchflower and Johnny Berry, were so severely injured that they never played seriously again.

Charlton was picked up some 60 yards away from the Elizabethan airliner which crashed on its third attempted take-off after re-fuelling at Munich, West Germany. He had broken no bones, but there was a deep cut on his head, and he was still strapped in his seat severely shocked.

So shocked, in fact, that when he returned to Manchester some days later Jimmy Murphy, who had taken over as acting manager until Matt Busby recovered from his terrible injuries, despaired whether young Charlton would ever play again. It seemed that Charlton was still mourning the loss of so many close friends, so Murphy sent him back home to Ashington to be with his own folk for a week or two.

For a time Charlton appeared to have no interest in ever playing the game again. He says it was a talk with the family doctor that finally made the difference; off he went to kick a ball around in a local park and watch some kids doing the same. The experience convinced him that he could never be anything else but a professional soccer player.

When he returned to Manchester it was, said Murphy, a new and far more serious Charlton, who seemed determined to play his heart out in memory of and to keep faith with the friends who had died. Said Murphy:

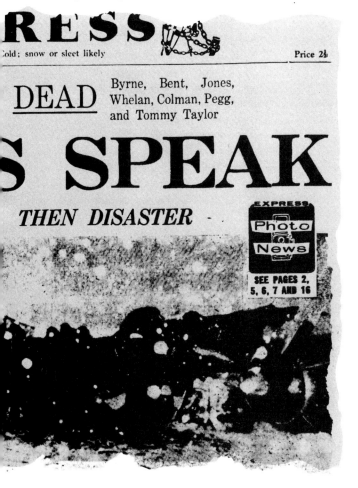

RE'SS

Cold; snow or sleet likely

Price 2½

DEAD Byrne, Bent, Jones, Whelan, Colman, Pegg, and Tommy Taylor

S SPEAK

THEN DISASTER

EXPRESS
Photo
News
SEE PAGES 2, 5, 6, 7 AND 16

114

'Before Munich, Bobby was playing as a striking inside-forward. After Munich, I thought we could get more out of him, and protect him, by switching to the left wing where he would have more room to use his obvious skills.'

The move paid off handsomely, for a few weeks later Charlton made a goal for Colin Webster in the last minute of a replayed quarter-final, so knocking out West Bromwich and putting Manchester United into the FA Cup semi-final against Fulham. Inspired by Bobby Charlton, United beat Fulham 5–3 after a drawn game and reached the Cup final.

For the second year running, Charlton ended on the losing side and sadly, for the second year running, he might so easily have changed the course of the game when one of his thunderbolt shots beat Eddie Hopkinson, the Bolton goalkeeper, smashed against a post and rebounded into the grateful arms of the 'keeper.

In a matter of weeks after the tragedy it seemed that this new, more serious, Bobby Charlton had matured, and he was honoured by being chosen to represent England against Scotland at Hampden Park, Glasgow.

It is a game still remembered for an astonishing Bobby Charlton goal when he met a Tom Finney centre with a violent volley. Naturally, the sporting press went into eulogies about the Munich survivor, hailing him as soccer's new 'golden boy'.

That description left Charlton cold. He has always been basically too shy a person to allow himself to be projected in that way. Once when described as the 'greatest ever English soccer player', he said, rather embarrassed, of the author: 'Well, he's entitled to his opinion.'

After the 1958 World Cup series he became an automatic choice for England as a left-winger, yet very often to the crowd and to the experts he was a frustrating enigma. Despite his reputation, there are those who say that he was never a great player; at least not in the way that Best, Pele or Puskas were great players. It was probably not until the 1966 World Cup that the Charlton on the field was really recognized as being much more than an emotional reminder of Munich.

Perhaps the answer was in Charlton's own self-effacing personality. In 1963 he was back at Wembley Stadium with Manchester United for his third FA Cup final appearance. That season Manchester United had struggled so badly in the League that for a long time there were fears they would be relegated. But Busby put the picture in perspective when he said to the team on the eve of the match with Leicester City: "If we can't win with men such as Charlton, Law, Quixall and Herd in the forward line, backed by Crerand at half-back we have no right to be at Wembley. This pitch was made for you . . . now go out and enjoy your game.'

United replied with a thrilling 3–1 victory in one of the best post-War finals. At last Charlton had his Cup medal and with it there came a dramatic change in his approach to the game. For some seasons he had appeared, at times, either diffident or dangerous. Now, with the sweeping tactical changes altering the face of soccer, Busby made his gambler's throw.

With men such as Denis Law, Johnny Giles and Albert Quixall on the books he decided to give the job of midfield general to Charlton because as he said: 'Where else in the world is there a player with such a range of playing ability. He can find a team-mate with a 40-yard pass; he can still come from behind the other forwards to have a crack at goal. Besides, Bobby is now at the stage where he needs responsibility. He can become one of the world's greatest players.'

Busby's plan and faith in Charlton brought dividends not only to his club but eventually for his country. For, in Bobby Charlton, Alf Ramsey, England's newly appointed team manager, saw the player around whom he could build his World Cup winning team. It is well known in soccer that at one time Ramsey was not exactly a Charlton fan. Like many other top managers in the game, he felt the Ashington wonder boy had never quite lived up to the exciting promise of his youth.

Charlton answered the call with a thrilling enthusiasm which is now history. There were three factors which probably caused him to burst through the straight-jacket of self-doubt. He had by now married a lovely model, Norma, who said of him: 'Bobby has always been devoted to soccer'. But when he started the maximum wage was still in force and he felt he would do well to save enough capital from his playing days to set up in a greengrocer's shop or something like that. He has never really lost that simple dedication to the game, although his career, of course, has bridged the vast financial change in the position of soccer players.

At the time of his switch, Manchester United's fortunes with George Best another exciting player in the line-up, began to improve. And, as United became a power in the game again, Charlton faced his greatest challenge . . . the challenge of the 1966 World Cup in England.

Charlton's contribution to that glittering success was perhaps not so dramatic as his skipper Bobby Moore's consistency nor the thrilling finality of Geoff Hurst's hat-trick in the Wembley final over West Germany. Yet few could deny that Charlton's presence on the field struck a disabling fear into many of England's opponents, and his ice-cool distribution of the ball in midfield played a big part in England's rapid breaks from defence to attack, a crucial factor in England's eventual triumph.

Certainly he scored one of the memorable goals of that series, when he ran from just inside his own half to crash the ball in from 25 yards against Mexico. Asked afterwards why he didn't score more goals like that one, Charlton gave a clue to his introvert personality by replying: 'You've got to be joking. I just ran forward looking for someone to pass to. But the Mexicans didn't come to tackle me. They just retreated so I ran on, until I saw a gap and let fly. Those shots either go in or miss by a mile.'

Even so, perhaps his most relevant contribution was almost negative. His running display against Portugal – when he scored two fine goals – so impressed the Germans that their most creative player, Franz Beckenbauer, was detailed to close-mark Charlton for the final and as a result the German attack lost much of its own fluency and potency.

'What else is there to win?' asked Jack, England's centre-half that day.

'Just one thing more,' said Bobby.

He was referring to the European Cup; the motivating force of his life, as it was in Matt Busby's. It was something they didn't speak about very often, but deep down Charlton, like Busby, felt that they owed it to the players who had lost their lives returning from that European Cup tie in 1958.

They had already thrown away one glorious opportunity losing in Belgrade to Partizan when favourites to win the trophy in 1966. And Charlton knew when Manchester United won the League Championship in 1967 that possibly this would be his very last chance of making that dream come true.

In fact, once again they very nearly made a mess of it. After beating the Polish side Gornik Zabrze, in the quarter-finals, Charlton and his men found themselves losing 3-1 to Real in the semi-final in Madrid. Now Charlton, with Crerand, took hold of the game and forced Madrid back and, quite unexpectedly and some would say undeservedly, United drew 3-3. Thus, having won the first leg 1-0 at Old Trafford, they were in the European Cup final at last.

On 29 May 1968, at Wembley, Bobby Charlton became one of the few soccer players ever to fulfil all of his major ambitions. It was a night of highly charged emotions; of agony and ecstacy, as Londoners linked arms with Mancunians and became Manchester United supporters for the night; United against Benfica in the final of the European Cup.

Charlton, trying desperately to keep his own nerves and those of his team-mates cool, scored a rare goal with his head to put United ahead early in the second-half. 'It must have skidded off my bald patch,' he modestly explained afterwards. Benfica equalized, almost won the match with a Eusebio thunderbolt and so the match went into extra time (overtime).

This was Charlton's finest hour, running, chasing, urging his flagging muscles to a final effort. Three times United scored in the next ten minutes; the last a matador's thrust from Charlton as he coolly swept a centre from Brian Kidd into the net.

They threw a big party for United's players, past and present, in the Russell Hotel, London, where they wined and dined and talked of the great days for hour after hour until dawn broke. There was one important absentee: Bobby Charlton. His wife Norma, looking elegant in evening gown, went bravely into the reception on her own to join all the other wives and sweethearts, while her husband who had done so much for the club slept soundly above: 'He was too tired and too emotional,' explained Norma.

He played for another five years, the same spirit and dedication remaining even in a struggling United side. He then had a spell in soccer management before opting for the quieter life as a director of a travel business.

Yet of all the honours that Charlton has won, the biggest and perhaps the most lasting is the respect he has earned from his fellow professionals. When the Bobby Moore affair blew up in Bogota and the England captain was falsely accused of the theft of an expensive bracelet, no one believed it. As everyone said: 'It couldn't have happened. Bobby Charlton was with him . . .'

Below: Two of soccer's all-time greats in direct confrontation as Bobby Charlton tries to get away from Pele. The encounter took place when England lost 1-0 to Brazil in Guadalajara, Mexico, during the 1970 World Cup. Charlton was to play his last game for his country only days later in the quarter-final of the competition. England were leading West Germany when Sir Alf Ramsey, the England manager, substituted Charlton to save him for the semi-final, but then the lead was lost and England went out.

Giorgio Chinaglia

With due reverence to 'King' Pele, the arrival of Giorgio Chinaglia on the doorstep of New York Cosmos in the early summer of 1976 represented a major breakthrough for the North American Soccer League. Pele had brought his glittering talents to the United States in his twilight years; he had already undergone one 'retirement.' At 29 Chinaglia came in his prime, the first fully active star player to be recruited full-time to the NASL.

At 6ft. 1 ins. and 190 lbs., Giorgio Chinaglia possessed that rare combination of agility and bulk that made him a feared goalscorer in the Italian League, the hardest division in the world in which to become a regular marksman. Against cynical, packed defences he survived the ruthlessly close marking with its ever-present provocation to become an idol of the Roman supporters of the Lazio club and to become an international striker. All the way controversy has never been far from his door.

That is the way it has been for Chinaglia – the big forward who was the one who got away from British soccer. Born in Carrara in Italy on January 24th 1947, his family emigrated to Cardiff, Wales, in the early fifties. His father took a job in the massive iron and steel works in the locality and later owned a cafe. Young Giorgio became 'George' and learned his first soccer lessons in an area that has provided the British game with an abundance of talent.

Playing for Cardiff Schools he was spotted by a scout for Swansea Town, then in the English Second Division. He signed as an apprentice and on his 17th birthday he became a full professional, with all the evidence pointing to a sound future in his adopted country. As a teenager he played four times in the Swansea first-team but a change of coach brought an abrupt end to his relationship with the Welsh club. Chinaglia could establish no rapport with Glyn Davies who had taken over from Trevor Morris, the man who had signed young George.

Chinaglia said later: 'We just didn't get on. He was always fining me for some breach of his rules or other. I suppose I was at fault too, but the club thought I was too much of a problem and they put me on the transfer list.' There was some talk of a transfer to nearby Cardiff City but Mr. Chinaglia Snr. stepped in to bring about the move that was to ensure that Italian soccer would benefit where Swansea had failed in spotting the potential of Giorgio.

His father made arrangements for Giorgio to try his luck with Massese, a Third Division club close to his birthplace. His immediate welcome was tepid, with the locals hardly impressed by the willingness of Swansea to release him. But once he had played they greeted him with all the adulation of a folk hero. Soon he moved up a rung with a transfer to Internapoli, and then in 1969 Giorgio Chinaglia reached the big time when he was traded to Lazio.

Right: Giorgio Chinaglia was rejected by a Welsh Third Division club as a teenager, but then found fame and fortune in his native Italy before joining the Cosmos.

Chinaglia gave a focal point to a club whose reputation was one of notoriety. On the field the side had an image of violence; off it their supporters transcended the line between bias and brutality. Lazio constantly fell foul of the European soccer authorities, a succession of ugly incidents culminating in a street brawl between players of both sides after Lazio had played the famous London side Arsenal in a particularly ill-tempered European tie. Chinaglia's skill in front of goal made him an instant idol in a country where soccer stars are feted with adulation.

Like many big men he did not always convince those who saw him less regularly. On a bad day his lumbering, round-shouldered style smacked of clumsiness, but bad days were few and far between and by June 1972 he had convinced the Italian selectors that his talent merited international recognition. Playing against Bulgaria in Sofia, in place of his great rival Pietro Anastasi of Juventus, he scored Italy's goal in the 1–1 draw. In September he scored again in Turin against Yugoslavia and the race was now on for the honour of wearing the number nine jersey for Italy in the 1974 World Cup finals.

It was a race Chinaglia won, though he was in and out of the national side in the year leading up to the climax of the competition. But for him and for Italy the experience in West Germany was not to be a happy one. Chinaglia was taken off for Anastasi in the opening game in which Italy struggled to beat Haiti 3–1. Anastasi kept his place in the draw with Argentina, and when Chinaglia was paired with his rival in the starting line-up for the crucial third match, against Poland, Italy were beaten among rumours of attempts to bribe the Poles on the field, and put out of the competition. Chinaglia was again withdrawn before the end of the game.

Within a year came the first rumblings about his possible transfer to the United States, a switch always likely from the moment he fell in love with and married his American wife Connie. Chinaglia was in fact hoist by his own petard; he had often said Lazio would not dare sell him because the fans would wreck the stadium in protest. When he wanted to leave the outcry, as expected, was immense. At one time there was an apparent change of heart; he appeared to be settling for the life-style which had brought him ownerships of a recreation centre and a fashionable man's clothing store, the luxury of his own cabin cruiser, a debut as a film actor and as a pop singer. But the draw of the United States proved to be too great. He was installed into the Cosmos organisation in time for the 1976 Bicentennial Tournament, ironically representing Team America against Italy.

His impact in the NASL was immediate. Over twenty-four thousand New York fans saw him score twice, claim an assist in a goal for Pele, and bring about two penalty-kicks which were converted by Keith Eddy in a 6–0 annihilation of Los Angeles. Two days later he scored both goals in the 2–1 victory over Boston. Within two weeks he was voted NASL player of the moment on the strength of three more goals which were key contributions to Cosmos wins at Minnesota and Portland.

He finished the season as the NASL leading scorer, even though he had missed the first month of competition.

Nineteen goals and eleven assists in only nineteen matches brought him four more points than Derek Smethurst of Tampa Bay Rowdies, and five more than Pele, who had played in three more games. But Cosmos failed to reach Soccer Bowl '76 when they fell 3–1 to Tampa in the Divisional Play-Offs.

It was a disappointment that Chinaglia was to put behind him twelve months later. In the regular season he lost his crown to Steve David of the Aztecs, finishing fourth top scorer with fifteen goals and eight assists from 24 appearances. He also lost his place in the NASL All-Star team, though he was in the eleven selected for an honourable mention. But in the play-offs he was a vital factor in a Cosmos triumph.

In the 8–3 thrashing of Fort Lauderdale he scored three times and played a part in another goal for Steve Hunt. The Cosmos then won through to meet Seattle Sounders in front of a capacity crowd at Civic Stadium in Portland for the NASL Championship – Soccer Bowl '77. It was an occasion magnified by Pele's impending and final retirement. Chinaglia played a minor role in a strange opening goal. His forward and hopeful pass had carried beyond Hunt and into the arms of Sounders' goalkeeper Tony Chutsky who then rolled the ball so casually along the ground that Hunt whipped it from him to score.

The Sounders equalised before half-time, but the game's climax was to belong to Chinaglia. Hunt worked his way up the left touchline before swinging over a perfect cross. The tall Italian guided in the winning goal, but even in triumph there was further irony; Hunt and Chinaglia, it was rumoured, had hardly been the best of friends. It was a fitting instalment in the career of a player who had never found controversy far from his side. And it was another note of triumph which was ruefully recorded back in South Wales by those who had let a player of international class slip away for nothing.

For Chinaglia himself the moment of glory would have come as no real surprise. In such a career of highs and lows his belief in his own ability had kept him in the forefront of his profession when men of lesser character might have cracked. For those whose job it is to do the hardest task in soccer, that of putting the ball regularly past the opposing goalkeeper, a touch of arrogance is a definitive asset. The tall Italian, who could have become one of the hottest properties in England, who grew to maturity against the most calculating and cynical defences in the world and who quickly recognised the financial and professional possibilities of transferring his allegiances to New York Cosmos, can never be accused of lacking in that respect.

Right: Giorgio Chinaglia's arrival in New York added to the cosmopolitan make-up of the roster, teaming up with Pele from Brazil and Beckenbauer from West Germany. Rumours were rife that it was not the happiest of marriages, but differences were set aside in the Soccer Bowl of 1977 when the Cosmos won the play-offs. They beat Seattle Sounders 2–1 in Portland, with Chinaglia becoming the hero of the hour. In the second half it was his header which clinched the match.

Charlie Cooke

'The sort of players I envy are those like Johnny Boyle. They may not be spectacular crowd-pullers, but they do their job well – all the time. And they're always in action.'

It might seem strange that Charlie Cooke, with all his splendid gifts, should be envious of his former team-mate with Chelsea in London and later the coach at Tampa Bay; Boyle, totally whole-hearted, was a journeyman. But then the obvious and the uncomplicated just do not associate themselves with Charlie Cooke.

In 1969, at a time when Cooke was an irregular member of Chelsea's first team and following his selection for the Scottish national squad, Hugh McIlvanney, the London sportswriter who knows him better than any other, wrote in *The Observer*. 'To be considered one of the best 22 players available to Scotland without being recognized as one of the best 11 available to Chelsea is by no means the greatest paradox in the life of Charlie Cooke.

'He is plagued by more fundamental contradictions, most of all by the dark suspicion that he is a hero without a role; that the excitement associated with his name is a capricious invention of the public, an aura to which he is not entitled.'

Cooke's unusual position is as much the result of his own searching self-examination as it is of his soccer playing prowess. He questions, for instance, the way his life has been organized: 'Professional soccer players are like babies', he once said. 'We go abroad and they count us on and off the bus, on and off the plane. They take our passports, look after our baggage, pay our bills, order our food. They don't stick labels round our necks, but that's about all.'

At times, when the whole business exasperated him, he reflected that playing soccer was a bloody silly way to earn a living, and asked himself why he did it: 'I'm one of the most selfish bastards alive, but when I'm out there I'm not doing it for personal glory. I'm not doing it for money to keep the wolf from the door. I'm not doing it for a 50,000 crowd. I'm doing it so that a handful of people I really respect can hold their head high in a pub when they say "Yes, I know Charlie Cooke".'

Whatever the personal doubts, Cooke's talent has never been the subject of controversy. From the schoolboy days in Greenock, to Juvenile Port Rovers to Renfrew Juniors, he stood out as a kid who could work the ball in what has come to be accepted as the classic Scottish manner. In addition he was blessed with a jagged streak of pace.

It was assumed, as with so many young Scots of real potential, that his ability would take him to one of the big Glasgow duo, Celtic or Rangers. But his partner at Renfrew was a sturdy wing-half called Jim Geddes, a lad who did Cooke's donkey-work for him. Jim signed for Aberdeen, who had one eye on Cooke, and within a few days of his 17th birthday Charlie joined his friend.

He spent five years with Aberdeen, a period in which his ability developed in the kind of soccer which does not stifle a player who knows he can do things with a ball. Then in 1964, a difference of opinion with his manager Tommy Pearson led to Aberdeen deciding to part with him.

Rangers were approached and told that the fee was £20,000 ($40,000); even with hindsight that was derisory. The Ibrox board, however, considered that the club had sufficient ball-players of Cooke's type, and the offer was declined.

Celtic were consulted and expressed a keen interest. Then suddenly Dundee, rushed in, slapped down £40,000 ($80,000) and whisked him off to Dens Park. It was a fine piece of boldness by Bob Shankly. One year later, Tommy Docherty, who signed the cheque for Chelsea, showed similar audacity to Shankly in his transfer dealing. A handful of English clubs had watched Cooke – wondered, considered, but waited. Docherty did not.

The signing of Cooke seemed an intriguing move for a man like Docherty to make. He was in the process of dismantling a young side who had faltered on the brink of great things – a brisk, urgent, single-minded side whose style apparently represented the kind of soccer in which Docherty believed.

Yet there he was bringing in a dreamer, a whimsical player, a fellow who put his foot on the ball and rolled it around and preferred the obscure to the obvious, often disappearing up blind alleys of his own making. One of the players who departed as Cooke entered expressed what a lot of people were thinking when he said: 'I don't understand Tom. He's been on at me for bloody seasons to do the simple, quick thing. "Give it and go, make early crosses" he says. Now he buys a bloke who reckons he owns the ball.'

Whatever the snipers thought of Cooke, the Stamford Bridge crowd quickly came to worship him. He was different. There was a little bit of the magician in him.

Chelsea reached the FA Cup Final that season. They had never been to Wembley Stadium before and Cooke helped to take them there. Spurs beat them that day, but then Spurs were used to winning Cup Finals. Chelsea's turn would come.

Docherty left the following season on a tide of acrimony and sensation, and his departure had a marked and lasting effect on Cooke's career.

The new manager, Dave Sexton, was less ready to indulge Cooke's anomalous ability than his predecessor had been. At first, he decided that the Scot was a luxury which Chelsea would not afford, and agreed to trade him. Cooke turned down the move, and he began to adjust.

'Dave Sexton made me a different player, a better player,' he reflected later. 'That "darling of the crowds" bit never meant much to me because I could always see qualities in other players that I wished I had.

'Dave asked for talent, but at the same time he asked for a commitment to a game which was a wee bit foreign to me – a harder, more physical game. I worked at it because I could see the merit of it.'

Sexton managed to utilize Cooke's reservoir of skill for the benefit of the team; he made him involve himself in the action; he encouraged him to use that acceleration to thrust out of tight situations, particularly in the middle of the field. And Charlie became a far more effective player, if a marginally less charming one.

He won his fifth Scottish cap, the first for two years, in Sexton's first season, dominating the match with a resourceful display in the 1–1 draw against England. At the end of the season, Chelsea supporters voted him their Player of the Year and, apart from a brief fracas over wages which resulted in a short-lived transfer request, Cooke settled comfortably into his role as a mature and gifted midfield player in a steadily improving side.

Chelsea showed what they thought of his talents when they turned down a £100,000 ($200,000) bid from Villa (managed by Tommy Docherty) in the summer of 1969. And the wisdom of that rejection was underlined the following season when they found themselves back at Wembley to face Leeds in the FA Cup Final.

When he looks back on his career at Chelsea, Cooke may well decide that the Final of 1970 and its replay were the most relevant matches he ever played for the club.

Leeds did everything to Chelsea but beat them at Wembley and, on an atrocious surface, Cooke was never allowed to deploy his skills to real effect. But he ran and fought and grafted as hard as anyone.

The replay struck Cooke as being the most important game he had ever played in, and he prepared accordingly. He went without food or water for 60 hours (from Saturday evening to Tuesday lunchtime) losing so much weight that he had to visit his tailor to have his trousers taken in.

'With less weight I was running farther and faster', he explained. 'At the start I was happy just to stop Billy Bremner destroying us. But as it went on I felt he was weakening and I was getting stronger. And that's when we took them.'

In a match remembered more for its brutality than the quality of its soccer, Cooke had one of the great displays. Aggressive, influential, blending deep-rooted skills with new-found strength, he made Chelsea's decisive contribution that night – his chip to Osgood for the equalizer was supreme – and Sexton was not slow to credit him for the victory.

The following season Chelsea won the European Cup Winners Cup with a victory over Real Madrid in Athens, again after a replay in which he had a fine game, playing deeper following an injury to John Hollins in the first match.

Cooke's attitude to his talent for soccer has always been ambivalent. He doesn't talk so often now about the 'degradation of being paid to take your trousers down in front of 50,000 people, for giving them licence to praise you or tear lumps out of you as they think fit.' And his pleasure after a good performance is not obscured by all

Charlie Cooke spent two spells of his distinguished career with the West London club Chelsea.
Above right: In the days when he moved south from Dundee.
Below right: The more mature Charlie Cooke when he re-joined Chelsea after a disastrous transfer to Crystal Palace.

the downbeat reaction to congratulations. 'Was that all right?' he said to a friend after he had outshone the stars of Real Madrid in Athens. 'Were you quite pleased with the wee man? I didn't let you down?'

But soccer has not always given him sustained satisfaction. The moments of exhilaration have sometimes been outnumbered by others in which he is left unmoved or even miserably disenchanted. It is largely because of this that he has been so vulnerable to distractions. When he is not inclined to be contemptuous about his role as a player, dismissing it as 'poncing about at a boy's game,' the surest way to prove to him that he's not being honest is to remind him of the time he found tears in his eyes as he watched England's defeat by Brazil in Mexico.

'When guys have the sort of qualities those England players showed and they lose, you've got to feel for them' he said. 'Maybe it's a boy's game, but they were men out there. Don't worry about that.'

Charlie Cooke had tears in his eyes for himself when in 1972 his career suddenly seemed to tumble away like a rock in an avalanche. Chelsea sold him to Crystal Palace where his impact was less than sensational. Personal problems took a grip on his sensitive nature; the magician could no longer conjure a trick.

This time others managed it for him, like an American girl, now his wife, who settled his domestic life; like Chelsea who to the surprise of English soccer critics bought him back in 1974. Like George Best he feels his playing days have been lengthened by seasons in the NASL. At 34, Chelsea brought him back into their side of youngsters at the end of the 1976–77 season to stabilise a faltering attempt to regain a place in the First Division. He did the job.

Following another summer with the Aztecs in Los Angeles, his English club again turned to him to help in the adjustment to the top division. So at 35, Charlie Cooke still played in England's First Division. He might have been surprised because ten years earlier he felt that long-service was a reward for only the journeymen he so admired. Charlie Cooke, one-time erratic crowd-puller, proved to be a super-pro.

Below: Packed defences have never deterred Charlie Cooke.
Right: The Dutch soccer master, Johan Cruyff.

Johan Cruyff

'Number 14 is dead' read the headline in a Dutch newspaper, as it described Johan Cruyff's transfer from Ajax Amsterdam to CF Barcelona in September 1973.

Cruyff, the brilliantly gifted forward who for the previous three years had superstitiously clung to a shirt once worn successfully as a substitute, had outgrown Dutch soccer. His speed, ball skills and ruthless finishing ability had been both knife and club in a series of successes that had brought Ajax a hat-trick of European Cup triumphs.

The fee commanded by such a talent was of unique proportions. Barcelona wrote a personal cheque for about £460,000 ($1,000,000), a new record for a player's services. It was chicken-feed; with Cruyff Barcelona leapt from the obscurity of the lower reaches of the Spanish League to the Championship in a matter of months.

At the same time he led Holland in cavalier fashion into the World Cup finals. There, Cruyff and fellow Dutch masters like Johan Neeskens, Wim van Hanegem and Ruud Krol wove a spell of fantasy around the tournament. Their fluid style of play, with Cruyff the conductor of the orchestra, swept aside Uruguay, Bulgaria, Argentina, East Germany – and even Brazil – only to fail in the final when the resolution in Dutch hearts failed to match the magic in their feet.

But that ultimate defeat was hardly a failure considering ten years earlier Holland had been a second-rate soccer country. Cruyff's development, and that of his contemporaries, had lifted the nation into first European and then world standings. From 1970–73, Dutch clubs won the European Cup; Cruyff, with Ajax, claimed three victor's medals.

Cruyff made his debut for Ajax in the 1965–66 season and quickly started to amass goals. In fact he scored in his first match. In 1966, at the age of 19 he was capped for Holland, but in his first international season he ran into trouble. Against Czechoslovakia, he was provoked by a defender, he retaliated and was sent off. That episode earned him a year's suspension from international soccer.

In the 1966–67 season he tore the Liverpool defence to pieces with three goals – two of them at Anfield – in Ajax's 7–3 win in the European Cup. Two years later, again in the European Cup, Cruyff played a major part. Though Ajax lost in the final to AC Milan, Cruyff scored in every round up to then. In the quarter-final against Benfica, with the score from the first two legs 4–4 on aggregate, Cruyff scored two in Ajax's 3–0 win in the play-off in Lisbon. An injury towards the end of that season slowed him down and consequently impaired the effectiveness of the team.

Cruyff's love for the game started at an early age, as he watched the Ajax elite of that time train and eagerly copied their skills. At 15 he joined Ajax, and his talents were quickly recognized.

The lithe youngster packed a lot of power in his right foot but was physically underdeveloped and had a weak left foot. Youth trainer Jany van der Veen made Cruyff train with weights attached to his legs.

In this atmosphere, Cruyff matured quickly. He developed a powerful shot and the ability to score from all angles. Yet this was not his greatest asset. His phenomenal speed, coupled with his superb ball control, made him stand out. He evaded tackles with the ease and grace of a leaping gazelle, leaving full-backs flat on their faces.

When younger he used to enjoy tormenting defenders, but after a couple of injuries he stopped that and concentrated on using his guile and his skill to crack open defences and create the easiest of chances for his fellow forwards. Like the great Real Madrid players, di Stefano and Puskas, the Dutch star had mastered variation of pace which bewildered defenders.

Rinus Israel, captain of Feyenoord and the Dutch national team, and undoubtedly one of the best central defenders on the continent, knew just what it was like to be left by Cruyff: 'Of course you can stop Cruyff,' said Rinus. 'You can stop any player. But his variations are so many, his skill so bewildering that many a time you don't know what he is going to do next. You only know when he has gone.'

In 1971 Ajax won the European Cup after beating the Greek side Panathinaikos 2–0 at Wembley. They didn't play very well, looking complacent, and they never really controlled the play as they could have done. Cruyff too had – by his own high standards – a poor game. Even so, three times in 15 minutes he came down the left flank and had the Greek defence in disorder.

But he was brilliant even by his own standards in the 1972 final against Inter-Milan when his two second-half goals won the game. And his skills stood out in a drab 1973 final in which Juventus fell victims to Ajax. Characteristically he left the Dutch club with a flourish early in the 1973–74 season with a magical solo goal in his last game.

Cruyff's talents are not confined to the soccer field. Under the guidance of his father-in-law he has become an astute businessman; he has marketed his own reputation better than any other soccer player in Europe. His sharp brain is sensitive to language and within a few months of his arrival in Barcelona he was happily chatting in Spanish to his new team-mates. To watch him in action in a post-match press conference after he has played is remarkable. Questions in Dutch, Spanish and English he digests and then provides a fluent answer in the correct tongue; in other European languages too he can make comprehensible comments.

Johan Cruyff is very much his own man, and he jealously guards his family life When he captained Holland to qualification for Argentina in 1977, he stated categorically that he would not be available for selection for the World Cup finals. After coming so near in Munich he refused to welcome another chance of the greatest prize. His wish was to remain with his wife and children.

All of Holland prayed he would change his mind. So too did soccer fans everywhere. The gallery of the World Cup would be vastly poorer for the loss of the Dutch master.

Right: Johan Cruyff sets off alarm bells in the Uruguay defence during the 1974 World Cup finals.

Alfredo di Stefano

If Pele was the undisputed King of soccer, there are only a handful of players who can be mentioned in the same breath – Beckenbauer, Best, Cruyff, Muller, Puskas . . . and Alfredo di Stefano. If Pele's skills won over the United States to soccer, di Stefano changed the concept of the game in Europe.

In the mid-fifties UEFA, the European Football Union, finally persuaded the insular-thinking clubs of a number of countries to take part in an international competition. The tournament, now the prized European Cup, might have been a nine-game wonder in that experimental year of 1956 had not Spain's Real Madrid unveilled a breath-taking style of soccer that made previously reluctant countries sit up and take notice. Real Madrid were to win the European Cup for its first five years and they were brilliantly led by Alfredo di Stefano.

His talents were abundant. He was a fine leader, had a sprinter's acceleration coupled with faultless control, and could pass the ball superbly – often to Gento, whom he could find instinctively on the left wing, or to Puskas, usually splitting the defence. And his accurate, powerful shooting brought him countless goals. These abilities were welded together by his exceptional stamina, and permeating his whole game was a mature understanding of soccer. His strategy was almost beyond analysis.

But after packing away his famous boots – he was past 40 then – he quickly realized that the aura of his playing days would not last for ever, nor would it carry him very far in the altogether different and uncertain managerial world.

He realized he had a new job to learn, one that involved diplomacy, handling men and the creation of a good press and public image. So di Stefano matured. He became more friendly and quickly appreciated the value of communication; he even started talking to the press.

Born in Buenos Aires on 4 July 1926, di Stefano received his first football lessons from his bus-conductor father, himself a useful amateur centre-forward. Alfredo says, 'I was right-footed, so he wouldn't let me play unless I shot only with my left foot. He always said that with one foot I'd never be a footballer.' It was sound advice for a six year old all those years ago.

However, when he was 15, di Stefano was nearly lost to football. His family, rallied by his mother, thought that he should become a farmer and carry on an old family tradition. But di Stefano's father was adamant. 'Alfredo was born and bred in the city . . . I'm not banishing him to the lonely prairie. Besides, he can't play soccer with cattle.' And so di Stefano entered a business college, where the facilities for sport gave him the opportunity to develop what – even then – were obvious football talents.

At 17, the young di Stefano was the veretan of his district team, Barracus ('We never lost a match'), where one day he was discovered by the manager of River Plate, Lubrowski, and signed as an amateur. 'In River's amateur teams there were so many of us that we were all substitutes for the substitutes,' recalls di Stefano.

He then moved to Huracan, on loan, for one year before returning to River Plate as a professional. Immediately he gained a first-team place and overnight he became the idol of River's crowds. During his three-year stay at River Plate, di Stefano won a league title medal and was once the league's leading scorer. He played in seven internationals for Argentina.

Then came the first di Stefano 'mystery'. In 1949–50, at the height of his Argentine fame, he suddenly left River Plate and signed for Los Millionarios of Bogota, a newly-formed club with ambitions to sign the best players. The Buenos Aires public were critical of a move that they could not understand.

But di Stefano maintained, 'There was no mystery.' Colombia were anxious to improve their soccer and badly needed experienced players. Los Millionarios offered financial terms that were 15 times higher than in Argentina. Many players accepted the carrot – an exodus that was responsible for the eclipse of Argentina in the 1958 and 1962 World Cups.

Di Stefano stayed with Los Millionarios for three and a half years, helping them win two league titles, in 1950 and 1952.

His departure surprised everyone and started another furore, this time in Spain. In September 1953, Spanish newspapers went wild with delight when Real Madrid announced they had signed the Argentinian star, then 27 years of age, for four years. Real paid Los Millionarios £10,000 ($25,000) for his transfer and di Stefano received £4,000 ($10,000) a year from them. His contract with Real was twice renewed on improved terms, and at the peak of his career, di Stefano was the highest-paid player in the world.

But within hours of di Stefano's signing for Real came a fierce protest from Barcelona. They, of course, had heard of his fame and ability and, behind the scenes, had made moves to obtain his signature. Their disappointment at losing him to their rivals created one of those 'affaires' which have rocked soccer in Spain through the years.

It was not until the president of Los Millionarios personally intervened in the public controversy over di Stefano, officially declaring that he had promised di Stefano to Real more than a year before, that the dispute in any way abated.

Madrid's president, D. Santiago Bernabeu, had been first impressed with di Stefano during Real's mid-40s South American tour. Bernabeu had wanted to sign him 'before anyone else realizes how good he is.' Fellow directors calmed his enthusiasm and persuaded him to wait. And he did. But in 1952, when Los Millionarios played in Real's Golden Jubilee Anniversary tournament, Bernabeu saw a more developed di Stefano and was even more obsessed with the idea of buying him. He spent hours trying to persuade the Colombian club to release their star player, and even enlisted the aid of di Stefano's wife. But he failed, although he was told by Millionarios 'When we decide to transfer him you will be first to know.' A year later the Bogota club kept its word.

Di Stefano scored in his first league game for Real Madrid, against Santander on 27 September 1953, and during the 11 subsequent years he was a Real player, he

remained continually in the world headlines . . . winning
five European Cup medals, one World Club championship,
eight Spanish League medals, becoming the league's
leading goalscorer five times and collecting countless
other honours. In 1957, after he had taken Spanish
nationality, di Stefano made the first of 31 international
appearances for Spain. His 23 goals for Spain were a
record for his adopted country.

His popularity was unbelievable, in spite of his strange,
temperamental character. The public worshipped him,
though for his talent alone; di Stefano never gained the
really deep affection that crowds would show for Bobby
Charlton, Puskas or Pele.

Indeed, many people attributed the fabulous, glittering
'Golden Era' of Real Madrid between 1956 and 1964
entirely to Don Alfredo. But though di Stefano undoubtedly
played a vital part in Real's success, the Spanish club's
world-beating displays were never a one-man show. Di
Stefano was the brain and, until Puskas arrived, scored
most of the goals, but the ceaseless service and cooperation of his often equally brilliant colleagues paved
the way.

In August 1958, Alfredo's 'wonderful world' was
disrupted a little by the signing of Didi, Brazil's key
World Cup midfield player. The talented Brazilian signed
for Madrid amid a fanfare of publicity. Nothing quite like
it had ever been seen in the capital, But, a few months
later, after completing only part of his contract, Didi
returned mysteriously to Buenos Aires. It caused a
sensation.

Years later, Didi gave his story. 'I arrived in Madrid
hailed as the best player in the 1958 World Cup in
Sweden. Everyone was talking about Didi. It was Didi,
Didi wherever you went. Di Stefano didn't like this
excitement; he naturally felt it might reflect on his own
popularity and he became very anti-Didi both on and off
the field. In many matches I was completely ignored.

'Naturally this kind of thing reflected upon the team's
form. Rather than see a great team disintegrate, I approached president Bernabeu for a release of my contract.
He understood the problem and we parted the greatest
of friends.'

When di Stefano was asked about the problem he said,
somewhat tersely, 'I had no problem with Didi. He
neither reached his normal form nor fitted into the side
as Real Madrid thought he would. If a player is in-
compatible, that is not the fault of another player. Didi
was just unable to produce his best form or fit into the
side. Nothing more.'

Whatever the reason, Didi certainly did not fit in.
And nor did a number of other stars like Canario, Tejada
and Kopa – though Kopa did last three years. But why
should so many players leave Real so soon after joining the
club?

*Top and above right; Di Stefano scoring two of his three goals
during the 1960 European Cup final at Hampden Park. It was the
fifth successive final in which he had scored.*
Right: Di Stefano practising in the Bernabeu stadium.

127

Their departure left di Stefano *the* player of Real Madrid, which of course, he liked, although with the arrival of Ferenc Puskas a little after Didi, the limelight had to be shared. The Hungarian was a different, more cheerful, carefree character than di Stefano . . . but the two became famous friends, linking almost magically on the field, and with Rial, Gento and Kopa, there emerged the greatest forward line of any team, anywhere in the world.

The story behind Puskas somehow hitting it off with di Stefano has passed into soccer's folklore. It concerns the last match of Puskas' first season with Real, when he and di Stefano were joint leading goalscorers in the Spanish First Division. Puskas, with an easy chance to score, made a gift of the goal to di Stefano, and from then on they were firm allies. In the 1960 European Cup final, when Real gave their memorable exhibition against Eintracht Frankfurt at Hampden Park, these two scored all seven of Real's goals between them.

Time marched on, slowly and successfully for Alfredo. Then in 1964 came the news of his move from Real Madrid to Espanol, the first division Barcelona side. The trade came as a shock, and gossip spread. 'Di Stefano was a law unto himself. The team had to conform to di Stefano. He was temperamental. The player had become at cross-purposes with his colleagues and Miguel Munoz.'

Real manager Munoz never once entered the controversy. Six years later he did break his silence, and although he still spoke cautiously, the point was taken. 'A manager had to do his job, and when the moment comes to fulfil his obligations on behalf of the club that pays him, he has to do what is necessary.' And so di Stefano left for Barcelona.

'I did not leave Real Madrid with enmity,' he remembers. 'Why should I? Every manager has his obligations and there always comes a time when he has to rescind the contract of a renowned player. If it's in the best interests of the club, well. . . .'

Di Stefano stayed with modest Espanol for two years, years that must have been frustrating, even an anticlimax. Later, after taking the Federation's managerial course, he took up his first appointment with Elche.

In 1968–69 Alfredo returned to his homeland and became personal adviser on technical matters to Don Alberto Armando, president of Boca Juniors.

Unfortunately, di Stefano's dour, unapproachable character had preceded him and from the beginning the Argentine press was anti-di Stefano. No one questioned his playing and his technical abilities or his experience. His remarkably unwavering dedication to the game was immediately held as an example to all. But his manner and his inability to establish cordial relations with people and the press brought the most bitter criticism from sensation-seeking sports writers. He was 'difficult', they said, and 'totally unsuitable as a presidential adviser and as a club official.'

But with one or two selected aides, he patiently made a thorough search of the country for new and unknown players. 'I want young players . . . players with spirit and fight . . . though but fair players . . . and most im-portant of all I want soccer players, not matadors.' And so the rebuilding of the ailing Boca Juniors began.

The following season, 1969–70, di Stefano was appointed manager-coach of the club, and the real transformation took shape. Defensive thinking and the old 4-3-3 system were discarded. Di Stefano had Boca Juniors play with two authentic wingers and at times with seven forwards. Ruthlessly he dropped long-serving players and blooded his discoveries – all of them promising youngsters, and all hitherto unheard-of players.

The most difficult task di Stefano had to face was telling the famous Antonio Rattin, captain of the national side and idol of Boca Juniors for 12 years, the greatest stopper centre-half Argentina had ever produced, he was the architect and pillar of the negative, defensive outlook which di Stefano maintained had caused Boca Juniors' decline.

Rattin took the news philosophically for, despite his martyrdom in the 1966 World Cup, he was a true professional. He retired gracefully into the shadows. But the newspapers erupted as never before. Rattin's photograph occupied the full front page of several newspapers. Leading articles demanded his immediate reinstatement, petitions were organized, demonstrations launched. The press demanded . . . and howled. But di Stefano rightly refused to be intimidated, remained unmoved and continued with his policy of rejuvenation. To his credit Antonio Rattin remained silent.

As the season progressed, di Stefano's radical policies brought success. Under his inspiration Boca Juniors won the national championship in a grandstand finish – an away draw – with their eternal rivals and his old club, River Plate. A record, police-limited crowd of 75,000 people acclaimed Boca's achievement.

When his year's contract with Boca Juniors ended, he unobtrusively rejoined his large family – six children – in Madrid. He just could not settle down in his homeland, he had become too Spanish. Soon after his return, Alfredo signed his first contract with Valencia on 2 April, 1970.

Twelve months later, Valencia became Spanish League champions for the first time in 24 long and very frustrating years. With a tradition of mediocrity, they acquired, through the guidance and influence of di Stefano, a professionalism and dedication which brought them the consistency so necessary in Spain's short league programme.

Di Stefano's comments on his success at Valencia show just how much he had changed. 'Everyone talks about my success. But it's not mine. The success belongs to the players. I have helped them in physical and technical preparation, but it was they who fought throughout the season with such unbelievable enthusiasm and determination.' That – giving credit to other people – was certainly not Alfredo.

There may have been better players than Alfredo di Stefano in some minor details, but few could challenge him as *the* complete player, the greatest forward of his time, and with the exception of Pele, perhaps the greatest of them all.

Eusebio

On 28 August 1976 in Seattle, another chapter was written in the glittering career of Portugal's most famous forward. In the NASL play-off final Toronto Metros beat Minnesota 3–0. The great Eusebio had taken a Cinderella team all the way to the ball.

The striker from Mozambique, who became known as the 'European Pele', had played a few games for Boston in 1975. In 1977 he switched to Las Vegas. As the soccer boom spread across America, the NASL could only benefit from the presence of one of Europe's legendary goalscorers and his talents, which were first unveiled on an international stage in October 1961.

He was stalking the midfield when the ball was pushed through to him. Gathering it and accelerating in one movement, he was streaking for goal before England's defence had time to form. Racing into the penalty area, he glanced menacingly at the far corner of the goal the second before his right foot pummelled the ball out of the goalkeeper's reach.

But for the second time in the match, the dark-skinned youngster was beaten by the cross-bar. His expressive face showed all the frustration and disappointment of a small boy who has found the sweet cupboard but cannot open it.

Luck was not with Eusebio that day. And when Wembley Stadium emptied, England had an unsettled defence and an alarmed goalkeeper, but two goals. Portugal had just Eusebio's near misses.

Eusebio had taken everybody unawares. Before the game, his name had meant nothing to players, press or public. But so devastating was his performance that he was soon the focus of everybody's attention. With each electrifying run past defenders, with each of his massive shots, there was a general shaking of heads and reference to the programme from the press box to the stands.

In the sports pages of the newspapers and in pubs all over the country, there was one topic of conversation the next day, and it was not England's victory.

The black, athletic forward – still a teenager – had won his first cap only days earlier against Luxembourg. Then, with only Eusebio's 25 appearances for Benfica to draw on for experience of top-class soccer, it had seemed that Fernando Peyroteo, the Portuguese manager, was either desperate for players or astonishingly confident in the youngster's abilities. He was not desperate.

And on his international debut, just 19 years old, Eusebio had justified his manager's confidence in him with the kind of goal that would become the hallmark of his game: pouncing on the ball, twisting and sprinting past two or three defenders, then smashing it into the net.

It is that shot, one of the most powerful in the history of association football, plus his speed of thought and action that made Eusebio one of the world's most explosive strikers. The European Pele could win matches on his own.

Top right: The power in the boots of Eusebio and, right, another example of his unerring finishing.

This was never more in evidence than in England in 1966, during Portugal's World Cup quarter-final against North Korea. As the lightweight Koreans scampered to a 3–0 lead over the powerful Portuguese, the 1,500 or so Iberians scattered around Goodison Park clung to Eusebio's reputation like a drowning man to a lifebelt.

And it was entirely due to the pride of Benfica that Portugal were not, after Italy and Brazil, the third fancied team to leave the World Cup prematurely.

Eusebio first struck terror into the Koreans with a murderous shot on the half-hour. His direct penalty minutes before half-time sounded the death knell. Fifteen minutes after the change round, Eusebio sent Simoes racing clear down the left touchline, then tore forward to meet his cross with a right-foot volley that ripped into the net and was just a blur on the action replay.

Once more Eusebio was to run on into the Korean goal, retrieve the ball he had put there and carry it urgently back to the centre circle. North Korea 3, Portugal – in the person of Eusebio – 4. Augusto added a welcome fifth, but the Korean's resistance had long since been destroyed.

Indeed 1966 was a very good year for Eusebio. The £1,000 ($2400) cheque for the top scorer in the World Cup found its way – via his nine goals – into Eusebio's luggage. And though he finished third behind Bobby Moore and Jack Charlton in the voting for the best of the World Cup soccer players, Eusebio was acclaimed in the world press as 'the most spectacular player in the World Cup, who is now greater than Pele.' 'Here is pure and instinctive genius,' commented one newspaper.

That Eusebio should be universally known by his Christian name is appropriate enough for one of the world's most popular players. One of eight children, the full name given him was Eusebio da Silva Ferreira. It was 25 January 1942, and Pearl Harbour had just changed the course of the War. But in the tiny house in the colourful native quarter of Lourenço Marques, Eusebio's birthplace and the capital of Portuguese East Africa, it was a happy time.

Eusebio was born to poverty. His father died when he was only five years old, and his mother had to bring up Eusebio and the rest of the family single-handed. It was while running errands for his mother than Eusebio played his first game of soccer, when the local youngsters were one short for a kickabout. From that day on, in Eusebio's own words, 'I had soccer under my skin.'

Soon Eusebio was going to school, and like most soccer-mad youngsters, he could not wait for school to end every evening – the signal for two hours' soccer. Eusebio was already a good basketball player, as well as junior champion at 400, 200 and 100 metres, sprinting the shortest distance in the excellent time of 11 seconds. Most sportsmen in Mozambique knew of Eusebio, few foresaw his destiny.

It was Hilario, at that time just a friend and neighbour and not yet an international, who eventually persuaded Eusebio to join his soccer club, the Lourenço Marques Sporting Club. It was not that Eusebio did not want to play soccer seriously, it was just that he had always been a supporter of Sporting's rival, Desportivo!

However, he at last agreed – a decision that was to have far-reaching consequences – and by 17, soccer was Eusebio's livelihood.

He scored a hat-trick on his debut for Sporting Club, against Juventude, and with his help Sporting reached second place in the Mozambique championships that season. There was soon talk in the Lisbon press of Eusebio heading towards Europe.

The first formal invitation came from Benfica, whose offer was worth nearly £3,500 ($6,000) to Eusebio alone. Promptly, Sporting talked in terms of £1,400 ($2,500) for him if he stayed. But it was too late. With the idea of going to Lisbon, to the great Benfica, Eusebio's mind was already made up. 'For me, Benfica was like a tale out of the Arabian Nights. I slept little that night as it happened.'

But as soon as Eusebio got to Lisbon, the trouble started. Sporting Club of Lisbon insisted that he belonged to them, because the Lourenço Marques Sporting Club had originally been formed by Sporting Lisbon fans, and the two clubs had for years had an agreement about promising players.

So Eusebio spent the next seven months training furiously on the beaches of the Algarve, while Sporting and Benfica and the lawyers wrangled over his signature. Eventually, in May 1961, everything was settled, and on the 23rd, Eusebio donned the Benfica red shirt. He got three goals for them in what was a private match against Atletico.

His official debut was less exhilarating. The second leg of a Portuguese Cup tie, Benfica kicked off 3–1 up against Setubal. Soon after half-time and 3–0 down, the aggregate

score favoured Setubal. Eusebio introduced himself to the crowd with a fine goal that squared the tie, and a penalty award to Benfica soon afterwards invited them into the quarter finals.

But Eusebio missed it, Setubal scored again, and Benfica were out. A crestfallen Eusebio found small comfort in the agreeable comments of the press about his own performance.

A few months later, Benfica, as European champions, met Santos of Brazil in the Paris final of the annual international tournament organized by Racing Club de Paris. With half an hour to go, Santos led 5–0 and it seemed a good opportunity to try out Eusebio in top-level soccer.

'I can't imagine any goal giving me a greater thrill than those I got against Santos,' recalls Eusebio. For those 30 minutes were enough for him to force a destructively in-form Pele to share the stage with him. Eusebio scored a hat-trick of superb goals, and all with ten minutes to spare. His reputation was growing – fast.

In September that same year, he was flown out to Montevideo for the third and decisive match in the World Club Championship series with Penarol. As a newcomer to the side he was strictly ineligible, but he played – Penarol, confident of victory, raised no objections – and scored. But his impressive 20 yard shot only brought him a runners up medal.

He collected another the following season. Earlier he had been at peak form in 'a game I will always remember for its emotion and suspense.' Amsterdam was the venue for the 1962 European Cup final between Benfica and Real Madrid. Puskas' first-half hat-trick gave Real a half-time lead, but two spectacular goals from Eusebio, both formidable right-foot shots, and his

part in Benfica's other three, clinched the man-of-the-match award for him, and the Cup for Benfica.

Eusebio's next three European Cup finals were less fruitful. At Wembley, London, in 1963, he gave his side the lead against AC Milan with a glorious shot, but could not prevent the Italians winning. Two years later, while on the domestic front he collected his third consecutive League championship medal, AC Milan's neighbours, Inter, saw that Eusebio was again on the losing side in the European Cup final.

In 1968, back at Wembley, Manchester United's goalkeeper Alex Stepney saved magnificently from Eusebio when he was clear with just minutes to go – and United sent Benfica to another European Cup final defeat in extra time (overtime).

But while those European set-backs were undoubtedly a tremendous disappointment for Eusebio, he has had his share of soccer's honours. In 1963 he was chosen for FIFA's Rest of the World side to play England, and two years later, he was voted European Footballer of the Year. And eleven years later he was to be a winner in another continent – not just as a player in a championship team but even more important as a key figure in soccer's American success.

Below: The apprehension of the Manchester United wall as they prepare to face a Eusebio free-kick during the 1968 European Cup final. The wall stood firm and Eusebio failed to score as Benfica lost the match 4–1 after extra time. Conspicuous amongst the United players are a youthful George Best, next to the referee, and next along the line, Bobby Charlton. Best, in fact, scored the crucial goal that gave United a 2–1 lead and two of the other goals on the night came from Charlton.

Geoff Hurst

Geoff Hurst didn't exactly set the Kingdome alight. His one season with the Sounders brought him only eight goals in 23 matches. From the only man to score three goals in a World Cup final, the Seattle soccer fan expected more. The big Englishman was not surprised. For years his special brand of soccer talent had escaped all but the most tutored eye.

Geoff Hurst may be best described as the exception which proved the rule that 'nice guys finish last'. No man in soccer has achieved a more certain place in the history of the game whilst so lacking in the qualities allegedly necessary to win fame. For a start he was not born with the exceptional skills that invite the description 'star'; nor, despite a dedication to self-improvement that bordered on the masochistic, was he ever able to acquire them. His game lacked the inventiveness of the genius, the blind courage of the true hero, while his temperament was without the streak of non-conformity that provides the 'character', the arrogance that supports the 'idol'.

It would be fatally easy, in fact, to regard him as a lucky man who somehow, on a sunny and portentious afternoon in July 1966, had stumbled into the right place at the right moment three times, and scored three goals for England against West Germany in the World Cup final. One writer's description of that occasion – 'Geoff Hurst may have proved that in soccer this is the age of the common man, just so long as he can do something as uncommon as scoring three goals in the final' – suggests that the temptation to dismiss the feat and the man was strong.

But too many factors mitigate against the 'lucky man' theory. For one thing, how was it that Hurst was playing in the match at all when, had a vote been taken on team selection, England would have voted 52 million to one to give the number ten shirt to Jimmy Greaves, a true genius and star by any standards.

It is clear now that Alf Ramsey, the man whose one vote counted, had seen in Hurst the man for the hour, had trusted in abilities that most were not to recognize until much later – and that some were never to appreciate at all.

Again, if Hurst's only claim to fame was the staggering consequence of one afternoon's happy incidents, then how was it that a full two years later he was the subject of England's first ever £200,000 ($400,000) trade bid (Manchester United made the bid, and West Ham rejected it in a one-word telegram 'No') at a time when half that amount was considered the ceiling for the best?

Yet again, even the euphoria of 'The Day the World Cup was Won' could not explain how, six years later, Hurst was still disrupting traffic in provincial market towns when making personal appearances in connection with his sports goods business, nor disguise the fact that from him grew a whole generation of attackers goaded through long hot afternoons of instruction with the common 'no, no . . . think of what Hurstie would do'. It is a fact that soon after paying a record £125,000 ($250,000) for Martin Chivers, Bill Nicholson, manager of London rivals Tottenham Hotspur, bought a ticket in a West Ham stand for his signing and told him: 'Sit there and watch the big fellow . . . that's how I want you to play.'

Hurst's physical attributes were not startling. He had two good strong shooting feet (the left better than the right) and a sense of timing and direction that made him a dangerously accurate header of the ball. Other men have boasted as much. He was strong and tall, his massive thighs giving him strength and balance to resist rivals' challenges and the stamina to persist with his own; but he was seldon the biggest or toughest man on the pitch in any game he played.

Hurst had enough instinctive ball control to be a more than competent schoolboy soccer player and later a promising young professional (he won six youth international caps in 1959). Careful application honed those skills to enable him to subsequently match tricks against all but the very best. He had, in total, the playing equipment of an unexceptional pro. It was the extra element, the *thinking* application of those skills, that eventually sent him to the peak of the international game.

The process began in 1961, when Ron Greenwood became the West Ham manager and struck an immediate spark off Hurst with his lectures. Hurst, until this time, had been a dogged wing-half and little more. Indeed, he had become so disillusioned with his lack of progress (he made only eight first team appearances in two seasons) that he was ready for a change of club.

But Greenwood saw in Hurst the strength of character and the eagerness to learn that he needed for the tactical revolution he was about to press. Until this moment centre-forwards were of a type and their duties were simple: big men, they were asked to battle with centre-halves from halfway to the goalmouth in a sort of ritual, and there patiently await the service of passes and centres that other forwards would eventually provide.

Greenwood wanted more, much more. He wanted a forward with the brains and vision to be a mobile target for passes from defence, to be an elusive, unpredictable 'wall' off whom attacks could be built in the opponents' half, and then to be the unfindable, unmarkable late-arriving finisher who would sweep in on goal to deliver the ultimate shot.

Hurst threw himself into the task of learning the role from scratch. He had no example to follow; he was the first, the original. And slowly, painfully acquiring his own precepts, he became magnificently gifted at proving Greenwood's theory.

When West Ham were under attack, Hurst was never still: moving a few paces this way, checking, then turning to sprint in another direction, stopping again to retrace his path, then sliding off on another angled run. It all seemed so pointless, like the meanderings of a man too nervous to keep still. But Hurst knew precisely what he was doing; with a skill that amounted to intuition he was placing himself where he could always be seen, and reached, by a pass the moment one of his defensive team-mates gained possession.

And when those passes came arching out to him, with a

133

consistency only the observant could have seen, Hurst's second task had to be done. With the care that hours of training over months had made possible, he would place the ball with foot, head or chest, precisely down into space, ready for collection by one of the advancing body of midfield men. Now Hurst's job was to disappear.

He found it easier than seems likely. Now rivals' eyes were glued to the swift movement of the ball and the men involved in the second phase of West Ham's play. Defenders found little to worry them in the sight of Hurst wandering off with apparent disinterest to a part of the pitch that seemed to have little connection with the move now building up elsewhere. And the next time they noticed him was often too late – for he would be halfway to the corner-flag saluting a goal struck on the run through a defence now preoccupied with the inquest 'Where the hell did *he* come from? . . . why didn't *you* pick him up? . . . why *me*? . . . didn't *you* see him? . . . where? . . . when? . . . how?'

For Hurst had learnt to become a different sort of scorer. There were the famous who got their many goals with the force of their shooting or heading. There were those who wrecked defences by improbable feats of dribbling. Those who took their goals through sheer agility, or pace or courage.

Hurst was different. He became, simply, the 'man who wasn't there'. Until he scored. 'You can't mark someone who is moving,' he explains. 'You can't impede someone who isn't there, you can't save a shot until it's made, you can't tackle a man who hasn't got the ball. My game was to keep away, keep out of it, out of the goalmouth, out of sight, until the ball was halfway towards the goal-keeper's hands. Then beat him to it.' And that is what he did, better than anyone has done before or since – racing from deep positions to edge his forehead to the ball an inch before the 'keeper's grab, a toe-cap in front of the full-back's clearance.

One move in particular became his trademark – the near-post goal. He made it famous, and was made famous by its effects. In the years before Hurst, centre-forwards by training, instinct, habit and instruction, always moved to the far side of goal to meet centres; the theory being that by waiting at the far post for passes they gave themselves the entire goal to aim at. Greenwood reasoned that the 'bad centre', apparently dropped too short, caused goalkeepers and defenders to relax and left them at the mercy of forwards arriving late from positions behind them and out of vision. Hurst proved the theory accurate.

A large proportion of the goals he struck in those learning years (from 1963 to 1966) came from this move. Greenwood, uncharacteristically, was once moved to gloat: 'Hurstie has been doing this for three seasons, and rivals still haven't worked out what he's doing. They reckon it's a fluke . . . that happens week after week.'

But if the rivals were slow on the up-take the fans, even West Ham's own, were hardly more perceptive. For Hurst was few people's idea of a good player; most of the praise for the success of West Ham in the early sixties went to his extravagantly skilled team-mate,

Johnnie Byrne, and Hurst was still being barracked as 'that great cart-horse' by the Upton Park following.

One important man, however, shared Greenwood's perception: Alf Ramsey. In the 1965–66 season Hurst was selected for the England squad for the first time – to the astonishment of most including Hurst himself. 'I suppose I'd rather come to accept most people's verdict on myself – a willing trier,' he said later. 'I felt I was doing a good job for West Ham. But England? It never seemed likely. I was terrified of mixing with all the big names of the game.'

Hurst's modesty put him in trouble with Ramsey right at the start. At the first England training session he made a point of keeping out of the limelight, backing hurriedly into the background, contributing nothing to discussions, and only an orthodox minimum to practice matches. 'I wasn't getting the passes as I needed them and I was too shy to say so. I mean, how could I start criticising people like Bobby Charlton.' Ramsey, as ever shrewdly alert to the nuances, spotted Hurst's problems and called him to one side. 'Listen here,' he said. 'I picked you in this squad because you're good enough to play for England. But I can't make you an international player. You've got to do that yourself, there's nothing I can do. All the players in this squad are equals. You're here on merit. So for God's sake stop hiding yourself and start taking part.'

A few days later Hurst exploded at the lack of perceptive passes he was receiving from England colleagues and began shouting at everyone in sight. 'It just came naturally. If I'd stopped to think I would never have dared do it. But the point is they all took it naturally, as though I was, in fact, their equal. From that moment on my problems just fell away.'

Well, not quite, Hurst, after making his debut against West Germany and holding his place against Scotland and Yugoslavia, still had to suffer a terrible pre-World Cup tour to Scandinavia, when his own play was appalling and Ramsey's faith was tested to the limit. And he still had to suffer the torment of sitting on the sidelines to watch England struggle through the first three matches of the finals without him.

It was after the third game, when Hurst returned to the hotel to find Greaves nursing a vicious gash in his shin, that he sensed he might after all have a part to play in England's greatest test. Hurst came into the team, scored the only goal against Argentina with a text-book copy of that West Ham near-post play (his club team-mate Martin Peters made the pass), helped England beat Portugal in the finest match of the series by making a goal for Charlton – and then sat down to wait to discover whether he or the now fit Greaves would be chosen for the final. 'The longest hours of my life,' Hurst has said of those pre-decision days. 'I knew Jimmy was getting better, but I didn't know how *much* better. I was afraid to even ask him how he felt — because he was a friend of mine and if he'd answered "fine" I would have hated him.'

History records that, finally, it was Hurst who got the vote, Hurst who got the goals, and England who won the trophy. What history does not say is the effect that afternoon's work had on the player and the man.

He knew within hours that his life would change. Suddenly he was 'someone' in the game. 'Before the final I used to ring up this posh restaurant for a booking, and tell them I was a friend of Bobby Moore's to make sure I got a table. Now I was able to ring up and give my own name. That's one thing that showed the difference.' There were soon to be many more changes.

Within days every post and every phone call brought an invitation or an offer; everyone wanted to meet, or to use, the man who had scored three in the final. Hurst, obviously, was in a position to capitalize on his fame. He was going places. The question was: did he need an 'image' to extract the full value from the commercial overtures?

Hurst and two journalists, friends who had been asked to help, debated the problem for hours. Perhaps he should grow his hair long (in 1966 that would have been a gimmick) . . . perhaps he should be 'coached' to pungent comments . . . perhaps he should start adopting mannerisms on the pitch that would stamp him a personality . . . perhaps he should begin sensationalizing his lifestyle. At every suggestion the two journalists looked at Hurst – and shook their heads. Nothing so contrived seemed to fit the man. Finally one blurted out, 'For God's sake, this is nonsense. What we have here is a straight, natural nice guy. Why not let him be himself and leave it at that?'

So it was decided. And in the next few years Hurst wrote columns for newspapers, appeared on television and radio, made speeches, opened stores, endorsed products and continued to play soccer in a manner that came naturally. The 'image' grew of its own accord: this was the son parents would have chosen for themselves, the boy the favourite daughter brought home to tea, the friend men would have liked to have had, the nice lad from next door, the star with the common touch, the idol with his feet on the ground.

On the pitch Hurst's image was different and, in a way, greater still. He went back to club football after Wembley bursting with confidence: 'I felt ten feet tall, and I found myself playing in a way I had thought only those others, the stars, would have dared.' A new dimension was added to his game overnight, as the unselfish maker of space for others started to turn with the ball and destroy defences with a deliberate-looking but oddly effective dribbling style.

This was a new and infinitely more dangerous Hurst – he scored 29 League goals in the post-World Cup season and six in one game against Sunderland in October 1968 – and it was now a talent that even the least aware of fans were forced to appreciate. Hurst recalls: 'The greatest encouragement of all was to notice the difference in attitude of rival players. Now I could hear them calling each other for help – "for chrissake don't leave me alone with this bloke. Get back quick." It did wonders for my confidence.'

But there was a price to be paid. Now Hurst had a shadow behind him in every match, and many of them were not particular how they chose to meet this new and

Geoff Hurst in the red and white stripes of Stoke City. Hurst went to the Potteries when his first-class career was nearly over, and he never really made a significant mark. He later moved to West Bromwich before dropping out of the League altogether.

greater threat. Hurst's speciality, arriving quickly to play that first ball back to midfield colleagues, left him particularly vulnerable to the deliberate late tackle from behind. The backs of his legs and, eventually his spinal muscles, were to take terrible punishment in the following seasons. He became, in fact, a symbol of the uncomplaining victim of a regime of defensive ruthlessness that went on unchecked until a referees' revolution in 1971–72. 'The crunchers are getting away with murder – look at what they're doing to Hurst' became the slogan of the swelling voice of the reformers.

Hurst's equanimity during these punishing years bordered on the miraculous. Fouled a dozen times a match, limping at the end of most, he never retaliated or lost his temper. Except once. And Greenwood still recalls that incident as his definition of professionalism. 'Geoff had been kicked in the back about ten times by this bloke and when it happened again something seemed to snap. He grabbed the ball, I could see his face white with rage, and rushed at the offender. I thought he was going to smash the ball in his face, and I could have understood and forgiven him if he had, it had been so blatant. Instead, Geoff got a grip on himself after about three strides, and while still running he put the ball down, took the kick and was sprinting for the return pass as this other bloke stood there petrified with his hands up to protect himself. *That* was professionalism.'

Two other stories illustrate Hurst's attitude to his chosen calling. In 1967, towards the end of his first and only discussion with West Ham about wages (he had been paid since 1966 at his old pre-World Cup rate), he signed a new contract that would tie him to the club for six years – with the spaces for the pay and bonuses still left blank, 'Ron Greenwood asked me to trust him, and I did. I knew I'd done my bit for the club, so why should they try and cheat me?'

The other story dates from 1969, when Hurst became dissatisfied with his game and talked himself into believing that a change of club would lift him out of a rut. He asked to be traded – only to discover to his horror that England team-mate Martin Peters had made precisely the same request 20 minutes earlier. 'I couldn't do that to the club, not the two of us on one day,' said Geoff. 'How would it have looked to outsiders? So I walked back in and withdrew my request. It seemed the only decent thing to do.' While Peters soon left for Tottenham Hotspur in British

soccer's first £200,000 ($400,000) trade, Hurst settled loyally back into the 'rut' with West Ham – though he knew Manchester United would have made him rich had he persisted with his demand.

Hurst was to remain a West Ham player for another three years. He also remained an England regular, though the criticism of his continued selection at international level grew steadily – along with that of Ramsey. He became the symbol of the manager's loyalty to the 'old guard' of 1966. As it was, none of his rivals for the job could match Hurst's consistency and, despite some unnecessarily cruel and often illogical, shallow attacks, he maintained both his contribution to the side and his place in it.

Hurst certainly did well from the game. By 1972 he, his wife Judith and two small daughters were living in a house in Essex worth perhaps twice the £20,000 ($50,000) it cost him, he drove a Mercedes and was sufficiently established in a sportsgoods business to think briefly about an offer to give up the game and concentrate on selling soccer boots.

That offer came at a moment of rare despair. Hurst had just been dropped from the England squad for the return match with West Germany in the European Championship – the news coming all the harder in that he heard it secondhand and not directly from Ramsey. Two days of hard thinking persuaded him that, while he could live without the money from soccer, he was not ready to live without the game.

Finally, in 1972 he left West Ham; 'You can be too long in one place.' He teamed up with Stoke City and later had a spell with West Bromwich Albion, about the time of his flirtation with the NASL. But business commitments kept him in England – he owns two flourishing traditional British pubs – and he remained in the game as manager of semi-professional Telford United. When Ron Greenwood became England's team manager in 1977 he turned to Hurst for assistance with coaching. The former England warrior jumped at the chance to help out his country again.

Two tributes paid to him towards the end of his career emphasize his quality. Nobby Stiles said of his old England team-mate: 'Watching Hurst at first, casually, you see nothing. Studying him carefully you start noticing qualities in his play that surprise you. Then when you play against him you realize he's a bit special. He must be the game's most solid ghost. You can't pin him down or keep him out. But it's when you play *with* him that you really know. He's got an instinct for being in the right place at the only right time, and he chases so hard it's almost impossible to give him a bad ball.'

One journalist wrote, at the time of a testimonial dinner to Hurst: 'A few have played more often for England, some may have scored more League goals. There may have been players who have shown equal courage, similar determination, introduced to tactics as much thought, or taken greater punishment with less complaint. But it is the total claim of the man that makes it clear that the bitter remark "Fame, somehow, seems too precious to be wasted on the famous" was *not* directed at Geoff Hurst.'

137

Kevin Keegan

For Kevin Keegan, the 1976–77 season was the culmination of a marvellous seven years with Liverpool Football Club. He won his third League championship medal. He gave the outstanding individual performance against Borussia Monchengladbach as Liverpool became only the second English club to win the European Cup. And he became the most expensive player in British history when he was traded to SV Hamburg for £500,000 ($900,000), a move so personally lucrative that it ended any money worries for the rest of his life.

Yet twelve months earlier Keegan lay in the casualty ward of an English hospital while doctors debated whether to perform a major operation. On his way back to his farm-house home in North Wales after appearing in, and winning, the British Superstars competition, he had been crippled with internal pains. In the end the diagnosis was a type of colic, a reaction to the unrelenting pace of his life-style.

The story tells much about the man who followed George Best as the idol of the young. A restless inventive player, adept in midfield, on the flank and particularly as an outright front man, his style on the field is indicative of his personality. Intelligent, competitive and abounding in energy and improvisation. In that appearance in Superstars which had finally caused his body to cry enough, he had crashed to the track during a cycle-race, but insisted on re-mounting to finish and gain a vital point towards his overall win. The tournament was in the off-season, the precious few weeks that top-class soccer players have to recharge their batteries. Keegan preferred the challenge to the more recommended resting on the beach, fitting in the days of competition into a schedule already crammed with personal appearances and business interests.

In hospital he vowed to his charming and loyal wife Jean that he would heed the warning. He kept his word . . . for a week! 'As a professional soccer player I consider I owe the public something. I want to give something back to a game that has been exceptionally good to me. Consequently I find it difficult, and at times impossible, to turn people down. Without knowing the ins and outs of every individual cause, it's impossible to decide which are the more worthy. By doing as many of them as possible I am disappointing fewer people.'

But it took soccer a while before the game decided to be good to Kevin Keegan. His round of schoolboy trials ended in rejection, mainly on the grounds of size – even now he is only 5ft. 8 ins. and weighs around 150 lbs. He eventually joined Scunthorpe United in England's Fourth Division, and it was there that Liverpool's scouts were drawn by reports of an effervescent youngster. Liverpool and Scunthorpe had done business before – two years earlier when they bought Ray Clemence, the goalkeeper who was to become a regular member of the England team. In May 1971 Bill Shankly, the Liverpool manager, invested £30,000 ($70,000) for Kevin Keegan to take his first step along the same path.

His first taste was of the big-time. The very week he signed Liverpool were playing Arsenal at Wembley Stadium in the FA Cup Final. Keegan travelled to London as a spectator and though his new club lost the match he liked what he saw and vowed to reach that level himself. He did not have long to wait.

His first match in the first team, the following August, was nationally televised. His talent shone out like a light. His exuberant style of perpetual motion added another dimension that readily appealed to the English spectator who has been weaned on non-stop action. Kevin Keegan was on his way.

Within eighteen months he made his debut for England, playing against Wales at Ninian Park Cardiff. He was a stimulating ingredient in the Liverpool recipe which won the championship in 1973 and 1976. A mere three years after he had sat gawping at that 1971 Cup final he became a Wembley hero himself scoring twice in Liverpool's 3–0 triumph over Newcastle United. He personally spread his reputation throughout Europe with a series of sparkling performances in the European competitions, helping Liverpool to win the UEFA Cup in 1973 and 1976, in addition to that final flourish in the European Cup.

And yet behind that catalogue of triumphs for Kevin Keegan there have been times of tearfulness. With England not qualified for the 1974 World Cup finals, England went on a summer tour to provide warm-up opposition for certain nations who had earned their place for the extravaganza to be held in West Germany. England did well, drawing with East Germany and beating Bulgaria and it was a high-spirited party which landed at Belgrade airport for the third and final game, against Yugoslavia.

Too high-spirited perhaps because one player started some horse-play as the squad waited for their baggage. That player was NOT Kevin Keegan, but when the Yugoslav security guards took violent exception to the fun and games, it was Keegan they seized. When he was finally released gifts bought for his family had been smashed and his body was not entirely unmarked. An emotional man, his self-control was remarkable and he found a way for revenge by scoring England's second goal in a 2–2 draw when the match was played.

If he had been an innocent victim of mistaken-identity on that occasion, he had no defence two months later. The now-established opening to an English season is a Wembley spectacular between the League Champions and the FA Cup Winners. Keegan's two goals against Newcastle had ensured that it would be Liverpool who would meet Leeds United on August 10th 1974. This time there were only jeers. Along with Leeds' Scottish international Billy Bremner, Keegan was sent off – for throwing retaliatory punches. In the long walk back to the locker-room he tore off his shirt, an act which was interpreted by the soccer authorities as a gesture of disgust. For both offences he was suspended for a month and fined £500 ($1,000). 'It was the second time I'd been hit and you can't just stand there and take it,' was his sad but combative description of the incident.

The following May the pressure told on him again. England were to visit the trouble-torn city of Belfast for a full international for the first time in four years. There were the expected rumours of violence; Keegan is an Irish name and as the most charismatic member of the England party he was an obvious target for threats to his life before the game. Don Revie, the England manager, gave him the opportunity not to travel. Characteristically Keegan replied that he had worked hard to gain his England place and he wanted to keep it whatever the risks.

He played no worse than any other player in a poor England performance in a goalless game. Three days later, back at Wembley, Revie made several changes for the match against Wales. Kevin Keegan was among those omitted. Feeling that he deserved more after risking his life in Belfast he quietly packed his bags and slipped unnoticed out of the team hotel. When the news broke, immediately after the Wales match that seemed to be the end for the Liverpool star. Nobody turned their back on England and got asked again.

Nobody, that it is, until Kevin Keegan. By the end of the week he had put his case to Revie, been forgiven and been selected to play in the final match of the British Championship against Scotland. The already happy ending had another warming twist when England beat their traditional rivals 5–1.

Under Revie, Keegan's international career continued to flourish to a level that few who saw his early matches in an England side would have thought he was capable of attaining. Sir Alf Ramsey had not used Keegan in his club role and he made little impact. Keegan admitted later: 'I have nothing against Sir Alf whom I greatly respected for his success as England manager, but I didn't really fit into his way of things. It was much better for my career when Don Revie took over from him.'

So much better, in fact, that in March 1976 Revie picked him to take over from the injured Gerry Francis as captain of his country. 'I couldn't believe it. I was really thrilled. Playing for England is one thing, but to captain them as well – well that's a bit special, isn't it?'

In 1976 the Soccer Writers of England voted Kevin Keegan Player of the Year, but already his restlessness was reaching the surface once more. Before that 1976–77 season he announced that he wanted to leave Liverpool to play abroad. The Liverpool supporters are the most passionate, the most loyal, and the most humorous throughout Britain; they had taken Keegan to their hearts. His desire to get away bewildered them. Players never volunteered to leave Liverpool. A place in their first-team had, for a decade and a half, been a guarantee of winning medals.

Keegan was adamant, but he was to leave them with a lasting memory. Even by Liverpool's standards that year produced remarkable success. For much of the season they pursued a unique treble. Only an unfortunate defeat by Manchester United in the FA Cup Final thwarted them. Yet they still won the League Championship after a long and tiring tussle with Manchester City and Ipswich. And the real glory came in the lavish setting of Rome's Olympic Stadium in the European Cup Final.

For Keegan the beautiful arena, set in the hills of the Italian capital, held no happy memories. Eight months earlier he had been captain of an England side that had been demoralised, defeated and, in effect, dumped out of the 1978 World Cup finals. But this time he wore the red shirt of Liverpool, not the white of England, and it was as though blood had been pumped into his veins.

Borussia Monchengladbach gave their most experienced defender Berti Vogts – a dogged, disciplined player with the savoir faire to be the successor to Franz Beckenbauer as captain of the national side – the task of subduing Keegan. Vogts was to finish a very poor second in that contest. He had already been twisted and turned by a virtuoso Keegan display before a lunging tackle on his tormentor conceded the penalty from which Liverpool sealed their European Cup triumph.

Adopting an if-you-can't-beat-him-get-him-to-join-you philosophy, Monchengladbach immediately entered the negotiations to try to be the club with which Keegan began his European challenge. But by then the deal had been struck with Hamburg.

With his track record Kevin Keegan would have been ready to cope with any upset in his new career. And he needed to be. Not speaking German he found communication with his new team-mates almost impossible. On the field as well. He earned an eight-week suspension for flattening an opponent who had set out to maim him (interrupted only by a marvellously intuitive performance for England against West Germany when he was completely out of match practice). He even had to endure the taunts of the Liverpool supporters when Hamburg were beaten 6–1 at Liverpool in the Super-Cup competition between European Cup winners and the European Cup Winners Cup winners.

But he bounced back to his best, winning the respect of his new team-mates. Such is his honesty that Hamburg will gain the benefit of the best of Kevin Keegan. But only until the restlessness in his soul rises to the surface once again.

Right: Kevin Keegan on the attack during the game that may eventually be remembered as his greatest performance—the 1977 European Cup final between Liverpool and Borussia Monchengladbach. Keegan led West German and Borussia captain Berti Vogts a merry dance and helped create the atmosphere and the opportunities which gave Liverpool a famous and thoroughly deserved 3–1 victory. The third goal came from a penalty after an electrifying run from Keegan. He started on the halfway-line and was well into the penalty area when Vogts could stand it no longer and brought him down. Neal scored from the penalty and Liverpool were home and dry. That was Keegan's last game for the English champions for he was to move to Hamburg days later for a fee and salary which made him the most expensive and best paid English footballer of all time. He said at the time that this was the way the stars would go—the salaries and tax structure in Europe and America being far more conducive to men in a career which could last, at best only a quarter of a life-time. At Hamburg, though, there were problems and his old club showed their strength over his new club by winning a friendly at Anfield embarrassingly easily, 6–1.

Stanley Matthews

Created OBE in the birthday honours in 1957 and knighted in 1965 'for services to football', Stanley Matthews was a player for 35 years; and for most of that time he was known all over the world as the greatest in English football. He played more than 50 games for England and appeared in three Cup Finals, gaining a winners medal at the third attempt, when he was 38. He was still playing in 1965 and, living in the sunshine of Malta, he was still not an old man in the early sixties; yet his fame, especially to the younger addicts of the game, was already that of a historical figure, a portrait in the select gallery that holds the frozen likenesses of such heroes as Steve Bloomer and Billy Meredith.

What was it like then, to see him in action at the height of his talents? The first feeling, as he runs out on to the field, seemingly unaware of his reputation, is one of surprise. His figure, neither noticeably tall nor short, is unimpressive; his face spare; his skin not ruddy nor brown, as might be expected of an athlete, but pale, tight over his cheekbones and forehead, with the thin hair drawn well back. His raised eyebrows and hooded eyes give him an almost Chinese air of impassivity. He holds himself nervously, with a kind of brittle stiffness, his hands closed and his arms slightly bent. He tries his legs, shifting his weight from one to the other – carefully, as if he were taking an inventory of his muscles, confirming that he has overlooked nothing in his meticulous preparations. There is a tension in him, a restrained anxiety, suggesting that of a schoolboy who hopes he will do well. He pays no attention to the crowd.

As the whistle goes and the ball moves upfield, he jogs forward with that same careful movement, wasting no energy, but with his cool eye shifting, watching intently. He is a little behind the rest of the forward line, with a clear space ahead of him, when the ball comes to him for the first time – as he likes it, straight to his feet. The ball comes fast, but he stops it dead as it reaches him. It is already perfectly controlled as he turns and, at little more than a fast walk, takes it towards the back.

The back, like every other in the game, has heard all about Matthews. He knows that Matthews likes to beat his man by going outside him; he knows that if he rushes his tackle, Matthews will be round him; so he stays near the touchline, watches, and retreats. Matthews continues, in his leisurely way, to bring the ball to him; retreat becomes dangerous. The back holds his ground. Another man comes across in support. Matthews is now very close; the back is within a stride of the ball. Matthews shrugs his shoulders and sways to the left. In that second, with a kind of desperate clarity, we can read the back's mind; this time Matthews is going inside. The ball is held in the curve of Matthews' right foot and that lean, wonderfully balanced figure has swayed so far to the left that it is almost too late to catch him. But not quite – he is a quick strong back, and he goes across in a swift lunge. There is no one there: Matthews is gone – on the outside – flying past him, already yards beyond him, imperturbable as ever; slowing down now to his trot as he obligingly shows the ball to the next crouching defender.

The speed of that sudden sprint, over those few yards, was Matthews' essential secret. With all his other gifts he could still outwit and wrong-foot his opponents, but he would not have left them grotesquely and completely beaten, staggering off-balance, or sitting helplessly facing in the wrong direction – all of which he did, over and over again, to the best defenders in the world.

It would be difficult to convey, to anyone who had never seen Matthews, the extraordinary *moral* effect of his presence in a team. A side facing Matthews – particularly a foreign side whose players had not seen him bundled about in League matches on muddy Saturdays – expected the impossible. They thought so hard about stopping Matthews that they often forgot to give proper attention to the rest of the forward line. It is true – and this is the main point his critics always had against him – that he often gave the defence time enough to assemble its forces; but then the assembly tended to take place around Matthews himself. Wide spaces were left in the middle, and Matthews always knew exactly where those spaces were.

He was never a purely ornamental dribbler. He would stop the game sometimes, standing still over the ball, or tap-tap-tapping it with three men round him, but it was more than ball-control: it was command. With all his certainty of touch, he could look away from the ball, watch the other man's feet, take in the disposition of the field with one cool flickering glance, and place his passes to an inch. No other player in English football ever carried such an atmosphere with him, and his opponents' knowledge of his reputation and fear of his mastery was a weapon for him; and he used it mercilessly. For all his diffidence, skill and delicacy, he was a ruthless player. He would never foul a man, or retaliate when fouled, he was never vicious; but he would beat a man, expose his inferiority, beat him again, and coldly destroy his confidence.

Matthews was a maker of goals. He often scored during his early years with Stoke City, he scored in his first international and (playing at inside-right) he had a hat-trick against Czechoslovakia in 1937, when England won 5–4. But after a few years he changed his tactics. Out on the touchline, he would take the ball right down to the corner-flag, and work in towards goal. His characteristic high centre curved across to drop just beyond the far post, out of reach of the goalkeeper; his ground pass was angled back to the edge of the penalty area.

In both cases the forwards were running on to the ball and the defenders had to turn. Matthews was so far forward with the ball that it was almost impossible for the man receiving it to be offside, his control was so extraordinary that he could hold the ball until a clear opening was made. He was not rushed into bad passes and he never passed at random. The principle is simple. The execution of it, as he did it, required a peculiar temperament and a skill that was almost genius – in fact it required a Matthews. He was a school of football in himself.

This page: Stanley Matthews, the legend whose career spanned three decades and whose name came to be regarded as the equivalent of football in so many corners of the globe. Starting at Stoke, his spell at Blackpool led to his only and massively celebrated club honour (bottom right) when he won a winners' medal in the 1953 Cup final, known forever afterwards as 'Matthews' Final'.

His father was a boxer: Jack Matthews, 'The Fighting Barber of Hanley', with a record of 350 fights, and good enough to appear at the National Sporting Club. He, too, was a lean smallish man, a featherweight, quick and skilful, and by all accounts exceptionally fast and neat on his feet. He drank no alcohol, never smoked, and wore waxed moustaches. Matthews remembers that when he was only a small child the clothes were pulled off his bed at six o'clock every morning, and he had to join his father and two brothers at their dawn exercises; first deep breathing at the open window, then a spell with the chest expander.

Matthews says that, looking back, he is grateful for his father's severity. As a footballer he had reason to be: his wonderful durability was the direct result of that foundation of rigid physical habit – one which he continued – but it must have been hard going at the time.

His unusual quality as a footballer was discovered early. He was a centre-half when he played for his school at 11 – certainly not a defensive one, because he scored eight goals one afternoon – but they soon made him into an outside-right, and within a year of the change he was an office-boy at Stoke City Football Club; at 15 he played two games with the reserves; at 16, 22 games; and on his 17th birthday he signed as a professional, making his first-team debut in March 1932.

Through these years he was still under the severe eye of his father. The physical training continued, and when he was an office-boy his father took charge of his money. With no bus fares, the boy walked the two miles between Hanley and Stoke every day, because the exercise was good for him; when he became a player, half his wages went into a Post Office savings account.

At 18 he was in the first team, Stoke City were promoted, and young Matthews won a Second Division Championship medal; at 19 he played for England. That first international, against Wales at Cardiff, was in September 1934; his last was to be against Scotland in April 1957, when he was over 40.

If Matthews had retained his place throughout that period he would have gained 119 caps in official matches. As it was he won 54 (plus 26 in wartime and victory games) in a rather sporadic international career. Indeed the start was not a good one: the first two displays, against Wales and Italy, even induced one of the leading football writers of the time to accuse him of 'slowness and hesitation' and to conclude that 'perhaps he has not got the big match temperament'.

But Matthews undeniably became a great star, and there was an intensely dramatic quality in the way his great performances were matched to great occasions. Yet none of this was reflected in his personality off the field. There was no flamboyance, no distinction in his manner or his dress, little variety in the flat intonations of his voice, with its accent of the Potteries. His manner was understated and self-contained, his only interest the playing of football, his obsession that of physical fitness. He was rarely in the news except for his performances on the field.

But he had a precise notion of his own value. He stayed 16 years with Stoke, and twice asked for a transfer. The

Matthews (dark shirt) finds Ron Burgess of Tottenham Hotspur difficult to pass in a 1948 FA Cup semi-final. Blackpool won 3–1.

first time produced an extraordinary local demonstration. Thousands of handbills and posters appeared all over the city, bearing the words 'Stanley Matthews Must Not Go'; 3,000 people attended a public protest meeting, and a thousand more paraded outside with placards. Matthews stayed – for nine more years, and then, after being out for a few weeks through injury, he was asked to play in the reserves, rather than force a change in a winning team. He refused, and in 1947 he was transferred to Blackpool. He owned an hotel there (he was thrifty, as one might expect from his background), he trained on the Blackpool ground, and had made it clear he would go nowhere else. So Blackpool got him for what was even then a bargain price – £11,500.

He stayed with them until 1961, and with them found the opportunity to capture a major honour: an FA Cup winners medal. These were Blackpool's good Cup years. They reached the Final in 1948, against Manchester United, and on the eve of the game the Football Writers' Association named Matthews as their first Footballer of the Year. But United won the Cup. 'I would have liked the medal,' Matthews said. 'It's always been my great ambition. I wanted to give it to my son Stanley' – the talented son who did not follow his father into football but, with his approval, made a name for himself some years later in tennis.

Against all probability, Blackpool were back again at Wembley three years later, up against Newcastle United. Matthews was 36 and must have been sure it was his last chance; but Jackie Milburn scored twice and Blackpool lost again.

By this time Matthews' medal, like Gordon Richards' Derby win, had become an object of popular mythology. Thus when Blackpool reached the Final again in 1953 the most unexpected people seemed to be emotionally involved in the result, and the stage was set for what was possibly Matthews' greatest game – though this is an almost impossible selection to make. There had been, for instance, the game against Czechoslovakia in 1937 and the 6–3 win over Germany in Berlin the following year; there were yet to come the 1955 match with world champions Germany at Wembley – when towards the end it was the young men who looked tired and clumsy – and England's 7–2 trouncing of Scotland the same year, with Matthews making five of the goals. That was Duncan Edwards' first international, and Matthews had been playing for England before he was born. These were only a few of the thousands of games he played; yet for most people the Cup Final of 1953 has to be the most memorable.

With only 20 minutes to go, Blackpool were 3–1 down. Then Matthews, at 38 the oldest man on the field, lifted his play into a new dimension – faster, lighter, younger than all the rest, covering the field in his search for the ball, doing miraculous things with it when he captured it, slipping through the narrowest openings, dancing over lunging tackles. His opponents seemed pinned to the ground by their own weight as he flitted through them. His high cross found Mortensen by the far post, and it was 3–2; with two minutes to go, Mortensen slammed

in a free kick from outside the penalty area, and Blackpool were level. With less than 30 seconds left Matthews had the ball again, went inside the back this time, feinted and went outside the next man, took the ball right down to the line, and cut back a hard ground pass – behind them all, behind the defence, and Mortensen racing in – but right into the path of Bill Perry, who met it first time. Blackpool had won the Cup in the most theatrical fashion and Matthews had achieved his last ambition.

Perhaps not quite the last. In 1961 he went back again to Stoke City, then 19th in the Second Division and drawing an average gate of 10,000, for a nominal £2,500. There were 33,000 in the ground on 18 May for the last match of the 1962–63 season, against Luton Town. Matthews was 48. Again the situation seemed dramatically contrived: Luton had to win to avoid relegation, while Stoke needed a point for the Second Division championship and promotion. At half-time they were one up – not enough. Then just after the interval came the goal that settled it – and Matthews scored it. It was his only goal of the season and his last in professional football.

It was a fine finale to an astonishing playing career. There followed a brief period on the administrative end of the game, which ended unhappily. Matthews went from Stoke to take over as general manager of Port Vale, in the Fourth Division, and in 1968 the club were fined £4,000 and expelled from the Football League for making illegal payments to players. They were immediately re-elected but he, much distressed by the affair, resigned. He later managed Hibernian of Malta – just one of the corners of the world where, for years, Matthews *was* football.

Matthews became something of an ambassador for the footballing authorities. He was part of FA tours abroad for many years – here in newly independent Ghana in 1957.

Rinus Michels

'I am often asked which man has influenced my career most of all. Well the answer is simple – Rinus Michels.' That often-stated testimonial comes from Johan Cruyff for a fellow Dutchman who amongst many coaching successes can rightly claim to have transformed Cruyff from a rebellious youth into a player of world class.

'Iron Rinus' has become Michels' nickname because, apart from his obvious flair for developing young players, his is a reputation built on a platform of stern discipline. When he was brought in as managerial overlord to the Dutch squad for the 1974 World Cup finals, he found a set of players of supreme talent bent on destroying their own considerable chances of success. The most publicised problem was a dispute over pay and bonuses involving nine players including Wim Suurbier, Ruud Krol, Arie Haan and Johnnie Rep, all of whom were to play in the World Cup final.

Michels refused to be intimidated and told the rebels that if they didn't want to play for Holland in the world's greatest competition there were plenty of players who did. But it was no grand gesture on his part; instead he shrewdly manipulated the situation so that a compromise was reached and the Dutch squad did not lose the services of the valuable players who were in dispute.

In fact the performance of the Dutch in West Germany in the summer of 1974 finally brought universal appreciation for the coaching and tactical skills of Rinus Michels. With Cruyff implementing his instructions on the field Holland added flair, invention and a dash of magic to the World Cup recipe. Crucial victories over Argentina, East Germany and Brazil – all without conceding a goal – were achieved with breathtaking fluency. Beneath the glitter there was a strength that ensured, particularly against Brazil when the game took on an ugly dimension, that no opposition would be allowed to destroy the skill by violent means.

Michels was denied the ultimate accolade, which fell to Helmut Schoen, of being in charge of the world champions when in the final Holland lost the on-the-field discipline he had imposed and with it their hopes of success. But of that tournament it was the brilliance of the Dutch, more than the victory of the Germans, which left the deepest imprint on the memory.

Like Cruyff, Michels had returned to the Dutch squad from self-imposed exile. The two men who had done most to make the world sit up and take notice of Dutch football had been re-united in Spain at the CF Barcelona club. Michels left Holland in 1971 to take over from Vic Buckingham in Barcelona. It was a strange irony because six and a half years earlier Michels had also followed in Buckingham's shoes at the Ajax club in Amsterdam.

In January 1965 Michels began his duties, still remembered as a midfield player, blessed with unlimited capacity for graft rather than individual technique, but who had still been good enough to play in five internationals for Holland at the beginning of the 1950s. Buckingham had already given the 17-year-old Cruyff his initiation into first-team soccer but the youngster's willful and headstrong temperament had hardly helped him make the most of the opportunity. Cruyff, like many of the older players, did not take easily to the stricter regime imposed by Michels. But when they knuckled down to business the results began to come with impressive regularity.

In Michels first full season in charge, Ajax won the Dutch Championship for the first time in six years. It was no one-off affair. He masterminded Championship wins in the next two seasons and again in 1970 as Ajax came out on top. The domestic success in itself was a considerable achievement but the extra proof of the quality of the Ajax side was more clearly shown in European soccer. Until then, the impact of Dutch clubs on the European Cup had been minimal, but in the 1966–67 competition Ajax reached the last eight, only going out by one goal in the home and away tie against Dukla Prague. In the previous round they had made England sit up and take notice with a 7–3 aggregate success over Liverpool.

Two years later the progress was even more dramatic; this time in the quarter-final Ajax won a famous victory over Benfica from Lisbon in a play-off in Paris. Spartak Trnava from Czechoslovakia were beaten in the semifinal, but Ajax were overcome by the occasion when they lost 4–1 to AC Milan in the final in Madrid. Michels had to wait another two years before the skill of his team-building brought true reward.

Then again Ajax reached the final, this time held in London's Wembley Stadium. The opposition was from Greece, Panathinaikos, coached by the legendary Hungarian, Ferenc Puskas. Ajax won comfortably, 2–0, to start a sequence which was to bring them a hat-trick of triumphs, a run that confirmed them as indisputably the top club side in Europe. But Michels was not there to share in the second and third victories.

The offer which took him to Barcelona was far too lucrative to turn down but when he needed to strengthen his new club his eyes turned again to Holland. His relationship with Cruyff enabled him to bring off a major coup in the transfer market. In 1973 Barcelona stepped in when Cruyff publicly declared himself disenchanted with Ajax and paid a record £925,000 for his services. Cruyff himself received around half that sum but it had not been the money which had made him choose Barcelona. He opted for the mentor who had made him grow up. At the time of his transfer he said: 'What I particularly admire about Rinus is the way he approaches discipline. He's definitely a stern disciplinarian but always a fair one. Our relationship has always been that of player and coach and from him I've gathered a lot of tactical knowledge. His great quality is that he understands just how players think. He also makes it very clear exactly how he is thinking so you get an ideal rapport which makes the squad settled and relaxed.'

Above right: Johan Cruyff, who for much of his career has been guided and motivated by Rinus Michels.
Right: Often stern-faced, Michels endures one of the regular chores of top-class coaches, facing the microphones and interrogation of the media.

Michels' ability to obtain Cruyff and then integrate him into the Barcelona life-style is often underestimated. Cruyff's talents should guarantee him success everywhere but others equally gifted have been lured to Spain in the past and fallen foul of problems of life-style, language and dressing-room jealousies. Barcelona had started the 1973–74 season badly which prompted Michels to make his move for Cruyff. They finished that season as champions of Spain.

Respect for Rinus Michels provided the attraction for another of Barcelona's big money trades, the purchase of Johan Neeskens, another Ajax and Holland star. But after ten years of unqualified progress Michels finally ran into trouble at the end of the 1974–75 season. Barcelona reached the semi-finals of the European Cup but rather surprisingly were beaten by Leeds United. Master and pupil seemed for a time to have fallen out, though both firmly denied it. Michels, none the less, took what blame there was going and Barcelona asked him to leave. He proclaimed that he was going to write his memoirs but turned up again in Amsterdam as coach to once mighty Ajax.

It was something of an ill-fated move and he resigned before the end of the 1975–76 season, and his name was linked with Valencia. But to general surprise Barcelona announced that Michels was re-joining them. It was a test for the coach about whom one Dutch international said, when asked about why Michels was such a great motivator, 'He really makes his players perform for him because they know that if they don't they are out. Even Johan Cruyff.'

Bobby Moore

Sadly the North American Soccer League did not see enough of Bobby Moore. England's greatest defender played just 24 games in the 1976 season for San Antonio Thunder. It seemed he would return when the franchise switched to Hawaii, but a deal could not be struck, and the NASL was poorer for that failure.

Moore is the one soccer player who makes the phrase 'Golden Boy' seem something more than a glib, facile tag. If you asked a computer to come up with an idealized version of the captain of a pro soccer team it would produce a blond six-footer, rich and tolerably handsome with an attractive wife, two children, an equable temperament and the ability to do his job better than anyone else in the world.

His on-field character gave the impression that all his attributes came too easily. There was no passion about his game. One felt that he long ago thought it through and decided that emotion would impair effectiveness, thus it was discarded. His one outstanding gift, that of reading a game more quickly and comprehensively than any other defender, enabled him to reduce frantic chasing and desperate tackling to the minimum so he was rarely seen in any physical distress. And his preference for the curt command rather than the brandished fist suggested that he was not putting too much sweat into his captaincy.

But such impressions could be no further from the truth. Bobby Moore played 108 times for England, more than any other player. Nobody wins a record number of caps without being an exceptional player. And there is no question that he was a very exceptional player.

Born in Barking, East London, in 1941, he attended the Tom Hood School, Leyton, and cherished the ambition common to most kids in that area. At first it seemed he would be disappointed: 'I was choked when the time came for me to leave school,' he recalls. 'All my mates had gone off for trials with clubs around London but nobody seemed to want me. I thought I'd missed out . . . then West Ham called me up for a trial.'

The development was steady. He played a record 18 times for England Youth, turned professional in June 1958 and followed the conventional route towards the international team with eight Under-23 caps and an international debut in Peru in May 1962.

As a 20-year-old international, his earning potential – both inside and outside the game – was considerable. But when, after 17 caps, he was made England's youngest-ever captain for the match against Czechoslovakia in May 1963, that potential became enormous.

The comparison between Moore and another blond defender who himself had been England's youngest-ever captain is itself a comparison between soccer's past and present. Billy Wright's international career had yielded him 105 caps, and while the 105th was being won his weekly wage was around £20 ($50). Moore was about to establish a new pattern.

In 1964 he began to be aware of the limitations of his club. West Ham United was a friendly club, packed with amiable, civilized people. It had risen from the Second Division in 1958, and was mightily pleased to sit among the elite. But it did not look like winning anything.

Spurs, on the other hand, were the side by which other teams measured themselves. The memory of the Cup and League double was still fresh and, with the talent available at White Hart Lane, there were still things to achieve. But Dave Mackay had broken a leg and Spurs were searching for a top-class replacement. Moore, in a newspaper interview, admitted that he would not mind a move to a bigger club. Only a successful West Ham team, it seemed, could change his mind. However, West Ham worked their way to the FA Cup Final and were improving all the time. They won the Final, beating Preston, and Moore was elected Player of the Year.

The Cup victory sent West Ham into Europe. The team just kept on getting better and, on a warm spring evening at Wembley in 1965 they produced what many people still regard as the finest performance by a British side in Europe to take the European Cup Winners Cup by beating Munich 1860.

Moore grew immeasurably during those two seasons. His leadership of West Ham had established his place as one of the most influential people in the British game and the pace at which other West Ham players, notably Geoff Hurst and Martin Peters, were progressing was eloquent tribute both to the influence of Moore and the stewardship and brilliant coaching of West Ham, and later England manager, Ron Greenwood.

Moore's own talent had passed from precocity to maturity. He was now in the front rank of international defenders, his natural ability refined by Greenwood and his England manager, Alf Ramsey, his temperament steeled by seasons of world-class competition.

The business interests were developing apace. By August 1965 he owned a sports shop opposite West Ham's ground, he appeared in hair cream and anti-smoking advertisements ('I wouldn't lend my name to anything unless I really believed in it,' he said), and he was a director of Bobby Moore Ltd, a company formed to exploit his name, which among other things, purchased land, constructed buildings and acquired inventions.

But the big test was ahead, the World Cup of 1966 when he was to lead an England team with the finest chance of winning the trophy any English side had ever possessed.

Yet three months before the competition began, Moore stunned West Ham with another request for a move. He had, by now, played more than 250 games for the club; he had led them to another Cup Winners Cup semi-final. But, just a few days before that important match was to be played, he asked for a move for the reason he had cited two years before . . . he wanted a bigger club.

Greenwood reacted angrily. He took the club captaincy from Moore and announced: 'If the West Ham image does not suit him, then he is better off where the image does suit him.' But that storm, like the previous one, blew itself out within a couple of months and, freed from distracting considerations, Moore was able to work and worry about the series of matches which were to secure his reputation and ensure his fortune.

His form before that 1966 World Cup fell far below the standards he had set himself – indeed, there was talk in some quarters of Leeds' Norman Hunter taking over Moore's England shirt and George Cohen assuming the captaincy.

If Ramsey was aware of such speculation he made no move towards vindicating it. Close observers of the England organization in the late sixties and early seventies tend to agree that Ramsey and his captain were something less than bosom friends. That is not to say that there was antagonism, but they had their own distinctive ideas and attitudes. However, they shared a strong belief in the futility of finishing second. They were winners; and they recognized that they needed each other if victory were to be achieved. They were, of course, absolutely right.

A year before the World Cup of 1966, a soccer writer was asking Ron Greenwood what he thought England's chances were of winning. Greenwood just pointed across the pitch to where Bobby Moore was practising with a ball. 'We're going to win,' he said, 'and that man's the reason why. He can already see in his mind's eye a picture of himself holding up the World Cup, and he's calculated down to the last detail just what that will mean to him and to his career.'

If the England side of 1966 was steeped in the dogma of Ramsey then it was inspired by the example of Moore. Over six matches he was as near impeccable as anyone can be in a team game. 'Bobby Moore is my representative on the field. He is responsible for seeing that the plans we have worked on are carried out,' said Ramsey.

Moore fulfilled that role with distinction, but he embellished it with the finest soccer of his career. As the competition wore on he became more of a presence than a player, capable, comforting and totally assured.

He won the Player of Players award at the end of the tournament, and such was the calibre of his performance that a competition which had featured all the world's finest players could come up with no conceivable alternative.

The indirect financial rewards for World Cup success were prodigious, and Moore began to capitalize on his fame with a shrewdness and single-mindedness which impressed even experienced businessmen.

'Soccer has obviously opened a lot of doors to Bobby,' said one business associate. 'But he'd have made money if his name had been Fred Bloggs and he'd never kicked a ball. He's got this East End shrewdness, he knows what he wants and he's prepared to work to get it. He'll never starve.'

As a further precaution against starvation, Moore became a partner in a suede-leather manufacturers producing expensive and high-quality coats for men. He discovered that he had a flair for design and this was put to useful effect in the business. And all the time he

Right: Bobby Moore's own favourite picture. Shirts and the warmest mutual feelings are exchanged after the classic contest between the attacking genius and the defensive maestro in the 1970 World Cup in Mexico.

149

obeyed Henry Ford's dictum 'Money is like an arm or a leg . . . use it or lose it.'

By now, of course, one of the more popular pastimes among Football League managers was to discover a weakness in Moore's game. The discussions usually boiled down to three facets of his play: his pace, his heading and his tackling.

Moore himself would admit that he was not the fastest defender in the League – or even in East London. He was inclined to be one-paced, and only a brave man would back him against some of the fliers in the First Division. But you could count on one hand the number of times in a season Moore allowed himself to be drawn into these situations of direct conflict. Similarly with his heading.

The myth that he could not tackle he exploded. Again, he preferred to decline direct confrontation, but he tackled to win the ball, and both West Ham and England had cause to be grateful for a number of goals which had their origins in Moore winning a tackle around the fringe of his own area and setting up a situation with a fast, 30-yard-pass.

If anything, he actually became a better player in the seasons which followed his 1966 triumph. West Ham started to fall on relatively hard times, but Moore's own game was completely unaffected. At the end of one trying season, Greenwood (who singles out individuals as reluctantly as Ramsey) was heard to say: 'I think we all take Bobby too much for granted. His level of performance is so high that people only notice him when he makes a mistake. I've never seen a player put together so many good games as this fellow does.'

His life-style attracted a growing number of sneers. An indifferent performance would inspire a quota of tedious, carping articles about the Moore's French maid, their gardener, their lavish home in a select London suburb. Tina's television advertising, Bobby's two dozen hand-made suits, three dozen hand-made shirts and his West End manicures all added fuel to the fires.

Their effect upon Moore's composure was rather less than nil. Yet nobody really knew how ingrained was that composure until in May 1970 there occurred a distasteful episode which was to make 'Bogota' a dirty word in the vocabulary of English sport.

It happened in the last few weeks before the start of the World Cup finals in Mexico. The English planning, under Sir Alf Ramsey, had been immaculate in its detail and as part of the attempt to accustom players to altitude it was decided to play matches in Bogota, Colombia and Quito, Ecuador.

Colombia were beaten 4–0 and Ecuador were defeated with similar ease. The confidence of the English team – led, of course, by Moore – was at an encouraging peak when they returned to Bogota on the way back to Mexico City.

Below left: Though never renowned for his heading, Bobby Moore rarely came off second best in aerial challenges.
Below: The coolest head in a confused goal area.

Five hours later, when the team's plane set off for Mexico, Moore was left behind in Bogota, under house arrest, accused of stealing a £625 ($1125) emerald and diamond bracelet from a boutique at the luxury Tequendama Hotel a few days earlier.

His accusers were a shop assistant and a witness, produced a week after the incident, who claimed to have seen Moore slip the bracelet into his pocket while two other English players distracted the shop-girl.

It was the biggest sports story in years; the world champions deprived of their captain only a few days before they began the defence of their trophy; the bizarre panto-mime of South American justice involving dramatic reconstructions of the 'crime' with large and noisy crowds and hundreds of reporters and television camera-men; the conflicting stories of the prosecution; the back-ground of Latin resentment to England's triumph in 1966; the fact that similar charges had been laid against other sports stars in previous years at the same shop; the appeal for urgent justice by the British Prime Minister Harold Wilson . . . and in the middle of it all the figure of Moore, looking just he would when West Ham were victims of a bad decision and saying simply: 'I am inno-cent. All I want to do is go to Mexico. I don't know why they picked on me.'

His colleagues in the England party were furious but conscious of the need to watch their words until their captain was freed. Sir Alf described the whole affair as 'a sick joke', saying 'I should have thought the integrity of the man would be answer enough for these charges.' Team-mates were scornful: 'Steal a bracelet? With Bob's money he could have bought the shop. It's ridiculous.' And that was the conclusion at which the judge arrived when he decided there was no real evidence against Moore.

The England team, now established in their head-quarters in Guadalajara, gave him a hero's welcome on his return four days later, and Moore himself said he wanted to forget the whole thing with the match only days away.

He was left with only one lasting impression. 'You find yourself looking in jewellers' windows with your hands stuck in your pockets, pointing at things with your nose,' he was to say, a month later.

Moore performed in the matches with Rumania, Czechoslovakia and even in the losing game with Brazil in the same magisterial manner he had exhibited in England four years earlier. But the results were not to follow the same pattern.

Pele, the player for whom Moore has a great and abiding respect, named England's captain the finest defender in the world after their epic battle in Guadalajara. The soccer world eagerly waited for the return duel between the two men which was to have been in the final in Mexico City. But things went catastrophically wrong for England against West Germany when a two-goal lead was squandered and an extra-time (overtime) defeat was inflicted.

Odious though the whole South American affair must have been to Moore, the publicity he received at home – both for his conduct in Bogota and his playing perform-ances in Mexico — was entirely favourable.

The only wholly bad publicity Bobby Moore has received in his whole career lay six months ahead. In November 1970 West Ham played Glasgow Celtic in a testimonial match for Moore; the game raised £10,000 ($18,000). Two months later, on the eve of a third-round Cup tie with Blackpool, Moore and three others players were spotted in a Blackpool night-club. West Ham lost the Cup tie 4–0, and Moore had a wretched match.

The contrast between the lavish testimonial and the late, late night was too brutal even for the Londoners who had followed his career with loyalty and pride from the earliest days, and there is little doubt that the mass of fans were behind Greenwood's action in handing out a hefty fine and keeping him out of the side for five weeks. Ramsey, too, punished the indiscretion and left his captain out of one international. But for club and country the set-back was a short one, and he resumed for both with that almost inhuman consistency.

But one slip, sadly proving his mortality, could not have come at a worse time. In Poland in a World Cup qualifier on a summer's evening in June 1973 he allowed Lubanski to purloin the ball from him to shoot a match-clinching goal – a goal which severely threatened England's chances of reaching the finals.

That match was his 105th international. Within eight days he had added two further caps to break Bobby Charlton's England record. However, he was to play only once more for his country.

But Bobby Moore was not finished. In the spring of 1974 West Ham traded him to Fulham for a bargain £25,000 ($40,000) and he responded by helping the homely West London Second Division club reach the FA Cup final the following year. His summer with San Antonio was to include appearances for Team America in the Bicentennial Tournament, including playing against his beloved England.

He played the last match of his career at the end of the 1976–77 season before looking for a career as a team manager. In doing so he gave a final reminder of the class of the man. Totally unplanned, that final match happened to be his 1,000th in senior soccer. Above all else, Bobby Moore always had style.

Above left: The big occasion always brought the very best out of Bobby Moore, who seemed to come alive when the challenge was its toughest. Here the England captain assesses the situation while Brazil take possession.

Right: Moore in more colourful garb during a spell in the United States. Moore played for San Antonio Thunder during the 1976 season, leaving when the franchise moved to Hawaii, but it was long enough for American crowds to appreciate the skills of the best defender in the world.

Left: Moore played in 108 internationals for his country, more than any other Englishman. He captained the side by example rather than by any raucous and demonstrative verbal motivations. His greatest quality lay in his uncanny ability to read play, a speed of thought that more than compensated for his own average speed of movement. Here he aims to intercept a ball during a spell with The Portland Timbers in the NASL.

Gerd Muller

The cross was played behind him, and would have confounded most other strikers in the world. Gerd Muller simply checked his run, twisted back and controlled the ball with one touch. Another turn, a second touch and the ball was in the back of the net. So casual was the exercise you might have thought it was a practice match. In fact it was the winning goal in the 1974 World Cup final.

There was an inevitable air about the moment. Holland were beaten by Muller's highly developed sense of opportunism. In 1970, when West Germany finished third in the World Cup, Muller's ten goals had made him the top scorer in the finals. Two years later he scored two more as West Germany won the European Championship. But the deadly thrust that killed off Holland was to be the last of the man for whom the term striker could have been invented. It provided his 68th goal in his 62nd international and after it he settled for club soccer and more time with his treasured family.

Gerd Muller, born to score goals.
Left: A winner for Bayern Munich against Dusseldorf.
Below: Knocking England out of the 1970 World Cup.
Right: Making West Germany 1972 European Champions.
Right inset: Yet another gesture of triumph.

The Germany of 1945, even in the comparatively remote Bavarian village of Zinsen, was not the ideal place to bring up a future European Footballer of the Year. But in the November of that year Frau Muller gave birth to a fourth child, a son, Gerhard.

He was only 15 when his father died and the young Muller was sent out to work in the weaving trade, because his mother could no longer afford to keep him at school. Soccer became strictly a Sunday affair. Muller joined the local club, TSV 1861 Nordlingen, where he gave some indication of his talents by scoring 46 goals for them in two seasons. His marksmanship soon came to the attention of the more senior sides.

Nordlingen's coach, Conny Kraft, a professional with Nuremberg in the 1950s, intended Gerd to sign for his old club. There were others in the market as well – among them Stuttgart Kickers, Augsburg, and Munich 1860 – but they were all upstaged by Bayern Munich's sudden and decisive interest.

Wilhelm Neudecker, president of Bayern, sent his two best men to persuade Frau Muller that her son's future lay in joining the club.

The deal had not been completed when the rush to sign Muller reached its peak. There was a barrage of telephone calls from interested parties and even the Mayor of Nordlingen called on the Mullers, requesting Gerd not to leave the local club. But Muller said simply 'I have given my word', and moved to Munich in the summer of 1963.

Despite Muller's record, one man at Bayern was not immediately impressed by the new prodigy. The club coach, Yugoslav international 'Tshik' Cajkovski, indignantly asked Neudecker 'Do you want me to put a bear among my racehorses?' Within a year Muller had dispelled all doubts by scoring 35 goals in the Regional League South and helping Bayern to win promotion to the national division, the Bundesliga.

It is tempting to regard Muller's flair for goalscoring as the product of sheer instinct, as a skill impossible to analyse, like that of a great musician or painter. He himself admits that he's not sure how he does it – 'Somehow, something inside tells me "Gerd go this way, Gerd go that way, Gerd move up" – and the ball is coming over and I score. I know that's not a very satisfactory answer, but I can't explain it any better than that. After all, if I don't know how to do it, no one can find out how to stop me.'

But in fact Muller is a great exploiter of free space, playing the percentages so that should the ball escape the defence, it falls prey to his deadly finishing. Muller has such rare powers of concentration and anticipation that he can assess a situation instantly without moving his head to betray his intentions to an opponent.

If someone were to sit down at a drawing board and attempt to design the ultimate striker for the crowded penalty boxes of today's tight-marking game, the chances are he would come up with something like Gerd Muller – stocky, about 5ft. 8 in. (small enough to weave his way through the crush but not so small that he can be pushed easily off the ball) and with short thick legs, giving him a low centre of gravity which enables him to keep his balance in the tightest of turns. Add to these his sense of anticipation and concentration plus his excellent coordination and you have the ideal modern striker.

Muller is at his most dangerous in the physical challenge, for the strength of his hips and thighs enables him to evade opponents, jockeying for position in a swift twisting movement that can often bring him clear through to goal. He showed this in the 1970 World Cup semi-final against Italy, when Poletti, screening the ball on the assumption that Muller was directly behind him, suddenly found the German wriggling through to beat Albertosi, Italy's goalkeeper, with the merest, stretching touch.

Some centre-halves have countered this trick of Muller's by holding off their tackle until the last possible moment, but in doing so they take an enormous risk. The centre-forward showed his stunning speed on the turn against Scotland's Ron McKinnon – no raw recruit – when, during a 1969 World Cup qualifying match in Glasgow, Muller left him like a bale of straw and shot the ball sweetly past Lawrence for West Germany's only goal of the match.

Muller played a subordinate role in his first season in top-class soccer (1965–66), scoring just 14 goals and appearing in the Bayern side that won the German Cup, but it was in the following season that he began to confirm his true ability.

His tally of goals in Bayern's 1966–67 season encouraged the West German team manager, Helmut Schoen, to give him a chance in the national side. Muller did not score in his first game, against Turkey in October 1966, but he justified himself with a vengeance by scoring four in his second appearance, albeit against Albania. In doing so, Muller became the first German player to score four goals in an international since 1942.

In the 1966–67 season, Muller, still only 21, had helped Bayern take both the German Cup and the European Cup Winners Cup, scoring 47 goals altogether (28 in the League, eight in the Cup Winners Cup, seven in the German Cup and four in the international against Albania). He went on to win the Footballer of the Year award by 417 votes to team-mate Franz Beckenbauer's 60.

The goals continued to come for both club and country. In 1968–69 Muller helped Bayern to a League and Cup double and was once again voted Footballer of the Year. The silver cannon, the top-scorer's trophy, and the golden ball, the Footballer of the Year trophy, were both presented to him before Bayern's opening match of the 1969–70 season, against Rot-Weiss Essen. Muller responded appropriately by scoring a hat-trick.

In the World Cup qualifying competition, only Muller's ability seemed to stand between West Germany and complete disaster. In the games against Austria, Scotland and Cyprus he scored in every game, totalling nine goals from six matches.

Right: Gerd Muller's short stocky frame, with his low centre of gravity, gives him the ability to turn quickly, a technique which has helped him reach balls played into the penalty area ahead of most marking defenders.

Though West Germany managed to qualify for the 1970 World Cup, the team was far from settled, and Muller himself was unhappy with some of the experiments made by their manager Schoen. Following the second match against Austria, in which Germany snatched two points thanks only to Muller's goal two minutes from the end, he complained to reporters that his style simply did not fit in with certain members of the team, and either they would have to go, or he would. In the heat of the moment, Muller replied to a question, 'Yes, that even applies to Uwe Seeler.' (West Germany's former striker). From such small beginnings came a series of headlines about a Muller-Seeler feud. Muller and Seeler may not have been exactly life-long friends, but they always had the sense to put the team's interests above their own personal rivalries. The rumours were finally quashed only when Schoen cleverly made them share a room together for five weeks in their Mexican World Cup Headquarters.

Bayern qualified for the 1971 German Cup final against Cologne, and Muller was lucky to play in the match. In January of that year he had been sent off in distant Lima, against Universitario, in what was euphemistically described as a friendly match. In Germany sendings-off (dismissals) abroad are treated more sternly than in other soccer playing nations, and although Bayern tried to keep the case out of the hands of the disciplinary committee, it came up a fortnight before the end of the League season. Muller received a two-month suspension, which should have kept him out of the cup final, but after an appeal by his club, the German FA relented and allowed him to play.

Gerd Muller is essentially an easy going fellow who, despite two suspensions, lacks the callousness on the field that some stars find essential for success. Off the field too, he is hardly what one would call a hard-headed businessman.

He also fights a constant battle between his stomach and his professional common sense. His weakness for food has given him weight problems – his colleagues play on his sensitivity by calling him 'Der Dicker', 'The Fat Fellow'. Unfortunately his shy wife Ursula, or 'Uschi' as she's known, has constant fears of him wasting away, and likes nothing better than to heap platefuls of potato salad in front of him.

However, he always retained his sharpness – even after his decision to retire from international soccer. Two months before the 1974 World Cup final, he scored twice as Bayern Munich became the first West German club to win the European Cup. They cemented that initial success into three consecutive wins – with Muller a scorer in the 1975 victory over England's Leeds United.

It was the only opportunity he was given in the ninety minutes, but he took it. That's the way it has been throughout his career. And that's the way it was when the world looked on in the Olympic Stadium in Munich in July 1974, where, quite appropriately, the world's best striker won the World Cup.

Right: Gerd Muller races clear in a 1974 international against Scotland in Frankfurt. West Germany won 2–1.

Pele

Pele placed the ball for a free-kick and paced out his approach. The flowing ease of his run might have suggested a nonchalance if you failed to notice that in striking the ball with his right foot he lifted himself off the ground. Bullet-fashion, the ball sped past the goalkeeper. Another memorable goal for Pele. But this one was unique. His last.

Seventy-six thousand fans crammed Giants Stadium in final tribute to a soccer player whose name most had known for little over two years. For the greatest player the world has seen it was a second retirement, at the end of a second career.

The legendary Brazilian signed for New York Cosmos on 10 June 1975 – a three year deal involving almost $4 million (£2¼ million). In doing so he gave the NASL a credibility it had been struggling to achieve. More than that, Pele's mastery of the game enlightened a public for whom, hitherto, soccer had been a pastime for foreigners. In America, Pele made soccer come alive.

Joao Saldanha, former manager of the Brazil national team, said of Pele, 'If you ask me who is the best full-back in Brazil, I will say Pele. If you ask who is the best wing-half I would say Pele. Who is the best winger? Pele. If you ask me who is the best goalkeeper, probably I would have to say Pele. He is like no other player. He is to Brazilian football what Shakespeare is to English literature.'

Pele has climbed every mountain available to the great soccer player, won two World Cup winners medals, scored more than a thousand goals in his senior career and been recognized for almost twenty years as the most lavishly equipped exponent of his sport, probably the most exceptional it has ever known.

Of all the great players of the last 30 years or so, only one, Alfredo di Stefano, the magnificent Argentinian who was the central influence in the Real Madrid side who were irresistible in Europe in the 1950s, has been regularly compared with Pele in terms of personal capacity to control a match. But even di Stefano, with his iron will, his marvellous perception and superb skills, should take a place just slightly beneath Pele in the pantheon of the game. Di Stefano did not have the Brazilian's gymnastic grace or liquid fluency. There was a hard, functional angularity about his game, and while that quality, by emphasizing his strength and authority, carried its own excitement, it did not produce the shiver in the blood that came with the sight of Pele in full flow.

When Pele burst upon us in the 1958 World Cup in Sweden he was the prodigy of a team brimming with the highest skills; Djalma and Nilton Santos, Didi, Garrincha, Vava, Zagalo; these were giants. When the young Pele proved himself at least as exciting, scoring two goals in an unforgettable victory over Sweden in the final, no one could doubt that soccer had gained a star of the first magnitude.

Left: One of the last competitive touches of the ball for Pele in his final match in 1977.

The success in Sweden was followed by another in Chile in 1962, but injury prevented Pele from playing in more than two matches and it was left to Garrincha to dazzle the assembled *aficionados*. Despite their win, there was disturbing evidence that, as one writer said, the Brazilian team had begun to suffer from hardening of the arteries. But the warnings were ignored and so the World Cup of 1966 became as much a disaster for Brazil as it was a triumph for England. The selectors in Rio, afraid to desert venerated players who were palpably in decline, travelled to Europe with a party that looked more like a pensioner's club than a World Cup squad.

Even the outstanding young Brazilian players had been ill-prepared and when Pele was systematically kicked out of the competition by Morais of Portugal, a miserable exclusion from the quarter-finals became inevitable. This was an experience to scar the Brazilian psyche and it did so much personal damage to Pele that he talked for a while of turning his back on the Jules Rimet trophy for ever. In his career to that point, his country had taken the prize twice and yet Pele himself had never played a full series of matches in the finals. He muttered grimly that he saw no virtue in offering himself as a sacrifice to the hard men. What was the point of his taking the field in the World Cup if violence was to be allowed to invalidate virtuosity?

Fortunately for everyone, Pele's pessimism was short-lived and his spirit was fully restored by the fresh impetus imparted to Brazil's drive towards the World Cup of 1970. The Brazilian players, under Saldanha, were withdrawn from club soccer four months before the Mexico finals. It was the first time that Pele had known the luxury of a period of sustained training. Previously he had always been too pre-occupied playing matches (as many as 140 a season by the time he had earned the large fees Santos charged for his appearance in exhibition games) and the novelty of preparation had a wonderful effect on him.

Pele announced that he felt really fit for the first time in years. Tension between himself and Saldanha, the one factor that might have undermined his performance in Mexico, helped to persuade the ruling body of Brazilian soccer that Saldanha should be replaced. Mario Zagalo, Pele's ally on the field of ten years before, took over the managership and Pele's last and greatest assault on the Jules Rimet Trophy was launched.

What happened in Guadalajara and Mexico City in that burning midsummer of 1970 can be seen as a dramatic summation of Pele's contribution to soccer. Encouraged by his sense of physical well-being, his confidence in the vast, mature range of his abilities, and his knowledge that Brazil had been properly prepared, he went to Mexico with a calculated resolve that he and his team would dominate the ninth World Cup competition to a historic degree.

Right: Although closely marked, as here, throughout the 1970 World Cup final, Pele still managed to score the opening goal. He also laid on goals for Jairzinho and Carlos Alberto.

Far right: What will happen next? For twenty years defenders struggled to find an answer when Pele was on the ball.

One of the Brazilian officials said 'Pele has created his mood. We have timed everything to come to a peak at precisely the right moment. We are ready to explode.' We knew the kind of explosion to expect from Pele. He was probably the most exhilarating runner with the ball the game has known, exercising such astonishing control that he hardly seemed to play the ball deliberately at all. It seemed to be juggled adhesively between his feet and shins while he moved at maximum speed, free to concentrate on his next decisive stroke. Other players, even great ones, have to caress the ball constantly as they run, but Pele seemed to make it a natural appendage.

'Sometimes you tackle him and you are convinced you have the ball,' said Bobby Moore. 'You have felt solid contact with it and you know it's yours. Then you look round and he's ten yards past you and it's at his feet. He'll play it against your legs and then catch it on the rebound and carry on.'

The first time Pele used that insolent skill, Bobby Moore said he thought it had been an accident. 'But after the sixth or seventh time, I had to realize that, incredibly, he was doing it on purpose. Nothing is too outrageous for him.'

There was the same total lack of inhibition about Pele's passing and finishing. He passed the ball over, round, past and sometimes apparently through opponents,

curving the flighting and driving the ball with bewildering variety and relentless precision. And when Pele struck at goal, his athletic elasticity, inspired timing and spontaneous force gave him a deadliness no one has every exceeded.

His vision on the field, his awareness of what is going on all around him, was so amazing that he gives the impression of having his eyes on the sides of his head, like a bird's. But his sense of what is happening during a match went far beyond any question of sight. His was a deep, instinctive perception.

In the 1970 Mexico World Cup, in Brazil's opening match of the competition, against Czechoslovakia, Pele brought the first half to an amazing climax with one of the great moments of the World Cup. Moving into possession well inside his own half of the field, he gave a barely preceptible glance in the direction of Viktor, saw that the goalkeeper had stepped out some yards from the posts, and struck. Pele was still in the Brazilian segment of the centre circle when, raising his right leg in a prodigious backlift and swinging it through with a flowing, effortless precision worthy of an iron shot by Jack Nicklaus, he sent the ball in a fast arc towards goal. Viktor's contorted features revealed the extent of his painful astonishment as he scrambled back under the ball, then spun helplessly to see it swoop less than a yard outside a post. Through the interval the stadium throbbed with the special excitement crowds feel when they have seen something remarkable and know there is more of the same to come.

In the semi-final against Uruguay, a match fraught with the severest pressures for Brazil because of the history of their confrontations with their South American neighbours, there came this crucial moment.

Having adopted a stance about as fluidly aggressive as Fort Knox's, Uruguay were presumably content to hope that an opponent's error would give them a chance of a goal. Such a shamelessly barren philosphy hardly deserved the extraordinary vindication it was granted as early as the eighteenth minute when Brazil contributed not one but two unbelievable mistakes. First Brito, without any excuse, pushed the ball straight to Morales, who curled his pass behind Everaldo to Cubilla. Cubilla controlled the ball on his chest but had to take it too close to the bye-line, so that the shot was struck slackly across the face of the goal. Felix then supplied the second blunder. Moving like a man trying to walk on golf balls, he stumbled and groped across his line as the ball bounced languidly into the net.

Felix looked disgusted. Several of the other Brazilians were on the verge of despair, none more obviously than Gerson, who held his head as if to staunch a wound. Pele ran through the shattered ranks of the team and

collected the ball to bring it back for the kick-off. All the way to the centre cricle he was talking soothingly to those around him. He knew how debilitating mutual recriminations could be and he did not intend to let anything stand between him and the World Cup. One of his colleagues later recounted what Pele said as he placed the ball for the kick-off. 'Right. Now let's see who's going to be the first to score against these bastards.'

During that game, Pele was not only at his most vigorous, exploding into unforeseen runs as if in response to a gun that only he could hear, checking and swerving and doubling back, the religious medal around his neck glinting in the afternoon sunshine. He was also at his most outrageously ambitious, attempting plays that the heroes of our comics would have found taxing.

For at the heart of Pele's game was a joyful pursuit of the impossible. He dominated the mythology of world soccer as no man before him ever did, scoring over a thousand goals and creating ten thousand moments of exhilarating beauty. But he is happily dissatisfied. He did not hide the instant desire to score one goal that would stand apart from all the others, a goal that would be impossible until he made it possible, one that nobody else can emulate: Pele's goal.

That was the goal he had sought with his incredible arched shot from the middle of the field against the Czechs and he reached for it twice more against Uruguay, first with an instantaneous volley from 35 yards after the goalkeeper, Mazurkiewicz, mis-hit a goal-kick, and then with a dummy on Mazurkiewicz that neither he nor anyone else who witnessed it will ever forget. The miraculous goal did not come, though, but a superb victory did, when Italy were outclassed in the final match, and Pele went home happy in spite of the knowledge that his legend would now be even more difficult to live with.

Pele (born Edson Arantes do Nascimento) long ago gave up any hope of living a normal life. Indeed, all the members of the poor black family into which he entered on 21 October 1940, in common with his white wife Rosel and two children, have found their daily existence overwhelmed by the most pervasive adulation ever accorded to a sportsman.

Autograph-hunting is the mildest form of pestering that Pele is subjected to. More often he is asked for money. In Brazil there were television programmes which promised cash rewards for anybody who succeeded in bringing Pele in front of the cameras. The day Pele played his last match for the Brazilian team (18 July 1971) a television programme announced that whoever succeeded in bringing Pele to the studio would receive £1,000 ($2,250).

When Pele came back to his hotel he found, shoved under the door, a number of messages written by the hotel staff, each one explaining in painful detail precisely why it was so important for him and his family to get the £1,000 ($2,250). Pele did not go to the programme but he helped the staff out of his own pocket.

Right: Pele breathing life into the NASL in New York.

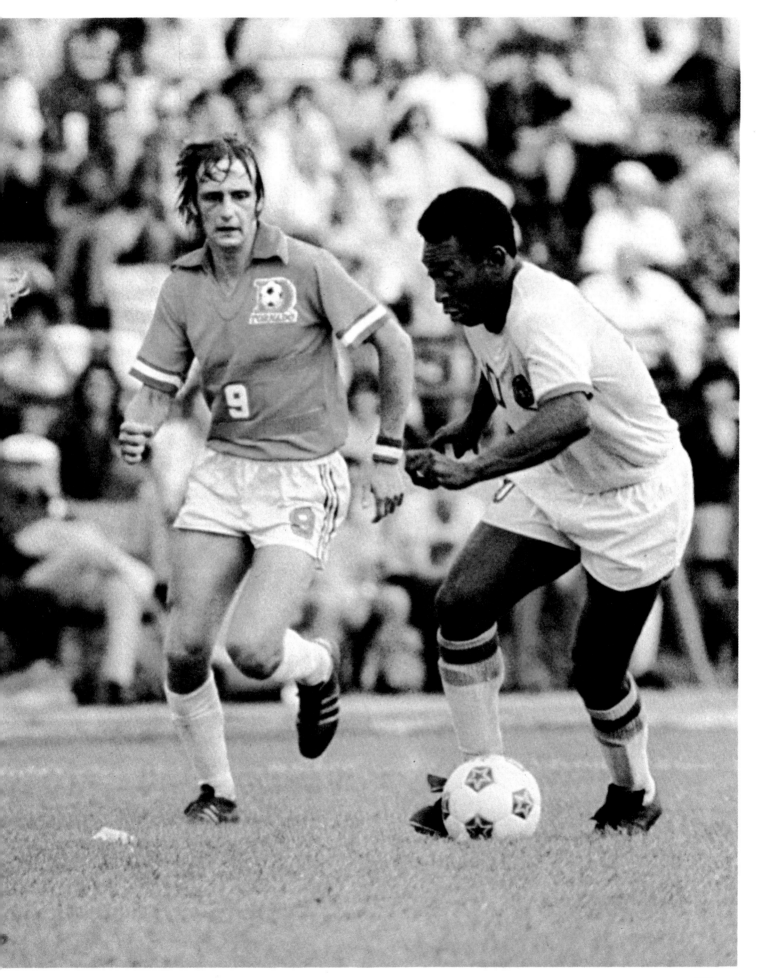

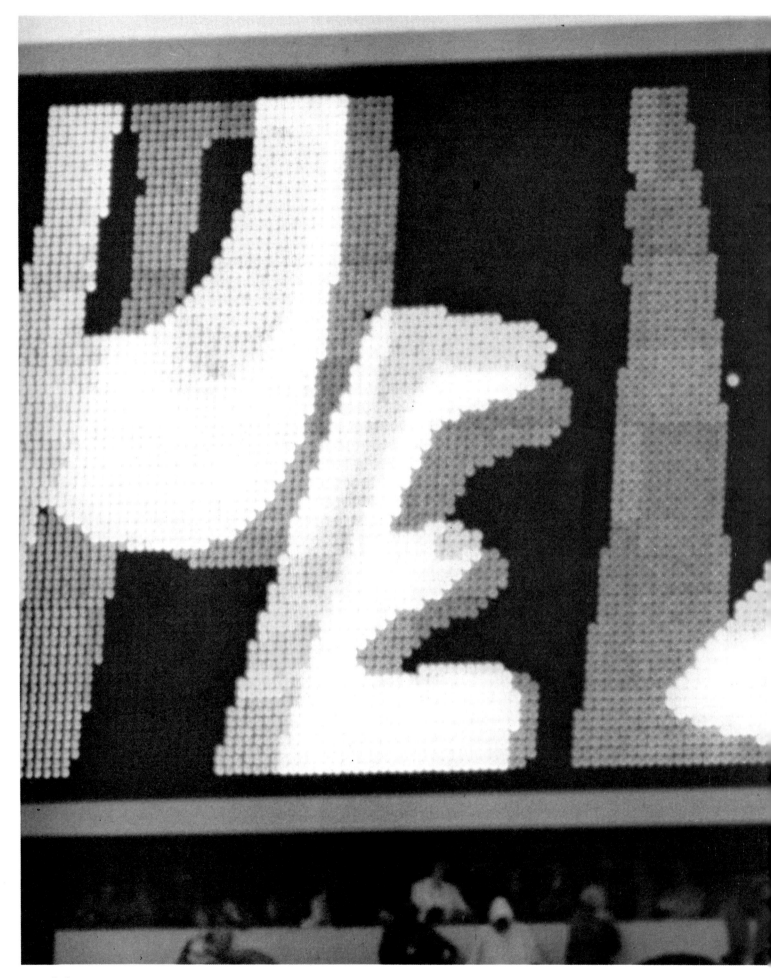

'If I were to go to a programme they would have to pay me £10,000 ($22,500) Pele said. 'Not because I want the money or because I need it. But because that is how I can make certain that they are not going to ask me. If I went on one programme. I would have to accept all the other invitations.'

Tres Coracoes (Three Hearts), the city where Pele was born, unveiled his statue in 1971. Politicians, army officers, everybody striving for publicity was there, standing by Pele to have their photograph in the newspapers. There were speeches, fireworks, the usual scenes.

Pele's brother Zoca, who is four years younger, wanted to be a soccer player and he was promising enough to be given a contract by Santos at the age of fifteen, but he never had a chance to make his way in the game. Whenever Santos included him in any team sent into the interior of Brazil the stands would be packed with people prepared to see miracles and prepared to condemn anything else. Zoca was a reasonable player but the pressure on him was intolerable.

Pele's own life has been irrevocably shaped by his talent. He has earned, vast amounts of money from soccer.

Pele even has the looks of a star, a handsome face, especially when he smiles, and the impossibly white teeth offset the overlong nose. The eyes are large and slightly protruding and the wary steadiness of their gaze emphasizes the overall impression of earnestness. His torso is thick (in the Brazil training camp of 1970 he sat at 'the fat man's table' set aside for those who had to watch their weight) and the back of his neck is heavy with muscle. His legs inevitably are remarkable. The thighs are vast slabs of muscle, the calves slim and tapering. They were once thinner, Pele explains, before the endless succession of kicks left an accumulation of permanent swellings. His feet are surprisingly splayed out.

When he talks of the special capabilities of those feet, he disclaims any personal credit. For Pele is a devout Catholic and is sincerely convinced that his talent for soccer was a divine gift.

'I feel the greatest skill I have on the soccer field is the ability to make something out of nothing. Of course, you need balance, and speed of mind and body, and strength. But there is something else, something God has given me, maybe some extra instinct for the game. Sometimes I can take the ball and no one can foresee any danger, and then in two or three seconds there is a goal. This does not make me proud. It makes me humble, because this is a talent that God gave me. All I can do is work to use it well, to make a good life for my family and to give pleasure to the people. Aside from anything I do, there is always the Finger of God. He made me a soccer player and he keeps me a soccer player.'

God did more. He made Pele *the* soccer player.

Left: The scoreboard in New York offers its tribute after a Pele goal – this a unique one, his last. In his final game he appropriately added this goal to his prodigious tally – a magnificently driven free-kick that left all those who saw it with one final memory.
Previous page: Another Cosmos goal.

Ferenc Puskas

In the great Hungarian team of the fifties, the team that sensationally destroyed England's unbeaten home record against foreign opposition, Hidegkuti was regarded as the perfect artist, Kocsis the master header of the ball. Yet it is Ferenc Puskas who is best remembered, because Puskas always had an air of the 'con-man' about him, full of swagger and impudence, which made everything he did look just that bit better.

The Ferenc Puskas story is the classic rags-to-riches story – but with a difference. For few players in the history of soccer have ever carved out two such separate, equally dazzling careers – both of them studded with remarkable achievement.

Puskas, the son of a mediocre soccer player, was born on 2 April 1926. His parents' second son, he was immediately nicknamed 'Ocsi', which means 'kid-brother', and Puskas has always signed his letters with this affectionate childhood tag. The dusty streets of Kispest were not as picturesque as the sandy beaches of Copacabana in Brazil, but nevertheless barefoot boys still kicked a ball about – a ball made of rags and old socks – just as enthusiastically. 'Ocsi' often says that his father could only afford one pair of shoes between him and his brother. He always wore the right one and did not dare kick a ball with it – and that was how, he said, he had developed the greatest left foot in the game.

At the age of 13 Puskas joined the local First Division club, Kispest, as a 'cub' player, and under the watchful eyes of his father, then a coach, began a career which made the name Puskas famous throughout the world. It was obvious from the outset that this stocky little lad had exceptional talent, and after playing for Hungary at youth level he made his League debut for Kispest when he was just 16. Immaculate ball-control, a deadly shot, intelligence, and speed of thought and action were the hallmarks of Puskas' play. Surrounded by average players, the young star was able to turn a match by creating and taking chances with both coolness and precision.

Puskas' sense of humour and flamboyance, the marks of an exceptionally gifted player, were demonstrated perfectly in a match against Hungary's most popular club, Ferencvaros. With the score at 1–1, Ocsi clashed with one of the opposing defenders and was stretchered off the field. The hushed crowd looked on in sympathy as the young man lay motionless, apparently badly injured. But as the ambulance men reached the tunnel leading to the dressing-rooms, Puskas jumped off the stretcher, ran to the touchline and, as the ball was out of play, rejoined his team-mates. Seconds later he picked up a loose ball in midfield, moved effortlessly past the Ferencvaros defence, and from 25 yards hit a stunning goal. The Ferencvaros fans, incensed by this mixture of clowning and artistry, bayed for his blood, but the youngster returned to the centre circle with an unashamed grin on his face.

At 17 years old, Puskas made his full international debut, against Austria, wearing a number ten shirt.

Puskas dies in battle says report

HUNGARY'S king of the Soccer field, Ferenc Puskas has been killed

Top left: Two of Ferenc Puskas's three goals in Real Madrid's 7–3 victory over Eintracht Frankfurt in the 1960 European Cup final.
Centre left: As manager of Panathinaikos he shows admirers his ball skills.
Left: Second from the right Puskas as a member of Real Madrid's forward line.
Top: Exchanging penants with Billy Wright before Hungary beat England 6–3 in 1953.
Above left: Incorrect reports that he had been killed in fighting in Budapest during the 1956 Hungarian uprising. He rebuilt his career in Spain.
Above: Puskas, the businessman; but this sausage factory lost money.

Officially an inside-left, he was the general of the team which included such seasoned forwards as the Ujpest pair, Szusza and Szengeller. Szengeller made Puskas an early goal which no doubt gave him added confidence, and Hungary won 5–2: Puskas was to keep his place in the team for the next 11 years.

That match against Austria took place in 1945. Soccer in Hungary had been virtually unaffected by the War, and the players had suffered no restrictions; indeed, rather than call them up, the government had found them work in hospital depots and the like, and had been uncharacteristically liberal with leave to play soccer. Not until March 1944, and the siege of German-occupied Budapest by the Russians, did soccer have to make even a temporary halt – because of fierce fighting in the capital.

With the speedy resumption, a new era began in the history of Hungarian soccer – an era to which young Puskas was to contribute much.

The Magyars, World Cup finalists in 1938, were past masters of the typical Central European game, one which suited Puskas. They shunned physical contact, relying instead on sheer ball control and clever, short passing moves. The emphasis was solidly on attack. By then, the 'W' formation was the universally accepted tactic for clubs and national teams alike. Within the rigidity of this system forwards like Puskas flourished, because they only had to beat one man, either with the ball or by intelligent positioning, and the way was clear towards goal.

Besides a style of play that admirably suited Puskas, as the much-battered capital came back to life, the Hungarian FA, following political directives, re-organized club soccer – to Puskas' advantage.

Kispest became the official Army club and was renamed Honved. In order to create exceptionally strong teams, several leading players were ordered to join either Honved or MTK, who had suffered a great deal during the previous ten years; indeed they had disbanded in 1943. So, suddenly, the hitherto struggling teams, including the newly christened Honved, became the stronghold of Hungarian football.

Honved could field such notable players as goalkeeper Grosics, wing-half Boszik and forwards Kocsis, Puskas and Czibor – all members of the legendary Hungarian side. Now, at last, Ocsi found himself playing regularly with top-class soccer players and the responsibility of 'carrying' a team was taken off his shoulders. As a result his game improved dramatically, because he could safely leave more of the donkey-work to others and concentrate on scoring goals.

Despite his international status, Puskas was still not content with his prowess and worked endlessly to perfect his skills. He would spend hours after training kicking a ball against a brick wall, controlling the rebound with his body, or balancing it up and down his thighs. This master-and-slave game was patiently played out night after night until he had achieved complete mastery over the ball.

Puskas and his Honved team-mates were ostensibly members of the People's Army, but they did very little military training. They fought on soccer pitches, not battlefields, for promotion and higher earnings, and Puskas rose to the rank of major without ever carrying a rifle. However, these crack soccer players were at times supposed to sleep in the barracks – not the most convivial accommodation – and so, after curfew, Puskas and company would put on their best suits, wave a cheerful goodbye to the understanding guards, and walk out into the night life of Budapest. They were caught only once, drinking in a bar around midnight by an officious captain who disliked soccer and was jealous of the freedom and affluence the players enjoyed.

Next morning, the commander sent for Puskas and ordered a 50 mile march as a punishment for the escapade. 'Thank you sir,' said Ocsi. 'But you realize that we won't be able to play against MTK next Sunday. It's up to you, sir. Either we march, or we play.' Luckily for Puskas the commander was a Honved supporter and readily succumbed to this obvious piece of blackmail.

In the meantime, Gustav Sebes had taken over control of the national team and was working hard on a new tactical plan, a kind of 4–2–4. Nandor Hidegkuti became the first ever withdrawn centre-forward, and Sebes gave Puskas, as well as Kocsis, a free-wheeling, buccaneering role. The combination of this tactical ploy and the presence of Puskas and several other brilliant players produced a near invincible team. Their magnificent soccer expressed the philosophy, 'No matter how many goals we concede, we can always score at least one more.'

Ocsi, by then known as the 'Galloping Major', was the kingpin of this excellent Hungarian team, and was largely responsible for the effectiveness of their attacking style of play. Puskas scored 85 goals in 84 internationals for Hungary, a remarkable average over such a large number of games. He got most of his goals with shots hit with his famed left foot, many from outside the penalty box. This ability to regularly fire goals from a distance of 20 yards and upwards was perhaps his finest attribute, one he used to good effect throughout his international as well as his club career.

Of Puskas' 84 internationals for Hungary – he also played four for Spain later on – three games stand out, all of them part of the golden era of Hungarian soccer; the unforgettable 6–3 win over England in 1953 at Wembley, the subsequent 7–1 thrashing of England in Budapest, and Hungary's tragic 3–2 defeat in the 1954 World Cup final against West Germany.

Ocsi played a major part in that sadly important setback, as well as those previous triumphs, when he did much of the damage to England. For earlier in the 1954 World Cup finals he was injured and could not play in the quarter- and semi-finals. He passed a late fitness test on the morning of the final, but his inclusion was still a brave gamble on the part of Sebes – a gamble that failed. The struggling Puskas had a relatively poor game for Hungary, even missing an easy chance at a vital stage of the game, and the winner's medals went to West Germany.

Right: Puskas, number 10, raises his arms in triumph after a magnificent individual goal against England in 1953.

Two years later he was on tour with Honved when the 1956 uprising erupted in Hungary. Puskas, like Kocsis and Czibor, decided not to return home because of the possible personal consequences of the Russian intervention. It was a hard decision for Puskas to make. Hungary was his home, and in his own words, Hungary had 'treated me like a king'. He had probably enjoyed a better standard of living there than the head of state. He was paid well, if somewhat furtively, in goods. When he went abroad he and the other Hungarian players were allowed to bring back virtually what they liked – 25 bolts of cloth or a few thousand razor blades for example – to be sold in Hungary. In this way they were able, provided they won their games often enough, to live quite well.

Now, however, Puskas left all that behind to set up home in Vienna. There he was joined by his wife and daughter.

After a year in the soccer wilderness – Puskas could not get a player's permit – he was approached by Emil Oestereicher, the ex-manager of his former club. Oestereicher, a likeable man and an excellent coach, was eager to work in Spain, and saw Puskas as the trump card he needed to clinch a job there. So, with Puskas' agreement, Oestereicher offered a package deal to the greatest club side of the time, Real Madrid. The package included a 30-year-old overweight player and a coach who could not speak the language. But despite these handicaps, the offer was accepted by Real Madrid's chairman, Santiago Bernabeu, and a partnership began which turned out to be as beneficial for Puskas as it was for Oestereicher and Real Madrid.

Puskas became part of the best club side ever to run the European gauntlet, and besides the satisfaction this brought to such a talented craftsman, it was also financially rewarding. Puskas amassed over £250,000 ($650,000) during his stay in Spain, though he lost a considerable part of that money with the collapse of a business in which he was involved. He invested in a sausage factory, but others took advantage of the little time Puskas could afford to devote to the business, and the value of his investment dwindled.

The intial problem that Puskas had to overcome when he moved to Madrid was to regain his match fitness. Once he had lost weight he then had to establish himself in the Real Madrid team – no easy task for even the most accomplished soccer player. For this was the era of Alfredo di Stefano. Di Stefano was the acknowledged boss of the Real Madrid dressing-room, and a newcomer, no matter how much he cost or however good his credentials, had to earn the maestro's approval before he was fully accepted as one of the team. Before Puskas' arrival, such outstanding foreign internationals as Brazil's Didi and Sweden's Simonsson had failed to impress di Stefano, and their stay in Madrid had been both short and far from sweet.

But Puskas still had a swagger and a personality which endeared him to the afficionados of Madrid. He did not go to Spain cap in hand but as a rival to di Stefano's hitherto unchallenged leadership, and during the first few months there was an uneasy atmosphere in the Real camp. Di Stefano and Puskas hardly spoke to each other, and both players had their small and separate group of friends. But the issue was to resolve itself in quite a dramatic fashion.

In Spain it is a greater honour to finish top scorer in the first division than in most European countries; the player is publicly crowned and receives cash prizes and gifts from various sources. At the end of one particular season Puskas and di Stefano were way ahead of their rivals with 26 goals each. Real had just one more game to play, against Elche.

The championship was already won – as usual – and the crowd had turned up merely to celebrate and crown the king of goals. In the first-half, the two stars scored a goal apiece and everything depended on the last 45

minutes. Neither of them had increased their total, when, just before the final whistle, Puskas waltzed past the defence and drew the goalkeeper. But instead of shooting past him, Puskas merely pushed the ball sideways for di Stefano to bang it into the net. At the end of the game, Alfredo ran over to Puskas and warmly embraced him. Di Stefano was the top scorer, but Puskas, once again using his wits, had won an important victory in cleverly settling the difference between them.

From then on they blended perfectly. And they never played better together than in the marvellous European Cup final in Glasgow, when di Stefano scored three goals and Puskas four to give Real a 7–3 victory over Eintracht Frankfurt.

In 1962 Pancho (Spain's affectionate nickname for him) scored another hat-trick in a European Cup final. But nonetheless Real lost, 5–3 to Benfica. Puskas also ended four seasons as top scorer in the Spanish first division, the honour he had selflessly allowed di Stefano to steal in that game with Elche.

Puskas was vastly amused when Pele was feted as the only man to score 1000 goals. 'I got at least 1,500, but

Left: Puskas still wore the famous white uniform of Real Madrid at the age of 41, but by then his expanding waist line had become a problem that he found hard to overcome.

Above: Puskas and Billy Wright lead out their teams when England entertained Hungary at Wembley Stadium in November 1953. What followed was a match that has gone down in the annals of soccer history. England had never lost a home match against opposition from outside the British Isles, and though Hungary were Olympic champions in 1952 they were not expected to pose any massive problems in the defence of that proud record. Instead Hungary settled their nerves with a goal inside ninety seconds, and went on to record a famous victory with Nandor Hidegkuti claiming three goals and Puskas scoring twice. England were fortunate that the margin of defeat was not greater than 6–3, so superior were Hungary on the day.

who's counting?' he said. This kind of remark is typical of Puskas. He is a difficult man to interview, because he has a habit of puncturing pompous questions with wry remarks. 'Was the Wembley game your best match?' 'No, I played better against Turku in Finland, when we won 17–0.' 'Which team would you most like to manage?' 'One which wins every game.'

Puskas however, is more open when talking about his old Hungarian team-mates. 'Hidegkuti was the finest centre-forward I ever played with, and Grosics certainly the best goalkeeper.' Puskas was always fiercely loyal to his Hungarian colleagues. 'They would have been an asset to any side. They always gave their best and that was usually more than good enough.'

Puskas himself overstayed his welcome as a player. He loved his soccer so much that he was reluctant to step down.

When he finally retired from playing, he was just a shadow of his old self, slow and ponderous. After his retirement he took up coaching with a small-town Spanish outfit, and afterwards tried his luck in Canada.

Then came an offer to take over the management of the Greek champions, Panathinaikos. The offer was worth £20,000 ($40,000) a year to Puskas, as well as a rent-free villa in Athens. He happily accepted the offer, and began commuting between Athens and his own villa in Madrid. He used his immense personal prestige to fix up lucrative friendlies for this little-known semi-professional team, and this experience against strong foreign opposition, plus Puskas' persuasive multi-lingual tongue, transformed these part-timers and took them into the final of the 1970–71 European Cup – a competition where previously no Greek team had ever reached the semi-finals. Panathinaikos achieved this distinction because they were completely dominated by Puskas' confident personality.

Puskas marched with his team into an hotel in London, where the final was to be played, like the manager of a travelling circus. A great showman, he always had an entourage of admirers around him. Now Hungarians from all over the world, Spaniards who remembered him with affection from his days in Madrid and Greek shipping magnates who just wanted to grab some of the reflected glory were there. The match was lost, as Puskas had quietly predicted all along, but Panathinaikos gave Ajax Amsterdam a hard fight.

Towards the end of 1971 Puskas was guest of honour at a dinner where he presented prizes to some outstanding players. After the meal, two of England's most famous players, Billy Wright and Bobby Moore, praised in their speeches the contribution Puskas had made to soccer, and other notable guests applauded him. Puskas said afterwards, 'Until today, I thought of myself as a professional doing a job just like a dentist, a plumber or anyone else. But hearing people like Billy and Bobby Moore speak so highly of me makes me feel that perhaps it is a little bit special to be Ferenc Puskas.'

Left: Puskas wearing the green and white of Panathinaikos from Athens during his time as their manager.

Kyle Rote Jr.

In 1977 Kyle Rote Jr. was back in business. With 11 goals and 6 assists, he stood as the Dallas Tornado's leading scorer in the North American Soccer League regular season games. In doing so he was justifying his tag as a soccer pioneer in the United States, where it mattered, on the soccer field.

More than three years earlier Rote had helped elevate the status of the game in the United States with a dramatic victory in television's 'Superstars', the trial of strength in a series of athletic events between the world's top professional sportsmen. At the start of the competition Rote would have been the least known entrant, except that his father had made the name famous as an All-Pro running back. By the end he was much more than his father's son.

He had earned his ticket into 'Superstars' by becoming, in 1973, the first American-born player to head the NASL scoring lists. His total of ten goals and ten assists began in Dallas's first game of the season, Rote's own first appearance in the starting line-up. The artificial turf at Texas Stadium was soaked by the sort of downpour that can devastate spectator interest in a sport with relatively new roots. Yet almost 20,000 turned up for the visit of the Toronto Metros. Rote made their journey worthwhile by scoring from a Mike Renshaw cross and playing a key part in the other goal in a 2–1 victory, his debut evening was crowned by the honour of being named the player of the game.

The Tornados were to lose the play-off final to Philadelphia but Kyle Rote Jr. exceeded the expectations of team coach, Ron Newman, during their valiant run for the championship. Half-way through the season, Rote came off the bench to tilt a critical game against close rivals, the St. Louis Stars. With less than twenty minutes to play he broke the deadlock with a shot from just inside the penalty area which sped into the back of the net. With the match still balanced on a knife edge, he then found the decisive pass which set Ilija Mitic free to claim a decisive second goal. Dallas had seen off St. Louis not just for the night but for the rest of the season.

His scoring record also arrived in dramatic circumstances, in the very last match before the semi-final play-off. He needed a goal to pip Warren Archibald of Miami who had edged ahead in his own final appearance the previous evening. The game, which meant more to New York than to Dallas who were assured of their play-off spot finished in a 4–3 defeat but Rote got his goal thanks to his team-mates who pushed him forward to take a penalty when the job usually fell to Mitic. A quirk of the competition then paired the same two sides in the semi-final and it was Rote's goal, again with Renshaw's help, which took Dallas through to the final.

During his hot-spell he found the net in five successive matches, against Montreal he broke new ground for the Tornados by scoring twice and claiming three assists and his goals, combined with the general success of the team, brought him the end-of-season accolade of 'Rookie of the Year'. It was an impact on the game which was that

much greater because he had turned aside the opportunity to make a career in the sport which had made his father famous.

Kyle Rote Sr. and his wife were students at Southern Methodist University in Dallas, when Kyle Jr. was born on Christmas Day in 1950. The story goes that his mother, with the opportunity of a Caesarean birth, was asked whether she wanted her baby delivered in the dying minutes of Christmas Eve or whether she would wait past midnight; she opted to extend her labour pains.

Rote Sr. began to catch the public eye at SMU where he became an All-American tailback. The pressures of his pro-career with the New York Giants accounted in part for the break-up of the marriage and the divorce saw his wife take her family back to Dallas. Kyle Jr. exhibited the same natural aptitudes for sports as his father, but perhaps because of his father's reputation and the inevitable comparisons he looked towards a different pastime.

Originally he used soccer at Highland Park High School as a means of keeping fit in the summer months before the start of the conventional football season. At the same time the United States was beginning its disastrous first flirtations with a professional soccer set-up. Kyle and his friends took the opportunity to watch Dundee United who represented Dallas in the old United States Soccer Federation. They liked what they saw.

After a year on a football scholarship at Oklahoma State University he switched to more academic pursuits at the University of the South at Sewanee in Tennessee. Soccer, though the poor relation on the campus, fitted easily into his curriculum, the soccer team played solely for fun. In the vacations in Dallas he helped form a new outfit, provocatively named the Black Bandits. The venture was designed for pleasure but it shaped the professional career of Kyle Rote Jr. In a match between the Bandits – 'Black' because of the members admirations of black athletes – and a team representing the Tornado in 1969, the 6.0 ft. forward caught the eye of Ron Newman. It would be three years before Rote's name would appear on the draft, but when it did Newman recalled that friendly match and picked him as his number one choice.

After the impact of the 1973 season, closely followed by his Superstars win in Rotunda, Florida over baseball heroes like Pete Rose, and Reggie Jackson, Olympic athletes like Brian Oldfield and Bob Seagren, tennis stars Rod Laver and Stan Smith, and the legendary O. J. Simpson, there had to be some degree of anti-climax. Contract hassles with Tornado owner Lamar Hunt were inevitable, Rote's superstars earnings of a little over $50,000 were almost *forty* times what he had earned from the 1973 soccer season!!

Left: The cycling race was just one of many events in Superstars which showed the all-round strength of agility of Kyle Rote Jr. of Dallas Tornado.
Right: Rote's quite remarkable achievements in the renowned competition between the leading performers in a whole variety of sports drew great attention to soccer. Here Rote and his father, Kyle Snr., a former American professional football star, pose for the cameras with one of Juniors awards.

The Dallas organisation were anxious to capitalise on the 'Superstars' publicity, and sometimes sent Rote on publicity missions to boost attendances on occasions when he should have been training with his team-mates. Even though he imposed a strict daily schedule of exercise on himself his performance declined. Many lesser men would have been unable to cope with the inevitable neuroses.

Kyle Rote Jr. proved himself to be made of sterner substance. His marriage to Mary Lynne, a fellow student at Sewanee, gave him a stable base, but for both of them strength came from deep religious convictions. When Superstars came round again in 1975 O. J. Simpson gained his revenge but Rote again performed well in this circus of swimming, cycling, golf, running, baseball hitting and other strenuous events to finish in third place.

Over the next two years 'Superstars' competitions tended to overshadow his soccer playing career. In 1975 his five goals and six assists made him the most productive Dallas attacker but was an indication of a poor season in which the team went 9–13 and failed for the first time in five seasons to reach the play-offs. He became a member of the United States international squad under Dettmar Cramer, but the impetus stimulated by the appointment

of the famous coach rather disappeared when he left for a job in West Germany. In 1976 Rote spent less time in the Dallas line-up than in any of his previous three seasons and managed only three goals.

But in Superstars he reached new levels to regain the crown, in 1976 and, incredibly, to retain it a year later. In 1976, he trained intensively for three months and in each of the seven events he entered he scored points. Soccer was also well represented by Bob Rigby, then the goalkeeper for the New York Cosmos, who finished fourth. After the contest Rigby gave a clue to Rote's success: 'You want to get into the science of it,' he said, 'then talk to Kyle. He has it broken down scientifically, every event, the training, the tactics. He earned his win. He put his time in.' Certainly no American would ever think again that soccer was a sport for second-class athletes.

By now an enormously marketable commodity he signed a contract with Mark McCormack's International Management Group – voluntarily surrendering a commission of *thirty* per cent on the premise that such an unusually high percentage would stimulate the agency to greater efforts on his behalf. 'I'd rather have 70 per cent of a lot rather than 90 per cent of very little,' he said at the time. His self-imposed values only allowed him to promote for companies in which he could feel an involvement. Lines from bread to breakfast cereal from toothpaste to oil filters plus the normal quota of endorsements of sporting goods and games have borne the Kyle Rote label. And with genuine integrity he always uses the products that he endorses.

His lessening impression on the soccer field in no way deterred companies who wished to use his name. As long as he performed with distinction in 'Superstars', it didn't seem to matter that he warmed the Dallas bench during the season. In 1976 he started only 11 of the Tornado's 26 games; in only six of those eleven was he still on the field when the final whistle was blown. In five matches he wasn't required, even as a substitute.

Though the sponsors didn't seem to care, Kyle Rote Jr., sensitive and totally incapable of a take-the-money and what-the-heck philosophy, kept his disappointment to himself and resolved to do better. With the soccer boom at last beginning to happen in America, Rote whose professional career had begun when the future of the NASL was less than clear realises more than most that the real key to a secure growth for the game in the United States rests with the development of the American-born player.

That is why his best-ever goals total in 1977 was so significant. For all his protracted negotiations with Lamar Hunt he, in keeping with most US-produced players, would hardly challenge the wealth of the Rockefellers from his soccer earnings. But it was a return to form that spelt out satisfaction.

Left: Rote takes a cut during the baseball Superstars event.
Right: Wearing the Tampa Bay Rowdies uniform for a change, Rote does the tackling against the People's Republic of China.

Helmut Schoen

When Franz Beckenbauer lifted the World Cup for West Germany in Munich's Olympic Stadium in July 1974, the wheel had turned full circle for Helmut Schoen. After the disappointments of second place in 1966 and third four years later, the West German coach had finally matched the achievement of his predecessor and mentor, Sepp Herberger, who had masterminded the coup that had brought Germany the World championship in 1954.

Helmut Schoen came into coaching from a pedigree background. As a player in the late thirties, he represented his country on sixteen occasions, scoring seventeen goals. In November 1937 he had set out on his international career by scoring twice against Sweden. But for the war Schoen's would have been an even more impressive record. His coaching achievements were, however, to compensate him for the loss of those precious years as a player.

Herberger called Schoen to his side in 1956; he served an eight-year apprenticeship until Herberger's retirement put him into the most stable coaching position anywhere in soccer. Herberger had succeeded the first German national coach, Otto Nerz, who was in charge from 1926–36. The German soccer authorities, so renowned for their patience, again stuck by their choice even though Schoen has suffered scathing criticism at times.

In 1966 some thought he placed too much emphasis on defence after the team had shown its exciting potential for attack in a 5–1 win over Switzerland in their first game. It was even suggested that his decision to consign Beckenbauer to close-marking Bobby Charlton cost West Germany the final against England.

In 1970 even the players began to question his thinking. At every tactical conference Schoen reiterated his belief that the German team had to be a defensive one. He insisted on playing Karl-Heinz Schnellinger as an orthodox sweeper while Beckenbauer, who in Schoen's words 'is best moving between midfield and defence rather than midfield and attack', played deep. Uwe Seeler, spokesman for the players, wanted greater flexibility and virtual autonomy on the field so that he, in his role of captain, could make fresh tactical dispositions as the situation demanded. It was on Seeler's insistence that Schoen introduced the substitute Jurgen Grabowski when the Germans were struggling for an equalizer against humble Morocco.

But the problems began to sort themselves out on the field as Germany fought their way through to the semi-final, thanks largely to Grabowski's decisive contributions as substitute.

Schoen's use of substitutes in the game against Italy in the semi-final, was more dubious. For the first time Grabowski started the game, while Reinhard Libuda, whose direct running at the full-backs had previously done so much to soften the defenders in readiness for Grabowski's arrival, was this time put on the bench. By the end of the first ninety minutes Schoen had no less than five front runners in the team – Grabowski, Libuda,

Muller, Seeler and Held. Germany paid the price in extra time when their over-exposed defence allowed the Italians to score three times.

Schoen's tactics might have sometimes been questionable but his ability to handle men and the thoroughness of his preparations are beyond doubt. Before the 1970 World Cup there was some suspicion about the compatibility of Muller and Seeler. Schoen's solution was simple and effective. He put them in the same room in the hotel. It was not long before the two were reconciled and they proved one of the most effective combinations in the tournament. Without resorting to the somewhat severe measures of Herberger, Schoen had little difficulty in disciplining his squad. None of the team which won the European Championship either drank or smoked. Under Schoen, as always, the Germans were supremely fit.

Although the team in 1970 might have fallen short of what they were capable of, to reach third place was still a considerable achievement. All the more so since the German team was then in a state of transition. Two years later half the side had given way to new faces. The skill with which he guided the change was one of Schoen's greatest achievements.

The turning point came in January 1972 when four of the established players, Bertie Vogts, Wolfgang Overath, Wolfgang Weber and Karl-Heinz Schnellinger were badly injured, while Klaus Fichtel, who had played so well against England in Mexico was excluded because of his alleged involvement in a scandal over bribing in the West German League.

Schoen hit on the ideal answer. He formed a national team out of six players from Bayern Munich and three from Borussia Monchengladbach, who between them had monopolized the German championship in the previous four years. The other two players, Hoettges, from Bremen and Kremers from Schalke were former Borussia Monchengladbach players.

Thus while most managers have to blend an assortment of eleven individuals, most of whom have probably only met on opposing sides in League matches, Schoen had only to blend two sets of players, the one from Bayern and the other from Borussia Monchengladbach. With the likes of Beckenbauer, Muller and Gunter Netzer at his disposal, the task did not prove too difficult.

The fluent style that evolved from this blend of club cohesion brought West Germany a memorable 3–1 victory over England at Wembley in the quarter-finals of the 1972 European Championship. Hungary were swept aside in the semi-finals to take Schoen's side into a final against Russia. There two goals from Muller and another from Wimmer were the key moments in a display of such dominance that West Germany were immediately installed as favourites for the next World Cup, to be staged on their own soil.

The forecasting was to prove accurate though not without some alarms for Schoen. He discarded Netzer, the key play-maker of '72, for Wolfgang Overath, the veteran of the '66 and '70 World Cups. West Germany actually lost a match in the finals, the first meeting between East and West on the soccer field with more than World

Cup status at stake. East Germany won by a goal from Sparwasser and the tide of criticism turned against Schoen. Speculation arose that Franz Beckenbauer, not Schoen, held the influence on team selection, and that other members of the squad were resentful.

Schoen would have drawn comfort from the knowledge that twenty years earlier Herberger's side had been beaten in a group match and had still gone on to win the World Cup. And so it was to be for the West Germany of 1974. Though their form improved with wins over Sweden, Yugoslavia and Poland, and though the final was to be in Munich, home of six of the side, West Germany were no longer favourites to win. The bookmakers favoured Holland.

But this time Helmut Schoen was not to be denied even after West Germany conceded a penalty and goal in the first minute. The responsibility and competitiveness that have been qualities in all Schoen's teams finally allowed the skills to flourish and West Germany were worthy winners. This time there was no criticism of defensive philosophies. The World Champions played with two wingers, and their campaign to retain the cup in Argentina was based on a similar formula.

Helmut Schoen was still at the helm, a firm but avuncular figure. Tall, bald and sad-faced he still looked for the most part like the bank clerk he was at the end of his playing career. Yet his effect on European and World soccer has been immense, and there can be no finer epitaph than the headlines of a German newspaper the day after West Germany won the World Cup – a sentiment every soccer student who has marvelled at the scintillating skills of the West German national side would echo . . . 'Danke Schoen!'

Top right: Old adversaries Helmut Schoen and Sir Alf Ramsey.
Right: Sepp Herberger, Schoen's mentor.
Below: Beckenbauer at the moment of Schoen's greatest triumph, the end of the 1974 World Cup final.

Index

Abegglen, Trello 42
Aberdeen 88, 120
Aclmovic 68
Adamache 60
Ademir Marques de Menses 45
Aebi 42
Afonin 63
Ajax (Amsterdam) 68, 79, 123, 124, 146, 147, 175
Albania 156
Albert, Florian 51, 54
Albertosi, Carlos 55, 63, 64, 65, 156
Albrecht, Jorge 54, 55, 58
Amancio 54
Amarildo 51, 52, 54
American Amateur Football Association 86
American Football Association 86
American Soccer League 86, 87, 88
Anastasi, Pietro 64, 69, 83, 118
Ancheta 63
Anderlecht (Brussels) 80
Anoul 47
Anselmo, Pelegrin 40, 41
Archibald, Warren 177
Argentina 39, 40, 41, 42, 49, 51, 54, 55, 56, 57, 59, 68, 69, 70, 86, 118, 123, 126, 134, 146
Arsenal 82, 97, 113, 118, 139
Asatiani 60
Asparoukhov, Georgi 59
Astle, Jeff 61, 62
Aston Villa 113, 121
Atletico Bilbao 82
Atletico Madrid 79, 80, 130
Augusto, Jose 54, 56, 130
Australia 54, 59, 68, 69
Austria 13 19, 39, 41, 42, 47, 49, 54, 68, 156, 158, 170, 172
Ayala 68
Ayra 43
Aztecs (Los Angeles) 104, 109, 118, 122

Baartz 68
Babington 68, 69, 70
Bahr 86
Bakhramov 57
Bakhuijs 42
Ball, Alan 54, 57, 61, 62
Baltazar 46
Banks, Gordon 57, 59, 61, 63, 95, 96, 97, 98
Barbosa 45
Barcelona 78, 80, 82, 123, 124, 146, 147
Battle of Berne 47
Bauer, Jose 46
Bayern Munich 71, 79, 80, 83, 99, 100, 102, 156, 158, 180
Baylon 60
Beattie, Andy 47
Beckenbauer, Franz 56, 57, 62, 63, 64, 65, 69, 71, 79, 93, 99, 100, 101, 102, 103, 115, 126, 140, 180, 181
Belgium 13, 39, 40, 41, 42, 47, 58, 60, 62, 68, 80, 83, 86
Bell, Colin 62, 63
Bellini, Luiz 50, 54
Bene, Ferenc 54, 56
Benetti, 69
Benfica (Lisbon) 58, 78, 79, 104, 116, 130, 131, 146, 174
Bent, Geoff 113
Bermuda 58
Berry, John 113
Best, George 79, 93, 104, 105,

106, 107, 108, 109, 110, 115, 122, 124, 139
Bicentennial Tournament 118, 152
Birmingham City 81, 113
Blackpool 145, 152
Blanchflower, Danny 49
Blanchflower, Jackie 113
Bloomer, Steve 142
Boca Juniors 128
Bolivia 39, 40, 44, 45, 54, 59
Bonetti, Peter 63, 97
Bonev 60
Bonhof, Rainer 70, 71
Boninsegna, Roberto 64, 65
Borghi 45, 86
Borussia Dortmund 80
Borussia Monchengladbach 79, 82, 139, 140, 180
Boszik, Jozsef 47, 48, 49, 172
Boyle, Johnny 120
Brabook 50
Brazil 16, 20, 39, 40, 41, 42, 43, 44, 45, 46, 47, 48, 49, 50, 51, 52, 54, 55, 57, 58, 59, 60, 61, 62, 63, 64, 65, 66, 68, 69, 70, 86, 90, 97, 122, 123, 130, 146, 151, 161, 162, 163, 164, 169
Breitner, Paul 69, 70, 71
Bremner, Billy 66, 69, 121, 139
Brindisi 68, 70
Brito 64, 163
Broadis 47
Brown, Bobby 49
Brulls 54
Brustad 42
Buchan, Martin 69
Bulgarelli 55
Bulgaria 51, 54, 58, 59, 60, 61, 62, 63, 68, 69, 70, 118, 123, 139
Buljan 69
Bundesliga (Western Germany) 100, 156
Burgnich 64
Busby, Matt 104, 105, 106, 110, 112, 113, 115, 116
Buzansky 47
Bwanga 68
Byrne, Johnnie 134
Byrne, Roger 48, 113
Byshovets 59, 60, 62

Cabrera 51
Cagliari 88
Calderon 54, 63
Canada 58, 68
Canario 127
Capdeville 43
Capello 70
Carapallese 45
Carbajal, Antonio 45, 54, 97
Cardiff City 112, 117
Carlos, Alberto Torres 57, 65
Carlsson, Henry 45
Carnevali 69
Carpegiani, Paulo Cesar 70
Carvajales 43
Carvalho 54
Castro, Hector 41
Caszely 69
Catterick, Harry 98
Cea, Pedro 40, 41
Celtic (Glasgow) 79, 120, 152
Charles, John 49
Charlton, Bobby 54, 57, 61, 63, 79, 100, 106, 110, 111, 112, 113, 114, 115, 116, 127, 134, 152, 180
Charlton, Jack 57, 62, 116, 130
Charlton United 113

Chelsea 80, 81, 97, 105, 120, 121, 122
Chesterfield 97
Chico 45
Chile 39, 40, 45, 50, 51, 52, 54, 55, 59, 68, 69, 86
China 9
Chinaglia, Giorgio 93, 117, 118
Chislenko, Igor 56
Chivers, Martin 132
Chumpitaz 60
Chutsky, Tony 118
Clarke, Allan 62
Clemence, Ray 97, 139
Clodoaldo Tavares de Santana 64, 65, 66
Cohen, George 59, 149
Colaussi, Gino 43
Colchester United 16
Colman, Eddie 113
Cologne 83, 158
Colombian League 45
Colombia 51, 54, 59, 68, 151
Colombo 45
Coluna, Mario 57
Combi, Giampiero 41
Conen 41
Connelly 54
Cooke, Charlie 120, 121, 122
Cooke, Jack Kent 88
Cortes 56, 58
Cosmos (New York) 85, 90, 99, 102, 117, 118, 161, 175, 177
Costa, Flavio 45
Crerand, Pat 115, 116
Cruyff, Johan 68, 69, 70, 71, 79, 123, 124, 125, 126, 146, 147
Crystal Palace 98, 106, 122
Cuba 42, 43
Cubilla, Luis 64, 163
Cubillas, Teofilo 60, 62, 63
Cush, Wilbur 49
Cyprus 156
Czechoslovakia 39, 41, 42, 43, 47, 49, 50, 51, 52, 54, 58, 59, 60, 62, 83, 123, 142 145, 146, 148, 151, 163, 164
Czibor, Zoltan 47, 49, 172

Dalglish, Kenny 66, 69
David 51
David, Steve 118
Davidson, Tiny 63
Delaunay, Henri 39, 77, 82, 83
Delfour 43
Del Sol 54
Dembrovski 62
Denmark 39, 58, 82
Dermendjiev 60
De Sordi 50
Deyna 70
Dickinson, Jimmy 47
Didi (Valdir Pereira) 46, 48, 50, 59, 127, 128, 161, 173
Dienst 57
Dino 49
Dinu 62
di Stefano, Alfredo 51, 78, 79, 124, 126, 127, 128, 161, 173, 174
Dobai 43
Dobias 83
Docherty, Tommy 108, 120, 121
Dockx 60
Domenghini 60, 63
Domingas Da Guia 43
Dorado, Pablo 40
Dubinsky 51
Dukla (Prague) 87, 146
Dumitrache 60, 62

Dundee United 120, 178
Dutch East Indies 42
Dynamo Kiev 80
Dynamo Zagreb 82
Dzajic 69

East Germany 49, 54, 58, 68, 69, 70, 80, 123, 139, 146, 180, 181
Eckel 47
Ecuador 59, 68, 151
Eddy, Keith 118
Edstroem, Ralf 68, 70
Edwards, Duncan 48, 112, 113, 145
Egypt 41
Eintracht (Frankfurt) 78, 128, 174
Eire 58, 68, 82
Eizaguirre 45
Elche 128, 173, 174
El Salvador 59, 60, 61, 62
Emmerich, Lothar 54, 56, 57
England 42, 44, 45, 46, 47, 48, 49, 50, 51, 54, 55, 57, 58, 59, 60, 61, 62, 63, 64, 66, 79, 80, 82, 83, 86, 87, 97, 100, 104, 110, 112, 115, 121, 122, 129, 130, 132, 134, 137, 139, 140, 142, 144, 145, 146, 148, 149, 150, 151, 152, 162, 170, 172, 175, 180
Espanol (Barcelona) 128
Esparrago 63
European Cup 20, 46, 77, 78, 79, 80, 99, 100, 102, 104, 113, 123, 124, 126, 127, 128, 131, 137, 139, 140, 146, 174, 175, 180
European Cup Winners Cup 77, 80, 121, 140, 148, 156
European Football Union Cup 77, 81, 126, 139 see also Inter-Cities Fairs Cup
European Nations Cup see European Cup
Eusebio da Silva Ferreira 54, 55, 56, 57, 58, 59, 78, 129, 130, 131
Evaraldo 163
Everton 87
Eyzaguirre 55

Facchetti, Giancinto 60, 65
Farkas 54
Felix 60, 62, 63, 64, 65, 70, 163
Feola, Vicente 48, 49, 54
Ferencvaros (Hungary) 82, 170
Ferrari, Giovanni 42
Ferreiro 56
Ferrini 50, 51
Festa 57
Feyenoord (Rotterdam) 79, 82, 124
FIFA 13, 26, 39, 41, 44, 46, 51, 55, 58, 59, 60, 67, 86, 90, 93, 131
Fichtel, Klaus 64, 180
Figueroa 69
Finney, Jim 56
Finney, Tom 45, 47, 49, 115
Fiorentina (Italy) 78, 80
Fontaine, Just 49, 50, 62
football
  history 9, 10, 11, 12, 13
  rules 25, 26, 27, 28, 29, 30, 31, 32, 33, 34, 35, 36, 37, 38
  scoring 33
  tactics 18, 19, 20, 21, 22
  techniques 15, 16, 17, 18, 19, 20, 21, 22, 23, 24
  terms 23
Football Association 12, 41, 113, 115, 120, 121, 139, 140, 145, 148, 152

Football League 13, 19, 97, 109
France 13, 39, 40, 41, 42, 43, 44, 46, 49, 50, 54, 58, 68, 82
Francis, Gerry 140
Franklin, Neil 45
French Football Association 39
Friaca 45
Fulham 109, 115, 152
Fuste 54

Gaetjens, Larry 45, 86
Galic, Milan 52
Gailardo 60, 63
Garrincha (Manoel Francisco dos Santos) 49, 50, 51, 52, 54, 161, 162
Geddes, Jim 120
Gelai 54, 56
Generals (New York) 88
Gento, Francisco 54, 126, 128
Germany 39, 41, 42, 145, see also East Germany, West Germany
Gerson de Oliveira Nunes 54, 60, 61, 63, 64, 65, 66, 163
Ghazouani 60
Ghiggia, Alcides 45
Giles, Johnny 115
Gillies, Matt 97
Gonzales 63
Gornik Zabrze (Poland) 80, 116
Grabowski, Jurgen 62, 63, 64, 70, 71, 180
Grahn 62, 70
Great Britain 9, 10, 11, 12, 13, 22, 39, 49
Greaves, Jimmy 51, 54, 55, 57, 132, 134
Greece 9, 58
Greenwood, Ron 132, 134, 137, 148, 149, 150, 152
Gregg, Harry 50, 104
Gren, Gunnar 45, 49, 50
Griffiths, Mervyn 47
Groscis, Gyula 48, 172, 175
Guaita 41, 42
Guatemala 68
Gustavsson, Julli 49
Gylmar 54

Haan, Arie 68, 146
Haiti 58, 59, 68, 69, 79, 118
Haller, Helmut 54, 56, 57, 59, 61
Hamburg SV 80, 139, 140
Hamrin, Kurt 49, 50
Hanegen, Wim van 68, 70, 83, 123
Hanot, Gabriel 77, 79, 83
Harvey, John 69
Hay 66
Held, Sigi 56, 57, 61, 64, 180
Hellstrom 60, 61
Herberger, Sepp 42, 46, 100, 102, 180, 181
Herbin 54
Herd 115
Heredia 69
Herrera, Helenio 20
Hertzka 43
Hibernians (Cork) 109
Hidegkuti, Nandor 47, 48, 170, 172, 178
Hilario 130
Himst, Paul von 60
Hitchens, Gerry 51
Hoeness, Uli 69, 70, 71, 83, 102
Hoettges 57, 180
Hofheinz, Roy 88
Hohberg, Juan 47, 49
Holland see The Netherlands

Hollins, John 121
Holzenbein 71, 83
Home International Championship 44, 106, 140
Honduras 59, 68
Honved 172, 173
Hopkinson, Eddie 115
Houseman 68, 70
Hrdlicka 60
Hungary 13, 20, 39, 41, 42, 43, 46, 47, 48, 49, 50, 51, 52, 54, 56, 58, 68, 80, 82, 83, 146, 170, 172, 173, 175, 180
Hunt, Lamar 88, 90, 178
Hunt, Roger 54, 57, 59
Hunt, Steve 118
Hunter, Norman 63, 149
Huracan 126
Hurst, Geoff 55, 56, 57, 60, 62, 97, 98, 100, 115, 132, 133, 134, 135, 136, 137, 148
Hutchinson, Tommy 66, 69

Ilyin 50
India 44
Indio 47
Inter-Cities Fairs Cup 77, 81, 82
Inter-Milan 20, 79, 124, 131
Internapoli 117
International Football Association 25, 26, 27, 28, 29, 30, 31, 33, 34, 35, 37
International Soccer League 87, 88
Internazionale (Milan) 78
Ipswich Town 140
Iran 68
Ireland see Eire see also Northern Ireland
Israel 49, 59, 61, 62
Israel, Rinus 124
Italian League 45, 54, 117
Italy 39, 41, 42, 43, 45, 47, 48, 49, 50, 51, 54, 55, 57, 58, 59, 60, 61, 62, 63, 64, 65, 68, 69, 70, 82, 83, 118, 130, 156, 164

Jair 45
Jairzinho 54, 59, 60, 61, 62, 63, 64, 65, 66, 68, 69, 70, 97
Japan 9, 59
Jeck 60, 62
Jeppson, Hans 45
Joel 49
Johnstone, Jimmy 59
Jones, Mark 113
Jongbloed 70, 71
Jonquet, Robert 50
Jordan, Joe 66, 69
Joseph, Jean 69
Jujica 60
Jules Rimet Trophy 41, 42, 43, 44, 50, 57, 58, 162 see also World Cup
Julinho (Julio Botelho) 47
Juskowiak 50
Juventude 130
Juventus (Turin) 79, 82, 118, 124

Kachalin, Gavril 59
Kakoko 68
Kaplichny 63
Karasi 69
Kasperczak 70
Katalinski 68
Kazadi 68, 69
Keegan, Kevin 138, 139, 140
Kelsey, Jack 49
Kerkhof, van der 71
Kevan, Derek 49

Khurtsilava 57
Kidd, Brian 116
Kispest 170
Kocsis, Sandor 47, 49, 50, 170, 172
Koerners 47
Kolev, Ivan 61
Kopa, Raymond 49, 50, 127, 128
Kopecky 43
Korea see North Korea, South Korea
Kostalek 42
Kreitlein 55
Kremers 180
Krol, Ruud 68, 70, 71, 123, 146
Kvasnak, Andrej 52, 60

Labone, Brian 62
Labruna, Angel 49
Landa 51, 52
Larsson, Bo 70
Larsson, Sven 61
Lato, Gregor 69, 70
Law, Denis 66, 115
Lawrence 156
Lazio 82, 117, 118
Leao 70
League of Ireland 109
Lee, Francis 60, 61, 62
Leeds United 66, 79, 82, 121, 139, 147, 149, 158
Lehner 42
Leicester City 97, 115
Leonidas da Silva 43
Libuda, Reinhard 61, 62, 64, 180
Liebrich, Werner 47
Liedholm, Nils 45, 49, 50
Liverpool 79, 82, 98, 123, 139, 140, 146
Lofthouse 47
Lohr 61, 62, 63
London 81, 82
Lopez 60
Lorimer, Peter 66, 69
Luton Town 145
Luxembourg 127

Mackay, Dave 49, 148
Mackay, Jim 68
Mai 47
Maier, Sepp 63, 69, 70, 71, 102
Malafeev 57
Manchester City 12, 20, 80, 97, 104, 140
Manchester United 48, 79, 104, 105, 106, 108, 109, 110, 112, 113, 115, 116, 131, 132, 137, 140, 145
Maneiro 60
Manga 55
Mannion, Wilf 45
Marcos 55
Maric 68, 69
Marinho, Francisco 68, 70
Marsh, Rodney 109
Masopust, Josef 52
Maspoli, Roque 45
Massese 117
Matrai, Sandor 54
Matthews, Stanley 45, 47, 142, 143, 144, 145
Matosas 64
Mattler 42
Mauro, Ramos de Oliveira 50
Mazurkiewicz, Ladislao 59, 62, 64, 68, 164
Mazzola, Sandrino 49, 65
Meazza, Giuseppe 41, 42, 43
Mcisl, Hugo 41
Meredith, Billy 142

Merrick, Gil 47
Messing, Shep 90
Meszoly, Kalman 54
Metros (Toronto) 129, 176
Mexico 39, 40, 45, 46, 49, 51, 54, 58, 59, 60, 61, 62, 63 68, 97, 115
Michaels, Rinus 68, 146, 147
Miguez 45
Milan AC 78, 79, 80, 102, 123, 131, 146
Milburn, Jackie 145
los Millionarios (Brazil) 126
Mitic, Rajko 45, 177
Mocanu 60
Montero-Castillo 68, 69
Monti, Luisito 41
Moore, Bobby 57, 59, 61, 80, 109, 110, 115, 116, 130, 135, 148, 149, 150, 151, 152, 153, 162, 175
Morais 55, 57, 162
Morales 60, 63, 64, 163
Morgan, Willie 66
Morlock 47
Morocco 59, 60, 62, 68, 180
Mortensen, Stan 45, 145
Moscow Dynamo 80
Mujic 51
Mullen 45
Muller, Dieter 83
Muller, Gerhard (Gerd) 59, 60, 61, 62, 63, 64, 70, 71, 79, 83, 102, 126, 154, 155, 156, 157, 158, 159, 180
Mullery, Alan 63, 82
Munoz, Miguel 128
Muntian 60, 62

NASL see North American Soccer League
Nacional (Uruguay) 59
National Professional Soccer League 88, 90, 92, 93
Neagu 60
Neeskens, Johann 68, 70, 71, 123, 147
Neill, Terry 106
Nejedly 42, 43
the Netherlands 13, 20, 39, 41, 42, 58, 66, 68, 69, 70, 71, 79, 83, 100, 102, 123, 124, 146, 147, 154, 181
Netzer, Gunther 69, 83, 99, 180
New Zealand 59
Newcastle 82, 139, 145
Newman, Ron 95
Newton 60, 63
Nicolas 42
Nigeria 59
Nordahl, Bertil 45
Nordahl, Gunnar 45
North American Soccer League (NASL) 26, 29, 31, 33, 49, 85, 98, 99, 109, 112, 117, 118, 122, 129, 148, 161, 176
North Korea 54, 55, 56, 59, 69, 130
Northern Ireland 49, 50, 58, 68, 82, 106, 109
Norway 42, 58
Nuremberg 156

Oblak 68
Ocwirk, Ernst 47, 102
O'Farrell, Frank 106
Olympic Games 39, 40, 49, 58
Orlando 50
Ormond, Willie 66, 69
Orsi, Raimondo 41, 42
Osgood, Peter 121
Overath, Wolfgang 57, 62, 65, 69, 70, 180

Paine, Terry 54
Pak Doo Ik 55
Pan Athinaikos (Athens) 79, 124, 146, 175
Panenka 83
Paraguay 39, 40, 45, 49, 54, 59, 86
Partizan (Belgrade) 77, 116
Patzke 64
Peacock, Alan 51
Pegg, David 113
Peiro 51, 54
Pele (Edson Arantes do Nascimento) 49, 50, 51, 54, 55, 59, 60, 61, 62, 63, 64, 65, 66, 85, 90, 92, 93, 97, 115, 117, 118, 126, 127, 128, 130, 131, 151, 161, 162, 163, 164, 165, 166, 167, 168, 169, 174
Pena 62
Penarol (Uruguay) 59, 131
Pereira, Luis 54, 57, 66, 69, 70
Perez 45
Perfumo 70
Perry, Bill 145
Peru 39, 40, 58, 59, 60, 62, 63
Pesser 42
Peters, Martin 54, 56, 61, 63, 134, 137, 148
Petkovic 68
Petras 60
Peucelle, Carlos 41
Piola, Silvio 42, 43
Planicka, Frantisek 41, 42, 43
Poland 42, 49, 54, 58, 59, 66, 69, 70, 118, 181
Poletti 156
Popuvic 51
Porkujan 55, 56
Portugal 44, 49, 54, 55, 56, 57, 58, 59, 68, 83, 116, 129, 130, 134
Port Vale 145
Pozzo, Vittorio 41, 42, 43
Prati 79
Preston 148
Probst 47
Puc, Antinin 42
Puskas, Ferenc 47, 49, 51, 78, 79, 115, 124, 126, 127, 128, 131, 146, 170, 171, 172, 173, 174, 175

Queen's Park Rangers 13, 109
Quintano 69
Quixall, Albert 115

Radakovic 52
Rahn, Helmut 47, 48, 49, 50
Rakosi 56
Ramirez 51
Ramsey, Sir Alf 20, 45, 54, 59, 60, 62, 63, 66, 115, 132, 134, 137, 140, 148, 149, 150, 151
Rangers (Glasgow) 80
Rappan, Karl 20
Rattin, Antonio 55, 56, 128
Ravens 63
Raynor, George 45
Real Madrid 54, 78, 79, 80, 113, 116, 121, 122, 124, 126, 127, 128, 131, 173, 174
Real Zaragoza 82
Red Star (Belgrade) 113
Redknapp, Harry 98
Reinoso 69
Rensenbrink, Rob 68, 69, 70, 71
Renshaw, Mike 176, 177
Rep, Johnnie 69, 70, 71, 146
Revie, Don 140
Rhodesia 59
Rial, Hector 128
Richards 69

Rigby, Bobby 90, 175
Rijsbergen, Wim 69, 71
Rimet, Jules 31, 77, 86
Ritchie, John 98
Riva, Luigi 63, 64, 65, 70, 83
Rivelino, Roberto 60, 63, 64, 65, 66, 68, 69, 70
River Plate 126
Rivera, Gianni 55, 60, 62, 63, 64, 69, 70
Roberto 43
Robledo, George 45
Rocha, Pedro 59, 68
Rojas, Eladio 52
Roma 81, 82
Rome 9
Romeau Pellicciari 42, 43
Rot-Weiss (Essen) 156
Rote, Kyle Jr. 90, 175, 176, 177, 178
Rowdies (Tampa Bay) 109, 118, 120
Rubinos 60, 63
Rumania 39, 40, 41, 43, 58, 59, 60, 62, 82, 83, 151
Russia see Union of Soviet Socialist Republics

Sabo 56
Sagalo 50
St. Etienne 79
Saldanha, Joao 59
Salvadore 55
Sanchez, Leonel 50, 51, 52, 55
Sanchis 54
Sandberg 68, 70
Sanon 69
Santamaria 51
Santos 90, 131, 169
Santos, Djalma 46, 47, 48, 50, 52, 54, 161, 162
Santos, Nilton 46, 47, 48, 161, 162
Sarosi, George 42, 43
Satmareanu 60
Schaefer, Hans 47, 48, 50
Scherer 52
Schiaffino Juan 45, 47
Schiavio, Angelo 42
Schnellinger, Karl-Heinz 54, 56, 59, 63, 64, 180
Schoen, Helmut 54, 59, 63, 66, 71, 100, 102, 146, 156, 158, 180, 181
Schulz, Willy 59, 64
Schwarzenbeck George 102
Scotland 13, 17, 44, 47, 48, 49, 59, 66, 68, 69, 104, 112, 115, 120, 121, 134, 140, 144, 145, 156
Scunthorpe United 139
Seculic 40
Seeldrayers, Rodolphe 39
Seeler, Uwe 49, 54, 59, 60, 61, 62, 63, 158, 180
Sekularac, Dragoslav 51
Setubal 130, 131
Sexton, Dave 120, 121
Shamrock Rovers 88
Shankly, Bill 97, 120, 139
Schroiff 51, 52
Shesternev, Albert 56, 59, 60, 63
Shilton, Peter 97
Shrove Tuesday Football 10, 11
Silva 56
Simeonov 61
Simoes da Costa, Antonio 54, 57, 130
Simon 54
Simonsson 173
Simpson 97
Sindelar, Matthias 41

Sionsson 50
Sipos 54
Skoglund, Nacka 45, 49, 50
Slovan Bratislava 80
Smethurst, Derek 118
Smith, Bobby 90
Sobotka 42
Soccer Bowl 118
Sotil 60, 63
Sounders (Seattle) 118, 132
South Korea 46, 47, 59, 68
Southampton 106
Spain 13, 39, 41, 42, 45, 51, 54, 58, 59, 68, 82, 127, 147, 172, 173
Spanish League 78, 123, 127, 128, 174
Spartak Trnava 145
Sparwasser, Jurgen 69
Spiegler, Mordecai 59, 61
Sporting Club (Lisbon) 77, 80, 131
Sporting Club (Lourenco Marques) 130
Springett, Ron 51
Spurs (Chicago) 88
Stabile, Guillermo 40, 41
Stars (St. Louis) 177
Stepney, Alex 91
Stiles, Nobby 54, 57, 104, 137
Stockport 109
Stoke City 97, 98, 137, 142, 144, 145
Strikers (Fort Lauderdale) 85, 95, 98, 118
Suarez, Luis 54
Sudan 59
Sunderland 135
Suurbier, Wim 146
Svehlik 83
Svensson 50
Svodoba 42
Swansea Town 117
Sweden 13, 39, 41, 42, 43, 45, 49, 50, 54, 58, 59, 60, 61, 62, 68, 69, 70, 100, 161, 162, 180, 181
Swift 45
Switzerland 13, 20, 39, 41, 42, 43, 45, 46, 47, 48, 50, 54, 58, 180
Szarmach 69, 70
Szengeller 42, 43, 172
Szentmihalyi 54
Szepan 42
Szusza 172
Szymaniak, Horst 48

Taylor, Jack 76
Taylor, Tommy 47, 48, 112, 113
Tejada 127
Telch 70
Thepot, Alex 40
Thunder (San Antonio) 148, 152
Tichy, Lajos 49, 51
Tilkowski 57
Tim (Elba de Padua Lima) 43
Titkos 43
Tomaszewski 70
Torino 45
Tornados (Dallas) 175, 176, 177, 178
Toro 51
Torres 51
Tostao, Eduardo 54, 59, 61, 63, 64, 65, 66
Toth 46
Tottenham Hotspur 80, 82, 105, 120, 132, 137, 148
Toye, Clive 90, 102
Tozzi, Humberto 47
Trautmann, Bert 97
Trinidad 68

Troche 54, 56
Tschenscher 60
Turek 47
Turesson 61
Turkey 44, 46, 47, 68
Turku (Finland) 175
Turnbull, Eddie 49

Ubinas 63
Union of Soviet Socialist Republics
48, 49, 50, 51, 55, 56, 58, 59, 60,
62, 63, 68, 80, 82, 83, 180
United States 13, 39, 40, 41, 42,
44, 45, 46, 47, 55, 58, 68, 85, 86,
87, 88, 89, 90, 91, 92, 93, 99, 102,
117, 118, 176, 178
United States Football Association
86
United States Soccer Association
88
United States Soccer Federation
86, 178
United States Soccer Football
Association 86, 87, 88
Universitario (Lima) 158
Uppingham School 12

Uruguay 39, 40, 41, 42, 44, 45, 46,
47, 49, 51, 54, 56, 59, 60, 62, 63,
64, 65 68, 69, 70, 86, 123, 163,
164

Valdivia 61, 62
Valdomiro 69
Valencia 82, 128, 147
Varela, Obdullio 45
Vava, Edvaldo 49, 50, 51, 52, 161
Venezuela 59
Viktor 60, 163
Vincente 55, 57
Viollet, Denis 112, 113
Vissoker 60
Vogts, Berti 69, 71, 140, 180

Waddington, Tony 97
Waiters, Tony 97
Wales 49, 50, 58, 139, 140, 144
Walter, Fritz 47, 48, 102
Weber, Wolfgang 54, 57, 180
Webster, Colin 115
Wembley Stadium 54, 57
West, Gordon 97
West Bromwich Albion 115, 137

West Germany 20, 46, 47, 48, 49,
50, 51, 52, 54, 56, 57, 58, 59, 60,
61, 62, 63, 64, 65, 66, 68, 69, 70,
71, 79, 80, 82, 83, 99, 100, 102,
115, 118, 132, 134, 137, 139, 140,
146, 151, 156, 158, 172, 180, 181
West Ham United 80, 97, 98, 132,
134, 137, 148, 150, 152
Wetterstroem, Gustav 43
Whelan, Bill 112, 113
Williams, Bert 45
Willimowski, Ernest 42
Wilson, Ray 57, 59
Wolverhampton Wanderers 82,
90, 106
Woosnam, Phil 90
World Cup 20, 39
1930   40, 41, 86
1934   41, 42
1938   42, 43, 47, 172
1950   44, 45, 86
1954   46, 47, 50, 59, 102, 172,
180
1958   48, 49, 115, 127
1962   50, 51, 52, 53, 60, 126
1966   54, 57, 97, 100, 115, 128,

130, 132, 148, 149, 162
1970   58, 65, 97, 151, 154, 158,
162, 180
1974   66, 70, 83, 99, 118, 123,
139, 146, 154, 158, 181
1978   72, 73, 74, 75
Wreford-Brown, Charles 12
Wrexham 45
Wright, Billy 45, 47, 60, 148, 175
Wunderteam 41

Yachin, Lev 49, 52
Yashin 56, 97
Yugoslavia 39, 40, 42, 45, 46, 47,
48, 49, 50, 51, 52, 54, 58, 59, 68,
69, 70, 82, 83, 118, 134, 139, 181

Zagalo 20, 59, 161, 162
Zaire 68, 69
Zamora 41
Zeman 47
ZeMaria 70
Zito 49, 50, 52, 54
Zizinho 45
Zoff 68, 69
Zozimo 50

Picture credits

Abril Press 44B; 51; 152;
Allsport Photographic 92/3;
160/1;
Associated Press 44T; 46; 48B;
75; 88T; 170/1;
Barratt's 55T;
Brian Bould 136;
Colorsport Endpapers; 2; 4/5;
12T; 14B; 17T; 17TR; 22C;
32B; 34; 38; 66/7; 71; 73; 84;
89; 91; 92; 98; 99; 102; 103;
107; 117; 121T; 122/3;
124/5; 135; 143T,L; 147T;
152B; 153; 155; 157; 158/9;
166/7; 168/9;
Gerry Cranham 57;

Diaramg 14T; 18; 19; 20; 26;
28T; 30; 31; 35B; 36/7; 37T; ;
64/5; 86/7; 96T,L;
Europa Press 147B
Mary Evans Picture Library
10TR; 11;
Fotosports International 116;
Fox Photos 36T; 55B;
Ray Green 14 (insets); 16/7;
17BR; 35T; 82; 94T; 105;
108/9; 110/1; 119;
John Hillelson Agency 88B;
Interpresse Geneve 78;
Keystone Press 16L; 32L; 43;
56/7; 144B;
L.E.N.F.S. 65; 81; 112/3;

150/1;
Manchette 58T; 62/3;
Mansell Collection 10TL; 62/3;
Mirrorpic 143TR; 145;
Newsport Press 121B;
Novosti Press 13TR;
P & L Photo Service 94B;
150L;
Popperfoto 48T; 143BR;
Press Association 22B; 28B;
56T; 129B; 130/1; 170/1;
Presse Sports 78/9; 127B;
Publifoto 41;
Radio Times Hulton Picture
Library 10B; 143BL;
Peter Robinson 22T; 76; 83;

164/5; 114B;
Sporting Pictures 6; 21; 58B;
138; 141;
Sportapics 24;
Sven Simon 154;
Syndication International 13B;
32TR; 33; 56C & B; 61T;
64L; 79; 80; 86/7; 100/1;
112; 122; 149; 162/3; 163;
courtesy of the Sunday Times
96R;
Topix 12B; 13TL;
U.P.I. 40; 50/1; 52; 52/3; 74;
129T;
A. Wilkes & Son 49;